Changing Properties of Property

Changing Properties of Property

Edited by
Franz von Benda-Beckmann,
Keebet von Benda-Beckmann
and Melanie G. Wiber

Berghahn Books
New York • Oxford

First published in 2006 by
Berghahn Books
www.berghahnbooks.com

© 2006, 2007, 2009 Franz von Benda-Beckmann, Keebet von
Benda-Beckmann and Melanie G. Wiber
Reprinted in 2007
First paperback edition published in 2009

Library of Congress Cataloging-in-Publication Data
Changing properties of property / edited by Franz von Benda-Beckmann,
Keebet von Benda-Beckman, and Melanie G. Wiber.
   p. cm.
   includes bibliographical references and index.
   ISBN 978-1-84545-139-4 (hbk) -- ISBN 978-1-84545-727-3 (pbk)
   1. Property 2. Right of property. 3. Commons. 4. Resource alloca-
tion--Decision making. 5. Culture and law. I. Benda-Beckmann,
Franzvon. II. Benda-Beckmann, Keebet von. III. Wiber, Melanie,
1954-

HB701.C526 2006
330.1'7--dc22

                            2006042832

British Library Cataloguing in Publication Data
A catalogue record for this book is available from the British Library
Printed in the United States on acid-free paper

ISBN 978-1-84545-139-4 hardback
ISBN 978-1-84545-727-3 paperback

Contents

List of Maps, Figures and Tables

Chapter 1
The Properties of Property*

Franz von Benda-Beckmann
Keebet von Benda-Beckmann
Melanie G. Wiber

The most serious single source of misunderstanding of the concepts of alien cultures is inadequate mastery of the concepts of one's own culture (Finnegan and Horton, quoted in Hirschon 1984: 2).

Introduction

Property is in. The media follows debates about patenting food crops and the human genome, while protesters around the world reject neoliberal privatisation. Academics and policy theorists tout various property forms, while the market turns ever more things into commodities. Throughout history, property has been at the centre of such intellectual, economic and political struggles. A number of recent developments force us to take a renewed look at property. One is the rapid increase in new types of properties, including social security rights, tradable environmental allowances, bioinformatics, cultural property and even such ephemeral things as air. Another development is the changing constellations of property relationships that form network-like structures sometimes reaching around the globe. These developments touch on fundamental issues of identity, social organisation and governance that have wide implications. They have also put classical property categories under increasing strain.

But to focus on property immediately entangles one in a long history of deeply intertwined conceptual discussions, social philosophies and

*This introduction began as the background paper for an international conference on 'The Properties of Property', held at the Max Planck Institute for Social Anthropology, Halle, 2–4 July 2003. The title was inspired by Bob Hunt's essay 'Properties of Property: Conceptual Issues' (Hunt 1998). We thank Brian Donahoe and Chris Hann for their thoughtful comments.

1

ideological justifications of past, present and future property regimes. This is not surprising as property concerns the organisation and legitimation of rights and obligations with respect to goods that are regarded as valuable. Property is thus the legitimate cloth of wealth as property systems structure the ways in which wealth can be acquired, used and transferred. Property is of central importance in all economies, but it cannot be reduced to 'the economic'. Property is always multifunctional (F. and K. von Benda-Beckmann 1999). It is a major factor in constituting the identity of individuals and groups. Through inheritance, it also structures the continuity of such groups. It can have important religious connotations. And it is a vital element in the political organisation of society, the legitimate command over wealth being an important source of political power over people and their labour, no matter whether we think of domestic or kinship modes of production, capitalism or communism. Property regimes, in short, cannot easily be captured in one-dimensional political, economic or legal models.

Property is the focus of struggles at all levels of social organisation, within and between families, communities, classes and states. The distribution of property objects has been contested throughout history, as have the legal property regimes themselves. Ruling elites have put much energy into regulating and changing property regimes in support of such variable objectives as accumulation of wealth for their own benefit, a public good such as equity, the efficient use of scarce resources, or the protection of the environment. And ordinary people have always had their own objectives, and their own corresponding views on how property should be organised.

As a result, property regimes and property rights have been a central theme historically in law and philosophy. More recently, they have also become central to many other disciplines including sociology, anthropology, political science, economics, geography and human ecology. Property figures as a prime mover in such diverse topics as social evolution, modernisation, globalisation, human rights, civil society, and sustainable resource management. Given this instrumental importance, many theories focus less on accurate descriptions and explanations of existing property regimes and more on desired (just, efficient) states of ideal property relationships, more on how property regimes *should* be instead of how they are (Reeve 1991: 111). One result is that property models that purport to be universal are in fact largely based on Western legal categories, the most important of these being the notion of private individual ownership, often regarded as the apex of legal and economic evolution as well as a precondition for efficient market economies. This has led to a misunderstanding of property both in Third World societies and in Western industrialised states, encouraging property policies that have unintended and deleterious consequences.

As a result, property as a concept has become loaded down with a heavy freight of political and ideological baggage. In this introduction, we refer to the individual contributions in the volume to unpack much of this freight. The volume as a whole also explores how the analysis of property regimes has been hampered by the lack of any sufficiently rigorous analytical framework. This lack can be redressed by returning to earlier foundations, such as the metaphor of 'property as a bundle of rights', which while useful, has rarely been used consistently. We demonstrate how to take the 'bundle of rights' seriously in order to capture the different roles that property may play, as well as the complexities and manifold variations of property in different societies and in different periods of history. We also incorporate the several distinct analytical layers at which property manifests itself, in ideologies, in legal systems, in actual social relationships, in social practices, and pay attention to the interrelations between these phenomena. What property is at these different layers may vary significantly and this variability cannot be reduced by collapsing one layer into another. Finally, we think it vital to address the fact that many contemporary states have a plurality of property ideologies and legal institutions, often rooted in different sources of legitimacy, including local or traditional law, the official legal system of the state, international and transnational law, and religious legal orders.

In what follows, we illustrate the importance of such an analytical framework for more accurate descriptions of the way property operates in the real world. These empirical descriptions in turn are a precondition for theorising about the place of property under conditions of social, economic and ecological change. While policy advice is not among the objectives pursued in this volume, many of the contributors do illustrate how past policies centred on the desirability of highly theoretical property regimes have failed. And given the recent developments alluded to earlier, we see the need for an analytically rigorous framework if such costly failures are not to be repeated. With technological and biophysical innovations, and with increasing government involvement in managing productive resources, new valuables have been created that were unthinkable until recently. These new properties raise new political, legal and ethical questions, and generate new conflicts. More importantly, they stretch the bounds of property categories, allowing us to study property concepts as they transform. This is particularly useful to order to counter the widespread tendency to think of property in terms of universal types (private, state, communal, open access) that are supposedly found widely distributed across space and time. We had these developments in mind when, together with Chris Hann, we chose the title of 'changing properties of property' for our conference. As we will show, one of the strengths of our analytical framework is in investigating to what extent these new properties are indeed new and whether they force us to rework our property categories.

In the following section of this paper we turn to the property freight we wish to unpack, including the ways that different disciplines have theorised property, and the interactions between disciplines that have continued to add to the theoretical baggage. Some of this baggage is well worth retaining, while much should be jettisoned. We then go on in subsequent sections to outline and illustrate the elements of our analytical framework before returning at last to the issue of new (and old) forms of property.

Unpacking the Freight

We cannot examine in detail the conceptual baggage built up over several hundred years of academic theorising and carried over into any new analysis of property. But it is useful to highlight some important developments in particular disciplines, and the subsequent interactions between disciplinary approaches, in order to better understand some of the misunderstandings that have taken root. Such a survey also suggests several ways in which property analysis needs strengthening.

Viewing Property from Different Disciplinary Perspectives

Contemporary property theory implicitly or explicitly relies on political economists such as Locke, Rousseau, Engels, Marx, Adam Smith and others, who taken together unfortunately generate many complex and contradictory views of property. Political scientists mine these particular theoretical lodes to address a spectrum of issues, including: the sources of legitimate property rights; the role of the state in protecting and distributing property rights; the role of property in delineating sovereignty, social justice and equity, and in shaping the relationship between the individual and the state. A significant contribution here has been the focus on the relationship between power and property, but unfortunately the tendency has been to resolve this important issue through the simple expedient of viewing the state as the sole legitimate font of property rights. This argument came to underpin much economic thinking (Demsetz 1967; North 1981). In this volume, Geisler revisits this state-centric viewpoint by pointing to the way that property rights are created, defined and protected by organisations other than the nation-state, both within the spatial boundaries of states and beyond.

The balance between the rights and freedoms for individual persons and the needs of the collective of which they are a part has proven another enduring question in political science. Over time, different societies have arrived at quite different solutions for this balance, and every legal system (including their property aspects) is a reflection of the political arrangements under which this ongoing balance is negotiated. The many quite different histories of property relations in various places around the world fall into broad patterns that have been labelled feudalism, capitalism or socialism. But they all illustrate quite different ruptures and continuities, particularly in the distinction between what is public and what is private, but also regarding the question of how (private) individuals may influence political decisions that affect entire groups (the public). Concepts of property as the foundation for civic responsibility, derived from Greek and Roman law for example, evolved and changed in the struggle for democracy and universal suffrage in Western Europe and in the Americas, and are changing again in the privatisation frenzy that has followed the end of socialist regimes. This is in part because political models for transforming former socialist countries have privileged private property rights as a mechanism to address the poor performance of socialist institutions in their public tasks. This poor performance was explained through the erroneous reasoning that all property was owned by the state and thus the state was overburdened and unable to satisfy basic needs. Where former autocratic regimes in the Third World have been dismantled, meanwhile, a somewhat contradictory approach advocates decentralisation and the devolving of responsibility to smaller geopolitical units, often by promoting community-based management. James (this volume) addresses both privatisation and decentralisation in her evaluation of the post-reform situation in South African black communities. Where appropriated land was restored but did not yield the expected benefits, James found part of the problem to be the under-funded restitution process, such that groups of people were forced to pool their restitution money to buy land. Unfortunately, the subsequent neoliberal devolution of state welfare responsibilities to these newly constituted communities caused significant problems, as the communities lacked the required resources.

Meanwhile, the concept of ethnicity as integral to natural political boundaries has resurfaced in current debates about aboriginal self-governance, often with collective property rights replacing territory as the foundation for group identities. Van Meijl (this volume) explores the challenges created by this approach in New Zealand, where the privatisation of fishing rights in the commercial fishery has resulted in conflict between Maori communities with claims to those rights. He notes how a misunderstanding of Maori social organisation that has been reified by state courts has privileged rural Maori over the larger urban Maori population, and has pitted North Island Maori against those of the South Island.

Such political debates tend to create a public/private dichotomy, despite the fact that both have multiple and overlapping meanings (Weintraub 1997; Geisler 2000).[1] Wiber (this volume), explores the way these several meanings are selectively applied in debates surrounding cultural property claims and illustrates the way that the, apparently, simple dichotomy depoliticises highly unequal power struggles in two cases from North America, one involving a religious artefact and another involving ancient human remains. She shows how repoliticising the public/private divide allows us to track the many political processes that make one set of claimants more persuasive than another. Recognising these different distinctions of public and private and their defining criteria (Weintraub 1997: 27, 37) allows us to expose the many and contradictory ways that these terms are used in political and legal thought.

Legal science, sharing many interests with political philosophy, has also viewed property as central to the sovereign state, law and governance, thus arriving at a similar distinction between public and private. In European and American legal systems, this distinction is largely derived from viewing the 'public' as closely linked with governance, and with relations of legitimate control and coercion by political representatives of the collectivity (public). On the other side lie the voluntary, equal, uncoerced, contractual relationships (private) as epitomised by 'the market'. The 'public' or 'private' character of rights has thus largely been determined by the difference between public and private law.[2] In European law, the legal status of the property object gives the public or private stamp to the associated rights. The property-holder may be a public body yet the status of the object may make it private property, with the public body then treated as a private property owner, subject to the sphere of private property law. On the other hand, individual citizens may have quite specific rights in property defined as public. Carol Rose (1994: 117) finds it helpful to distinguish two types of public property. The first is property 'owned' by the state as in government buildings, military supplies, or ministerial jets. The second is property owned collectively by the 'unorganised public' such as state forests or territorial waters, with claims independent of and perhaps superior to the claims of any purported governmental manager (ibid.: 110). Such porous barriers between public and private can lead to significant conflict between state and citizens, as Sikor (this volume) illustrates. Public (environmental) and private (agricultural) values come into conflict in some post-socialist societies, when the owners of newly restored private farms resist the effort of the state to download the cost of environmental reform onto them. In such cases, depoliticised notions of public and private do not further our understanding of the property aspects of these conflicts.

The practical and applied objective of legal science, meanwhile, is to create institutions and rules that defuse or manage such conflict. In this vein, the bundle of rights metaphor can help to identify the many possible interests associated with a single valuable (Maine 1861; Hohfeld 1923). Legal theory also addresses the question of the sort of social actors that should hold property rights and the relationship that should pertain between multiple holders of rights in a single good. A recent example of this problem is explored by Pálsson (this volume) with respect to the corporate appropriation of Icelandic family trees and genealogical information in the age of genome patents and genetic pharmaceutical/nation state partnerships. Who should own the genetic material we carry in our bodies, and in the Icelandic case, who should own the medical records that make possible the interpretation of the importance of selected genes? In bridging the different ways of conceptualising such problems, across both cultural and national boundaries, comparative scholars and legal practitioners have developed innovative property concepts (such as intellectual property) and have sought to make different kinds of property rights compatible in a practical way (Dezalay and Garth 1995; Arthurs 1997; C. Rose 2003).

In dealing with similar problems of comparison across different cultures and societies, classical anthropological theorists such as Maine and Morgan naturalised variation by adopting an evolutionary framework. Property as an institution was said to have evolved from types that privileged group rights to types that privileged individual rights (Newman 1983). When classical social evolution was later rejected in favour of more empirical and descriptive micro-theory, functionalist thinking and later neofunctionalist approaches, such as ecological anthropology, both treated property as an integral part of a wider systemic whole. In more recent scholarship, the notion of systemic interdependencies (often expressed as 'embeddedness') has been pursued through empirical studies of how property systems work on the ground. This empirical focus has been a particular strength in anthropology, documenting the role of kinship in property management, examining situations of legal pluralism,[3] problematising the state as holder of superior rights in all property, and generally deconstructing many Western assumptions.[4]

Much of this material was overlooked when the discipline of economics began to seriously theorise questions of property. Here the main focus has been on the theoretical significance of property in managing the social and economic effects of scarcity so that human needs can be efficiently satisfied. Maximisation of scarce resources is optimised where institutions clarify and regularise access to resources (Demsetz 1967; Barzel 1989; Libecap 1989, 1990). Property types are thus evaluated according to how they further this end with the result that economists distinguish what F. von Benda-Beckmann (2001: 296) calls the 'Big Four' theoretically significant types of property. Open access, a form of non-property, is the most ambiguous and thus the least desirable situation. Common property is only viable where there is a well-defined set of individuals with well-defined rights in the collective property, and where rules exist for regulating access and controlling for externalities.[5] State property is necessary where a powerful centralised agency is required to control otherwise unlimited access and withdrawal, as in marine fisheries.[6] But only private property, with clear identification of an owner and a full set of rights that include transmissibility will facilitate the gathering up of resources into the hands of the most efficient users (Barzel 1989: 7; Libecap 1989: 10). The central economic institution, the market, is the prime mover in this process. Thus, anything other than individual private ownership is regarded as inefficient, lacking the full specificity, legal security, and freedom of transfer that is considered fundamental to economic growth.

A number of contributions to this volume address this model. Kingston-Mann, for example, challenges economic assumptions about common property, particularly those archetypal examples frequently referred to in economic theory. Her close reading of the historical record on the productivity of both the British common lands and early Russian communes shows that in both cases, common property was actually much more efficient than previously thought. Further, poor rural commoners were more often the first to adopt agricultural innovations. In the British case, state subsidies for elite producers had far more to do with economic growth after the enclosures than did property reforms. Eidson's more recent historical analysis of the East German collective farm enterprise shows how property ideologies may be characterised by ambivalence creating effects comparable to those of legal pluralism. His example is the so-called cooperative plan of Lenin, which was less an ideology than an array of ideological possibilities providing charters for different – even contradictory – laws, relations and practices. Under such conditions, Eidson argues, property must be viewed in a broader context, including both legal and illegal uses of resources, because the determination of what is legal is subject to changing politics, variable perspectives, and shifting, though always unequal, power relations. Socialist collectivisation actually took quite different forms as a result of the varying social contexts in different socialist states. In the German case, for example, there were many opportunities for individual enterprise and for innovation within several distinct types of collective farm.

In the wake of the apparent failure of privatisation policy in rural Russia, Visser looks inside the 'black box' of the internal dynamics of collective enterprises to explain the rapid deterioration of rural productivity. His focus is on the labour relations within surviving large-scale agricultural enterprises, since Western advisors often blame rural workers who are said to block restructuring. But Visser finds that both agricultural workers and farm managers are caught in a trap of reform's making, unable to overcome chronic shortages and the structural disintegration which have crippled farm operations. As with the paper by James, the above contributions make a strong case for examining the real consequences of privatising social services, infrastructure, market facilities, and the environment along with productive resources. In each of these examples, changing one aspect of the property infrastructure nexus has led to serious impediments for putting resources to economic use. While Peters also addresses the fetishisation of private property rights common to both Africa and to post-socialist states, she goes further to query the anthropological solution of focusing on the embedded nature of property. She argues that anthropological models of embeddedness are too focused on resisting this fetishisation and not enough on developing significant theoretical alternatives.

Cherry Picking and False Comparisons

To properly engage with such recent developments as the global push for privatisation, one must grapple with the intellectual freight discussed above. While each of these disciplinary traditions has made important contributions to the understanding of property, they have also been limited by their particular focus. Many property theorists have been aware of this drawback and have striven to develop a cross disciplinary perspective on property. However, an additional problem has then developed as a result of scholars cherry picking very specific notions, lifting them from one disciplinary context and using them elsewhere. The result has often been over simplified property models, often based on conceptual misunderstandings and false comparisons, which in turn have been particularly damaging in the development and implementation of property policy.

Broadly speaking, property scholarship can be divided into two main approaches: the instrumental, normative and teleological on the one hand, and the empirical, descriptive and analytical on the other.[7] Particularly among the instrumental and policy driven approaches in law, economics and ecology, there has been a recent escalation of selective borrowing between disciplines. For example, the economics and property school drew on outmoded ethnographic studies to theorise about the evolution of property forms (Demsetz 1967). Law and development scholars and development economists borrowed from each other to advocate the transplant of Western property institutions into developing nations (see Johnson 2004), and to subsequently explain the poor success rate of such transplants. Ecological property theory more recently has been incorporated into economic models, while a reciprocal interest in economic property theory among ecologists has been fuelled by issues of natural resource management.[8] Ecologists have also dipped into ethnography in order to speculate about how property systems may have evolved to deal with certain kinds of resource constraints.[9] Such mixing and mingling of ideas, including cultural evolution, self-organisation in complex systems, rational choice theory, new institutional economics, the new norms literature, and chaos theory (see C. Rose 1999), eliminates a great deal of disciplinary context in order to sustain a positivist, methodological individualism and formal modelling (Johnson 2004: 409). While such modelling may facilitate the development of broad property policy direction, it may also explain why much of this policy fails in its objectives. One example of the resulting theoretical shortcomings can be illustrated through a discussion of property and ownership.

Instrumental theories and resulting policy are based on implicit or explicit assumptions about property that are empirically false for both Western and non-Western legal systems and societies. The most serious misconception lies in the area of private, individual ownership, which narrowly conceived, glosses over the many different kinds of rights and sets of obligations that can be involved both with respect to different categories of objects, and of categories of property holders. To illustrate some of the existing complexity here, both across time and space, we will return to the bundle of rights metaphor below. But first we want to draw attention to the way that much theory reifies the individual as an actor, granting owners far more agency than they have in real life. Examples are found in rational choice theory and in notions of absolute ownership (C. Rose 1998). Such ethnocentric (and erroneous) notions of free agency with respect to owned property are then taken to be the ideal to which all property systems should aspire, in both Western and non-Western legal systems.

In fact, rights are always political and frequently re-negotiated, and the terms of those negotiations are widely diverse across time and space. Schlager (this volume) for example, examines water right holders along the South Platte River in Colorado and their unique problems given the demands of an arid environment and of surface versus groundwater uses. In this context, water rights concepts imported from less arid regions were untenable, and many political compromises were developed over time that constrained both individual and public holders of water rights. Nuijten and Lorenzo (this volume) provide another example from Mexico where after recent constitutional reforms communal *ejido* lands are now open to privatisation. Nuijten and Lorenzo demonstrate how the many ongoing political negotiations between community members are more important to the changing patterns of production on the *ejido* commons than are property rights per se, and thus, few Mexican peasants are interested in the privatisation option.

In all state societies, the autonomy of owners with respect to their property has been increasingly limited under expanding public legal regulation of rights. The arguments for these limitations change over time, but have included: the common good, sound economic growth, protection of public environmental values, historic conservation, land use planning, or sustainable resource management. For example, European farmers of the past could place as many animals on their land as they could afford, but there are now serious limitations placed on land-animal ratios under either national or European law. Community or state permission is increasingly required for any change in the use or transfer of owned lands, forests or waters, and in some cases, owners have discovered heavy sanctions for taking actions that they were formerly allowed. Thus, while many rights that were unequivocally part of the ownership bundle in the nineteenth and early twentieth century have since disappeared or fallen under community or state control, the property object is still considered 'owned'. If the existing bundle of private property rights were to be measured against the mythical yardstick of 'total dominion', most European private ownership has never been ownership and is even further removed from ownership now.

Such errors have been compounded in interpreting the property systems of 'the other'. In many cases, the resulting misinterpretations have both academic and policy manifestations, with the two becoming inter-referential, taking on life in different circles and for different purposes. The colonial experience is a useful example of this as it allows us to briefly examine how such misunderstandings take on life of their own. Although the colonial academic and policy networks were separate and focused on quite different problems, they were mutually interdependent, giving academic legal comparisons wide political impact.

The main academic goal during colonial times was to describe and understand the strange cultures and sociopolitical organisation of other societies, and to translate and render them comprehensible to those at home. The major interpretative schemes of meaning, such as private and communal ownership, usufruct, and the distinction between public and private domain, were taken from European legal systems. The application of these to non-Western situations resulted in native concepts or institutions being viewed as more or less equivalent. Such assimilated concepts were then given the same legal and social consequences as the European concept had in European law. As the von Benda-Beckmanns (this volume) describe, for example, the distinction between the public and private domain as defined in Dutch law was imposed on indigenous Indonesian property regimes that did not make this distinction in the same way. The colonial government, as the public authority, was then justified in deciding when a valuable was a public good and when the greater good superseded local rights. With respect to what the colonial authorities termed 'waste lands', the term right of avail or right of disposal (Dutch *beschikkingsrecht*) was introduced in order to emphasise that indigenous cultures shared with the Dutch a notion of public goods, which could be strengthened under the colonial system.[10]

In contemporary developing nations, a similar process makes it possible to constrain local rights in favour of nature conservation, mining, lumber concessions or resettlement in, for example, the Indian Gir Forest, the Australian outback, or Indonesian and Philippine frontiers. The accompanying process of false comparisons has been criticised as 'backward translation' (Bohannan 1969: 410) or 'jamming into categories' (Nader 1965). It has seriously handicapped any understanding of and appreciation for other ways of organising property. A generous interpretation is that this process results from the naïve use of ethnocentric legal categories and leads to well-meaning state 'invention of customary law', which is ongoing in many post-colonial states. A less generous interpretation might see such legal distortions as driven by overriding political and economic incentives to 'develop' resources in a way that benefits outsiders.

Both interpretations may be too simple. Misinterpretations and false comparisons had two different types of consequences in colonial states. Western concepts were not only used as interpretative schemes of meaning but also as a standard for recognition under the state legal regime. In cases where local property rights were recognised within the administrative and judicial realm of the colonial state, the legal distortions did not have immediate consequences, although they sometimes affected and legitimised long-term changes in the distribution and inheritance of property and wealth within local social groups. But when recognition was denied, as when a right was not thought to sufficiently resemble European conceptions of ownership, the consequences were grave indeed, as happened with the previously mentioned wastelands in the Dutch East Indies (see F. and K. von Benda-Beckmann, this volume).

Much academic effort has been devoted to understanding the consequences of such property restructuring, including Marx and Weber, and more recent work by law and development, modernisation, land reform, common property, and economic and property theorists. And the resulting property theories continue to have significant economic and political consequences. Many academics, for example, are outspoken advocates of an 'appropriate' restructuring of property in relation to certain goals, such as individual freedom, a just distribution of wealth, or an efficient use of productive resources. Their ideas have sometimes guided or at least justified government policies, as when entire societal restructuring has occurred under capitalism or communism.

Given the misconceptions upon which they are constructed, and despite the fact that these ideas often gain a policy audience, it should not surprise us that idealised property models are not an accurate reflection of what we find in real life. Is our Western terminology at fault? Does it continuously lead us astray? Should we do away altogether with the term property? There has been support for this position.[12] It is true that the Western category 'property' led to ethnocentric bias and distortions when describing and analysing other non-Western property conceptualisations.[13] But we argue that the word property can be redefined as a general analytical category.[14] It may be difficult to distance oneself completely from ethnocentric understandings of certain terms, but it would be strange if a semantic determinism prevented anthropologists and other scholars from clarifying their concepts to reduce specific ideological content. In the following section, we develop the criteria for undertaking a cross-cultural, comparative analysis of property. Since such basic criteria must be capable of embracing a variety of empirical manifestations, they will inevitably be rather general. Only when these general criteria are in place, and the major dimensions identified along which wide variation occurs, will it be possible to adequately address the potential role of property in social change and transformation.

An Analytical Framework for the Analysis of Property

Property in the most general sense concerns the ways in which the relations between society's members with respect to valuables are given form and significance. Such relations are comprised of three major elements that include: first, the social units (individuals, groups, lineages, corporations, states) that can hold property rights and obligations; second, the construction of valuables as property objects; and third, the different sets of rights and obligations social units can have with respect to such objects. All three are set into time and space.[15] Property in this analytical sense is not one specific type of right or relation such as ownership. It is a cover term that encompasses a wide variety of different arrangements, in different societies, and across different historical periods. The metaphor of a 'bundle of rights' has been used to conceptualise these arrangements, mostly in two ways: first to refer to the totality of property rights and duties as conceptualised in any one society and second, to refer to any specific form, such as ownership, which by itself can be thought of as a bundle.[16] It could also be used, as we will illustrate below, in two further ways; first, to characterise the specific rights bundled in one property object and second, to characterise the different kinds of property held by one social unit.

Empirically, property finds expression in a wide variety of social phenomena, in cultural ideals and ideologies, in legal institutions, in actual social relationships and in social practices. We call these sets of phenomena 'layers of social organisation'.[17] What property is at one layer cannot be reduced to what property is at another layer. They concern different kinds of social phenomena, just as marriage ideologies and legal rules about marriage are different from the actual relations between two married people and their daily interactions.

These layers are interrelated in manifold ways, and these interrelationships must also be part of the analysis. For example, social practices of various kinds create, maintain and change what property is, having differential effects at the level of ideologies, of legally institutionalised categorical property relations, and of concretised property relationships. We can broadly distinguish between two general types of such practices. The first are (inter)actions that deal primarily with *concrete* property objects, relationships and rights, and that occur when people simply use, transfer, inherit or dispute a relationship with a property object. A second type of practices are those in which *categorical* property law and rights are reproduced and changed, and in which the nature of property law is explained, discussed or disputed in interaction settings such as courts, parliaments, universities, the mass media or local forums. Under conditions of legal pluralism,[18] these practices can include disputes over which body of law is relevant.

While elements of property relations at the different layers become interconnected in social practices, they have a sufficiently independent character to also warrant an examination of their independent characteristics. This is particularly useful to document and better understand the wide variation in property forms. Decades of highly detailed anthropological study have demonstrated the myriad ways in which the elements of property relations can vary across cultural boundaries.[19] And within each society, each layer of a property regime may change with different speed and for different reasons. Rather than employing a deductive approach that pins property down to one of these layers, we prefer a point of departure that is empirically grounded, and that analytically delineates property relations within a field of social organisation.

In the following sections, we illustrate how this analytical framework allows one to identify the three major elements (social units, property objects and rights and responsibilities) of any particular property constellation, as well as how they are conceptualised as bundles of rights, at the level of the ideological, of the legal institutional, of the social relational, and of quotidian practice. Further, we illustrate the utility of such an approach when comparative analysis across cultural variation is undertaken. We then rely on the contributions in this volume to illustrate how this analytical framework better explains situations of transformation and of change, particularly as relates to new forms of property.

Categorical Property Relationships at the Legal-institutional Layer

Given the social, economic and political significance of valuables, property relationships are legally formalised to a high degree in most societies. The resulting legal-institutional forms provide a legitimising and an organisational blueprint for property relationships, as well as a procedural and substantive repertoire to clarify problematic issues, notably disputes. At this layer, we call property relationships 'categorical'. This is to say that general categories of property relations are constructed by specifying property-holders, property objects, and the rights and obligations attached to these. Legal-institutional categories spell out rules and procedures for the appropriation and transfer of rights. Examples would include normative expressions of property rights such as: 'the owner of a thing can dispose of it freely so long as he does not violate the rights of others', or 'inherited lineage property can only be pawned under the following conditions: ...'.

At this legal-institutional level, cross-cultural variation ranges along a continuum of differentiation. Some basic principles may guide *ad hoc* decision making processes for dealing with property, or a large set of formal rules and procedures may become institutionalised. In highly institutionalised and differentiated legal orders, property relations are conceived of as a relatively isolated legal sub-field and are differentiated from such social or political relationships as family or political relations.[20] Many less differentiating legal orders, on the other hand, do not separate out property categories in the same way, but treat them as one aspect or 'strand' of many-stranded relationships, including kinship ties, property relations and relations of political authority. In Minangkabau, for instance, lineage membership, lineage leadership and property rights were (at least from the point of view of those external to the lineage) just different aspects of one social relationship (F. and K. von Benda-Beckmann, this volume). Further, even in those cases of high differentiation, the systemic interrelation between property and other institutions is likely to have a significant impact. For example, property relations (as a legal subfield) may be structured by tax law, environmental law, family law and corporate law, to name but a few. Moreover, property is typically linked with and made useful through a number of other institutions, including the market, transportation, education and public health, among others.[21]

The bundle metaphor is useful in dissecting the different aspects of rights in such categorical property relationships. First, it helps to capture analytically the *total range of rights and obligations*, the potential totality of 'sticks' that can be bundled and distributed over different holders of rights and obligations. Such sticks not only refer to access to a valuable and to a variety of uses and benefits, but also to its management, the possibilities of transfer and inheritance, and the political or religious authority to regulate and to distribute. In most societies a major distinction is made between rights to regulate, supervise, represent in outside relations and allocate property on the one hand, and rights to use and exploit economically property objects on the other. Many current economic theories see the former set as superior and as inherently encompassing the latter.[22] Thus, all exploitation rights are derivative. Muttenzer (this volume) however, rejects this approach, and instead sees the two as arising from quite different sources of justification.[23] In state legal systems, as we have mentioned, these issues are often addressed in terms of public and private law, but even there, significant overlap exists. In societies with less hierarchical political organisations and with less reified legal systems, there may not be such a distinction between public and private law spheres, however many aspects of sociopolitical authority and of use and exploitation remain distinct. Control and management rights may also be constructed in a tiered fashion, and are increasingly so with international levels of authority and regulation. In such cases, the rights may be delegated among various levels of political and administrative organisation. We can therefore speak of 'relative publics' (F. von Benda-Beckmann 2000). Many such relative publics, for example, are contesting for some degree of control over commercial aspects of the human genome or over various kinds of cultural property (Pálsson, Wiber, this volume).

Aside from this total set of all possible analytically distinguishable rights associated with the concept of property, the bundle metaphor can also be used to elucidate the wide variation of *specific categories* of property objects and rights (however legally elaborated) such as private ownership, as forming a bundle of rights in themselves. In most societies, there are a few 'master categories', such as private ownership, lineage property or state domain, with a range of quite specific rights bundled together and attached to them. This master category bundle metaphor is useful in two ways. First, it allows us to examine how the individual sticks in the master category bundle have been distributed among potential holders under processes of production or of historical accommodation. Second, it allows us to track variation in what is meant by a master category, such as private ownership, across cultural examples.

With respect to the first use, for example, we can track how lesser, conditional and temporary rights can be derived from the master category bundle and transferred to other holders (for instance through leasing or pledging). Eidson (this volume) shows how individual farmers in socialist Eastern Germany were pressured into delegating rights over their private farms to managers of collective enterprises. They did not, however, lose their residual rights as owners, and were able to reactivate their rights after the end of the socialist regime, albeit not without difficulties. The holder of the master bundle in such cases maintains residual rights, since many or most of the benefits are temporarily transferred in a provisional way. Note, however, that residual and provisional are relative notions. A provisional right is provisional only in relation to the residual right from which it is derived, but may also become residual itself if the right is again delegated on to yet another party. An absentee landlord, for example, can grant rights to a tenant, who in turn delegates them to a sharecropper.[24] Such delegated rights may be derived not only from private law but also from public law. The Icelandic government, for instance, created legally protected economic positions by gathering genetic/medical information from the public and then handing out the rights to the resulting data bases to pharmaceutical companies, and these rights are also provisional in nature (see Pálsson, this volume).[25]

In those situations where more than one set of legal orders specifies property objects, property-holders, rights and obligations, and acquisition and transfers quite differently, economics and policy science has tended to privilege state law and property rights, although some attention has been paid to non-state normative systems or processes of private ordering in industrialised states (Ellickson 1991). But in Minangkabau, for example, state law, village level adat and Islamic law coexist. State law and adat classify the same natural resources as different kinds of property belonging to different property-holders, while adat law and Islamic law direct the flow of property after death to quite different heirs (F. and K. von Benda-Beckmann, this volume). In other contexts of legal pluralism, as in the case of *ejidos* common lands in Mexico (Nuijten and Lorenzo, this volume), partially articulated property norms are treated as valid locally without real opposition to the state law as the primary legal system. Thus, as Peters (this volume) notes, the actual character of coexistence for plural legal orders may vary significantly from relatively peaceful coexistence, to open conflict, to combination into hybrid forms. In some cases, hybrid forms may become institutionalised. Colonial and post-colonial history provides many examples, as does the establishment of joint management for restored (private) property among black communities in South Africa (James, this volume). Such plural legal situations can also provide alternative procedural avenues to pursue where claims based on different rule systems may be played out against each other in 'forum shopping' strategies (K. von Benda-Beckmann 1981, 1984).

Concretised Social Relationships

We distinguish the above categorical property relations from 'concretised' relations that find expression at the layer of actual social relationships, that is in relationships between actual property-holders with respect to concrete valuables. Examples would include such statements as: 'I am the owner of this house', or 'Mrs Syamsiah holds these three ricefields that have been allocated to her as part of the lineage property', or 'Mr A receives water at this time in the rotation scheme in irrigation system X.' Such statements refer to property relationships that substantiate but are not the same as categorical rights. In addition, these categorical rights are based on criteria (defining holders, objects, rights and responsibilities) that are often subject to negotiation, dispute or open struggle, and in the process property relationships often change. We see an example of this in the emerging arrangements for water rights in Colorado (Schlager, this volume), where established patterns of water rights were renegotiated to deal with the consequences of widespread groundwater pumping. In many cases this emergent character of concretised property relationships is the consequence of plural legal situations that provide rich opportunities to construct different property relationships by reference to diverse normative legitimation for claims and counterclaims (F. and K. von Benda-Beckmann, this volume).

Concretised property relationships should also be interpreted within the context of the wider social networks where they form one important component of multiplex relationships. Visser (this volume), for example, shows why managers of large farm enterprises in post-reform Russia can rarely downsise their farm workforce, or even dismiss negligent workers, given their multistranded relationship with the farm labourers. A similar situation pertains between legitimate members of the Mexican *ejido* described by Nuijten and Lorenzo (this volume) and more recent residents without *ejido* rights. Members of the *ejido* find it difficult to deny non-members within their community a plot of land to work given their many social ties.

Concretised property relationships can also be analysed through the bundle of rights metaphor.[26] First, we can look at the concretised distribution of the individual sticks bundled in one master category to one actual property object, let us say an individual owner with respect to a specific farm. As mentioned above, she may be the owner, but may have conferred rights to manage the farm to another. The latter may have leased it to a tenant, who may have contracted a sharecropping arrangement. In such a case, sticks of ownership rights normally considered as forming a unit are in fact widely distributed over different holders. Behind the mask of private ownership often lurk such complicated arrangements, and management rights often become much more important than the residual ownership aspect of property.

Second, we can examine the several bundles of property interests held by a single person or property holding unit (corporate group, lineage). The property-holder may be the owner of a house, of financial property, of pawned land, of some form of lineage property, and of their own medical history, including information collected into the genome database. This use of the bundle metaphor allows us to examine the ways in which a single property-holder can collect rights that subsequently form interacting sets, with implications for the uses and exchange value of any one piece of the total property in which they have rights. If we examine more deeply the human genome example in Pálsson (this volume), for example, we can ask critical questions about the outcome of a single pharmaceutical corporation that seeks to acquire rights to the human genome, and who also owns the laboratories that do the genetic testing, the patents that emerge from the testing, the databases that place the results in a broader genetic context, and the medical products generated from this research. This use of the bundle metaphor allows us to investigate the relationship between accumulated property rights and economic or political power.

Third, we can examine the rights that over time have accreted to, or are 'bundled in', a single property object. This may involve both private and public law rights. For instance, a single house of historical interest can be the object of quite different rights held by an owner, a tenant, and a municipal government or heritage organisation. Such sets of rights are even more complicated when we look at different kinds of collective property; many of the contributions to this volume show that a careful unpacking of what is hidden behind the 'communal' label will often disclose quite complicated sets of rights that have become associated over time with a single resource or valuable (the von Benda-Beckmanns, James, Van Meijl, Muttenzer, Nuijten and Lorenzo, Peters, and Visser). For example, Wiber attempts to tease out the various types of collectives that have all lodged quite legitimate claims to a single shaman's drum, or to skeletal remains of significant antiquity. Various other sorts of 'new property' (Reich 1964) provide more complex examples (see also K. von Benda-Beckmann 1995). Consider a DNA test based on two genes (BRCA1 and BRCA2) that helps to predict the risk of developing breast cancer (Godrej 2002; New Internationalist 2002: 25). Myriad Genetics, a Utah-based biotechnology company, first patented the test to identify the genes, and then placed over twenty-five patents on them, and the proteins related to them, effectively limiting any further medical uses.

They argue that testing for these genes must be done through their labs, regardless of where in the world the patient is located. European labs flout the patents by continuing to test for the genes, and in May 2004 the European Patent Office revoked the European patent on the breast cancer genetic test (Pollack 2004: 16). If we consider BRCA1 and BRCA2 as individual property objects, we can investigate that total package of rights claims that they have acquired over the process of their discovery, documentation, patenting and use in medical testing. Such investigation should begin with whether such valuables qualify as property objects. Different legal regimes are taking different approaches here.

Property Relationships at the Layer of Ideology

Property relations are also expressed at the layer of general cultural ideals, ideologies and philosophies. In contemporary societies, property relationships at this layer all tend towards considerable plurality as we discussed in our 'Unpacking the Freight' section. Consider the competing ideologies of capitalism and communism, possessive individualism and the moral economy, welfare state ideologies and neoliberalism. Such ideologies differ considerably in their representation of and justification for both legal-institutional and existing or desirable property relations, and most diverge sharply from the reality they purport to represent. Kingston-Mann (this volume), for example, illustrates just how far common understandings of the period of the enclosures in Britain have strayed from the historical evidence.

Property at the ideological layer, then, needs to be distinguished from legal-institutional expressions, because of the way they can deviate markedly from each other. Because property regimes have evolved over long periods of time, and because different ideologies and philosophies have made an imprint on such regimes at any one point in time, neither ideology nor the legal-institutional property regimes are internally fully coherent. The diverse ideological expressions find some correspondence in the legal frameworks in the sense that general and vague notions are specified and delineated into formal property categories and rights. But as many of these notions are contradictory, both legal frameworks and actual property relations will also contain many contradictions, as most of our contributors point out. Given this divergence, the ideological layer must be treated as a quite separate phenomenon from both the legal-institutional layer, with its categorical property relations, and the layer of concretised social relationships. Taken together all these layers constitute important conditions that potentially constrain and enable people's dealing with property. Distinguishing these layers cautions one not to draw false conclusions about 'gaps' between actual practices and a conflated ideological-legal-institutional complex (see Moore 1969).

Working With the Analytical Framework

The analytical uses of the bundles of rights metaphor and the distinction between the different layers at which property is expressed allow for a systematic elucidation of the variations that pertain to property relationships. They also provide important points to be considered when theorising about property at the layer of actual social practice. With respect to both points we come back to our critical dialogue with the 'Big Four' conventional property categories (open access, state/public, common/communal and private property). We argue that these categories do not form a useful and consistent set that applies uniform criteria to the classification of diverse property categories. We further maintain that the 'Big Four' reduce complexity in misleading ways and form a poor point of departure for theorising.[27]

Descriptive Utility

We argue that our approach has a number of advantages both in terms of longstanding property forms and of 'new' properties that have emerged due to political and technological developments. Our framework allows for an examination not only of legal property categories, such as individual or state ownership, but also of the range of other rights pertaining to any actual property object. And within state spaces, it takes both the realm of private law and the public rights pertaining to each kind of property into consideration.

The conventional four categories are inconsistent in this respect and conflate criteria in different combinations of sources, types of rights, types of holder and categories of objects. As a result, the categories do not cover the range of variations one wants to distinguish empirically and to theorise about. Private property, for instance, is usually identified with private individual ownership. This ignores the very real possibility that private property is held by groups, associations, corporations, or as joint or communal ownership. Moreover, private rights are not necessarily ownership rights; they can for example, be sharecropper rights or tenancy rights. In the category of common or communal property, radically different mixes of rights of individuals, or smaller and larger social groups are thrown together. And this is an important point, as it is usually multiple holders that is the selected criterion for the definition of common property, while the type of holders and kinds of rights remain unspecified. Holders of common property can in fact be everything from spouses, to some or all members of a village, or the entire state.[28] Common rights may be ownership rights or use rights and in fact, much communal property may be held as private rights (see Lynch 1992). This leads to a great deal of confusion in the analysis of collective choice practices and the future of common property management.

With respect to open access resources, on the other hand, the difference between the legal status of the property object and the rights pertaining to it is usually effaced.[29] The rights concerned are legally unrestrained access and use of the resource. The question of what happens to those parts of the presumed open access property that *are* appropriated, as for example with the transformation of land declared *terra nullius* into private or state property, is usually ignored despite the fact that, under some legal regimes, 'virgin' resources retain this status after some kinds of use and appropriation. Moreover, when open access resources in Third World states are discussed, it is no longer the legal status of resources but actual social conditions and practices of open access that suddenly become prominent. For instance, it is regularly mentioned that when states take over resources, thereby undermining local traditional rights, yet not able to exert full control, these resources factually turn into open access, no man's or everyone's property in the conceptual schema. Legally speaking, however, these resources have the legal status of state domain or state ownership, and at the same time, of clan, tribal or common village land under local law. As we have mentioned, these differences in analysis are not just an academic quibble but have very different political implications.

Theoretical Utility

As the contributions in this volume show, the 'Big Four' actually collapse a variety of property bundles under the same category. Using them as a point of departure for empirical or theoretical generalizations, therefore, eliminates essential differences within the categories and makes useful propositions or policy unlikely. It is symptomatic that the close (sometimes causal) link between specific property categories and certain patterns of economic or ecological performance has somewhat fallen out of favour. It is now more frequently avowed that high degrees of unsustainable resource use can take place with all types of property (Dietz et al. 2003), with the explanation for this sought in variables external to property. Yet our contributors often demonstrate that with more specificity in the unpacking of property relationships, we can better understand the property dimensions of some of these phenomena. For example, when Sikor (this volume) explores the environmental consequences of the restoration of private property rights in the Czech republic, he is able to illustrate how state agents and the restored farm owners have very different conceptions of the sticks in a private property bundle, particularly as relates to the responsibility of sustaining rural environmental amenities.

A significant problem is that much property theory fails to distinguish between categorical and concretised property relationships. In most writings on the relationships between property and economic or ecological development, *categories* of property rights are assumed to inform people's behaviour and to affect resource allocation or sustainability of natural resources directly, while actual property relationships remain largely unnoticed.[30] While categorical and concretised property relationships cannot be dissociated from each other because concretised property relationships are in various ways shaped by categorical criteria, they are different social phenomena and constitute different constraining and enabling elements for social interaction.

Understanding Property Practices

Property ideologies, legal institutions and concretised property relationships are all part of wider contexts that form the conditions under which social interaction takes place. They constitute a set of potential factors motivating, constraining and enabling actual dealings with property. In everyday dealings with property, and especially in disputes, property ideologies and legal rules provide a repertoire of social resources through which people can rationalise and justify their interpretations of current property conditions or claims for change. But the kind of social relationships that interacting parties are involved in, the range of property they hold, and the embedded nature of property relationships may have a much stronger influence on people's dealings with property than property rules and types of rights. The question of Maori identity in the New Zealand case recounted by Van Meijl (this volume) is a good example. Many factors other than the legally recognised fishing rights allocated to the Maori community are influencing those who self-identify as Maori.

The way any person deals with a resource will largely depend on the other property relationships they are involved in and on the economic wealth and opportunities these embody. This is important with respect to dealings with any type of property. For example, the much debated 'tragedy of the commons', taken seriously on the level of an open access model, can only be understood in relation to privately owned cattle that require grazing. Most people, as we have pointed out, have rights in property of different kinds. What they do with those rights is likely to depend on the mixture of rights they have and their wealth (see Balland and Platteau 1999; F. von Benda-Beckmann 2001). Poor people who hold only provisional and temporary rights in a property object owned by someone else, or who have very few resources to invest in their private land (as in the James' examples from South Africa), have different options and are likely to employ the resource differently than might others better endowed.

We have already spoken about the issue of the embeddedness of property relations in other social relations as an important factor. One further point to make here is that while property interactions maintain (or change or create new) social relationships, the maintenance or change are also outcomes of wider interactions with wider intended and unintended consequences. In the many examples already given, both production *practices* and social *relationships* are shaped by the principles and rules of property law, but they are not the same as those principles and rules. All these (inter)actions contribute to the maintenance and change of concretised property rights as actual social relationships. In a more indirect way, they also contribute to the maintenance or change of the categorical property order which is inscribed into these relationships. This becomes more obvious in situations where both categorical and concretised relationships are undergoing new stresses and strains, as in the many situations recounted by our contributors who focus on the restitution of land rights, either in post-socialist states or in Africa.

Theorising Property and Change

These examples show that ideologies, legal property systems and actual property relationships are different factors necessary to the analysis not only of existing property practices but also for imputed economic or ecological significance of specific property types under processes of change. We have already highlighted the need to distinguish categorical and concretised property relationships. Most economic property theories focus on the categorical property rights rather than concretised property relationships. Further, what often seems to be an outcome of rules and categorical property rights may in effect be a result of actual accommodations or innovations in property objects, property-holders or property practices. Moreover, if categorical and concretised property relations are not kept separate, it will be impossible to analyse their potential interrelations. It becomes difficult to explore, for instance, whether certain types of property rights are likely to lead to concentration and accumulation of property by a few or to a relatively secure access to resources for the many; whether they will have weaker or stronger affects on social security and economic development, or whether they are likely to lead to more or less sustainable resource use.[31]

The ways in which property law is embedded into the wider legal system also has implications for change. While legal institutional orders are rarely fully systematised, changes in other parts of the legal order may spill over into property law, or changes in property law may be constrained by the structure of the wider order. Alexander (2004) has shown how this systemic nature of property has turned large parts of former socialist states into economic wastelands, as a factory here or a retail outlet there was privatised, while the rest of the infrastructure fell into collapse, rendering the new private property profitless and depriving the workers of many social services that used to be part of the socialist industrial complex. Many societies have undergone dramatic change in the balance of property rights between individuals, groups and the public sphere, that in turn affect the entire system of property rights. Property law reforms of land or water rights, where specific property rights are promoted and substituted for others without taking into account the existing interconnections, often run into great difficulties of implementation and trigger off undesired and unintended consequences.

It goes beyond the scope of this paper to attempt a comprehensive analysis of the relations between categorical and concretised property relations and socioeconomic change. We only want to point out here that a clear association or congruence cannot be assumed between the dominant categories of property and sets of property relationships and their economic significance in a given historical situation or development. This is true whether speaking of old or new forms of property. Sometimes categorical property rights remain unchanged over long periods, while being flexible enough to facilitate quite different economic and social arrangements, as the example of *ejido* common lands in the Nuijten and Lorenzo contribution illustrate. Without any change in the legal status, Mexican village common lands have supported the grazing of privately owned herds of cattle, the production of illicit drugs, the household production of subsistence maize and the rental of land to neighbouring villages, whether sequentially or at the same time.

Categorical and concretised property relations may change with different speed, and the factors underlying their maintenance and change may also be different. One example is the pressure on existing intellectual property rights (as in copyright) as a result of downloading music off the internet. There are other examples where property law frameworks remain stable, yet concretised property relationships and economic organisation undergo significant change.[32] One reason for this may be that many rules and procedures concerning property rights, distribution, transfers or inheritance leave considerable room for autonomous decisions of property-holders over use, sale, pawning or devolution. In similar fashion, there may be periods where the categorical property system is transformed, yet concretised property relationships hardly change. The reforms of land law in many Third World states have demonstrated that the intended transformation of property rights rarely has the expected outcome because right holders may refuse to redefine their property relationships in terms of the new categories or to use the opportunities to change concretised relationships through the new options for transfer offered by the categorical system.

Finally, under yet other conditions, changed property law may also bring about significant changes in concretised property relations and economic (re)organisation. The creation of some new property categories (gene patents, cultural property, fishing quotas), and their commoditisation may change the property object considerably, often by splitting it up into smaller units that then become subject to different property rules (as in the human genome example) and to different concretised property relations.[33] Many quota regimes are examples where certain aspects of the previous ownership right to land, cattle or fish are excised and are (re)distributed via an administratively created quasi-market to the holders of the quotas while older practices become illegal or negatively sanctioned by the state,[34] both with far reaching consequences. The new quota rights often accrued, not to the former property-holders, but to wealthier persons and to larger corporations, as in van Meijl's New Zealand example. But these redistributions facilitated by new kinds of property are not different in kind from older examples, such as land rights reform. When reforms were taken up by rural people in the Third World, with the result that many rights based in traditional law were transformed into ownership rights, concretised property relations were considerably changed because many lesser rights under traditional law could not be translated into the new property categories and were repressed. The unintended consequence was often a particular change in the gendered distribution of property rights, to the disadvantage of women. In the privatisation and distribution of the commons to the poor in India, other quite substantial changes in actual property relations took place. This privatisation successfully redefined the property relations to the commons, such that within a short period of time a significant amount of these new property rights had been sold and accumulated by the richer farmers (Jodha 1986). Recognising the various layers at which property is expressed can help to explain all of these very diverse relationships.

Conclusion

The heavy intellectual freight attached to property has derailed our understanding of the 'work of property' (Verdery and Humphrey 2004). Unpacking this freight has proven fruitful. On the way we have touched upon a range of disciplines and academic traditions that all deal with property, each with different assumptions and with a different focus of interest. We have also warned of some of the dangers of borrowing and of cherry picking ideas and assumptions across disciplines. The high inter-referentiality in the study of property has generated interesting insights, but has also led to some pernicious problems of analyses and comparison. Rather than providing a new theory of property, we have attempted to provide the outline for an analytical framework that could serve as a basis for dissecting property relations and thereby generating more adequate theory building. It is an approach that builds on the metaphor of property as a bundle of rights, but it makes much greater use of the metaphor. We have argued that ideologies, institutions, concretised property relationships, and the social practices affecting all three, are the basic layers that allow us to understand property, especially in conditions of legal plurality. These analytical distinctions between layers of social organisation are useful for whatever domain or aspect of social organisation one is interested in. They go beyond the frequent dualisms between ideal/real, law/practice, ideology/practice, institutions/interaction, structure/agency, which still dominate methodological assumptions. This is particularly relevant in property issues because most property theories fail to go beyond a distinction between legal institution and actual practice. The layers have to be analysed in their mutual interdependence, and none should be privileged over the others. We think that such an approach is an advance over institutional approaches that either put too much emphasis on the categorical legal institutional framework (rules of the game)[35] or treat institutions as compounds in which 'complexes of norms, rules and behaviors that serve a collective purpose' are lumped (De Janvry et al. 1993: 566).

Paying attention to the systemic nature of property and to the contexts in which property relationships and property practices are embedded allows one to study property change in its wider contexts without inferring too much about how changes on one layer affect the other layers. More specifically, it allows us to see in what respect the new properties are really new. We have seen that what seems to be totally new turns out to be new in some limited respect only. Increasing state regulation that diminishes the scope of entitlements for property-holders is not new, but fishing quotas and human genetic patents are new types of objects. But more than that, they are examples of the mechanism through which state regulation inadvertently creates new property simply because people start using these instruments of state regulation as property. Partitioning off parts of what used to fall under the older bundle of ownership, has a long tradition as the examples from wastelands appropriation in colonial states show. The human genome is an extreme example, and an example that has deep emotional underpinnings. However, some of the partitioning that took place in colonial forests and wastelands probably had similar emotional repercussions for those newly excluded. Other contributions in this volume have shown how changes in regulation and in the character of property objects have often generated changes in categorical property relationships and practices. The examples we have discussed here show that changes in property are not one-way processes. Change may be initiated at any specific layer, and that change then typically feeds back into other layers, leading to imbricated adjustments. Once we have understood the characteristics of these loops of influence within the layers of property regimes and in their wider contexts, we can begin to understand the relationship between specific property categories and political, economic or ecological change.

Notes

1. See also N. Rose (1987); Goodall (1990); F. von Benda-Beckmann (2000).
2. Public law constitutes state institutions and regulates their relationships, as well as the relationships with non-state organisations and individual persons in their legal status as citizens. Private law pertains to the legal status of and the relations among citizens.
3. Surveys of the concept of legal pluralism include Merry (1988); K. von Benda-Beckmann (2001); F. von Benda-Beckmann (2002); Griffiths (2002).
4. See among others Leach (1961); Goody (1962); Allott et al. (1969); Gluckman (1972, 1973); F. von Benda-Beckmann (1979); Wiber (1993); F. and K. von Benda-Beckmann (1994); Spiertz and Wiber (1996); Hann (1998, 2003); Hunt and Gilman (1998); Van Meijl and F. von Benda-Beckmann (1999); Juul and Lund (2002); Verdery (2004).
5. The commons literature is enormous but a good start is McCay and Acheson (1987); Ostrom (1990); Cole (2002); Ostrom et al. (2002). Recent contributions to adaptive management of the commons can be found in Gunderson and Holling (2002); Hanna et al. (1996); Dietz et al. (2003). For a critical review of the applied work of the 'commons professional', see Goldman (1998).
6. Some economists advocate private property rights even in the fisheries. For a list of citations and a critique of this position, see Wiber (2000).
7. Of course, social actors pursue many different and often quite contradictory objectives. To simplify our discussion, we reduce this diversity to a single distinction between instrumental and purely academic interests in property.
8. One can track such borrowing through the expansion of cross disciplinary journals such as *Natural Resource Economics and Policy, European Journal of Law and Economics,* and *Ecological Economics.* See also Costanza and Folke (1996); Taylor (1998).
9. The 'Big Four' were fundamental to the analysis by Schlager and Ostrom (1992) and Ostrom and Schlager (1996) that subsequently shaped common property studies (see Berkes 1996: 89; 1999; Richards 2002). Frank Muttenzer (this volume) rejects many of Schlager and Ostrom's core assumptions in his analysis of community-based (mis)management of forests in Madagascar.
10. See F. von Benda-Beckmann (1979); Holleman (1981: 43). Similar developments occurred in other colonies. These interpretations were later criticised as 'creations of customary law'. See Clammer (1973); Chanock (1985); Peters (2002).
11. See Wiber (1993); McCarthy (2002); Povinelli (2002); Randeria (2003); Trigger (n.d.).
12. The notion of property *rights* is sometimes said to convey a selective and specifically Western legal character to property relationships. Strathern (1999) has further argued that even the notion of *relationship* relies on a Western distinction between subject and object, one perhaps foreign to the way that

others conceptualise human beings and their interaction with the natural environment.

13. For some, this is reason enough to drop the concept or to speak of property only as a specific folk category of the West. While Verdery (2004) and Verdery and Humphrey (2004) express the same doubts, they continue to use the concept.

14. The problem of translation is ubiquitous, affecting concepts of economy, marriage, religion, household and law. All these words have culturally specific meanings, all have been used and abused in evolutionist and ideological discourses and have had political instrumental uses. Yet they have remained central and useful concepts in scholarly analysis.

15. This approach builds on earlier work (F. von Benda-Beckmann 1979, 1995; F. and K. von Benda-Beckmann 1999).

16. The bundle of rights metaphor in legal anthropology goes back to Maine's *Ancient law* (1986 [1861]) and his *Dissertations on early law and custom* (1883) and has been adopted by social and legal anthropologists for the analysis of legal institutions, such as ownership or marriage. See for instance Leach (1961); Goody (1962); Gluckman (1972); F. von Benda-Beckmann (1979); Wiber (1993); Hann (1998); Verdery (2004). For more on the metaphor of the total rights bundle, see F. von Benda-Beckmann (1995); K. von Benda-Beckmann et al. (1997). See also Pospíšil's formal analysis of Kapauku land and water tenure (1971: 273–339).

17. References to the embedded nature of property usually emphasise the deeply intertwined nature of property (and of the economy in general) with wider social, religious and political institutions, but without specifying how these interconnections work out in daily life (see Verdery and Humphrey 2004; Peters, this volume).

18. As mentioned above, in most contemporary states there are many, often contradictory legal orders where property objects, rights and obligations, property-holders, acquisition and transfers are institutionalised in different and frequently contradictory ways. We give examples in the sections to follow.

19. See Goldschmidt (1966); Nader (1965, 1969); Bohannan (1969); F. von Benda-Beckmann (1979, 1995, 2000); Wiber (1993); K. von Benda-Beckmann et al. (1997); Hann (1998); Hunt (1998); F. and K. von Benda-Beckmann (1999).

20. Maine (1861) saw this distinction in terms of historical evolution, arguing that in ancient law the law of things was not (yet) divorced from the law of persons.

21. On the systemic nature of law, see K. von Benda-Beckmann (2003).

22. Perhaps the confusion arises from the fact that the sticks representing sociopolitical control are usually held by political authorities. In state-organised societies, these sticks are one element of state sovereignty (Beitz 1991: 243).

23. On this distinction see F. von Benda-Beckmann (1979: 43); Bruce (1988). Some anthropologists speak of sovereignty and ownership (Lloyd 1959; Vanderlinden 1969). Gluckman (1972: 89) called these two levels 'estates of administration' and 'estates of production'.

24. See Goodenough (1951); F. von Benda-Beckmann (1979: 45).

25. One of the more interesting features of the human genome debate is the question of who has rights in this new valuable or set of valuables, and which rights are provisional and which are residual.

26. While both categorical and concretised property relations can be usefully seen as bundles of rights, they are bundles of a quite different nature. We see this if we extend the use of the metaphor more systematically to actual property relationships.
27. It is notable that many scholars who use them frequently begin by acknowledging that the 'Big Four' have their limitations. Unfortunately, they then go on to argue that the simplifications remain the best categories available.
28. See also Cole (2002).
29. After Hardin's (1968) essay on the commons, many scholars attempted to clarify that commons, such as grazing lands, were rarely open access resources, but rather institutionalised property resources. However, little has been done in analysing actual open access resources.
30. See Feder and Feeny (1993: 241). When the embeddedness of property relations is concerned, however, the focus is usually on the embeddedness of the property *relation* in other social relationships, while other sorts of embeddedness, such as of categorical property rights in the legal (or ideological) realm, are ignored.
31. For example, see the F. von Benda-Beckmann (2003) critique of De Soto (2000). For examples in which some of these distinctions have fruitfully been made, see Sugarman (1981); Berry (1988); Bruce (1988); Chambers and Leach (1989); F. von Benda-Beckmann (1990); Thompson (1993); Van de Ven (1994); Peters (2002).
32. Renner's (1929) study of European property systems is probably the first to show that in the transition from petty commodity production to capitalist production, important changes in the constellation of property relationships and their social, economic and political functions (*Funktionswandel*) could occur without any important change in categorical legal construction of property and labour relationships (*Normwandel*). Similar patterns have also been demonstrated in studies on rural development in the Third World. See also for Europe, Tigar and Levy (1977); Sugarman (1981); Thompson (1993). For the Chagga in Tanzania, see Moore (1986).
33. On intellectual properties, see Coombe (1998).
34. See F. von Benda-Beckmann (1992); Wiber (1995, 1999, 2000, 2005); Wiber and Kearney (1996); Wiber and Kennedy (2001).
35. See North (1990); Ostrom (1990); Feder and Feeny (1993).

References

Alexander, C. 2004. 'Value, Relations, and Changing Bodies: Privatisation and Property Rights in Kazakhstan', in *Property in Question: Value Transformation in the Global Economy*, eds K. Verdery and C. Humphrey, Oxford, New York: Berg, 251–73.

Allott, A.N., A.L. Epstein and M. Gluckman 1969. 'Introduction', in *Ideas and Procedures in African Customary Law*, ed. M. Gluckman, Manchester: Manchester University Press, 1–81.

Arthurs, H.W. 1997. 'Globalisation of the Mind: Canadian Elites and the Restructuring of Legal Fields', *Canadian Journal of Law and Society* 12(2): 219–46.

Balland, J.M. and J. Ph. Platteau 1999. 'The Ambiguous Impact of Inequality on Local Resource Management', *World Development* 27: 773–88.

Barzel, Y. 1989. *Economic Analysis of Property Rights*. Cambridge: Cambridge University Press.

Beitz, C.R. 1991. 'Sovereignty and Morality in International Affairs', in *Political Theory Today*, ed. D. Held, Oxford: Polity Press, 236–54.

Benda-Beckmann, F. von 1979. *Property in Social Continuity: Continuity and Change in the Maintenance of Property Relationships through Time in Minangkabau, West Sumatra*. The Hague: Martinus Nijhoff.

——— 1990. 'Sago, Law and Food Security on Ambon', in *The World Food Crisis: Food Security in Comparative Perspective*, ed. J.I.H. Bakker, Toronto: Canadian Scholars' Press Inc., 157–99.

——— 1992. 'Uncommon Questions about Property Rights', *Recht der Werkelijkheid* 1: 8–14.

——— 1995. 'Anthropological Approaches to Property Law and Economics', *European Journal of Law and Economics* 2: 309–36.

——— 2000. 'Relative Publics and Property Rights. A Cross Cultural Perspective', in *Property and Values. Alternatives to Public and Private Ownership*, eds C. Geisler and G. Daneker, Washington, D.C.: Island Press, 151–73.

——— 2001. 'Between Free Riders and Free Raiders: Property Rights and Soil Degradation in Context', in *Economic Policy and Sustainable Land Use. Recent Advances in Quantitative Analysis for Developing Countries*, eds N. Heerink, H. van Keulen and M. Kuiper, Heidelberg: Physica-Verlag, 293–316.

——— 2002. 'Who's Afraid of Legal Pluralism?', *Journal of Legal Pluralism* 47: 37–82.

——— 2003. 'Mysteries of Capital or Mystification of Legal Property?', *Focaal - European Journal of Anthropology* 4: 187–91.

Benda-Beckmann, F. von and K. von Benda-Beckmann 1994. 'Property, Politics and Conflict: Ambon and Minangkabau Compared', *Law and Society Review* 28: 589–607.

——— 1999. 'A Functional Analysis of Property Rights, with Special Reference to Indonesia', in *Property Rights and Economic Development*, eds T. van Meijl and F. von Benda-Beckmann, London, New York: Kegan Paul International, 15–56.

Benda-Beckmann, K. von 1981. 'Forum Shopping and Shopping Forums', *Journal of Legal Pluralism* 19: 117–59.

——— 1984. *The Broken Stairways to Consensus: Village Justice and State Courts in Minangkabau, Verhandelingen van het Koninklijk Instituut voor Taal-, Land- en Volkenkunde*, Dordrecht, Leiden: Foris Publications, KITLV Press.

——— 1995. 'Private Ownership of Air-shares: An Appropriate Way of Letting the Poor Profit from the Global Natural Resource Base?', in *Proceedings of the Legon Conference of the Commission on Folk Law and Legal Pluralism*, ed. H. Finkler, Ottawa: DIAND, 283–98.

——— 2001. 'Legal Pluralism', *Tai Culture* VI(1 & 2): 11–17.

——— 2003. 'The Contexts of Law', in *Legal Pluralism and Unofficial Law in Social, Economic and Political Development. Papers of the XIIIth International Congress, 7–10 April, 2002, Chiang Mai. Thailand*, ed. R. Pradhan, Kathmandu: ICNEC, 299–315.

Benda-Beckmann, K. von, M. de Bruijn, H. van Dijk, G. Hesseling, B. van Koppen, L. Rys 1997. *Rights of Women to the Natural Resources Land and Water*. The Hague: Ministry of Development Cooperation.

Berkes, F. 1996. 'Social Systems, Ecological Systems, and Property Rights', in *Rights to Nature. Ecological, Economic, Cultural, and Political Principles of Institutions for the Environment*, eds S. Hanna, C. Folke and K.-G. Mäler, Washington, D.C.: Island Press, 87–107.

—— 1999. *Sacred Ecology*. Philadelphia: Taylor and Francis.

Berry, S. 1988. 'Concentration without Privatisation? Some Consequences of Changing Patterns of Rural Land Control', in *Land and Society in Contemporary Africa*, eds R.E. Downs and S.P. Reyna, Hanover and London: University Press of New England, 53–75.

Bohannan, P. 1969. *Justice and Judgement Among the Tiv*. London: Oxford University Press.

Bruce, J.W. 1988. 'A Perspective on Indigenous Land Tenure Systems and Land Concentration', in *Land and Society in Contemporary Africa*, eds R.E. Downs and S.P. Reyna, London: University Press of New England, 23–53.

Chambers, R. and M. Leach 1989. 'Trees as Savings and Security for the Rural Poor', *World Development* 17: 329–42.

Chanock, M. 1985. *Law, Custom and Social Order: The Colonial Experience in Malawi and Zambia*. Cambridge: Cambridge University Press.

Clammer, J. 1973. 'Colonialism and the Perception of Tradition in Fiji', in *Anthropology and the Colonial Encounter*, ed. T. Asad, Atlantic Highlands: Humanities Press, 199–220.

Cole, D.H. 2002. *Pollution and Property: Comparing Ownership Institutions for Environmental Protection*. Cambridge: Cambridge University Press.

Coombe, R. 1998. *The Cultural Life of Intellectual Properties*. Durham: Duke University Press.

Costanza, R. and C. Folke 1996. 'The Structure and Function of Ecological Systems in Relation to Property Rights Regimes', in *Rights to Nature*, eds S. Hanna, C. Folke and K.-G. Mäler, Washington, D.C.: Island Press, 13–34.

De Janvry, A., A. Sadoulet and E. Thorbecke 1993. 'Introduction – State, Market and Civil Organisations: New Theories, New Practices and their Implications for Rural Development', *World Development* 21: 565–75.

Demsetz, H. 1967. 'Toward a Theory of Property Rights', *The American Economic Review* 57(2): 347–59.

De Soto, H. 2000. *The Mystery of Capital*. New York: Basic Books.

Dezalay, Y. and B. Garth 1995. 'Merchants of Law as Moral Entrepreneurs: Constructing International Justice from the Competition for Transnational Business Disputes', *Law and Society Review* 29(1): 27–64.

Dietz, T., E. Ostrom and P.C. Stern 2003. 'The Struggle to Govern the Commons', *Science* 302: 1907–12.

Ellickson, R.C. 1991. *Order Without Law: How Neighbors Settle Disputes*. Cambridge, MA: Harvard University Press.

Feder, G. and D. Feeny 1993. 'The Theory of Land Tenure and Property Rights', in *The Economics of Rural Organisation*, eds K.A. Hoff, A. Braverman and J.E. Stiglitz, New York: Oxford Press, 240–58.

Geisler, C. 2000. 'Property Pluralism', in *Property and Values. Alternatives to Public and Private Property*, eds C. Geisler and G. Daneker, Washington, D.C.: Island Press, 65–86.

Gluckman, M. 1972. *The Ideas in Barotse Jurisprudence*. Manchester: Manchester University Press.

———— 1973 [1955]. *The Judicial Process among the Barotse of Northern Rhodesia (Zambia)*, 2nd edn, Manchester: Manchester University Press.

Godrej, D. 2002. '8 Things You Should Know about Patents on Life', *New Internationalist* 349 (Sept): 9–12.

Goldman, M. 1998. 'Inventing the Commons: Theories and Practices of the Commons' Professional', in *Privatizing Nature*, ed. M. Goldman, London: Pluto Press, 20–53.

Goldschmidt, W. 1966. *Comparative Functionalism*. Berkeley: University of California Press.

Goodall, K. 1990. '"Public" and "Private" in Legal Debate', *International Journal of the Sociology of Law* 18: 445–58.

Goodenough, W.H. 1951. *Property, Kin and Community on Truk*. New Haven: Yale University Publications in Anthropology No. 46.

Goody, J. 1962. *Death, Property and the Ancestors*. Stanford: Stanford University Press.

Griffiths, A. 2002. 'Legal Pluralism', in *An Introduction to Law and Social Theory*, eds R. Banakar and M. Travers, Oregon: Hart Publishing, 289–310.

Gunderson, L.H. and C.S. Holling 2002. *Panarchy. Understanding Transformations in Human and Natural Systems*. Washington, D.C.: Island Press.

Hann, C.M., ed. 1998. *Property Relations: Renewing the Anthropological Tradition*. Cambridge: Cambridge University Press.

Hann, C.M. and the 'Property Relations Group' 2003. *The Postsocialist Agrarian Question: Property Relations and the Rural Condition*. Hamburg: LIT Verlag (Halle Studies in the Anthropology of Eurasia, no. 1).

Hanna, S.S., C. Folke and K.-G. Mäler eds, 1996. *Rights to Nature. Ecological, Economic, Cultural, and Political Principles of Institutions for the Environment*. Washington, D.C.: Island Press.

Hardin, G. 1968. 'The Tragedy of the Commons', *Science* 162: 1234–48.

Hirschon, R. 1984. 'Introduction: Property, Power and Gender Relations', in *Women and Property – Women as Property*, ed. R. Hirschon, London, Canberra, New York: Croom Helm, St. Martin's Press, 1–22.

Hohfeld, W.N. 1923. *Fundamental Legal Conceptions as Applied in Judicial Reasoning and Other Essays*. New Haven: W.W. Cook.

Holleman J.F., ed. 1981. *Van Vollenhoven on Indonesian Adat Law*. The Hague: Martinus Nijhoff.

Hunt, R.C. 1998. 'Properties of Property: Conceptual Issues', in *Property in Economic Context*, eds R.C. Hunt and A. Gilman, Lanham, New York, Oxford: University Press of America, 8–27.

Hunt, R.C. and A. Gilman, eds 1998. *Property in Economic Context*. New York, Oxford: University Press of America.

Jodha, N.S. 1986. 'Common Property Resources and Rural Poor', *Economic and Political Weekly* 21, 5 July 1986: 1169–81.

Johnson, C. 2004. 'Uncommon Ground: The "Poverty of History" in Common Property Discourse', *Development and Change* 35(3): 407–33.

Juul, K. and C. Lund, eds 2002. *Negotiating Property in Africa*. Portsmouth: Heinemann.

Leach, E. 1961. *Rethinking Anthropology*. London: The Athlone Press.

Libecap, G. 1989. 'Distributional Issues in Contracting for Property Rights', *Journal of Institutional and Theoretical Economics* 145: 6–24.

——— 1990. *Contracting for Property Rights*. Cambridge: Cambridge University Press.

Lloyd, P.C. 1959. 'Some Notes on the Yoruba Rules of Succession and on Family Property', *Journal of African Law* 3: 7–32.

Lynch, O. 1992. 'Securing Community-based Tenurial Rights in the Tropical Forests in Asia: An Overview of Current and Prospective Strategies', *Issues in Development*: 1–11.

Maine, H. 1986 [1861]. *Ancient Law*. London: J. Murray.

——— 1883. *Dissertations on Early Law and Custom*. London: J. Murray.

McCarthy, J. 2002. 'Contesting Decentralisation: Law, Power and Access to Property in Central Kalimantan, Indonesia', paper presented at the workshop 'Mobile people, mobile law: Expanding legal relations in a contracting world', Halle/Saale, Germany.

McCay, J. and J.M. Acheson, eds 1987. *The Question of the Commons*. Tucson: University of Arizona Press.

Meijl, T. van and F. von Benda-Beckmann, eds 1999. *Property Rights and Economic Development: Land and Natural Resources in Southeast Asia and Oceania*. London: Kegan Paul International.

Merry, S.E. 1988. 'Legal Pluralism', *Law and Society Review* 22(5): 869–96.

Moore, S. F. 1969. 'Descent and Legal Position', in *Law in Culture and Society*, ed. L. Nader, Chicago: Aldine Press, 374–400.

——— 1986. *Social Facts and Fabrications: 'Customary' Law on Kilimanjaro 1880–1980*. Cambridge: Cambridge University Press.

Nader, L. 1965. 'The Anthropological Study of Law', *American Anthropologist* 67(6): 3–32.

——— , ed. 1969. *Law in Culture and Society*. Chicago: Aldine Publishers.

New Internationalist 2002, Special Issue: Patents on Life. *New Internationalist* 349 (September).

Newman, K.S. 1983. 'Theories of Legal Evolution', in *Law and Economic Organisation*, ed. K.S. Newman, Cambridge: Cambridge University Press, 6–49.

North, D. 1981. *Structure and Change in Economic History*. New York: W.W. Norton and Co.

——— 1990. *Institutions, Institutional Change and Economic Performance*. Cambridge: Cambridge University Press.

Ostrom, E. 1990. *Governing the Commons*. Cambridge: Cambridge University Press.

Ostrom, E. and E. Schlager 1996. 'The Formation of Property Rights', in *Rights to Nature*, eds S. Hanna, C. Folke and K.-G. Mäler, Washington, D.C.: Island Press, 127–56.

Ostrom, E., T. Dietz, N. Dolžak, P.C. Stern, S. Stonich and E. Weber, eds 2002. *The Drama of the Commons.* Washington, D.C.: National Academy Press.

Peters, P.E. 2002. 'The Limits of Negotiability: Security, Equity and Class Formation in Africa's Land Systems', in *Negotiating Property in Africa*, eds K. Juul and C. Lund, Portsmouth: Heinemann, 45–66.

Pollack, A. 2004. 'European Patent on U.S. Gene Test is Revoked', *International Herald Tribune*, 20 May 2004: 16.

Pospíšil, L. 1971. *Anthropology of Law.* New York: Harper and Row.

Povinelli, E. 2002. *The Cunning of Recognition, Indigenous Alterities and the Making of Australian Multiculturalism.* Durham & London: Duke University Press.

Randeria, S. 2003. 'Glocalisation of Law: Environmental Justice, World Bank, NGOs and the Cunning State in India', *Current Sociology* 51(3–4): 307–30.

Reich, C. 1964. 'The New Property', *Yale Law Journal* 72: 733.

Reeve, A. 1991. 'The Theory of Property: Beyond Private Versus Common Property', in *Political Theory Today*, ed. D. Held, Oxford: Polity Press, 91–114.

Renner, K. 1929. *Die Rechtsinstitute des Privatrechts und ihre soziale Funktion.* Tübingen: Mohr.

Richards, J.F. 2002. 'Toward a Global System of Property Rights in Land', in *Land, Property, and the Environment*, ed. J.F. Richards, Oakland, California: ICS Press, 13–37.

Rose, C.M. 1994. *Property and Persuasion. Essays on the History, Theory, and Rhetoric of Ownership.* Boulder: Westview Press.

—— 1998. 'Canons of Property Talk, or, Blackstone's Anxiety', *Yale Law Journal* 108(3): 601.

—— 1999. 'Expanding the Choices for the Global Commons: Comparing New Fangled Tradable Allowance Schemes to Old-fashioned Common Property Regimes', *Duke Environmental Law and Policy Forum* 10(1): 45.

—— 2003. 'Romans, Roads, and Romantic Creators: Traditions of Public Property in the Information Age', *Law and Contemporary Problems*: 89–111.

Rose, N. 1987. 'Beyond the Public/Private Discussion: Law, Power and the Family', *Journal of Law and Society* 14: 61–76.

Schlager, E. and E. Ostrom 1992. 'Common Property and Natural Resources; a Conceptual Analysis', *Land Economics* 68(3): 249–52.

Spiertz, J. and M.G. Wiber, eds 1996. *The Role of Law in Natural Resource Management.* Themanummer Recht der Werkelijkheid 1996/2.

Strathern, M. 1999. *Property, Substance and Effect: Anthropological Essays on Persons and Things.* London: The Athlone Press.

Sugarman, D. 1981. 'Theory and Practice in Law and History: A Prologue to the Study of the Relationship between Law and Economy from a Socio-historical Perspective', in *Law, State and Society*, eds B. Fryer, A. Hunt, D. McBarnet and B. Moorhouse, London: Croom Helm, 70–106.

Taylor, M. 1998. 'Governing Natural Resources', *Society and Natural Resources* 11: 251–58.

Thompson, E.P. 1993. *Customs in Common.* New York: The New Press.

Tigar, M.E. and M.R. Levy 1977. *Law and the Rise of Capitalism.* New York and London: Monthly Review Press.

Trigger, D. 2003. 'Mining Projects in Remote Aboriginal Australia: Sites for Contesting Visions of Economic and Cultural Futures', paper presented at 'Mining Frontiers: social conflicts, property relations and cultural change in emerging boom regions'. Max Planck Institute for Social Anthropology Workshop, 16–18 June 2003.

Vanderlinden, J. 1969. 'Réflexions sur l'Existence du Concept de Propriété Immobilière Individuelle dans les Droits Africains Traditionnels', in *Ideas and Procedures in African Customary Law*, ed. M. Gluckman, Manchester: Manchester University Press, 236–51.

Ven, J. van de 1994. 'Members Only: Time-sharing Rice Fields and Food Security in a Sumatran Valley', in *Coping with Insecurity: An 'Underall' Perspective on Social Security in the Third World* 22/23, eds F. v. Benda-Beckmann, K. v. Benda-Beckmann and H. Marks, Yogjakarta: Pustaka Pelajar, 85–96.

Verdery, K. 2004. 'The Obligations of Ownership: Restoring Rights to Land in Postsocialist Transylvania', in *Property in Question: Value Transformation in the Global Economy*, eds K. Verdery and C. Humphrey, Oxford, New York: Berg, 139–59.

Verdery, K. and C. Humphrey, eds 2004. *Property in Question: Value Transformation in the Global Economy*, Oxford, New York: Berg.

Weintraub, J. 1997. 'The Theory and Politics of the Public/Private Distinction', in *Public and Private in Thought and Practice. Perspectives on a Grand Dichotomy*, eds J. Weintraub and K. Kumar, Chicago and London: University of Chicago Press, 1–42.

Wiber, M.G. 1993. *Politics, Property and Law in the Philippine Uplands*. Waterloo, Ont.: Wilfrid Laurier University Press.

—— 1995. 'Everyday Forms of Violence: Farmer's Experiences of Regulation in the Canadian Dairy Industry', *Journal of Legal Pluralism and Folk Law* 35: 1–24.

—— 1999. 'Caught in the Cross-hairs: Liberalizing Trade (Post M.A.I.) and Privatizing the Right to Fish. Implications for Canada's Native Fisheries', *The Journal of Legal Pluralism* 44: 33–51.

—— 2000. 'Fishing Rights as an Example of the Economic Rhetoric of Privatisation: Calling for an Implicated Economics', *Canadian Review of Sociology and Anthropology* 37(3): 267–88.

—— 2005. 'Mobile Law and Globalism: Epistemic Communities Versus Community-based Innovation in the Fisheries Sector', in *Mobile People, Mobile Law: Expanding Legal Relations in a Contracting World*, eds F. von Benda-Beckmann, K. von Benda-Beckmann and A. Griffiths, Aldershot: Ashgate, 131–51.

Wiber, M.G. and J. Kearney 1996. 'Stinting the Commons: Property, Policy or Powerstruggle? Comparing Quota in the Canadian Dairy and Fisheries Sectors', in *The Role of Law in Natural Resource Management*, eds M.G. Wiber and J. Spiertz, 's-Gravenhage: Vuga Press, 145–66.

Wiber, M.G. and J. Kennedy 2001. 'Impossible Dreams: Reforming Fisheries Management in the Canadian Maritimes after the Marshall Decision', *Law and Anthropology* 11: 282–97.

Chapter 2
Ownership in Stateless Places*

Charles Geisler

Introduction

First among the properties of Western property is its embeddedness in
state law, authority and sovereignty. Failed property systems, we are told,
are a hallmark of weak states. For many, property without the state is an
oxymoron; the state is the ultimate guarantor and trustee of property.
This canon is the parent property of property. It typically reads as follows
(Hackworth 1940: 465–66): 'Ownership, in its essential features … is
secured to the owner under the authority of the Government exercising
the right of sovereignty …' (cited in Pop 2000: 278).

As the introductory essay to this volume suggests, however, Western
property is a mix of legal concepts, myths and ideological propositions. It
may be instructive to ask whether the parent property is flawed and
whether too tight a coupling between property and state blinds us to state
abuses of property. I pose these possibilities en route to a deeper, perhaps
more heretical question: must contemporary property presuppose a
working state? I suggest that our ability to fully imagine property and its
future properties suffers from our tendency to grant the state too
permanent a seat at the property table.[1]

In this chapter, I revisit the intellectual history of the parent property
to underscore the difficulties of disembedding it. I then turn to the twin
dilemmas of state perishability and state perfidy. Together, they give
readers critical distance on the state-property nexus and challenge its
indelible nature. Next, I survey the growing storefront of non-state
spaces (or 'counterpaces') in support of the claim that state-centric

---

* I am grateful to Keebet von Benda-Beckmann, Shelley Feldman, Paul Gellert, Jason Cons and
coauthors in this book for providing valuable feedback on earlier chapter drafts.

property overdetermines common conceptions of property. The final section returns to our originating question, answers it in the negative, and points to non-state-property precedents in concluding that diverse social organisations – not just nation states – sanction and protect property.

States and Ownership

The marriage of state and property is deeply inscribed in Western thinking (Pollock 1896; Appadurai 1996; Taylor 1996). John Locke, to whom we largely owe its modern formulation, welded property and state together by writing that the protection of property is the 'sole reason for the state to exist' (1690: Ch. 9, Sec. 124).[2] According to Thompson (1975: 21), 'The British state, all eighteenth-century legislators agreed, existed to preserve the property and, incidentally, the lives and liberties, of the propertied.' Despite Locke's reputation as a liberal breaking with the old regime, his formulation grafts comfortably onto feudal tenure theory keyed to a sovereign monarch. All title in the (pre-state) realm hinged on the king's power to defend the kingdom, to subdivide it, and to protect the subdivision (Gray 1995).

The cement between the 'state' and property seems changeless, as indicated in scholarship since the appearance of Locke's *Two Treatises of Government*. Such work clings to the notion of state as the sine qua non of property and draws more or less consciously on Locke's two-stage historical account of private property replacing state-of-nature property (*terra nullius*) as money and markets became prevalent (Lasslett 1970; Tully 1980). We will have more to say about terra nullius later; a quick excursion into the scholarship nourished by Locke's ideas says much about the parent property.

Louis Henry Morgan's work, *Ancient Society* (1877), was widely translated and read in the nineteenth century. Morgan, like Locke,[3] divides history into two epochs, one ancient ('Societas') and the other modern ('Civitas'). The latter was founded on property. Human nature 'craves' privilege and power, for which property, in the form of inheritance, becomes the repository. Instead of liberty, equality and fraternity (hallmarks of Societas and Locke's 'state of nature'), in Civitas there are tendencies towards inequality. Property and inheritance become driving forces and shape key institutions, including the state itself. With embellishments, Morgan arrives at Locke's position: 'Government, institutions, and laws are simply contrivances for the creation and protection of property' (White 1937: 269).

Slightly more enigmatic is Herbert Spencer, the social evolutionist, who strenuously argued against state involvement in human affairs. Yet his influential *Social Statics* (1850) clearly and eloquently advocated fundamental human equality and rights, including the right to equal landownership for all.[4] Therein, Spencer draws on Locke's 'prepolitical' state of nature to support Locke's post state-of-nature conclusions. Spencer's uncharacteristic call for state protection of property rights is noteworthy because of his general skepticism over any positive role for the state in society. The real duty of the state for Spencer is to administer justice, which consists of maintaining the law of equal freedom (his basic tenet) and of protecting the life and property of the citizens from internal robbery, fraud, and external invasion (Spencer, Chapter 21 in *Social Statics* 1850 [1970] and Barnes 1948: 130).

The tight coupling between states and property rights continues vigorously through Hegel, Marx and Engels into the present era. A neoclassical version of this state-property affinity is present in the work of Nobel Laureate, Douglas North (1981: 21):

> ... A state is an organisation with a comparative advantage in violence, extending over a geographic area whose boundaries are determined by its power to tax constituents. The essence of property rights is the right to exclude, and an organisation which has a comparative advantage in violence is in the position to specify and enforce property rights ... One cannot develop a useful analysis of the state divorced from property rights.

This said, North adopts the now-familiar two-stage human history. Stage one (North's first economic revolution) begins with the dawn of agriculture and lasts until the nineteenth century. The exploitative or 'predatory state' evolves therein ('an endless saga of war, exploitation, and enslavement') and was tolerated because individuals preferred it to anarchy. The predatory state specifies property rights that maximised the revenues of the group in power, regardless of the impact on society as a whole (North, 1981: 22). The modern state that follows behaves like a 'discriminating monopoly', separating constituent groups and devising property rights for each to maximise state revenue.

In a landmark work, Alvin Gouldner (1970) appeals for a fresh sociological perspective on property. As with North, modern property is not about solidarity and trust (Locke's world of communal property) but about power and privilege shielded by the state. Says Gouldner (1970: 313):

> The state provides ready and willing protection for property, and, in return, owners provide the state with the resources and moral support needed to maintain its activities on behalf of 'law and order.' ... [t]he state and property owners commonly develop mutual understanding and appreciation. For in the end the greed of the state is less costly to property owners than would be the needs of the disadvantaged. Relatively willing and able to support the state, and defined therefore as responsible, loyal, and reliable, property owners can commonly rely on the state's reciprocal responsiveness to their interests.

Oddly, both North and Gouldner reveal dark sides of the parent property master frame – to which I return below – without abandoning it.

Similar conclusions of these and other authors add weight to the bunker assumption under discussion: property somehow 'needs' states. Felix Cohen (1954–55: 357) spoke for many in the legal profession when he defined private property in terms of 'exclusions which individuals can impose or withdraw with state backing against the rest of society.' Yet perils were and are at hand. The state's ability to protect property is far from guaranteed, if only because states perish. Furthermore, even if states were immutable, their public interest record – uncritically assumed in the parent property – would give most observers pause. We will review each of these perils in turn.

The Perishable State

The withering of the state, whether toppled from without, or crumbling from within, is in constant debate.[5] Half a century ago Arendt (1951) offered powerful critique of the state model. Today, states are widely viewed as constructed and contingent rather than natural and eternal. Scholars busily profile 'weak states', the weakest typically being those lacking domestic order, including dominion over land and territory (Muir 1997). The vulnerability of states is implied in Harvey's (1996) generic discussion of places as 'permanences' created from space. Herein he cautions: 'The permanences – no matter how solid they seem – are not eternal: they are always subject to time as "perpetual perishing", and contingent on the processes that create, sustain and dissolve them.' (1996: 261, cited in Benda-Beckmann 1999: 133).

The cumulative forces eroding states and state-centric logic are immense, as is the literature assessing them (see Brenner 2004). I will refer to three among many: globalisation, citizen disenfranchisement, and evolving non-state warfare. Globalisation itself is multidimensional. It refers to transboundary technologies; to evolving international bureaucracies (the World Trade Organisation, the International Criminal Court, the European Union, the European Central Bank, the United Nations, etc.); to transnational economic interests (roughly half of the world's largest economies are multinational corporations (Horsman and Marshall 1994); to the proliferation of nongovernmental organisations with regional and global offices; and to off-shore trends in production, consumption and finance. Some organisations competing with states for allegiance are secretive (e.g., those that launder some $1.5 trillion each year (Dresner 2001) or illegal (cartels, mafias, terrorist networks). International trade agreements (e.g., NAFTA and the pending Free Trade Area of the Americas) empower individual investors to sue foreign governments, thereby overturning social and environmental laws created by elected officials (Greider 2001). A new political economy is emerging in which state survival is precarious and organs external to the state are thriving.[6]

Just as ominous, states are disenfranchising the people for whom they speak and in whose name they protect property. Disenfranchisement takes many forms. Eviction, exile, forced migration and asylum-seeking leave growing numbers of people uprooted, homeless and potentially stateless (Appadurai 1996). Still other forms of displacement are in situ (i.e., loss of civil rights, services, shelter, secure employment, citizenship and identity) (Feldman et al. 2003). State policies frequently undermine environmental rights by degrading ecosystem services and life-support systems (Jacobson 1998). Nor, as North forewarned, is the state a safe haven for citizens who escape displacement. The number of peopled killed by states (massacres, executions, forced labor, induced famines, genocide) between 1900 and 1987 was four times the number of deaths from international and civil wars in the same period (Rummel 1994, 1997). As Kibreab (1999: 387) states, '... the "right to remain" ... does not make sense unless it means the right to stay in that territory in safety ...' The view that the world is an orderly mosaic of relatively benign sovereign units filled with enfranchised citizens is a seriously arrested framework (Olwig 1999).

Warfare has long threatened individual states, but a new generation of warfare threatens the state model of governance as a system. Given the disenfranchisement just referred to, few readers will be surprised that states as 'homelands' is a contested subject. The world's 5,000 ethnic groups currently reside in 200 nations; many of the former lack sovereignty over territory in the latter (Byers 1991).[7] States find themselves internally convulsed by a new form of opposition called 'fourth generation warfare' (Van Creveld 1991; Lind 2003) unfolding not between states, but between states and networks, sects and ethnic nations. 'At the core of Fourth Generation warfare', according to Lind (2003: 20), 'is a universal crisis of legitimacy of the state ... In virtually every country, including the U.S., one of the biggest growth industries is the private security business. Nothing testifies more clearly to the failure of the state.' New warfare strategies are sidelining states, their armies and their peace processes.[8]

States as a system of sovereign governments and territories are in crisis and transformation (McChesney 2003; Rotberg 2003). U.S. Secretary of Defense, Donald Rumsfeld recently expressed concern that an increasing number of areas in Latin America were falling outside of government control (Robinson 2003: 36–44). These were accurate perceptions. The state model is perishable, as are individual states. This short registry of major state difficulties and dysfunctions calls the parent property into serious question. So do certain aspects of state performance with respect to property.

State Perfidy

First and foremost, 'states' are not unitary entities. They vary radically in internal agencies, organisation and interests. They are dissimilar in their laws, their accountability and their due process. When it comes to property, 'the state' means quite different things. In some contexts, a central state bureaucracy determines the rules and distribution of property; in others, these prerogatives are devolved to powerful sub-states. In almost all matters of property, 'state' in the U.S. refers to 50 separate entities with different statutes, constitutions and interpretations of their police powers (Philbrick 1938). The Declaration of Independence says nothing directly about property, and the Constitution limits itself to instruction on takings and due process in its Amendments. More substantive issues of what constitutes antisocial uses of property vary widely within and between nation states (Benda-Beckmann 2000), an on-going vexation to planners, land reformers, and advocates for social and environmental justice.

More troubling is the issue of 'whose state?' State power not only jumps between levels and public agencies, but is highly susceptible to capture by private property interests who invert the relationship and tarnish public trust. As Beard (1923) documented long ago, the U.S. Constitution originated among and reflected the interests of privileged propertied groups of the day. At base, the document is an economic blueprint, based upon the concept that 'property rights should be beyond the reach of popular majorities' (1923: 324).[9] Few litmus tests of this view are as telling as the checkered life of eminent domain in the U.S. and elsewhere. Repeatedly, this extraordinary power of the state over property has been used to take property from one owner (or sector, class, or ethnic group) and bestow it on another (Scheiber 1973), blatantly subsidising the welfare of some at the expense of others. With horrifying regularity, states reinterpret the public interest to align with what private interests believe they are entitled to and have the power to claim.

It is a short step from the above to important conflicts of interest with respect to property to which few states are immune. The state is the senior owner of and landlord over property. By law the state is entrusted to manage what is public and regulate (and tax) what is private. Employing this trust, states can legally make as well as break property (Coward 2001; Kruekeberg 2004). That is, they can grant title to themselves or their supporters (and award windfalls through these entitlements) and can extinguish title (or decrease value) in targeted or capricious ways (Runge et al. 2000). The abuses of public lands and resources by the world's states would fill a small encyclopedia; regarding private property (land and other), the state is perpetually caught between condoning property concentration and its redistribution and conservation (Geisler 1995). In short, states are seldom neutral arenas warranting the ownership rights of more-or-less equal citizens, and state 'protection' is politically constructed and structurally compromised (Philbrick 1938; Mitchell 1998). As aptly summarised by Vandergeest and Peluso (1998), there is a lack of fit between abstract state property and lived state property.

Finally, it is naïve to assume that the liberal state of Locke enjoyed a clean break with the 'prepolitical states' of feudalism and other *ancien regimes* thought to be less enlightened. Not only do prior forms of political organisation not end punctuality, but 'old' and 'other' property systems, as legal pluralists have long insisted, have a way of confounding, enriching and complicating later property relationships (Benda-Beckmann 1999). Britian's Parliament terminated feudalism in 1660 but completed the task only in 1922 (Gray 1995). Scotland officially abolished feudalism only in the new millenium (Chenevix-Trench and Philp 2001). Who is protecting what for whom under what legal mandate in the name of 'the state'? It is far from clear.

Counterspaces

We arrive, then, at a turning point in conventional thinking on the parent property of property. The state-based framework is a popular though restraining myth, riddled with validity problems with respect to permanence and performance. I turn now to non-state places and property systems; some are categorical departures and others are more relative shifts away from the parent property framework. Having seen that a strong state is not essential to property and may in fact abuse or corrupt it, we ask who protects property in non-state spaces and by what authority?

One window on non-state space is found in legal scholarship on *terra nullius*, or domains which, borrowing a slightly awkward term from Gray (1991), were never 'propertised.' Recall that Locke painted all early property with this brush, expecting it to become private with state protection as property improvement (the investment of labour) and the medium of money spread. Gray maintains, however (1991: 257), that 'Contrary to popular perception, the vast majority of the world's human and economic resources still stand outside the threshold of property and therefore remain unregulated by any proprietary regime.'[10] In a similar vein, Pop (2000) reviews legal opinions on ownership in outer space (seemingly remote, but once again relevant with current space probes) in the absence of state sovereignty. He concludes that, despite non-appropriation treaties for sovereign states, private appropriation remains a legal option (only state-led claims are banned in the treaties). That is, property does not require a strong (or any particular) state.

Some will be uncomfortable using the *terra nullius* window, seeing it as far afield from state realities at present. James Scott (1998) and others explore the less exotic case of non-state places and property therein. For Scott (1998: 37), many traditional property systems are too complicated or anachronistic for 'efficient state management and administration.' From a mainstream Western perspective, they are irregular and recalcitrant – neither public nor private. Though numerous, they are difficult to map, inventory and tax. Practically speaking, they are illegible to state administrators.[11] States therefore reclassify such property into more legible systems or deny their legitimate existence altogether; history suggests that the latter invites state or private appropriation, which facilitates legibility. In a similar and somewhat earlier vein, Lefebvre (1974) recognised the 'continuous struggle over and within the organisation of space, including the production of "counter spaces" by social actors opposed to the dominant order.'

Scott's work alerts us to the tip of a counterspace iceberg. Van Schendel (2002) describes hundreds of property enclaves along the border of West Bengal and Bangladesh lacking legal integration in either state. 'The issue of unadministered enclaves,' according the Van Schendel (2002: 140) 'points ... to the spatial limits of states and to the importance of identifying non-state spaces in the modern world.' These range from no-man's lands, frontier societies, and war zones to disputed islands; they also include spaces well within state territories, e.g., the high mountains, marshes, dense forests, deserts and mangrove swamps that appear 'empty' but in which permanent or seasonal human colonies (and illegible property systems) flourish.[12] They include but are not limited to zones of state opposition in, say, apartheid South Africa (Cross 1991), the Philippines (Chapman 1988), northern and southern Iraq (Vick and Williams 2003), Colombia (Robinson 2003), Chiapas (Lappe et al. 1998), Sri Lanka (Vije 1986), in Chechnya (Gall and De Walle 1998) and a long list of global squatter settlements (Durand-Lasserve and Royston 2002).

Yet not all non-state spaces are opposed to the state. Indeed some may supplant the state and, despite Scott's interpretation, have the state's conditional blessing. Indeed, they may be vested with powers conferred by the state. Cases include religious land grants, proprietary domains and frontier trading companies (Sakolski 1957). Britain's East India Company was chartered by Queen Elizabeth I in 1600 and thrived until 1874 with breathtaking independence – including its own army, currency, presses, cartographic bureaucracies, legislative powers, taxation prerogatives and expansive property rights. Other trading monopolies included the Dutch East India Company (1602 to 1798) and the French East India Company (1664 to 1769). So powerful was the British East India Company charter that Edmund Burke questioned, in a famous speech to Parliament, whether its charter amounted to a Magna Carta granting the company independent political power (Mehta 1999: 134).

Counterspaces are and were a familiar circumstance on colonial frontiers in a quasi-oppositional form as well: self-proclaimed independent republics. The Commonwealth of Massachusetts was chartered as an independent colony by Charles I. With this charter, the Bay Company managed its affairs as an independent, religious republic. Freemen elected their officials and made their own laws (something not widely practiced in England itself). Property rights were spelt out in the General Court's Body of Liberties; grants of six square miles went to clusters of fifty to one hundred people for commons, proprietary use and settlement. When England pitched towards Civil War, Puritan emigration to the colony intensified (nearly 20,000 people between 1628 and 1650). The King's Privy Council ordered that the colony's charter be returned to England; the colony threatened armed popular resistance and did not comply (Loury 1987). Its local theocratic sanctions over property prevailed.

The American War for Independence stirred many counterspace experiments, some quite bloody, as have independence movements elsewhere (e.g., Van Schendel's case). For the most part, assertions of sovereignty and self-determination over property matters by indigenous 'nations' were brutally suppressed by settler states.[13] Yet settlers themselves were often insubordinate, and collectively challenged the property prerogatives of colonial and post-colonial governments. In North America, the new states were required by the Continental Congress to relinquish western property claims, some of which spanned the continent to the Pacific Ocean (Sakolski 1957; Loury 1987). Some regions, which lacked former administrative status, left the Union altogether, taking their real estate with them. For example, Vermont was an Independent Republic for more than a decade after Independence (Singer 2000). Half a century later, Texas became an independent republic as well, after American settlers colonised northeast Mexico in 1821. They voluntarily became subjects of the Mexican government, developed their own land system, assembled a militia (Texas Rangers), and eventually revolted from Mexico. For ten years, until the Mexican War, Texas was a breakaway republic with self-made property rules (Webb 1931).

Conclusion: Disembedding Property from the State

The question on which we embarked in this chapter was whether contemporary property presupposes a working state. We have now seen that property rights predated the state model of governance, they have survived outside of states for centuries, and not all property rights systems within states have positive sanctions. Still others are undecipherable to states, by design or default. We have further seen that the state itself is a problematic protector of property. The counterspaces presented here range from *terra nullius* and frontier colonies (at times run by nonstates) to autonomous enclaves within states. Some counterspace property is formal and legal (religious, corporate); some is informal and extralegal.[14] The parent property of property is indeed tenuous.

This conclusion may be dramatised with two final examples, one from pre-Civil War America and the other still unfolding in eastern and central Europe. Like Texas, California belonged to Mexico in the nineteenth century. When war between the United States and Mexico ended in 1848, California entered jurisdictional limbo until statehood in 1850. During the two-year hiatus, some 200,000 miners flocked to the territory to prospect. By 1850, '… miners had organised into groups and had agreed upon explicit contracts in which exclusive and transferable rights to land were assigned to individuals within a given mining area or district' (Umbeck 1981: 5). By 1866 over 500 separate districts had formed, each with their own system of property rights. So property, as we suspected (e.g., Becker 1992), presupposes a strong state only some of the time. A second example is contemporary – the property systems that prevailed after the termination of the Soviet Bloc in 1989–91. There, new states replaced old states, but property protected by the latter persisted – or at best remained highly ambiguous – despite commitment by the former and powerful international support for privatising ownership. So this 'Second Great Transformation' (Hann 1998) existed more on paper than in practice from a property standpoint (Verdery 1998). Just as the prior socialist states were unable to command complete socialist property, the post-socialist states have been unable to decree universal private property. The 'recombinant property' that followed was neither foreseen nor prescribed by state laws or constitutions (Stark 1996).

Exactly where does this leave those seeking to understand non-state property niches and their properties?[15] In what is property embedded if not the state? California's jurisdictional limbo between 1848 and statehood was not absolute limbo, as we have just observed, nor was Australia's vast *terra nullius* a property void, though declared as such by the British Crown in the nineteenth century.[16] Even Locke's famous theoretical division between the world of expanding private ownership and state-of-nature communal ownership did not contest the existence of property beyond the reach of the state. Communal ownership was merely a property form of little account because it lacked a labor signature assigning it to individuals and a money system to hasten its privatisation.

More significantly, it lacked Locke's conceptualisation of a sovereign state to protect it. Yet it existed. There was a property 'there'. *Terra nullius* was not a land 'of nobody', as is widely (mis)understood (Mitchell 1998), but a propriety place subject to non-state sanctions and terms of reference.

The final point, then, is that property is embedded in social, political and economic organizations, which may or may not be working states.[17] State-centric thinking dominates cartography and geography, theories of trade and nationalism, business cycles and arms races, the world of patents and foreign policy, the logic of sovereignty and 'national' identity, and remains the main counterweight to globalisation. Is it any wonder that we have used it to overdetermine the origins of property since the time of Locke? As indicated earlier, a close look at 'the state' yields a web of interests that are contradictory and at times dysfunctional for property protection. The state's much vaunted monopoly on violence and power are absolute in theory but not in practice. The state has alter egos including the Vatican, major corporations, international cartels, mobile mafias, global indigenous networks, warlord fiefdoms, and a long list of 'offshore' interests that are not state-centric. Most define and defend property of their own making on their own terms, while coexisting with states and state property.

Notes

1. For useful commentary on 'seeing' property in unfamiliar ways, see Rose (1994). As for a familiar definition of state – one used here – see the definition by North (1981) which appears later in the text.
2. For elaboration of the political-philosophical context in which Locke produced his ideas on property, see Alexander (1997) and Hann (1998). His Two Treatises were a rebuttal to Robert Filmer's powerful defence of absolute monarchy (Mehta 1999), and possibly the competing property logic of Catholics (converting heathens and thereafter annexing heathen lands) in Rome, in the New World (Spain was a threat to Virginia and Locke's proprietary lands in North Carolina), and England itself (see Bond et al. 2002).
3. Locke equated 'the world owned in common' with *terra nullius* because it contained no human labour, the basis for possession (Mehta 1999).
4. At first glance Spencer may seem impossibly idealistic using this standard. But consider Locke himself in accounting for (and explaining away) the concentration of land (see Tully 1980 and Kruekeberg 2004a).
5. Wallerstein's exploration of absolutism and statism is relevant here. He cautions that '... [e]ven the strongest states in the sixteenth century were hard pressed to demonstrate clear predominance within their frontiers of the means of force, or

command over the sources of wealth, not to speak of primacy of the loyalty of their subjects.' (1974: 94).

6. Some authors are sceptical that globalization weakens nation states (e.g. Brenner 2004).

7. In additional to ethnic nationhoods we might add loyalty to Appadurai's (1990) 'scapes' (ethnoscapes, mediascapes, technoscapes, finanscapes and ideoscapes) as transboundary alternatives to states in organising peoples' time, interests and loyalties.

8. From this perspective, national security is no longer equivalent to state security. Hannah Arendt's much-read essay on 'The Decline of the Nation-State and the End of the Rights of Man' (1951) speaks at length about what is now called deterritorialisation (e.g., Ohmae 1990; Debrix 1998; Ferguson and Gupta 2002). Arendt portrays the dysfunction of nation-states before and after the First World War, particularly for stateless minorities. Prior to that war, minority populations constituting 100 million people enjoyed neither freedom nor self-determination in the European states they inhabited. Afterwards, up to half of the populations in some European states were legally forgotten, the victims of states which closed their borders in crude attempts at ethnic cleansing. Cultural nations and political states pulled apart and continue to do so.

9. See Underkuffler (1991) for a list of authors who have built on Beard's analysis.

10. Byers (1991) would dispute the claim that global commons have not been enclosed; about 40 percent of the oceans are now claimed by states.

11. These surely number in the thousands; see Burger et al. (2001) for discussion of the expanding spatial scale of common property regimes taken cumulatively.

12. In relative terms, statelessness occurs where population density is low, temporary or nonexistent (e.g., Saudi Arabia's Empty Quarter, arctic barrenlands, Australia's Outback, or even the 'internal frontier zones' of the contemporary U.S. – veritable no-man's lands on a grand scale (Popper 1984; Popper et al. 2000).

13. Illustrations of this phenomenon abound. An interesting exception are resistant Mayan zones in the Yucatan and Quintana Roo and the substantial homeland zone of the Miskito, Sumo and Rama Indian nations in northern and eastern Nicaragua (Hale 1994).

14. Informal property should not be conflated with customary ownership. Informal property, or more accurately ownership arrangements, range from the gift-based systems (Mauss 1967), to pawn shops, to rights of trespass, and access to a wide range of informal market products and processes (Peluso et al. 1994), rental agreements (Grossman 2000), and reciprocal norms within and between families usually not encoded in law (Hirtz 1998). Household spaces serve as informal non-state places for women in (some) societies where state protection is problematic (e.g., Emmott 1996; Ilcan 1998).

15. The useful notion of property niches appears in Fortmann and Nhira (1992)

16. Mabo v Queensland (No 2), (1992) 175 CLR 1 (see Gray 1995)

17. I owe this insight to Keebet von Benda-Beckmann. She points out that the British did not recognise the political organisation of indigenous Australians, thus claiming *terra nullius* and asserting territorial sovereignty, but did recognise

such organisation among the Maori of New Zealand (and made no *terra nullius* claim). Both positions were consistent with the parent property which went largely unchallenged in the mid-nineteenth century.

References

Alexander, G.S. 1997. *Commodity and Propriety: Competing Visions of Property in American Legal Thought 1776–1970.* Chicago: University of Chicago Press.

Appadurai, A. 1990. 'Disjuncture and Difference in the Global Cultural Economy', in *Global Culture: Nationalism, Globalisation and Modernity*, ed. M. Featherstone, London: Sage, 295–310.

——— 1996. 'Sovereignty without Territoriality: Notes for a Postnational Geography', in *The Geography of Identity*, ed. P. Yaeger, Ann Arbor: University of Michigan Press, 40–58.

Arendt, H. 1951. *The Origins of Totalitarianism.* New York: Harcourt, Brace and Co.

Barnes, H.E., ed. 1948. *An Introduction to the History of Sociology.* Chicago: University of Chicago Press.

Beard, C.A. 1923. *Economic Interpretation of the Constitution of the United States.* New York: Macmillan.

Becker, L.C. 1992. 'Too Much Property', *Philosophy & Public Affairs* 21: 196–206.

Benda-Beckmann, F. von 1999. 'Multiple Legal Constructions of Socio-Economic Spaces: Resource Management and Conflict in the Central Moluccas', in *Frontiers and Borderlands: Anthropological Perspectives*, eds M. Rösler and T. Wendl, Frankfurt: Peter Lang, 131–58.

——— 2000. 'Relative Publics and Property Rights: A Cross-Cultural Perspective', in *Property and Values*, eds C. Geisler and D. Daneker, Washington, D.C.: Island Press, 151–74.

Bond, E.L., J.L. Perkowski and A.P. Weber 2002. 'Father Gregorio Polivar's 1625 Report: A Vatican Source for the History of Early Virginia', *The Virginia Magazine of History and Biography* 110: 69–86.

Brenner, N. 2004. *New State Spaces: Urban Governance and the Rescaling of Statehood.* Oxford: Oxford University Press.

Burger, J., B.D. Goldstein, R.B. Norgaard, E. Ostrom and D. Policansky, eds 2001. *Protecting the Commons. A Framework for Resource Management in the Americas.* Washington, D.C.: Island Press.

Byers, B. 1991. 'Ecoregions, State Sovereignty and Conflict', *Bulletin of Peace Proposals* 22: 65–76.

Chapman, W. 1988. *Inside the Philippine Revolution: The New People's Army and its Struggle for Power.* London: I.B. Taurus.

Chenevix-Trench, H. and L.J. Philp 2001. 'Community and Conservation Land Ownership in Highland Scotland: A Common Focus in a Changing Context', *Scottish Geographical Journal* 117: 139–56.

Cohen, F. 1954–55. 'Dialogue on Private Property', *Rutgers Law Review* 9: 357, 373, 378.

Coward Jr., E.W. 2001. 'Making Property in the Taos Valley', paper presented at conference 'Moving Targets: Displacement, Impoverishment, and Development', Cornell University, 9–10 November 2001.

Cross, C. 1991. 'Informal Tenure against the State: Landholding Systems in African Rural Areas', in *Harvest of Discontent: The Land Question in South Africa*, ed. M. de Klerk, New York: R. Schalkenbach Foundation, 31–49.

Debrix, F. 1998. 'Deterritorialised Territories, Borderless Borders; the New Geography of International Medical Assistance', *Third World Quarterly* 19: 827–46.

Dresner, D.W. 2001. 'Sovereignty for Sale', *Foreign Policy*, September/October: 76–77.

Durand-Lasserve, A. and L. Royston, eds 2002. *Holding their Ground: Secure Land Tenure for the Urban Poor in Developing Countries*. London: Earthscan.

Emmott, S. 1996. '"Dislocation", Shelter, and Crisis: Afghanistan's Refugees and Notions of Home', *Gender and Development* 4: 31–38.

Feldman, S., C. Geisler and L. Silberling 2003. 'Moving Targets: Displacement, Impoverishment, and Development', *International Social Science Journal* 175: 1–7.

Ferguson, J. and A. Gupta 2002. 'Spatializing States: Towards an Ethnography of Neoliberal Governmentality', *American Ethnologist* 29(4): 981–1002.

Fortmann, L. and C. Nhira 1992. 'Local Management of Trees and Woodland Resources in Zimbabwe: A Tenurial Niche Approach', *Occasional Paper*, no. 43, Oxford: Forestry Institute.

Gall, C. and T. de Walle 1998. *Calamity in the Caucasus*. New York: New York University Press.

Geisler, C. 1995. 'Land and Poverty in the United States: Insights and Oversights', *Land Economics* 71: 16–34.

Gouldner, A. 1970. *The Coming Crisis in Western Sociology*. New York: Avon Books.

Gray, K. 1991. 'Property in Thin Air', *Cambridge Law Journal* 50: 252–307.

———— 1995. 'Property in Common Law Systems', in *Property Law on the Threshold of the Twenty-first Century*, eds G.E. van Maanen and A.J. van der Walt, Antwerpen: MAKLU, 235–83.

Greider, W. 2001. 'Sovereign Corporations', *Nation*, 30 April 2001: 21–29.

Grossman, M. 2000. 'Leasehold Interests and the Separation of Ownership and Control in U.S. Farmland', in *Property and Values*, eds C. Geisler and G. Daneker, Washington, D.C.: Island Press, 119–48.

Hackworth, G.H. 1940. *Digest of International Law*, vol. I. Washington, D.C.: US Government Printing Office.

Hale, C.R. 1994. *Resistance and Contradiction: Miskitu Indians and the Nicaraguan State 1894–1987*. Stanford, CT: Stanford University Press.

Hann, C.M., ed. 1998. *Property Relations: Renewing the Anthropological Tradition*. New York: Cambridge University Press.

Harvey, D. 1996. *Justice, Nature & Geography of Difference*. Oxford: Blackwell Publishers.

Hirtz, F. 1998. 'The Discourse that Silences: Beneficiaries. Ambivalence towards Redistributive Land Reform in the Philippines', *Development and Change* 29: 247–75.

Horsman, M. and A. Marshall 1994. *After the Nation State*. London: HarperCollins.

Ilcan, S. 1998. 'Challenging Settlement: Rural Women's Culture of Dis-placement', in *Transgressing Borders: Critical Perspectives on Gender, Household and Culture*, eds S. Ilcan and L. Phillips, Westport: Bergin and Garvey, 55–73.

Jacobson, D. 1998. 'State and Society in a World Unbound', in *Public Rights, Public Rules: Constituting Citizens in the World Polity and National Policy*, ed. C.L. NcNeeley, New York: Garland, 41–57.

Kibreab, G. 1999. 'Revisiting the Debate on People, Place, Identity and Displacement', *Journal of Refugee Studies* 12(4): 384–428.

Kruekeberg, D.A.2004a. 'The Lessons of John Locke or Hernando do Soto: What if your Dreams Come True?', *Housing Policy Debate* 15: 1–24.

——— 2004b 'Property without Community: The (Frequent) Consequences of Tax Exemptions for Non-profit Institution', in *Private Property in the Twenty-first Century*, ed. H.M. Jacobs, Cheltenham, U.K.: Edward Elgar, 125–42.

Lappe, F.M., J. Collins and P. Rosset 1998. *World Hunger: Twelve Myths*. New York: Grove Press.

Lasslett, P. 1970. *Two Treatises of Government / John Locke; A Critical Edition with an Introduction and Apparatus Criticus by Peter Laslett*. London: Cambridge University Press.

Lefebvre, H. 1974. *Production of Space*. New York: Blackwell.

Lind, W.S. 2003. 'Wars without Countries', *American Conservative*, 7 April 2003: 19–21.

Locke, J. 1690. *Two Treatises of Government*. London: Awnsham Churchill.

Loury, G. 1987. *How the Nation was Won*, vol. I. Washington D.C.: Executive Intelligence Review.

Mauss, M. 1967. *The Gift: Forms and Functions of Exchange in Archaic Societies*. New York: Norton.

McChesney, F.S. 2003. 'Government as Definer of Property Rights', in *Property Rights: Cooperation, Conflict, and Law*, eds T.L. Anderson and F.S. McChesney, Princeton: Princeton University Press, 227–53.

Mehta, U.S. 1999. *Liberalism and Empire: A Study of Nineteenth-Century British Liberal Thought*. Chicago: University of Chicago Press.

Mitchell, J.H. 1998. *Trespassing*. Reading: Addison Wesley.

Morgan, L.H. 1877. *Ancient Society*. Calcutta: Bharati Library.

Muir, R. 1997. *Political Geography: New Introduction*. New York: Palgrave Macmillan.

North, D. 1981. *Structure and Change in Economic History*. New York: W.W. Norton and Co.

Ohmae, K. 1990. *The Borderless World*. London: Collins.

Olwig, K.F. 1999. 'Caribbean Place Identity: From Family Land to Region and Beyond', *Identities* 5: 435–67.

Peluso, N., L. Fortmann and C. Humphrey 1994. 'The Rock, the Beach and the Tidepool: People and Poverty in Natural Resource-dependent Areas', *Society and Natural Resources* 7: 23–38.

Philbrick, F.S. 1938. 'Changing Conceptions of Property in Law', *University of Pennsylvania Law Review* 86: 691–732.

Pollock, F. 1896. *The Land Laws*. London: Macmillan.

Pop, V. 2000. 'Appropriation in Outer Space: The Relationship between Land Ownership and Sovereignty on the Celestial Bodies', *Space Policy* 16: 275–82.

Popper, D.E., R.E. Lang and F.J. Popper 2000. 'From Maps to Myth: The Census, Turner, and the Idea of the Frontier', *Journal of American and Comparative Cultures* 23: 91–102.

Popper, F.J. 1984. 'Survival of the American Frontier', *Resources* 77: 1–4.

Robinson, L. 2003. 'Special Report: Why Special Forces are America's Tool of Choice in Colombia and around the Globe', *U.S. News and World Report*, 10 February: 36–44.

Rose, C.M. 1994. *Property and Persuasion: Essays on the History, Theory, and Rhetoric of Ownership*. Boulder: Westview Press.

Rotberg, R., ed. 2003. *When States Fail: Causes and Consequences*. Princeton: Princeton University Press.

Rummel, R.J. 1994. *Death by Government*. Piscataway, NJ: Transaction Publications.

—— 1997. *Statistics of Democide*. Center for National Security Law. Piscataway: Transaction Publications.

Runge, C.F., M.T. Duclos and J.S. Adams 2000. 'Public Sector Contributions to Private Land Value: Looking at the Ledger', in *Property and Value*, eds C. Geisler and G. Daneker, Washington, D.C.: Island Press, 41–62.

Sakolski, A.M. 1957. *Land Tenure and Taxation in America*. New York: Robert Schalkenbach Foundation.

Scheiber, H.N. 1973. 'Property Law, Expropriation, and Resource Allocation by Government: The U.S., 1789–1910', *Journal of Economic History* 33: 232–51.

Scott, J.C. 1998. *Seeing Like a State*. New Haven: Yale University Press.

Singer, J. 2000. *Entitlement: The Paradoxes of Property*. New Haven: Yale University Press.

Spencer, H. 1970 (1850). *Social Statics*. New York: Robert Schalkenbach Foundation.

Stark, D. 1996. 'Recombinant Property in Eastern Europe's Capitalism', *American Journal of Sociology* 11: 993–1027.

Taylor, P.J. 1996. 'Embedded Statism and the Social Sciences: Opening up to New Spaces', *Environment and Planning* A28: 1917–28.

Thompson, E.P. 1975. *Whigs and Hungers: The Origins of the Black Act*. New York: Pantheon.

Tully, J. 1980. *A Discourse on Property: John Locke and his Adversaries*. New York: Cambridge University Press.

Umbeck, J. 1981. *A Theory of Property Rights: With Application to the California Gold Rush*. Ames: Iowa State University Press.

Underkuffler, L.S. 1991. 'The Perfidy of Property', *Texas Law Review* 70: 293–316.

Van Crefeld, M. 1991. *The Transformation of War*. New York: Free Press.

Vandergeest, P. and N.L. Peluso 1998. 'Territorialisation and State Power in Thailand', *Theory and Society* 24: 385–426.

Van Schendel, W. 2002. 'Stateless in South Asia: The Making of the India-Bangladesh Enclaves', *The Journal of Asian Studies* 61, February: 115–47.

Verdery, K. 1998. 'Property and Power in Transylvania's Decollectivisation', in *Property Relations: Renewing the Anthropological Tradition*, ed. C.M. Hann, New York: Cambridge University Press, 160–80.

Vick, K. and D. Williams 2003. '"Kurdish Experiment" Continues in Northern Iraq', *The Ithaca Journal* (Friday, 3/7): 3A (from The Washington Post).

Vije, M. 1986. *The Militarisation of Sri Lanka*. London: Tamil Information Centre.

Wallerstein, I.M. 1974. *The Modern World System*. New York: Academic Press.

Webb, W.P. 1931. *The Great Plains*. New York: Grosset & Dunlap.

White, L.A., ed. 1937. *Extracts from the European Travel Journal of Lewis H. Morgan*. Rochester Historical Society Publications XVI: 269–70.

Chapter 3

The Romance of Privatisation and its Unheralded Challengers: Case Studies from English, Russian, Soviet and Post-Soviet History

Esther Kingston-Mann

The spirit of property doubles a man's strength – The possessor of property desires a wife to share his happiness, and children to assist in his labors. His wife and his children constitute his wealth. The estate of such a cultivator, under the hands of an active and willing family, may become ten times more productive than it was before. (Voltaire 1769)

Introduction: Axioms, Economics and the Challenge of Empirical Evidence

In every culture, there are values so widely accepted that they are rarely discussed. They are 'what everybody knows' and require no explanation. That private tenure enhances economic performance is one such axiomatic belief, repeatedly validated – in the eyes of a wide range of Western economists, philosophers, historians, poets, policy makers, and progressives of the Right and Left – in every time and place. This paper explores the link between private tenure and economic performance – not as an axiomatic truth, but as a hypothesis to be tested. It will further consider the possibility that axioms, however useful, may impose constraints upon our understanding, and lead us to ignore significant empirical evidence to the contrary. To wit:

In the 1970s and 1980s, the policies of the World Bank fostered the establishment of a worldwide property regime that unequivocally privileged individual ownership. In sub-Saharan Africa, the Bank's structural adjustment programmes required a wholesale privatisation of common, public and socially controlled resources. These policies failed to generate higher productivity rates. Instead, economic output fell by 30 percent in the 1980s; by the mid-1990s, per capita income in sub-Saharan Africa stood at 80 percent of the 1980s level (Gibbon et al. 1993: 103–10; Peters, this volume). In the 1990s, similar privatisation strategies were introduced – with similar consequences – into the states of the former Soviet Union. By December 1996, per capita monthly income in the Russian Republic stood at 47 percent of its 1992 level (Caskie 2000: 206). By 2004, the population of the Russian Federation was declining at a rate of 500,000 per year, with less than half of today's sixteen year olds expected to live until the age of sixty (*Argumenty i Fakty*, 1 June 2004). Overall rural production has fallen by more than 40 percent over the past decade (Visser, this volume).

How is one to understand a truth unshaken by data of this magnitude? It is useful to consider – among others – the following explanation: In discourses on privatisation, we enter a world of myth and romance where courageous architects of private property rights confront starkly dichotomised choices between progress and backwardness. As this adventure unfolds, the lazy and malevolent attempt to thwart the property-owner's effort to construct the only possible gateway to a more productive modern world. It should be noted that such romantic scenarios are not wrongheaded; it is quite appropriate to highlight private initiatives that inspire others to produce material benefits that reach beyond the individual. However, a characteristic feature of the romantic narrative is that its heroes and heroines overshadow – and are too often prone to demonise – the non-elite individuals and social groups who play out their lives offstage or behind the scenes. In the context of these time-honoured omissions, the following discussion will explore the relationship between property rights and economic performance by considering a significantly wider range of actors in England's Agricultural Revolution and in Russia from the late nineteenth century to the present day.

England: Model or Cautionary Tale?

Who would be at the pains of tilling [the earth] if another, might ... seize upon and enjoy the product of his industry, art and labour? (William Blackstone, *Legal Commentaries*)

In the course of a centuries-long Agricultural Revolution, radical innovations in field use and large-scale land improvement transformed the English landscape and excited the imagination of progressives the world over. In a process remarkably free of external threat or challenge, England's three-field system and strip cultivation were replaced by consolidated fields and multiple-field crop rotations, convertible husbandry made use of all of the agricultural land each season, and great quantities of marsh and swamp were transformed into ploughland. Although these changes were triggered neither by technological breakthroughs nor by the enclosure of common lands, these two factors nevertheless came to dominate both the historical accounts and the economic analysis of England's transformation.

Innovators in the English Countryside: Actors and Non-actors on the Historical Stage

The symbolic mainstay and hero of England's Agricultural Revolution was the 'improving landlord'; in the eighteenth century, his struggles against the 'country bumpkins' of the open fields and the 'medievalism' of local and national officials became the stuff of legend (and of classical economic theory). Foreign observers ranging from Voltaire and Diderot to the Russian serfowner, Ivan Petrovich-Belianin, internationalised this message, attempting to convince progressives in their home countries that miracles of economic innovation and productive economic behaviour could be unleashed by a landlord-dominated enclosure movement. However, although the evidence of landowner ingenuity has understandably carried great weight, researchers have in recent years begun to complicate the rather one-sided historical canon that awarded to landowners a virtual monopoly on economic initiative.

The most neglected economic actor in England's Agricultural Revolution was the English tenant. As the agricultural historian P.J. Perry long ago observed, 'one of the remarkable features of high farming is its development by tenant farmers enjoying little or no security' (Perry 1981: 156–66). Although tenants are generally understood to have been at the forefront of initiatives for agricultural innovation, modern scholarship has tended to ignore their history. As a consequence, we possess no body of systematic comparative data that would permit us to draw useful conclusions about the degree of tenure security or insecurity that either promoted or constrained innovation and change among tenants and owners. In the years to come, it is to be hoped that researchers will engage in more study of this topic.

Somewhat more is known about innovations by smallholders who made use of common lands and open fields, and rooted their ownership claims in a history of occupation or labour on the land. Despite their lack of schooling and the meagreness of their resources to bear the costs and risks of change, open field farmers in seventeenth-century Oxfordshire appear to have secured the consent of their neighbours to the village-wide introduction of multiple-field systems of crop rotation. Available evidence suggests that the use of fodder crops spread more rapidly on the open fields than on the large-scale private estates of the Thames district (Havinden 1961: 73–83). Some innovations turned out to have been particularly well suited to open field systems, because the preparatory measures required could be more easily implemented by communities than by solitary small producers (Dahlman 1990: 174–76).

On occasion, even champions of enclosure like Arthur Young conceded that private ownership was not always the decisive factor in decisions to innovate. In some areas under open field cultivation, he found crops were 'inexplicably' good, with open field farmers who 'agreed among themselves to sow turnips instead of fallowing on many of their lands'; equally puzzling to Young was the evidence indicating that farmers might use the same outmoded techniques in both open *and* enclosed fields. Unfortunately, despite the vast scholarly literature on the enclosure movement, there is little empirical data to indicate either (1) the degree and extent of rural innovation in open field communities, or (2) whether English communities – like their Russian counterparts – devised systems of reward for individual innovation within the community framework (see below, pp. 112–13).

Moving down the social ladder, we find the agricultural labourers. In the eighteenth- and nineteenth-century English literature of agricultural transformation, members of this group were more often the object of ridicule than of empirical research, and have rarely been a topic for study by modern scholars. Although I have been able to locate a single scholarly article in the 1980s that explored the relationship between 'user-modification' by intelligent agricultural labourers and the success of agricultural innovation (MacDonald 1981: 84), the literature of the Agricultural Revolution has tended in general to emphasise the labourers' penchant for 'wild, irrational, ungodly and undisciplined behavior' (reformer John Sinclair), or inventor Jethro Tull's claim that he was driven to devise new tools as a way to thwart the 'deceit and idleness' of his workers. While innovators like George Boswell praised gifted labourers who adapted new tools and techniques for use in a particular context, he seems to have been something of a rarity among the leading agricultural writers of the day (Kingston-Mann 1999b: 14–15).

Women were the social group whose agency was probably most drastically constrained by the privatisation of common lands, because they (and their children) were the gleaners, the cutters of wood and of peat for fuel. It was women's work to scavenge the commons for nuts, berries, mushrooms and herbs that supplemented the diet of their households. The commons supplied products whose use or sale enabled women to contribute significantly to the household's domestic comforts and livelihood. With few exceptions, there has been relatively little research on the role of women in the changes that comprise England's Agricultural Revolution (Humphries 1990: 22).

If we set aside the routinely derogatory references to their backwardness, the vast majority of the rural population are largely absent from the master narrative of England's Agricultural Revolution, and are joined in obscurity by the British Parliament. Anti-statist Liberal reformers and scholars declined to acknowledge Parliament's substantial role, either as planner and founder of vast regional swamp drainage projects, or as the provider of generous subsidies to 'improving landlords'. As a consequence, the heterogeneous realities of economic change fostered by a variety of agents gave way to more heroic scenarios that highlighted the owner/innovator's uphill battle to foster rational economic behaviour despite the machinations of ignorant commoners and corrupt bureaucrats.

England's Enclosure Movement: Either/Or

In England, enclosures were first documented in the fifteenth century, when a variety of coercive and non-coercive strategies facilitated conversion of the commons (and even cultivated holdings) into private sheep pastures to serve the developing English wool trade. Privatising initiatives gathered momentum in the wake of a seventeenth-century civil war that threatened the survival of England's landed elite, and generated a discourse of improvement that demonised opponents of enclosure as 'primitives' and denied the complexity of their motives, aims and intentions. Like low-status populations in other times and places, some English smallholders engaged in compromise and selective adaptation while others expressed their opposition by destroying deeds and fenceposts and sending threatening letters to local authorities. In general, scholars have tended to focus on the yeoman farmers who concluded voluntary enclosure agreements with the landed gentry, in order – according to economic historian D. McCloskey – to break free from the 'archaic land tenure arrangements of the past'.[1]

In general, smallholders were not the major beneficiaries of enclosure. Owners who possessed the most land beforehand received the lion's share of the common lands enclosed, and a gentry-dominated Parliament privileged land claims based on deed and contract over the traditional claims of labour, occupation or need. In the eighteenth and nineteenth centuries, productivity rates rose on giant, privately owned estates managed by tenants who in turn hired the labourers who introduced convertible husbandry, fenced the moors and drained the marshes. Based on the meagre evidence available, it may be fair to say that (1) England's agricultural reforms were introduced not only by owners but by tenants, and to some degree by open field communities, as well as by yeoman farmers; (2) changes introduced by estate owners were far more extensively documented and studied than open field innovation; (3) land clearing and swamp drainage projects were largely financed by local and national government authorities. In this process, Parliament legitimised the private claims of rural entrepreneurs, criminalised the traditional claims of open field cultivators, and ignored efforts by the latter to engage in farming innovation.

Dilemmas of Freedom, Constraint and Agency

In the eighteenth century, reforming landlords and liberal economists contended that having to seek the consent of others was not only an obstacle to productive economic behaviour but an unconscionable constraint on the individual's freedom. To its advocates, unrestricted rights of private ownership established England as the standard-bearer for freedom in every possible sphere of human activity. These quite extraordinary claims tended in many cases to overshadow some of the important historical contradictions within which eighteenth-century private property rights and its burgeoning claims were embedded. Alongside the freedom-loving yeoman farmer, Liverpool slave merchants purchased freehold landed property and proclaimed themselves advocates of human liberty, while legal theorist William Blackstone argued that individual freedom resided above all in the despotic power to exclude the claims of others. In his words, 'There is nothing which so strikes the imagination and engages the affections of mankind, as the right of property; or that sole and despotic dominion which one man claims and exercises over the external things of the world, in total exclusion of the right of any other individual in the universe' (cited in Rose 1986: 711). Few among England's unlettered commoner population were capable of contending with theorists like Blackstone. But in the writings of the nineteenth-century ploughman-poet, John Clare, we find the suggestions of a counterargument. Turning Blackstone's claims upside down, Clare argued that true independence was manifest above all in the right of rural inhabitants to freely make use of common lands accessible to all. According to Clare, the erection of fences on previously open land left both 'men and flocks imprisoned, ill at ease' (cited in Heys 1987: 10–11). To Clare, fences were not symbols of freedom because they served to *narrow* the choices and opportunities available to the rural lower classes.

Although Blackstone's celebration of the unfettered individual inspired would-be entrepreneurs the world over, his arguments also served to reify the individual actor by attributing to the latter far more agency than was likely to have been acquired by the simple purchase of a deed of ownership for a piece of common land. The modern preoccupation with constraints imposed by open field communities frequently masked the quite powerful constraints that enclosure imposed upon the agency of commoners. Before enclosure, the income that open field farming households obtained from their varied economic activities provided them with the option to decide whether to accept, refuse or negotiate the terms offered by landlords in return for their labour. Commoners thus possessed the power to disrupt large-scale farming operations at key periods in the agricultural cycle. It was precisely the exercise of this sort of freedom that troubled a Shropshire reporter to the Board of Agriculture who complained in 1794 that rights to common land encouraged among labourers 'a sort of independence' indistinguishable from insubordination. However, once rights to common land were eliminated, hired labourers would 'work every day in the year/ Their children could be put out to labour early', [thus reinforcing] 'the subordination of the lower ranks of society which in present times is so much wanted'. With the countryside enclosed, the open field farmer's wife (and children) would have no choice but to make themselves available as a seasonal reserve labour force to be hired and fired as needed by estate owners for hay-making or harvest activities (Neeson 1984: 134 and Humphries 1990: 28–30).

Instead of asking whether greater constraints were imposed by open field communities or by enclosure, it may be more useful to ask whose agency is constrained under each of these systems of landholding – all rural inhabitants or only certain groups (e.g., landlords or women)? As an Africanist legal scholar has suggested in a very different context, our assessment of 'the seriousness of the constraint and the appropriateness of the strategy for dealing with it will depend on the answer to this question' (Bruce 1993: 35–55).

The Supposed Enemies of Innovation

In practice, the much-despised 'foot draggers' in the enclosure movement did not invariably oppose either change or enclosure. The seventeenth-century 'Diggers' defended open field farming as part of their appeal to commoners to use fertiliser to enrich the soil. When they attempted to 'dig up' the commons to plant fodder crops, the Diggers were imprisoned for infringement of private property rights. In the eighteenth century, the radical Thomas Spence demanded that public authorities lease out land allotments for terms long enough to benefit the individual and allow for innovation, and in sufficient quantities to give the poor a chance at survival. Repeatedly imprisoned for his anti-enclosure activity, Spence was denounced as a 'primitive' by Thomas Malthus for contending that the welfare of small farmers was fully compatible with the cause of agricultural improvement (Rudkin 1927).

Eighteenth-century 'anti-enclosure' letters reflected ambivalence as well as opposition to change. An anonymous 1798 letter warned that 'heartless' enclosers would be 'sorted out from the land of the living', but included as well the poignant promise that if the gentry could only bring themselves to compromise, they would gain the 'Poore's hearts and their all'. Rather than calling for a halt to all enclosures, the letter's unknown author(s) demanded a more equitable division of enclosed and privatised lands among smallholders. Although we do not know how the Parish of Cheshunt responded, a Draconian Parliament enacted legislation that made the sending of anonymous letters a capital crime (Thompson 1975).

In many respects, the history of England's enclosure movement reveals the workings of an almost 'totalitarian' privatisation strategy. As it played out, the unequal power relations between commoners and landlords turned out to be more decisive than the laws of Parliament in determining the outcome of struggles to re-shape, resist or foster the enclosure movement. Contemporary observers tended to reduce the interaction between enclosers and the hostile, undecided or flexible elements within the rural populace to a romantic struggle between landlord improvers and those described by Arthur Young as the 'Goths and Vandals of the open fields' (Mingay, 1975: 111).

From a twenty-first-century perspective, both the claims advanced for the benefits of enclosure and the contention that utter stagnation represented the only possible alternative seem overdrawn. However, without data on the economic behaviour of tenants, or systematic comparative study of commons users and yeoman farmers, it remains exceedingly difficult to sort out the complex relationship between tenure and economic performance in the English case.

Russia: a Developing Society

If you guarantee to a man the rights of property in the desert, he will turn it into a smiling garden, but if you lease the garden to the same man for nine years, he will turn it into a howling desert. (Finance Minister Witte, citing John Stuart Mill, citing Arthur Young)

England's popularity as a model for rural transformation is easily attributable to its extraordinary economic triumphs, its impact upon the plans and strategies of other nations, and its place in the cultural imagination of the Western and non-Western world. However, the Russian case is instructive for very different reasons. Most importantly, Russia possessed far more statistical and economic data about its pre-enclosure rural population than England or any other nation in the world before the second half of the twentieth century. Between the 1870s and 1905, Russian researchers interviewed 4.5 million peasant households and compiled an immense quantity of empirical evidence about rural economic behaviour (Kingston-Mann, 2005a). In contrast to England, Russian data permits a far more empirically grounded examination of the concretised property relations and social practices of creating, maintaining and changing property relationships.

Equally instructive was Russia's experience as a developing society engaged in an early version of a Third World, life-and-death struggle to catch up with the west (Shanin 1986). By the 1880s, the subjugation of predominantly peasant societies the world over by empires that fostered private property rights convinced many Russian radicals and conservatives that anti-communal strategies might enable Russia to avoid the dismal fate of nineteenth-century Ireland, India or China.[2] As the

Marxist Lenin urged peasants to abandon their 'medieval' communes, tsarist Minister of Finance Witte enthusiastically cited English reformer Arthur Young on the 'magic of property'. Whatever their differences, the tsarist regime and its Marxist critics agreed that productivity increase required the speedy advent of capitalism (Kingston-Mann 1999: 112–32, 166–80). While the findings contained in Russia's immense statistical database did not provide definitive answers to the tenure question, they would – as the following discussion indicates – profoundly illuminate both the complexities of communal tenure and the relationship between tenure and economic performance.

Communal Tenure and the Russian Peasant Commune (*mir*, or *obshchina*)

Above all, Russian statistical data demonstrated that the peasant communes to which the majority of the population belonged were mixed economies within which individual, household and community-wide rights to ownership coexisted in social configurations that varied regionally and over time. The object of centuries of idealisation and demonisation by a host of radicals, reformers and government officials (Kingston-Mann 1999: 126), the commune's distinguishing feature was the periodic repartition of land allotments among member households according to family size, the number of adult labourers per household, or some other collective social principle.

Peasant allotments were not private property. In keeping with the Emancipation of 1861, both allotments and common lands belonged to the communes and peasant households were accorded rights to land use only as commune members. At the same time, individual commune members owned their personal belongings and could bequeath them to others. Peasant women possessed unconditional ownership rights to a 'woman's box' (the product of poultry-raising, care of livestock and other gendered activities); these properties formed the basis for what meagre status women enjoyed within a male-dominated peasant household. Commune households possessed collective and hereditary rights to a house, garden plot and livestock – the latter properties constituted a key source of rural inequality (Kingston-Mann 1991: 23–22). In general, women assumed primary responsibility for work on the household's garden plot (Kingston-Mann 2005b).

Periodic repartition was relatively rare in the northern and western regions of the Empire, where most peasants held land in hereditary (*podvornoe*) tenure. However, even in these areas, peasants enjoyed community-based rights to the use of common lands. More like English commoners than yeoman farmers, *podvornoe* communities shared out and collected the obligations owed to landlords and to the state. Like their counterparts within the *mir*, they devised and enforced rules for the use of common lands, and provided welfare supports to their members. 'Private' in comparison with the *mir*, they were nevertheless far more 'communal' than their pre-enclosure English counterparts.

Although the powers exercised by the patriarch (the *bol'shak*) over the daily life of his household were virtually absolute, at his death, household property reverted to the household group under a new head (a son, a brother or sometimes a widow). When household divisions occurred, a village assembly (*skhod*) comprised of the heads of member households and led by elected village elders generally oversaw the distribution of property, and aggrieved parties could appeal to them for aid in the resolution of conflict. Although wealthier peasants exerted disproportionate influence within and outside the commune framework, scholars do not agree over the extent to which economic differences in the 1900s were being reproduced from generation to generation as class formations. Since commune repartitions usually apportioned allotments according to family size or labour capacity, larger households tended to be those 'richest' in land, while newer and smaller households received smaller allotments. Vulnerable to the corruption, nepotism and devotion to personal advantage that plague most economic and non-economic institutions, communes nevertheless obliged wealthier families to link their fate with their poorer neighbours (Kingston-Mann 1990: 23–51).

Obstacles and Incentives to Change

Although the commune-imposed obligation to obtain the consent and support of one's neighbours before introducing significant changes was clearly frustrating to some, it is unclear whether this constraint was decisive in determining whether or not peasants assumed the risks of innovation. In 1900, most peasants continued to struggle – like their parents and grandparents before them – against the obstacles posed by a Russian land and climate largely inhospitable to productive farming. In regions where rainfall was reliable, soils were poor; more fertile regions were routinely plagued by drought. These drawbacks persisted regardless of prevailing political or socioeconomic systems, and despite historical efforts either to privatise or collectivise the land (Kingston-Mann, forthcoming b).

As the most impoverished and least literate of the tsar's subjects, peasants in 1900 continued to bear the burdens imposed by a variety of more or less importunate social and political elites. Freed from serfdom in 1861, they constituted 80 percent of the population, the majority were women, and a substantial proportion were ethnically non-Russian. Regardless of whether private or communal tenure prevailed in a particular region, peasant economic opportunities were everywhere constrained by the absence of roads, schools, access to medical care, tools, and more hands to share in economic tasks (in addition to the financial burdens imposed by the terms of the Emancipation). As Russian economist A.I. Chuprov sarcastically observed, none of these issues were automatically resolved by the simple act of leaving the commune (Chuprov 1909: 22).

Innovation was a costly process. Peasants who attempted intensive cultivation in areas where grain prices only covered the costs of extensive farming, could rarely compete successfully with landlords, who practiced extensive cultivation, benefited from lower production costs and marketed goods more cheaply. In less fertile regions, peasants who rented land in addition to their commune allotments could face profit-oriented landlords who demanded that tenants fertilise rented land *as a condition* of their rental contracts. Forced to fertilise the landlord's land before their own, these peasants were frequently left without sufficient fertiliser to manure their own allotments. As a countermeasure, some communes prohibited the transfer or sale of manure by members to outsiders, and required members to use a certain quantity of manure on each allotment annually, *before* they could use any on non-commune land. Although these strategies sometimes enabled communes to preserve soil quality and avoid direct confrontation with the gentry, they also increased pressures on commune members who were renters. On the other hand, small private owners outside the commune were far more vulnerable to such gentry pressures (Kingston-Mann 1990: 39–46).

Commune Rewards for Innovation: Balancing Private and Community Interests

In many regions of the Russian Empire, the by-now familiar axiomatic opposition between collective and individual rights was strikingly contradicted at the level of peasant practice. While richer peasants in more privatised (but still commons-using) regions engaged in rural innovation, statisticians documented the operation of strategies specifically crafted to (1) reward individual innovators within the commune framework, and (2) reconcile the competing demands of private interest and social equity. For example, in the Siberian province of Tobolsk, commune assemblies divided scattered strips of member allotments into three categories on the basis of soil quality, location and degree of improvement. 'Improvers' received either first choice of the best-quality land, or the option of retaining their original allotments. In order to prevent the initial improvers from establishing a self-perpetuating monopoly of the best land; 'non-improvers' received first priority in the allotment of second quality land. Land in the third category was distributed on an equal basis to all commune members according to the assessed labour needs of each household. In the Volga province of Tambov, communes rewarded peasants who fertilised their allotments either by providing special monetary payments at the time of repartition, by providing a similar allotment, or by permitting innovators to retain their original holdings (Kingston-Mann 1990: 45). In some commune regions, changes spread quite rapidly – in 1900, 127 commune villages in a single district in Moscow province introduced many-field crop rotations; by 1903, 245 out of 368 villages had done so (Bazhaev 1902: 260, 331, Stepanov 1922: 112, 116). However, it is unclear how these changes – either by commons-using 'private farmers' or by commune members – related to the 'capitalist' and 'socialist' frameworks that so monopolised the attention of Marxists state capitalist reformers of the tsarist regime.

Land Rights: The Claims of Labour

In almost every sphere of peasant economic activity, statisticians noted an overriding emphasis upon labour as an economic necessity, and – as was the case with their English pre-enclosure counterparts – as the basis for claims to land use and status within the household and community. Communal allotment size was frequently determined according to the number of adult labourers per household. In times of unrest and rebellion, peasant petitions and proclamations declared that the land had been 'stolen' by gentry miscreants from the tillers of the soil who were its rightful claimants. In the Revolution of 1905, peasants demanded that land be 'returned' to the labouring peasantry. At no time did they acknowledge the legitimacy of claims to landownership by persons who did not labour on it. In the years to come, such time-honoured labour claims would pose serious challenges to a succession of Russian, Soviet and post-Soviet policy makers (Kingston-Mann, 2006, forthcoming, and see below, p. 78).

Russian Enclosure: Either/Or

In 1905, when Russia's first twentieth-century revolution erupted, communes emerged as organisers of land seizure and venues for peasant demands for land and liberty, elimination of private property rights, and the 'return' of land to the tillers of the soil. By 1906, their perceived revolutionary threat to the government and the landed gentry would unite both conservatives and reformers in support of a Russian-style enclosure movement led by Premier P.A. Stolypin. Convinced that the twin imperatives of stability and progress required the creation of a constituency of 'strong' and conservative private farmers, the Stolypin regime introduced a series of reforms that encouraged peasant households to break with the commune and establish themselves on enclosed, self-contained farms. In this process, the household's garden plot was transferred into the hands of the male head of the household (a measure that deprived women of an important source of livelihood).

In the rhetorically charged discourse of the reform era, the government placed its 'wager on the strong' farmer and celebrated the heroic individual who stood up against 'the needy and drunken' commune dweller. Attempting to foster peasant loyalty to the government that guaranteed their property rights, and to privilege individuals who established private farms at the expense of commune households, the government provided generous legal and extra-legal support, financial subsidies and preferential credit rates to 'separators' (who also were offered the sum of fifty rubles each) (Baker 1977: 152–53). To facilitate peasant withdrawal from the commune, a 1911 decree deemed a single household's request sufficient to dissolve the whole commune. By the outbreak of the First World War, as many as two million peasant households were involved in Russia's enclosure process.[3]

However, despite the government's efforts, the complexity of peasant responses to the Stolypin Reforms made a mockery of reformer assumptions about tenure transformation. The most disillusioning outcomes included the following: (1) While some requests to separate from the commune came from 'strong' peasants, many came from 'weak' households that had suffered disease or other misfortunes and feared land loss in commune repartitions that were based on family size or labour capacity (Zyrianov 1992: 111–15). (2) Communities that eliminated periodic land repartition generally retained not only their common lands but also the welfare supports that communes traditionally provided. (3) Peasants who adopted private tenure were not significantly more likely to innovate (Khauke 1914: 355). (4) Women were frequently discovered in the forefront of confrontations with the authorities because it was believed that soldiers were less likely to fire on them. At the same time, their opposition was fostered by Stolypin's recognition of the patriarch (*bol'shak*) as sole owner of the household's garden plot, a policy that weakened the position of peasant women whose income and status were intimately connected with labour on this land (Kingston-Mann, 2005b).

Between 1906 and 1916, women, like other 'foot draggers' in Russia's privatisation scenario, drew on a rich and varied repertoire of survival strategies that included subversion, compromise, petitions of complaint, and destruction of the fences that established the new private boundaries. In addition, communes devised ingenious strategies that made use of enclosure as a 'wrecking strategy against individual separators'. In one case, a commune pre-empted a single household's plan to separate by requesting a commune-wide enclosure that *excluded* the would-be separator but retained the commune's pre-enclosure claims to common pasture land (Pallot 1999: 194).

Stolypin himself was assassinated in 1911, and on the eve of the First World War, 'separators' began to return to the commune in increasing numbers; in 1916, the Reforms were suspended. Although 10 percent of the former commune peasants had become Western-style proprietors of consolidated farms between 1910 and 1914 (Diakin 1904: 367–68), Russia's tenure transformation did not succeed in eliminating the commune, or in demonstrating that enclosed private farms were either more or less innovative, productive or profitable. Within and outside the commune, the amount of arable land under cultivation and levels of agricultural productivity rose during the prewar years – with marginally superior levels in non-commune districts (Pallot 1999: 249–51). In general, government-sponsored reforms turned out to be no match for the staying power of property relations that peasants had themselves built up over the course of many generations. For the overwhelming majority of the rural populace, the social relations of peasant production remained largely untouched. At the same time, it should be noted that in the English case, it had taken three centuries – rather than Russia's single decade – before enclosure prevailed.

The Soviet Era: Either/Or

Between the outbreak of the First World War and the rise of Stalin, foreign invasion, civil war, and Soviet grain requisitions formed the backdrop for a successful but largely unheralded and rarely studied 'anti-Stolypin peasant revolution' that reinforced the dominance of communal tenure in the Russian countryside. By 1920, 96 percent of the rural population in thirty-nine out of forty-seven provinces were commune members. However, Soviet Marxists, ideologically blind to the resurgence of the peasant commune (deemed to be an obsolete and 'feudal' institution), proclaimed a policy of 'War Communism' and stubbornly categorised communes as 'individual' landholders. In 1921, as peasant hostility to War Communism began to threaten urban industrial centres with starvation, Lenin proposed a 'retreat to capitalism' that revealed in full measure the degree of Soviet ambivalence on the question of property rights.

However convinced they were that collectivist socioeconomic institutions were wholly preferable both to capitalism and to the 'feudalism' of the pre-1917 countryside, Lenin and Bukharin nevertheless proposed a New Economic Policy (NEP) that revealed their indebtedness to both of these 'inferior' systems. Courageous enough to concede openly that they needed both private ownership and markets, Soviet Marxists drew the line at any acknowledgement that they *also* needed to draw on the 'feudal' labour principles of the peasant commune. The Land Statute of 1922 reflected their dilemma. It guaranteed individuals the right to farm the land with their own labour, and hire labour on condition that employers worked alongside employees; at the same time, it abrogated Stolypin's transfer of household property to the *bol'shak*.

By 1926, peasants had successfully restored grain production to its pre-1914 level. While Soviet officials were prepared for a strong economic performance by farmers from more privatised regions like Nizhnii Novgorod, they were astonished by reports of commune-based innovation and productivity increase. In a single district in Moscow province, for example, 5,204 out of 6,458 commune villages introduced new systems of crop rotation during the year 1926 alone. In a tragically short-lived burst of enthusiasm, Soviet leader M.I. Kalinin suggested that perhaps the *mir* (*obshchina*) might change 'from an organisation of darkness, illiteracy and traditionalism into, as it were, a productive cooperative organisation' (Okuda 1990: 257–62).

In 1927, when adverse climatic conditions produced a harvest 6 percent lower than the previous year's bumper crop (Wheatcroft 1974: 157–80), Party leaders quickly abandoned the relative tolerance of the NEP era in order to target kulak sabotage and 'Asiatic' peasant backwardness. Although government figures indicated that the current size of the peasantry's 'upper strata' was negligible in comparison with the 15 percent level of the pre-1917 era, an increasingly Stalinist Party and government leadership eagerly denounced kulak 'hoarding' as part of a widespread capitalist conspiracy (Atkinson 1984: 282–87; Lewin 1994: 212). In 1928, the Party abruptly demanded a 50 percent upward revision of the state's grain procurement quotas, and a concomitant transfer of peasants to collective farms. In a series of hare-brained pronouncements, the government warned the rural populace to be prepared for a wholesale collectivisation of the nation's entire agricultural sector within one and a half years.

After 1928, peasant land, livestock and tools officially became the property of collective or state farms. A *Gosplan* recommendation that communes be considered one of many institutional variants that could facilitate a transition to collectivisation was ignored, and reports on commune-based innovation disappeared as well from Soviet publications (Okuda 1990: 266; Lewin 1994: 117). Henceforward, ploughing, sowing, weeding and harvesting were regulated according to state quotas and indicators, and enforced by means of mass killings, the murder of suspected kulak 'traitors' and deportations to forced labour camps. The RSFSR (Russian Soviet Federated Socialist Republic) Criminal Code was cited to justify the bombardment of peasant villages found guilty either of 'failure to offer goods for sale on the market' or unwillingness to meet state-assigned grain quotas.

In response, many peasants denied to the Soviet state the fruits of their labour and attempted to avoid the dread designation of 'kulak' by destroying massive quantities of grain and slaughtering their livestock. Collective resistance was an important feature of rural opposition, with women playing a particularly significant role. In 1930 alone, 3,712 mass disturbances (total 13,754) were almost exclusively by women; in the other cases, women constituted either a majority or a significant proportion of the participants (Viola 1996: 183–85). While *Pravda* attributed resistance by women to the 'individualistic female spirit', it should be recalled that women were also in the forefront of opposition to Stolypin's privatisation reforms. As in 1906, they resisted the appropriation – this time by the state rather than the *bol'shak* – of the household garden plot and livestock upon which a significant measure of their household status and security depended.

Although the rural populace was unable to block the government's onslaught, peasants – and peasant women in particular – nevertheless achieved an extraordinary, but largely unheralded, victory over the Stalinist regime. In 1935, the Soviet state's Model Collective Farm Code granted peasants modest household plots of land within the collective farm framework (Shmelev 1971: 110–11; Wadekin 1971). These lands were not – any more than the garden plots of the pre-1917 commune were – private freehold property in the Western sense of the term. They could not be sold or rented, and households were dependent on the collective for seeds, farm tools, hay from the common meadow and rights to pasture animals on common land. Nevertheless, the 'private' plots introduced – on however modest a scale – a traditional peasant notion of mixed economy into the dichotomised, 'all or nothing' collectivisation strategies of the Soviet state. As in the pre-1917 commune, women bore major responsibility for labouring on the 'new' private plots. In the 1930s and afterwards, Soviet officials downplayed both the magnitude of the state's capitulation and the significantly female peasant agency that triggered it. Stalin himself took care to trivialise the conflict as 'a little misunderstanding with collective farm women. This business was about cows' (Lewin 1994: 178–79).

Since collective farm wages were generally paid out only after the state appropriated its share, the 'temporary' and subsidiary (*podsobnoe*) properties became for many peasants their only secure source of livelihood. The slow agricultural recovery that began in the second half of the 1930s was disproportionately fueled by these holdings; by 1938, 45 percent of Soviet agriculture's total farm output was being produced on 3.9 percent of the sown (private) land (approximately 0.49 hectare per household). On this predominantly women's 'turf', women turned out to be the most productive and efficient – but by far the least acclaimed – economic actors in the Soviet countryside (Bridger 1987: 14; Kingston-Mann, 2005b).

The 'private' plots flourished within a radically transformed and collectivised Soviet agricultural sector. By 1940, a vast Moscow-based bureaucracy (*Gosplan SSSR*) was deciding what each republic, region, province, district and even state and collective farm should produce, with government quotas routinely set at levels beyond the capacity of the farms to fulfill. In this context, the Stalinist 'command' system fostered the emergence of a vast informal network of insider negotiations, nepotism and other forms of favouritism, and massive corruption all along the bureaucratic chain of command.

The Second World War and Its Aftermath

The era of the 1930s served as the brutal and brutalising prelude to the Second World War catastrophe of twenty-seven million dead, and the postwar resurgence of massive deportations and purges. However, when Stalin died in 1953 the Soviet state began to move away from mass murder and deportations as core instruments of state policy. During the late 1950s, the rural sector at last became a site for significant government economic and non-economic investment. Between 1953 and 1967, the average income of collective farm workers increased by a massive 311 percent in real terms (Schroeder 1983: 243). During the Khrushchev era, collective and state farms became important sources of social benefits, particularly in the area of education. In contrast to 1938, when only 9.4 percent of the rural population possessed eight years of schooling, 55 percent were literate by the 1960s, with women frequently better educated than men.

On the economic front, assessments of the Soviet agricultural sector present a quite contradictory picture. Ambitious agricultural initiatives were severely undercut not only by the usual climatic reversals, but also by the Soviet state's penchant for bureaucratic, top-down directives that ignored local conditions and local knowledge. Land reclamation projects in the northern Caucasus and Siberia inflicted massive ecological damage; in Kazakhstan, collective and state farmers were ordered to expand the land area sown with corn regardless of whether the necessary equipment or seeds were available. However, at the same time, according to United Nations' estimates, Soviet agriculture achieved a faster rate of growth in volume and per capita than any other major region of the world. Between 1950 and 1975, agricultural output more than doubled (Tompson 2003: 64–98). Reconciling these disparate indicators remains a challenge for students of the Soviet era.

The Brezhnev years are frequently described as an era of stagnation, but from the perspective of the rural populace, they were not. In the 1970s, collective farms were empowered to assign 'private' plots to member households based on pre-1917 commune principles of labour and need. Operating under fewer constraints than before, the rural populace began to create a world that differed from the Stalinist model, recalled the values of an older peasant community, and incorporated changes that not only widened village perspectives, but inspired many villagers to abandon the countryside for the city. Despite the omnipresent, Moscow-devised plans and quotas, deliberations by farm assemblies (*skhody*) were frequently skewed by gender and age considerations or by patronage connections between individuals, households and local authorities – but the latter no longer freely exercised the life and death powers of their predecessors. As farm wage levels rose, the private plots gradually became less crucial to a household's survival (Kerblay 1983: 87). Although most of the rural populace were state employees, they bore little resemblance to western-style hired labour. The state provided collective and state farm workers with education, health, shelter, old age assistance, one-month vacations, 112 days of paid maternity leave and old-age pensions. Possession of a job thus conferred far more than a wage; it also mediated a set of social, economic and cultural relations and obligations between individuals and a wider community (Bridger and Pine 1998: 7–8).

In the 1980s, a corrupt and stubbornly repressive 'command' economic and political system continued to exert control over the lives of a rural (and urban) populace that was no longer either malnourished or illiterate, but instead possessed of rising expectations. In important respects, the contradictions and tensions that eventually brought down the Soviet system were embodied in the career of Mikhail Gorbachev. Born on a collective farm and a star beneficiary of Soviet guarantees of education and social welfare, Gorbachev made his name as a proponent of incentive-based agrarian reforms and rose to the top of the Party hierarchy. From this vantage point, he spoke out in the name of others like himself and demanded an end to the Stalinist 'command' system.

Today's Russia: Privatisation and Its Challengers

The perestroika reformers of the 1980s did not initially envisage a wholesale repudiation of the nation's collectivist past. Instead, they called for the expansion of opportunities for autonomous action and decision making within and outside of existing collective and state enterprises. Unlike Yeltsin and his successors, who targeted collectivism as the chief obstacle to freedom and prosperity, sociologist Tatyana Zaslavskaia attributed the Soviet Union's failures to its political rigidity, hypercentralisation, pervasive corruption and bureaucracy, rather than to a wholly defective tenure system (Zaslavskaia 1986, 1987, 1990). Within and outside government, the 1980s saw historically unprecedented appeals by reformers for unscripted public input into the formation of rural economic policy.

On the agrarian front, the populace responded with an 'avalanche' of letters, proclamations, plays and poems demanding a revitalisation of farming communities, market socialism, rights to acquire land of one's own, rewards that were related to merit, respect and acknowledgement for local knowledge, experience and expertise (Shanin 1988: 14). In 1990, in a short-lived foray into economic pluralism, the Soviet Union's last government legitimised a variety of forms of tenure that ranged from outright ownership, possession for life, leasehold, and indefinite, permanent or temporary use (without eliminating collectivist economic institutions or Soviet welfare guarantees). These early reform years saw a 21 percent increase in health, education and other welfare benefits, a 48 percent rise in per capita income and an 8 percent increase in productivity rates – levels of improvement unheard of in the 1990s (Liefert 1993: 25–42).

When the Soviet Union broke up in 1991, perestroika efforts to balance the 'old' and the 'new' came to an end. Instead, 'shock therapists' launched a revolutionary effort at social engineering no less dramatic and far-reaching (albeit far less brutal) than Stalin's. The first step in this process was to disentangle and sever property rights and economic activity from the reciprocal social obligations within which – from the peasantry's perspective – they had always been historically embedded. Convinced that the 'natural' desire to receive a piece of national wealth for free would serve as a powerful engine for agricultural land reform, neoliberal reformers issued a series of rather hare-brained '500' and '1000–day' schemes for wholesale privatisation.

The new economics of the Russian republic was spelled out in a highly charged and dichotomised rhetoric that may at this point be familiar to the reader. Reformers like Yegor Gaidar sought far and wide for 'the new Russian', a man – shock therapy heroes were invariably male – who hated backwardness and bureaucracy, and devoted himself to property acquisition. Expectations were quite low for the rest of the population, routinely described as a 'peasant-like' mass, susceptible to 'populism' and suffering from such 'typical' Russian character defects as a deep-seated propensity for laziness, theft and violence, resistance to change, tendencies to hysteria and mob action (Popov 1990). As rural and urban output plummeted, reformers confronted by accelerating suicide, infant and adult mortality rates and deaths due to preventable disease, argued that these social costs represented a painful transition to adulthood for a tragically risk-averse Russian populace.

In the 1990s, a rather Darwinian romance of privatisation once again played itself out. Between 1992 and 1996, a catastrophic, 2,600 percent increase in Russian consumer goods prices was accompanied by a 47 percent decline in per capita monthly income. The rural populace reacted by turning back to their private plots, and to the collectives that had formerly provided them with seeds, machinery, fuel and for a measure of health and welfare benefits (Caskie 2000: 206–7). In 2003, many public opinion polls indicated that the majority of former collective farmers who still controlled three-quarters of Russia's arable land continued to oppose the private ownership of land.

Even if we set aside from the confusion and corruption of the 'land for shares' programme (Visser, this volume), it, has remained as difficult for Russian collective farmers as it was for England's eighteenth-century ploughman-poet John Clare to grasp the notion that property owners could legitimately possess absolute rights to exclude others from the use or benefits of land. Neither in the Soviet or pre-Soviet era was it possible for peasants to buy land but not use it, to claim rights to misuse land they owned, or buy land simply in order to sell at a higher profit. In the early 1990s, Western observers reported that peasant women denounced such individuals as 'speculators' (*spekulanty*) rather than 'true owners' (Hivon 1995: 18). Fearing that he would be bought out by a foreign agribusiness, the new private farmer A.K. Poprov declared: 'Ownership is an empty symbol. What's important is who possesses the land and how he uses it. Just because someone can afford to buy it doesn't make him a farmer' (Weir 2002).

In 2003, some 90 percent of Russian grain still comes from former collective and state farms, and there are few signs that privatisation reforms have exerted a positive effect on productivity rates (Ioffe and Nefedova 2000: 296). Frustrated enthusiasts like Boris Nemtsov complain that 'the primary hindrance to privatisation of land in Nizhnii

Novgorod province is the lack of people who want to become owners' (Ioffe and Nefedova 1997: 158). 'And to bring us full circle, there is evidence that in 2003 peasants apparently created new forms of the pre-1917 *obshchina* (*mir*) in sparsely populated regions all over Siberia' (Gray 2003: 293–321).

Conclusion

From a historical standpoint, the foregoing discussion suggests that although private owners have played a significant role in changes that produced substantial economic and non-economic benefits to other social groups as well, they are not the only group to have done so – they are simply the group whose achievements have been most widely documented, analysed, contemplated and publicised. A narrow scholarly focus on the private property owner has for too long deflected research away from the study of majorities – peasants, factory workers, women as well as men, commons-users, commune peasants and even collective farm members who may function as subjects as well as objects in a world 'in transition'. Our understanding is still constrained by the absence of evenhanded, comparative investigations of the productive economic potential of private, non-private and mixed tenure institutions. As we have seen, the either/or dichotomies of wholesale privatisation or collectivisation impose unacceptable human costs. In 1900 as in 2004, such strategies have been consistently contradicted at the level of peasant practice. Although we cannot prejudge the outcome of a more inclusive and balanced study of the potential agents of change – either in the past or in the present – it is time to pay attention to these alternative perspectives and to the research agenda that they require.

Notes

1. As might be expected, the historical record does not lend itself to easy generalisations on this score. McCloskey cites anecdotal evidence that enclosure increased productivity rates, but economic historian Richard Allen's data indicates that few documented improvements in agricultural productivity could be directly linked to enclosure. (McCloskey 1991, Allen and Grada 1988: 93–116).
2. Russian fears were quite well grounded. Even before Russia's First World War disaster, Russia's military defeats and humiliating setbacks included the Crimean, Russo-Turkish and Russo-Japanese wars. Famines erupted in 1891, 1897 and 1901, in tandem with the mixed blessing of massive foreign

investment. By 1914, France controlled three quarters of Russia's coal and iron output.

3. Different, and more positive interpretations of the Stolypin Reforms include Yaney (1982); Gerasimenko (1985) (a 'classic' Soviet text); Macey (1993: 97–120).

References

Allen, R. and C.O. Grada 1988. 'On the Road with Arthur Young', *Journal of Economic History* 48: 93–116.

Argumenty i Fakty, 1 June 2004.

Atkinson, D. 1984. *The End of the Russian Land Commune, 1905–1930*. Stanford: Stanford University Press.

Baker, A. 1977. 'Community and Growth: Muddling Through with Russian Credit Cooperatives', *Journal of Economic History* 37: 139–60.

Bazhaev, B.G. 1902. *Travopol'noe khoziaistvo v nechernozemnoi polose evropeiskoi Rossii*. St. Petersburg.

Bridger, S. 1987. *Women in the Soviet Countryside: Women's Roles in Rural Development in the Soviet Union*. Cambridge: Cambridge University Press.

Bridger, S. and F. Pine 1998. *Surviving Post-Socialism: Local Strategies and Regional Responses in Eastern Europe and the Former Soviet Union*. London: Routledge.

Bruce, J. 1993. 'Do Indigenous Tenure Systems Constrain Agricultural Development?', in *Land in African Agrarian Systems*, eds T. Basset and D. Crummey, Madison: University of Wisconsin Press, 35–56.

Caskie, P. 2000. 'Back to Basics: Household Food Production in Russia, *Journal of Agricultural Economics* 51(2): 196–209.

Chuprov, A.I. 1909. *Krest'ianskii vopros*. Moscow.

Dahlman, C. 1990. *The Open Field System and Beyond: A Property Rights Analysis of an Economic Institution*. New York: Cambridge University Press.

Diakin, V. 1904. *Krizis samoderzhaviia v Rossii 1895–1917*. Leningrad.

Gerasimenko, G. 1985. *Bor'ba krest'ian protiv stolypinskoi agrarnoi politiki*. Moscow.

Gibbon, P., K.J. Havnevik and K. Hermele 1993. *A Blighted Harvest: The World Bank and African Agriculture in the 1980s*. Trenton: Africa World Press.

Gray, P. 2003. 'Volga Farmers and Arctic Herders: Common (Post)Socialist Experiences in Rural Russia', in *The Postsocialist Agrarian Question: Property Relations and the Rural Condition*, ed. C.M. Hann, London: Transaction, 293–321.

Havinden, M. 1961. 'Agricultural Progress in Open Field Oxfordshire', *Agricultural History Review* 9: 73–88.

Heys, B. 1987. 'John Clare and Enclosures', *John Clare Society Journal* 6: 10–18.

Hivon, M. 1995. 'Local Resistance to Privatization in Rural Russia', *Cambridge Anthropology* 18(2): 13–22.

Humphries, J. 1990. 'Enclosures, Common Rights, and Women: The Proletarianization of Families in the Late Eighteenth and Early Nineteenth Centuries', *Journal of Economic History* 50(2): 17–41.

Ioffe, G. and T. Nefedova 1997. *Continuity and Change in Rural Russia: A Geographic Perspective*. Boulder: Westview Press.

—— 2000. 'Areas of Crisis in Russian Agriculture: A Geographic Perspective, *Post-Soviet Geography and Economics* 41(4): 288–305.

Kerblay, B. 1983. *Modern Soviet Society*. London: Methuen.

Khauke, O. 1914. *Krest'ianskoe zemel'noe pravo*. Moscow.

Kingston-Mann, E. 1981. 'Marxism and Russian Rural Development: Problems of Evidence, Experience and Culture', *American Historical Review*: 731–52.

—— 1983. *Lenin and the Problem of Marxist Peasant Revolution*. New York: Oxford.

—— 1990a. 'Peasant Communes and Rural Innovation: A Preliminary Inquiry', in *Peasant Economy, Culture and Politics of European Russia*, eds E. Kingston-Mann and T. Mixter, Princeton, New Jersey: Princeton University Press, 23–51.

—— 1990b. 'Breaking the Silence: An Introduction', in *Peasant Economy, Culture and Politics of European Russia*, eds E. Kingston-Mann and T. Mixter, Princeton, New Jersey: Princeton University Press, 3–20.

—— 1999. *In Search of the True West: Culture, Economics, and Problems of Russian Development*. Princeton, New Jersey: Princeton University Press.

—— 2005a. 'Statistics, Social Science & Social Justice: Zemstvo Statistics in Pre-revolutionary Russia', in *A Member of the Family: Russia's Place in Europe, 1789–1914*, eds S. McCaffray and M.Melancon, New York: Palgrave/Macmillan, 113–39.

—— 2005b. 'Claiming Property: The Soviet-era Private Plots as 'Women's Turf,' in *The Borders of Socialism: The 'Public' and 'Private' Sphere during the Soviet Era*, ed. L. Siegelbaum, New York: Palgrave.

—— forthcoming. 'Transforming Peasants: Dilemmas of Development in Imperial, Soviet and Post-Soviet Russia in the Twentieth Century', in *Cambridge Modern History of Russia and the Soviet Union*, ed. R.G. Suny.

Lewin, M. 1994. *Russia/USSR/Russia: The Drive and Drift of a Superstate*. New York: Norton.

Liefert, W. 1993. 'Food Problems in the Republics of the Former USSR', in *The Farmer Threat: Political Economy of Agrarian Reform in Post-Soviet Russia*, ed. D. van Atta, Boulder: Westview Press, 25–42.

MacDonald, S. 1981. 'Agricultural Improvement and the Neglected Laborer', *Agricultural History Review* 31(2): 81–90.

Macey, D. 1993. 'Stolypin is Risen! The Ideology of Agrarian Reform in Contemporary Russia', in *The 'Farmer Threat': The Political Economy of Agrarian Reform in Post-Soviet Russia*, ed. D. van Atta, Boulder: Westview Press, 97–120.

McCloskey, D. 1991. 'The Prudent Peasant. New Findings on Open Fields', *Journal of Economic History* 51: 343–56.

Mingay, G.E. 1975. 'Introduction', *Arthur Young and His Times*, ed. G.E. Mingay, London: Macmillan.

Neeson, J. 1984. 'The Opponents of Enclosure in Eighteenth-century Northamptonshire', *Past and Present* 105: 114–39.

Okuda, H. 1990. 'The Final Stage of the Russian Peasant Commune: Its Improvement and the Strategy of Collectivisation', in *Land Community in Russia: Communal Forms in Imperial and Early Soviet Society*, ed. R. Bartlett, Basingstoke: University of London, 254–71.

Pallot, J. 1999. *Land Reform in Russia 1906–1917: Peasant Responses to Stolypin's Project for Rural Transformation*. Oxford: Clarendon.

Perry, P.J. 1981. 'High Farming in Victorian Britain: Prospect and Retrospect', *Agricultural History* 55(2): 156–66.

Popov, G. 1990. 'The Dangers of Democracy', *New York Review of Books*, 16 August 1990: 27–28.

Rose, C. 1986. 'The Comedy of the Commons: Custom, Commerce and Inherently Public Property', *University of Chicago Law Review* 53: 711–81.

Rudkin, O. 1927. *Thomas Spence and His Connections*. London: Allen & Unwin.

Schroeder, G. 1983. 'Rural Living Standards in the Soviet Union', in *The Soviet Rural Economy*, ed. R. Stuart, Totowa: Roman & Allanheld, 241–57.

Shanin, T. 1986. *1905–1907: Russia as a Developing Society*. New Haven: Yale University Press.

———1988. 'Soviet Agriculture and Perestroika: The Most Urgent Task and the Furthest Shore', unpublished paper, revised and published as 'Soviet Agriculture and Perestroika: Four Models', *Sociologica Ruralis* 29(1): 7–22.

Shmelev, G. 1971. *Lichnoe posobnoe khoziaistvo i ego sviazi s obshchestvennym proizvodstvom*. Moscow.

Stepanov, I.P. 1922. *Neskol'ko dannykh o sostoianii sel'skogo khoziaistva v Moskovskoi Gubernii*. Moscow.

Thompson, E.P. 1975. 'The Crime of Anonymity', in *Albion's Fatal Tree: Crime and Society in the Eighteenth Century*, eds D. Hay, P. Linebaugh, J. Rule, E.P. Thompson and C. Winslow, New York: Pantheon, 313–14.

Tompson, W. 2003. *The Soviet Union under Brezhnev*. London: Longmans.

Viola, L. 1996. *Peasant Rebels under Stalin: Collectivization and the Culture of Peasant Resistance*. New York: Oxford University Press.

Wadekin, K. 1971. *The Private Sector in Soviet Agriculture*. Berkeley: University of California Press.

Weir, F. 2002. 'This Land is My Land', *These Times*, 11 November 2002.

Wheatcroft, S. 1974. 'The Reliability of Russian Prewar Grain Statistics', *Soviet Studies* 26(2): 157–80.

Yaney, G. 1982. *The Urge to Mobilize: Agrarian Reform in Russia 1861–1930*. Urbana: University of Illinois.

Zaslavskaia, T. *Sovietskaia kultura*, 23 Jan 1986 and *Pravda*, 6 Feb 1987.

———1990. *A Voice of Social Reform*. Armonk: M.E. Sharpe.

Zyrianov, P.N. 1992. *Krest'ianskaia obshchina evropeiskoi Rossii 1907–1914*. Moscow: Nauka.

Chapter 4

Beyond Embeddedness:
a Challenge Raised by a Comparison of the Struggles Over Land in African and Post-socialist Countries

Pauline E. Peters

Introduction

The premise of this paper is that there are intriguing parallels in the current debates and social processes surrounding property in land in the post-colonial countries in Africa and those in post-socialist countries.[1] Despite the obvious differences of history and culture (not to speak of climate, types of production, and so forth), current similarities include the following. Interpretation of current change is being discussed in terms of 'transition' – in the post-socialist case from state-centric, communist regimes to democratic, market systems, and in many African countries from one-party dictatorships and (often ineffective) centralised economic controls to multi-party democratic, market systems. The initial phases of this 'transition' depart significantly from the ideal ends projected in rhetoric, and are marked by precipitous declines in economic production and in welfare indices of health, mortality, education and general wellbeing. In the post-socialist countries, these are attributed to decollectivisation and related institutional dismantling, while in African countries, the imposition of structural adjustment and market liberalisation policies levy the same costs. In both regions, institutional dismantling and deregulation at the national levels have been unaccompanied by the projected growth in economy and civil society but, rather, with economic distress, increasing social inequality, social conflict, political turmoil, and a rise in illicit and criminal activities. In both regions, neoliberal development policies have 'proved to be a virtual economic and social disaster' yet continue 'to serve as the offical globalisation model' (Schierup 1999: 22). This broad typification of major changes is not elaborated here but merely indicates the necessary background against which to set the content of the paper, which is the 'family resemblances' between the debates about property in land now underway in post-socialist literature and societies and a much longer and still continuing argument on land and property in Africa.[2]

After discussing the key issues concerning land and land tenure in Africa, both the contemporary debates and those in the past that have shaped the present, I shall indicate where these might inform and be informed by current research on post-socialist countries. I conclude that we need to go beyond ever more detailed documentation of the social 'embeddedness' of property relations to develop analyses that specifically reject the asocial reductionism of economics and 'new' institutionalism.

Colonial Administrations, Anthropologists and Customary Tenure in Africa

There has been a long and protracted battle against the taken-for-granted 'liberal' model that makes 'property' the sine qua non of civilised society and a market economy. In Africa, the debate has been engaged since the early days of colonial and mission influence, during the post-colonial 'development' programmes, and more recently in face of the neoliberal renaissance.

The early colonial administrators and missionaries demonstrated a profound antipathy towards African modes of organisation they labelled 'communal'. Taken to describe both social organisation and the system of landholding, 'communal' was interpreted as primitive, as smothering individual initiative and inhibiting social 'progress'. Such thinking was challenged by anthropologists including Gluckman, whose simple statement that, 'rights to land are an incident of political and social status' (1965: 78), was a rebuttal of those models that separate 'property' from its social and political anchoring. Similarly, the revisionist interpretation of 'customary' law has been influential in the current thinking about the workings of customary tenure that still dominates rural Africa. Far from being a precolonial oral system merely being put into writing, the ideas and practice of 'customary tenure' were produced out of colonial misunderstandings and politically expedient appropriations and allocations of land (Colson 1971). The formation of customary law and communal tenure served to promote both state and private European interests in African colonies (Chanock 1991; Amanor 1999), yet Africans ended up defending the colonial constructions as one of the few ways to try (usually unsuccessfully) to fend off further appropriations (Chanock 1991).[3] This has continued into post-colonial times (Mamdani 1996).

A related revisionist point is that the 'legal pluralism' said to typify the mix of legal typologies (statutory, customary, Islamic) in African countries is not a neat parallel system but often a contradictory blend.[4] 'Customary' law and tenure need to be seen, not as 'informal' or 'traditional' systems separate from and opposed to 'formal systems' of 'law', but as mutually imbricated with the latter (Moore 1978; Chanock 1985; Merry 1988; Griffiths 1997), or as 'competing forms of institutionalisation' (Benjaminsen and Lund 2003: 2). The effects can be contradictory. Customary law can result in a form of 'decentralised despotism' in which so-called traditional leaders may benefit at the cost of those in their 'charge', as Mamdani (1996) has argued (cf. Ribot 2000). Yet the institutional separation of customary law can have the unintended effect of enabling a degree of 'local autonomy ... insulated from external interference', as Sally Moore documents for the Chagga of Tanzania (1986: 319). A perception in official circles that 'custom' is static can have certain advantages for groups seeking to keep officials ignorant of what they are doing (ibid.).

Post-colonial Development Policies on Land and their Critiques

The land policies formulated by governments and promoted by donor agencies, especially the World Bank, in Africa during 'the land reform decades' of the 1960s and 1970s (Bassett 1993a: 11), were all based on the premise that customary systems did not provide the necessary 'security' to ensure agricultural investment and productive use of land. The appropriate policy direction was taken to be the state creation of clearly defined and enforceable property rights. Most often, individual, private property rights were assumed necessary. These positions on land tenure echoed those of the colonial administrations in the 1940s and 1950s, in being premised on ideas about necessary trajectories of modernisation and economic development based ultimately on Western European experience,[5] although they gained a more technical cast from development economics.

Research in Africa rebuts the conventional policy premise that customary tenure fails to clearly define an individual's property rights, thereby producing insecurity of tenure, which constitutes an obstacle to investment and productive use of land. First, widespread cash cropping and 'price responsiveness' across Africa, the most quoted case being that of cocoa production by farmers on customary land in West Africa, clearly demonstrated that customary tenure did not inhibit agricultural investment or commercialisation. Moreover, studies showed that the vast majority of farms in Africa are worked by individuals and small familial units who have separable claims, rights and responsibilities over plots, crops and trees, even though authority over land, in its most general sense, is usually vested in collectivities such as chiefdoms or clans. In some places, so-called 'customary' tenure would be more accurately seen as 'family property' because individuals and family units have defined rights to specific areas of land (Francis 1984; Peters 1997). Authors have also documented many types of transfer of land and of rights to land, such as tenancy in the cocoa areas of West Africa (Hill 1963; Berry 1975; Gyasi 1994) and elsewhere (see Lawry 1993 for Lesotho), as well as rentals and sales (Allott 1968; Cohen 1980; Bruce 1988; Ng'ong'ola 1996; Besteman 1999). Longitudinal studies have shown that agricultural intensification and commercial production are not inhibited by 'customary' landholding as much as by broader social and political-economic conditions at local, regional and international levels (Linares 1992; Guyer and Lambin 1993; Netting 1993; Guyer 1997).

Furthermore, field research documenting how programmes of land registration and land titling actually performed from the 1970s to the late 1980s showed the fallacy of assuming that land title would improve tenure security and lead to increased agricultural investment and productivity. Not only did the programmes fail to achieve those ends, but they also encouraged speculation and fraudulent land claims in land by outsiders, thus displacing the very people – the local users of the land – who were supposed to acquire increased security through land title. As a result, the programmes frequently exacerbated conflicts and patterns of unequal access to land based on gender, age, ethnicity and class.[6] A similar literature has revealed the negative to disastrous effects of land titling and privatisation in livestock and range management schemes in Africa.[7]

There is now a very large body of accumulated research on the 'land question' in Africa. One currently influential approach in African Studies privileges flexibility, negotiability and indeterminacy in analyses of social relationships over land. One recent survey states: 'If a single lesson emerges from recent scholarship on African land-holding, it is that it is complex, variable, and fluid' (Shipton and Goheen 1992: 318; cf. Juul and Lund 2002). A major influence on this literature has been the prolific writing of Sara Berry on the dynamics of agrarian transformation, including her emphasis on people 'investing in social relations' as the primary way to guarantee them access to valued resources such as land. The revisionist studies, documenting the ways in which so-called customary tenure has allowed people to adapt to rapidly changing political and economic conditions throughout the continent, have supported Berry's stress on flexibility and negotiability in the relations over land. Much of the literature also supports her conclusion that, 'the strength of customary claims to land is the principal obstacle to the "enclosure" and concentration of landed property in rural Africa' (Berry 1993: 210).

This influential body of scholarship has had a role in the apparent recent conversion of the World Bank and other major aid agencies from seeing customary land tenure in Africa as inhibiting agricultural modernisation to lauding its adaptive and flexible character that, over time, allows 'evolution' towards more efficient forms of landholding (Bruce and Migot-Adholla 1994; Toulmin and Quan 2000). There are reasons to remain sceptical about this change that will not be rehearsed here. More relevant is that we have reached a point to be dubious about the 'negotiability' in social relations over land (see Peters 2004).

Struggles Over Land in Contemporary Africa

Already in 1988, the editors of a volume of essays on land in Africa stated that, 'the least equivocal finding' was that 'access ... to land ... has become increasingly restricted and insecure' (Downs and Reyna 1988: 18). Since then, a growing body of research reveals intensifying competition and conflict over land, deepening rifts between and within kin-based, ethnic and regional groups, and expropriation of land by local and non-local agents. The intensification of production, increased reliance on the market for inputs and many basic necessities, growing populations and movements of people, and state demarcation of forest and other reserves or conservation areas, have all intensified competition over land. There have been increased transfers of land through rentals and sales, even though the latter are illegal under most 'customary' systems. Bassett links such processes in Ivory Coast to 'the development of commodity relations through the intensification of cotton cultivation' (1993b: 143). Similarly, increased commodification of livestock and state programmes enabling large cattle owners in Botswana to obtain deep wells has led to increased inequality in access to grazing lands (Gulbrandsen 1987; Peters 1994). For Ghana, Amanor describes 'a new process of commodification ... taking place on lineage land arising from ... agricultural modernisation in the form of new seeds and inputs', which has produced new divisions within and between families, lineages and larger groups (1999: 140). In addition, social differentiation and political rivalry within countries are closely linked to competition over land (Odgaard 2003). Southgate and Hulme identify a key means in land appropriation to be 'the capacity of the patron-client chains that link the national elite to the local level to gain control over resources that offer opportunities for accumulation' (2000: 112; cf. Myers 1994 for Mozambique; Besteman 1999 for Somalia; Klopp 2000 for Kenya).

A key sociocultural dynamic driving the differentiation over land turns on a narrowing in the *definition of belonging*. Social conflict over land produces stricter definitions of those with legitimate claims to resources, that is, group boundaries become more exclusively defined. This has been described for Northern Ivory Coast (Bassett 1993b), Botswana and Malawi (Peters 1994, 1997), Ethiopia (Lastarria-Cornhiel 1995), Zimbabwe (Moore 1993), and Ghana (Amanor 1999). Metaphors of difference include those of 'stranger', 'immigrant' and 'squatter' as contrasted with local or original inhabitants (Worby 2001), producing increased litigiousness, violence and witchcraft accusations (Peters 1997; van Donge 1999; Hammar 2001; Nyambara 2001).

The mounting evidence on pervasive competition and conflict over land calls into serious question the image of relatively open, negotiable and adaptive customary systems of landholding and land use and, instead, reveal processes of exclusion, deepening social divisions and class formation (Amanor 2001; Peters 2002, 2004). This is not to deny the cases of ambiguous outcomes and 'standoffs' between competing claimants over land that may last generations (Berry 2002), and there is much to support a view of Africa as a continent with the majority of its population living on the land, without clearly defined classes of landed and landless. Nevertheless, current research suggests this is only part of the story. More emphasis needs to be placed by researchers on who benefits and who loses from instances of 'negotiability' in access to land, an analysis that, in turn, needs to be situated in broader political economic and social changes. This requires a theoretical move away from privileging contingency, flexibility and negotiability that, willy-nilly, end by suggesting an open field, to one that is able to identify those situations and processes (including commodification, structural adjustment, market liberalisation and globalisation) that limit or end negotiation and flexibility for certain social groups or categories.

The Strangling Power of Paradigms

The tendency for scholars and others alike to get caught within particular ways of thinking and talking is well-known. It has continually bedevilled the debates around 'land tenure' in Africa. The ability of the model based on neoclassical economics predominant in development policy circles, to withstand many challenges for so long is a crucial example, but paradigmatic perils remain. The 'new' development policy view bases itself on a so-called 'evolutionary' theory of property rights. This allows recognition of the adaptability and flexibility of customary systems of holding and using land and, thereby, raises a caution about 'intervention'. Some critics point to the danger of this view overlooking inequitable patterns within customary systems (Platteau 1996, 2000), and to the ability of national and local elites to capture the benefits of decentralisation (Carney and Farrington 1998; Ribot 2000; Woodhouse et al. 2000). More fundamentally, the underlying theoretical premises have not so much changed as merely introduced 'evolutionary time' thus delaying the pace of transition from communal to private but not relinquishing either the assumption that the latter is the ultimate end or the premise of self-interested individuals changing institutions ('rules') as these prove hindrances to the achievement of their aims. The *eventual* outcome, then, is exactly the same as before: privatised property that is assumed to be more efficient in enabling self-interested, rational users to invest, innovate and produce.

The academic Africanist literature on land tenure, which is credited for influencing the 'new' view in the World Bank, has not escaped the blinkers of reigning paradigms. Critics who mounted successful challenges to simplistic and economistic models that posited customary landholding to lack security of title and, hence, to fail to provide incentives for investment and modernisation, were able to reveal the fallacy of this conventional development thinking, and, recently, to achieve what appears to be a dramatic reversal of position among World

Bank researchers noted above. But in so doing, they have also overemphasised negotiability and indeterminacy as I have argued above.

The enormous effort needed since the 1970s to counter the hegemonic developmental position on customary tenure as an obstacle, has produced a reactive literature that has become caught within the very formulation it sought to dislodge. The result is a literature celebrating indigenous or customary systems as flexible and adaptive, thus reversing the hegemonic view of them as rigid and outmoded. A repeated theme through these years is that tenure is a social relation and that relations over land must therefore be seen as 'embedded' in broader matrices of social, cultural and political relations. The research in Africa needs to go beyond this formulation of relations over land being socially embedded, to ask more precise questions about the type of social and political relations in which land is situated, particularly with reference to relations of inequality – of class, ethnicity, gender and age. Amanor points out that privileging 'negotiability ... results in an overestimation of the ability of people to influence the debate about what constitutes tradition and to lay down the norms for contemporary access to resources. In reality, it is only the wealthy and powerful who can [do so] and who can make the necessary investments in "social networks" that Berry focuses on' (1999: 44). The processes identified by Berry, he continues, 'need to be rooted in structures of social differentiation and class' (ibid.).

It was with mixed feelings, then, that I read the use by Elizabeth Dunn of an Africanist interpretation in her analysis of Polish privatisation. Dunn summarises Sara Berry's (1993) argument on the ways in which competing interpretations of 'custom' have been deployed by governments, donor agencies and various African groups, as: 'instead of unilaterally changing patterns of production or access to resources, colonial governments and donor agencies have tended to create new social spaces in which social practice, tradition, and identity can be debated' (1999: 146). Dunn takes this perspective to analyse the ways in which 'socialism' is used in different ways by people 'negotiating' positions in the course of privatisation in Poland. She concludes that: 'The transition, then, is less a movement from one preordained state to another than a period of intensified struggle over resources' (ibid.: 147). She finds in the notion of 'negotiability', described by Berry as 'a pervasive feature of social and economic life' (1993: 13), a way of reconceptualising the transition in Eastern Europe.

Such reminders of social agency and warnings of overly deterministic views are valuable. Nevertheless, the Africanist research literature shows clearly that colonial and post-colonial governments, along with donor agencies, have often had a far more direct and negative effect than merely to 'create new social spaces'. The literature on titling has shown that not everyone could 'negotiate' a way out of, or subvert, the programmes that often had distorting and negative effects on landholding practices and certain groups, and many other stories out of Africa reveal the ability of the powerful to overcome even moderate local autonomy (cf. Amanor 1999: 44). The conclusion, then, is to refuse both deterministic and open-ended approaches, to recognise both agency and the fact that some are not able to 'negotiate' as well as others. We are back, then, at the old question of who is creating history for whom at whose expense? At this point, let me turn to some comparisons between Africa and the former Soviet world.

African and Post-socialist Comparisons

Both regions are dominated by theories of 'transition': in post-socialist countries the posited leap is from stagnant collectivism to vibrant market democracies, while in Africa, the posited transition is from 'traditional' societies to market democracies or from non-development to development. Both reflect 'mainstream modernisation theory's familiar model of contemporary history as that of a grand (functionally necessary) movement from "tradition" to "modernity"' (Schierup 1999: 33). Central to this model, of course, are the neoclassical nostrums about rational individual action, efficient markets and, in its most recent neoliberal guise, renewed emphasis is placed by the 'new institutionalism' on 'property rights'. Against this common framework, the research reveals some important talking points for researchers in Africa and post-socialist countries alike.

The current research on post-socialist countries is marked by a pervasive dissatisfaction with the simple dichotomies of transition such as collective versus individual, and by a call for recognising property as a social relation. Chris Hann has written voluminously about the inability of oppositions of collective versus individual to capture the social realities of relations around land, as well as the need to be cognisant of the ideological history and continuing power of the notion of 'property' in academic and policy discussions. He shows how, for instance, a particular type of cooperative in Hungary 'undermined the ideological opposition between collective and private property at the level of practices' (2002:

11; cf. 1993, 1996). His description of the interplay of individualised rights, collective action and public goods in Tázlár is highly reminiscent of the way in which rural societies across Africa manage their lives.

Similarly, David Sneath's discussion of the mismatch between development agencies' discourse about Mongolia's pastoralism and the actual reality parallels absolutely the extensive literature on how African pastoralist systems have been misinterpreted, often with tragic results, by colonial and post-colonial administrations and their aid donors. Both the Asian Development Bank and the World Bank attributed Mongolia's poverty to 'the lack of land ownership legislation and clarity on property rights' (Sneath 2002: 195). Sneath's exposition of how multiple and overlapping claims 'confuse' outsiders only because they fail to understand that management of grazing lands was part of the political organisation is also echoed in the Africanist literature.[8] The premise that 'clarity of property rights' is dependent on individualised rights is precisely that challenged over many years by Africanist researchers, but one that continues to mislead powerful donor agencies as well as the governments they fund.

The degree to which rights to land are highly complex, involving multiple and overlapping uses and claims, has been remarked not just for pastoralists but also for most rural societies in post-socialist countries. Katherine Verdery has described the 'elastic' quality of land in Transylvania, in that it is subject to multiple, competing claims (1994). Elsewhere, she has described rights as appearing 'fuzzy' 'because of their complex interrelations and the multiplicity of actors holding them' and in contrast to 'an idealised image of exclusive private property' typical of 'neoliberal property notions' (1999: 54–55). The complexity of property relations around land in Transylvania derives from 'conflicting definitions' of different claimants' rights, overlapping claims, and competing notions of the appropriate delimitations of private and public rights. Their analysis thus requires seeing 'property ... rights [as] bound up with power relations, with social identities and notions of self, and with embeddedness in social networks' (ibid.: 55).

Once this oft-repeated point is taken seriously, the social tensions and conflicts that have emerged in the moves to privatise land are not surprising. Here again, there are important points of comparison with Africa. In the attempts to create 'clear' property rights by governments and aid agencies, there is a necessary impetus towards simplification of the complex systems of resource management described for both African and post-socialist countries. The multiple, overlapping claims that are contingent on person, place, act, season and so forth, have to be distinguished, divided and labelled, a process that inevitably generates questions of which distinctions and whose rights gain priority. In such a process, the divisions that emerge follow pre-existing and reinvented social fault lines. In Africa, these are based on gender, age/generation, village, indigenous versus stranger, local versus immigrant, and these latter are often defined in ethnic or 'tribal' terms. The level of social conflict ranges from tensions between spouses or between elders and junior men, to sporadic fights between ethnic groups or between those claiming indigenous origin and those defined as strangers, to civil and cross-border raids and war. The literature on post-socialist countries documents similar processes. At the 'local' level, the new struggles over land involve a 'process of individuation ... that erodes the solidarities ... of socialism'. This process of division and exclusion gives priority to the rights of 'locals' over those of 'immigrants', and generates 'a new class struggle in the village' (Verdery 1994: 1089, 1093, 1108). The class struggle extends beyond village boundaries to include appropriation by elites, and unfair advantages are gained by those able to draw on networks and knowledge deriving from their former social status under communism (Verdery 1994: 1076, 1101; Mandel and Humphrey 2002: 6). These closely parallel cases in Africa where some see a 'new scramble' for the continent's rich resources – land, water, forests, game, minerals – ranging from the most local to national and transnational levels of action (Peters 2004).

Just as competing claims over land produce social conflict, so the more pervasive conditions of economic decline and social distress can lead to people fixing on land in ways that often intensify distress. Verdery argues that, in the face of institutional instability and mounting insecurity, people turn to 'the few things that appear as solid – such as land', even though they quickly find that the appearance of solidity is a mirage (1994: 1072). There is a parallel phenomenon in Africa, where mounting inequality and socioeconomic differentiation in the face of deepening poverty and insecurity, are associated with a proliferation of conflicts over land. Some of these conflicts are centrally about the use of and claims to land itself, but in some, although the focus is on land, the social struggles appear to be more broadly about legitimacy and authority (cf. Berry 2002).

While both regions suffer from increasing social competition and conflict over land, researchers stress the point that access to land is frequently *not* the single problem faced by rural populations. Contrary to the simple notions of aid agencies that see 'insecurity of land tenure' and 'lack of clarity of property rights' as the obstacles to increased production and to 'development' more broadly, the vast majority of rural producers in Africa are stymied by the loss of government-subsidised and - managed programmes of input delivery, credit, and other extension and market services, and by the overwhelming inequality faced by most African products in world markets. The post-socialist literature documents a strikingly similar situation: over and over again, one reads that there is low interest in full-time commercial or cash-cropping agriculture among most family farmers (see Swain 1996: 204), and that 'property rights' to land without the means to use land productively is 'a sick joke ... because they lack the basic capital resources, and their social rights are being whittled away all the time' (Hann 1993: 313). This 'whittling away' refers to the fact that the dismantling of the collective and cooperative institutions of the communist regimes also removed the wide range of services, or 'entitlements' as Hann calls them, for health, education, pensions and so forth (cf. Kaneff 1996: 112; Sneath 2002: 193).

The Africanist literature documents something similar. The rigours of the donor-imposed policies of structural adjustment and market liberalisation – entailing the removal of agricultural and other subsidies, reduction in social service expenditures and introduction of service payments irrespective of income, severe retrenchment in civil service jobs, and removal of most import/export controls – were all done in the name of market efficiency with the prognosis that the restructured economies would emerge as revived juggernauts. When this did not happen and, instead, indices of income and welfare plunged, the World Bank supported new programmes called the 'Social Dimensions of Adjustment' that were intended to moderate the 'social costs' of the restructuring. Needless to say, this finger in the dyke approach conveniently ignored the fact that market economies *always* produce inequality (hence the rise of the welfare state) and did little to ameliorate the situation. The people suffering under these processes felt a greater exposure and insecurity in precisely the way that seems to be the experience for many in the post-socialist countries. The social conflicts over land as well as the acceleration of more pervasive conflict within and between countries in Africa are resonant with the descriptions coming out of post-socialist countries. These will not be resolved in either region by the new land policies being written and implemented in both, because the focus on 'property rights' in land is misplaced. The premise of neoliberalism, new institutionalism and 'property rights theory' is that appropriate development takes place through the market and is mediated by property. The repeated reminders put forward, over several generations by social scientists, particularly anthropologists, that property is socially embedded, attempt to contextualise that premise. Perhaps versions of the welfare state can be seen as the political parallel to those attempts. Marx and Marxist visions of socialism went further and rejected that premise. This is an old battle that does not merely engage technocratic ideas of economic growth or the balance between growth and equity that have often dominated 'development' discourse, but that turns on different visions of society and sociality. Comparing the literature out of Africa and the post-socialist world has led me to wonder if it is being rejoined.

Recall the old debates we know so well. The rise of capitalism in England entailed the dismantling and privatisation of common lands, and the elaboration of an ideology of private property as the lynchpin of social progress.[9] With the rise of capitalism, including the push towards agricultural 'improvement', customary usage and common rights came to be defined as secondary, then as obstacles, and deprived of their legal standing. Part of the cultural dynamic of separation of poorer commoners from the commons was the increasingly powerful ideology of private property as the only basis on which legitimate claims to land could be made. The shift was from, hitherto recognised 'coincident' usage rights, to a priority given to the property rights of 'owners' over 'users', and entailed a gradual restriction through court decisions of the definition of 'owner'. Supporting this shift was an ideology that recast those depending on common rights as vagrants and idlers, and the enclosing of commons as 'the means of producing a number of additional useful hands for agricultural employment, by gradually cutting up and annihilating that nest and conservatory of sloth, idleness, and misery, which is uniformly to be witnessed in the vicinity of all commons, waste lands, and forests'.[10]

The glorification of property, understood always as private property, and the related demonisation of groups considered to be living in a pre-property state and seen as drags on the agricultural 'improvements' of progressive proprietors, were exported from England to France and Russia (Kingston-Mann 1999), as well as to the colonies of North America, Australia and Africa. As described above, development policy in Africa has been guided by essentially these views, albeit regenerated through neoliberal theories, re-emphasising 'liberalised' markets and linking property rights to institutional change and civil society.

The demonstrated 'human' costs of structural adjustment, market liberalisation and globalisation, clear to many researchers long before the World Bank and other aid agencies agreed, have now raised questions about totally 'free' markets in surprising quarters. Hence, the arch-capitalists George Soros and Francis Fukuyama have both expressed concern about a too rabid form of capitalism in the massive financial speculation involved in the East Asian 'crisis', while reservations about forced liberalisation and aspects of globalisation have been aired by the former chief economist at the World Bank, Joseph Stiglitz, along with other former 'shock therapy' market liberalisers (like Jeffrey Sachs). I say 'surprising', of course, because these are the very people who have been proponents of neoliberal approaches, and it is less surprising that their critiques tend to be moderate, not straying far from the conventional approaches in development (of growth with equity, for example). In contrast, the broader field of development studies is awash with more fundamental challenges, with ideas of 'alternative' development, 'third-way' approaches, 'post-development' and 'anti-development'. While one needs to be cautious about supposing that this widespread ferment will lead to real change, it does seem to me that the research coming out of Africa and the post-socialist world speaks to issues that range beyond the particulars of any one place or topic. The research on how property in land (and other key resources) figures in the re/construction of societies raises questions about the type of society and social relations envisaged and possible, and about the appropriateness of currently dominant models or frameworks through which the 'visioning' and action take place.

The research coming out of the post-socialist world poses questions that are important not just for those countries, but also for Africa and wherever else the 'magic of property' is misguidedly supposed to achieve economic and social progress. Through his analysis of a cooperative in Hungary, Chris Hann shows how a myopic focus on privatisation as *the* route to a better future obscures the productivity (in economic and social senses) of the creative mix of private and public/collective rights and practices (1993, 2002). Ensuring private property in land cannot be separated from other, equally important guarantees of access to material and social resources. Hann, along with many other researchers, shows that the separation of this private right from a range of other collective and public rights is a step backwards. There are many instances of people refusing total privatisation and holding onto and/or modifying the former socialist institutions precisely because they seek to maintain these other rights (cf. Kaneff 1996). Caroline Humphrey describes how, for Russia, many productive enterprises are 'not ... dominated primarily by the profit motive but rather are concerned with survival and the social protection of their members' (1999: 24). It is clear that the effect of changes in 'property' and 'ownership' cannot be understood only in terms of individual 'rights' and 'obligations', but necessarily involve the definition of social units. In Africa, a parallel is found in the dismantling and privatisation of marketing boards which, while they had serious problems as managers, nevertheless were often more successful in preventing famine than are the privatised companies. In both cases, the change in property status also involves the redesignation of what is private and what is public, and the priorities assigned to one or the other.

Similar conclusions come from Katherine Verdery's analysis of the dispute over whether a building that had been a granary in a Transylvanian village should be allowed to become the private property – and thereby a profitable venture – of a single person or should be retained in public ownership. The debates about 'property conceptions' turned on definitions of 'community' and 'person' and how the valued 'self' is formed in relation to them (1999: 73). The Africanist literature has many such examples that link self, identity and invested effort (whether of work in the physical sense or ritual or commensality) in debates over rightful claims to resources.

The new 'ideologies of ownership' not only displace previously existing guarantees to basic needs but also introduce new social divisions with new threats of fragmentation. The 'ideologies of ownership' in Romania are now often based on 'kinship (or blood) and work', thus 'property restitution entails reinforcing kinship ideology ... a potent addition to the new (renewed) class struggle emerging in Transvylania's villages' (Verdery 1994: 1105–106). The dangers of struggles over key resources, such as land, becoming entangled in divisions of 'blood', such as kinship or ethnicity or race, are potent, as current experience in parts of both Africa and the post-socialist world tragically reveals. While there are examples of innovative compromise in post-socialist countries, as Swain shows for the 'auctions' of property in parts of Hungary, so there are deep concerns about 'the politics of unreason' (1996) and the politics of disorder and violence (Schierup 1999). The Africanist research reveals the same mix.

Conclusions

Much of the research out of the post-socialist world is summarised by Mandel and Humphrey as 'we are not dealing simply with the clash of two mutually alien economic systems, "the market" and "the socialist planned economy", but with a much more complex encounter of a number of specific, culturally-embedded, and practical organisational forms' (2002: 2). This might be echoed in the Africanist literature, where another two 'sides' are the peasant and the market. I wonder, however, if this goes far enough. The challenge emerging from a comparative glance across the post-socialist and Africanist research on land, property and development, for me at least, is to make deeper theoretical inroads into what seems to be cast analytically as an in-between or liminal place. I fear that notions of 'embeddedness', of 'fuzzy' rights, of 'an indeterminate third sector' (between private and public) are further examples of how our attempts to reject the dichotomies and ideological proclivities of dominant theories may be co-opted by reigning models – another example of paradigmatic strangulation. Thus, we stress property as embedded *because* dominant theories have disembedded those social relations from others. We refer to 'fuzzy' rights *because* they appear so only from the premise that rights should be clearly defined. We speak of a 'third sector' *because* the dominant ideology is of a world bifurcated into private and public, while 'indeterminate' evokes the fuzzy and complicated quality of real existing social relations that are reduced to individual incentive and/or rights in dominant approaches.

The insightful discussions of how commonly held resources, creatively complementing private individual or family properties and public services, have played an important part in many parts of the socialist world, gave support to the conviction that converting 'customary' tenure in Africa to private property is as much a mistake as assuming it will 'evolve' itself. The flexibility that forms of customary tenure – more accurately seen as family or lineage tenure – give to small-scale producers across Africa in situations of extreme volatility of natural and political-economic systems will be one victim of the current rush to land reform throughout the continent. I have been inspired by the post-socialist literature to believe that challenges to long-established views of the magic of property in land must go beyond calling attention to the 'embeddedness' and 'complexity' of property rights. The assumption that property is the necessary mediator of social and economic progress must be rejected. The neoclassical economic/neoliberal logic posits that *property in land* is the vehicle to ensure a *market in land* and, thereby, guarantees *individual incentives* to produce and improve income. For this faith to be rejected requires not a notion of embeddedness but of fetichisation. Rather than fetischising the market and property, we need a political, economic and cultural analysis of 'real' targets of human health, income and work – social 'entitlements' without which one is likely to see 'the revival of … a rural under-class of second-class citizens' (as Hann 1996: 47 fears for Hungary), and an intensification in the widespread poverty and social distress seen across most of Africa. Echoing another critique of neoliberal thought (as exemplified in neoclassical economics and the 'new' institutionalism), I suggest we need an approach 'historically grounded in the societies under consideration for which capital and capitalism, for example, are more appropriate as both material and cultural categories than are the universal notions of property, institutions, and ideology' (Fine and Milonakis 2003: 568).

Notes

1. I follow current regional use of the term post-socialist to refer to countries of the former Soviet Union. The problems of the 'post' are similar to the use of post-colonial for African countries. I am aware of the dangers of implying a false homogeneity in referring to 'Africa' and 'African', but in this paper I sketch broadly in order to engage a new discussion.
2. Anthropologists have been centrally involved and their research dominates here, although I also draw from writers in history, politics, legal studies, geography, and so on.
3. This also applies to the anthropologists whose efforts to counter colonial misrepresentations of African 'tradition' and 'custom' ended, willy-nilly, in helping construct 'customary' law (see Colson 1971; Chanock 1985; Cheater 1990).
4. Cf. the chapter by von Benda-Beckmann et al. in this volume.
5. The Report of the Royal Commission on Land and Population in East Africa (Great Britain 1955), for example, called on colonial administrations 'to encourage the emergence of individual tenure … where the tribal customs governing the existing form of tenure are out of line with modern requirements'.
6. Among others, see Okoth-Ogendo 1976; Coldham 1978; Pala 1980; Shipton 1988; Haugerud 1989; Attwood 1990; Shipton and Goheen 1992: 316; Shipton 1994: 364–65; Besteman 1994, 1996.
7. Among others, see Galaty et al. 1981; Hitchcock 1982; Sandford 1983; Horowitz 1986; Baxter and Hogg 1990; Behnke et al. 1993; Peters 1994.
8. Where the unit may be the 'state' as in the Mongolian case, but also may be clans, lineages or age-grades.

9. See Peters 1998; Kingston-Mann, this volume.
10. From a survey in 1810 of Hampshire forests, cited in Thompson 1993: 163.

References

Allott, A.N. 1968. 'Family Property in West Africa: Its Juristic Basis, Control and Enjoyment', in *Family Law in Asia and Africa*, ed. J.N.D. Anderson, London: Butterworths, 121–42.

Amanor, K.S. 1999. *Global Restructuring and Land Rights in Ghana: Forest Food Chains, Timber and Rural Livelihoods*. Uppsala: Nordiska Afrikainstitutet.

——— 2001. *Land, Labour and the Family in Southern Ghana: A Critque of Land Policy under Neo-liberalisation*. Uppsala: Nordiska Afrikainstitutet.

Attwood, D. 1990. 'Land Registration in Africa: The Impact on Agricultural Production', *World Development* 18(5): 659–71.

Bassett, T.J. 1993a. 'Introduction: The Land Question and Agricultural Transformation in Sub-Saharan Africa', in *Land in African Agrarian Systems*, eds T.J. Bassett and D.E. Crummey, Madison: University of Wisconsin Press, 3–31.

——— 1993b. 'Land Use Conflicts in Pastoral Development in Northern Cote d'Ivoire', in *Land in African Agrarian Systems*, eds T.J. Bassett and D.E. Crummey, Madison: University of Wisconsin Press, 131–54.

Baxter, P. and R. Hogg, eds 1990. *Property, Poverty, and People: Changing Rights in Property and Problems of Pastoral Development*. Manchester: University of Manchester, Department of Social Anthropology and International Development Centre.

Behnke Jr., R.H., I. Scoones and C. Kerven, eds 1993. *Range Ecology at Disequilibrium: New Models of Natural Variability and Pastoral Adaptation in African Savannas*. London: Overseas Development Initiative.

Benjaminsen, T.A. and C. Lund, eds 2003. *Securing Land Rights in Africa*. London and Portland: Frank Cass.

Berry, S.S. 1975. *Cocoa, Custom and Socio-economic Change in Rural Western Nigeria*. Oxford: Clarendon Press.

——— 1993. *No Condition is Permanent: The Social Dynamics of Agrarian Change in Sub-Saharan Africa*. Madison: University of Wisconsin Press.

——— 2002. 'Debating the Land Question in Africa', *Comparative Studies in Society and History* 44(4): 638–68.

Besteman, C. 1994. 'Individualisation and the Assault on Customary Tenure in Africa: Title Registration Programmes and the Case of Somalia', *Africa* 64(4): 484–515.

——— 1996. 'Local Land Use Strategies and Outsider Politics: Title Registration in the Middle Jubba Valley', in *The Struggle for Land in Southern Somalia: The War behind the War*, eds C. Besteman and L.V. Cassanelli, Boulder: Westview Press, 29–46.

——— 1999. *Unraveling Somalia: Race, Violence and the Legacy of Slavery*. Philadelphia: University of Pennsylvania Press.

Bruce, J.W. 1988. 'A Perspective on Indigenous Land Tenure Systems and Land Concentration', in *Land and Society in Contemporary Africa*, eds R.E. Downs and S.P. Reyna, Hanover: University Press of New England, 23–52.

Bruce, J.W. and S.E. Migot-Adholla 1994. *Searching for Land Tenure Security in Africa*. Washington, D.C.: World Bank.

Carney, D. and J. Farrington 1998. *Natural Resource Management and Institutional Change*. London: Routledge/ODI.

Chanock, M. 1985. *Law, Custom and Social Order: The Colonial Experience in Malawi and Zambia*. Cambridge: Cambridge University Press.

——— 1991. 'Paradigms, Policies, and Property: A Review of the Customary Law of Land Tenure', in *Law in Colonial Africa*, eds K. Mann and R. Roberts, Portsmouth: Heinemann, 61–84.

Cheater, A.P. 1990. 'The Ideology of "Communal" Land Tenure in Zimbabwe: Mythogenesis Enacted?', *Africa* 60(2): 188–206.

Cohen, J.M. 1980. 'Land Tenure and Rural Development in Africa', in *Agricultural Development in Africa*, eds A.F. Bates and M.F. Lofchie, New York: Praeger, 340–400.

Coldham, S.F.R. 1978. 'The Effect of Registration of Title upon Customary Land Rights in Kenya', *Journal of African Law* 22: 91–111.

Colson, E. 1971. 'Impact of the Colonial Period on the Definition of Land Rights', in *Colonialism in Africa, 1870–1960*, ed. V. Turner, Cambridge: Cambridge University Press, 193–215.

Downs, R.E. and S.P. Reyna, eds 1988. *Land and Society in Contemporary Africa*. Hanover: University Press of New England.

Dunn, E. 1999. 'Slick Salesmen and Simple People: Negotiated Capitalism in a Privatized Polish Firm', in *Uncertain Transition: Ethnographies of Change in the Post-socialist World*, eds M. Burawoy and K. Verdery, Lanham, Boulder, New York, Oxford: Rowan and Littlefield, 125–47.

Fine, B. and D. Milonakis 2003. 'From Principle of Pricing to Pricing of Principle: Rationality and Irrationality in the Economic History of Douglass North', *Comparative Studies in Society and History* 45(3): 546–70.

Francis, P. 1984. '"For the Use and Common Benefit of All Nigerians": Consequences of the 1978 Land Nationalization', *Africa* 54(3): 5–28.

Galaty, J.G., D. Aronson and P.C. Salzman, eds 1981. *The Future of Pastoral Peoples*. Ottowa: IDRC.

Gluckman, M. 1965. *The Ideas in Barotse Jurisprudence*. New Haven and London: Yale University Press.

Great Britain, Colonial Office 1955. *Report of the Royal Commission on Land and Population in East Africa*. London: HMSO.

Griffiths, A. 1997. *In the Shadow of Marriage. Gender and Justice in an African Community*. London and Chicago: University of Chicago Press.

Gulbrandsen, O. 1987. *Privilege and Responsibility*. Bergen: Department of Anthropology.

Guyer, J.I. 1997. *An African Niche Economy. Farming to Feed Ibadan, 1968–88*. Edinburgh: Edinburgh University Press for IAI.

Guyer, J.I. and E.F. Lambin 1993. 'Land Use in an Urban Hinterland. Ethnography and Remote Sensing in the Study of African Intensification', *American Anthropologist* 95(4): 839–59.

Gyasi, E.A. 1994. 'The Adaptability of African Communal Land Tenure to
    Economic Opportunity: The Example of Land Acquisition for Oil Palm
    Farming in Ghana', *Africa* 64(3): 391–405.
Hammar, A. 2001. '"The Day of Burning": Eviction and Reinvention in the
    Margins of Northwestern Zimbabwe', *Journal of Agrarian Change* 1(4): 550–74.
Hann C.M., ed. 1993. *Socialism. Ideals, Ideologies and Local Practice.* London and
    New York: Routledge.
———— 1996. 'Land Tenure and Citizenship in Tazlar', in *After Socialism. Land
    Reform and Social Change in Eastern Europe*, ed. R. Abrahams, Providence and
    Oxford: Berghahn Books, 23–50.
———— 2002. 'The Idiocies of Decollectivization', paper presented to the Program on
    Agrarian Studies, Yale University.
Haugerud, A. 1989. 'Land Tenure and Agrarian Change in Kenya', *Africa* 59(1):
    61–90.
Hill, P. 1963. *The Migrant Cocoa Farmers of Southern Ghana: A Study in Rural
    Capitalism.* Cambridge: Cambridge University Press.
Hitchcock, R.K. 1982. 'Tradition, Social Justice, and Land Reform in Central
    Botswana', in *Land Reform in the Making*, ed. R.P. Werbner, London: Rex
    Collings, 1–34.
Horowitz, M.M. 1986. 'Ideology, Policy, and Praxis in Pastoral Livestock
    Development' in *The Anthropology of Rural Development in West Africa*, eds
    M.M. Horowitz and T. Painter, Boulder: Westview Press, 251–72.
Humphrey, C. 1999. 'Traders, "Disorder", and Citizenship Regimes in Provincial
    Russia', in *Uncertain Transition: Ethnographies of Change in the Post-socialist
    World*, eds M. Burawoy and K. Verdery, Lanham, Boulder, New York, Oxford:
    Rowan and Littlefield, 19–52.
Juul, K. and C. Lund, eds 2002. *Negotiating Property in Africa.* Portsmouth:
    Heinemann.
Kaneff, D. 1996. 'Responses to "Democratic" Land Reforms in a Bulgarian
    Village', in *After Socialism. Land Reform and Social Change in Eastern Europe*,
    ed. R. Abrahams, Providence and Oxford: Berghahn Books, 85–114.
Kingston-Mann, E. 1999. *In Search of the True West: Culture, Economics and
    Problems of Russian Development.* Princeton: Princeton University Press.
Klopp, J.M. 2000. 'Pilfering the Public: The Problem of Land Grabbing in
    Contemporary Kenya', *Africa Today* 47(1): 7–26.
Lastarria-Cornhiel, S. 1995. *Impact of Privatization on Gender and Property Rights
    in Africa.* Madison: Land Tenure Center, University of Wisconsin-Madison.
Lawry, S.W. 1993. 'Transactions in Cropland Held under Customary Tenure in
    Lesotho', in *Land in African Agrarian Systems*, eds T.J. Bassett and D.E.
    Crummey, Madison: University of Wisconsin Press, 57–74.
Linares, O.F. 1992. *Power, Prayer and Production: The Jola of Casamance, Senegal.*
    Cambridge: Cambridge University Press.
Mamdani, M. 1996. *Citizen and Subject: Contemporary Africa and the Legacy of
    Late Colonialism.* Princeton: Princeton University Press.
Mandel, R. and C. Humphrey, eds 2002. *Markets and Moralities. Ethnographies of
    Postsocialism.* Oxford and New York: Berg.

Merry, S.E. 1988. 'Legal Pluralism', *Law and Society Review* 22(5): 869–96.

Moore, D.S. 1993. 'Contesting Terrain in Zimbabwe's Eastern Highlands: Political Ecology, Ethnography and Peasant Resource Struggles', *Economic Geography* 69(4): 380–401.

Moore, S.F. 1978. *Law as Process*. London: Routledge and Kegan Paul.

—— 1986. *Social Facts and Fabrications:'Customary Law' on Kilimanjaro, 1880–1980*. Cambridge: Cambridge University Press.

Myers, G.W. 1994. 'Competitive Rights, Competitive Claims: Land Access in Post-War Mozambique', *Journal of Southern African Studies* 20(4): 603–32.

Netting, R.M. 1993. *Smallholders, Householders: Farm Families and the Ecology of Intensive, Sustainable Agriculture*. Stanford: Stanford University Press.

Ng'ong'ola, C. 1996. 'Customary Law, Land Tenure and Policy in some African Countries at the Threshold of the Twenty-first Century', in *Property Law on the Threshold of the Twenty-first Century*, eds G.E. van Maanen and A.J. van der Walt, Ontwerp: Bureau JA Vormgevers, 391–414.

Nyambara, P.S. 2001. 'The Closing Frontier: Agrarian Change, Immigrants and the "Squatter Menace" in Gokwe, 1980–1990s', *Journal of Agrarian Change* 1(4): 534–49.

Odgaard, R. 2003. 'Scrambling for Land in Tanzania: Processes of Formalisation and Legitimisation of Land Rights', in *Securing Land Rights in Africa*, eds T.A. Benjaminsen and C. Lund, London and Portland, OR: Frank Cass, 71–88.

Okoth-Ogendo, H.W.O. 1976. 'African Land Tenure Reform', in *Agricultural Development in Kenya*, eds J. Heyer, J.K. Maitha and W.M. Senga, Nairobi: Oxford University Press, 152–86.

Pala, A.O. 1980. 'The Joluo Equation: Land Reform = Lower Status for Women', *Ceres*, May-June: 37–42.

Peters, P.E. 1994. *Dividing the Commons: Politics, Policy, and Culture in Botswana*. Charlottesville: University of Virginia Press.

—— 1997. 'Against the Odds', *Critique of Anthropology* 17(2): 189–210.

—— 1998. 'The Erosion of Commons and the Emergence of Property: Problems for Social Analysis', in *Property in Economic Context*, eds R.C. Hunt and A. Gilman, Lanham: University Press of America, 351–73.

—— 2002. 'The Limits of Negotiability: Security, Equity and Class Formation in Africa's Land Systems', in *Negotiating Property in Africa*, eds K. Juul and C. Lund, Portsmouth: Heinemann, 45–66.

—— 2004. 'Inequality and Social Conflict over Land in Africa', *Journal of Agrarian Change* 4(3): 269–314.

Platteau, J.-Ph. 1996. 'The Evolutionary Theory of Land Rights as Applied to Sub-Saharan Africa: A Critical Assessment', *Development and Change* 27(1): 29–86.

—— 2000. 'Does Africa Need Land Reform?', in *Evolving Land Rights, Policy and Tenure in Africa*, eds C. Toulmin and J. Quan, London: DFID/IIED/NRI, 51–74.

Ribot, J. 2000. 'Decentralization, Participation, and Representation: Administrative Apartheid in Sahelian Forestry', in *Development Encounters: Sites of Participation and Knowledge*, ed. P.E. Peters, Cambridge: Harvard University Press for HIID, 29–60.

Sandford, S. 1983. *Management of Pastoral Development in the Third World.*
Chichester: John Wiley and Sons for ODI.

Schierup, C.-U., ed. 1999. *Scramble for the Balkans. Nationalism, Globalism and the
Political Economy of Reconstruction.* New York: St. Martin's Press.

Shipton, P. 1988. 'The Kenyan Land Tenure Reform: Misunderstandings in the
Public Creation of Private Property', in *Land and Society in Contemporary
Africa*, eds R.E. Downs and S.P. Reyna, Hanover: University Press of New
England, 91–135.

—— 1994. 'Land and Culture in Tropical Africa: Soils, Symbols, and the
Metaphysics of the Mundane', *Annual Review of Anthropology* 23: 347–77.

Shipton, P. and M. Goheen 1992. 'Introduction. Understanding African Land-
Holding: Power, Wealth, and Meaning', *Africa* 62(3): 307–25.

Sneath, D. 2002. 'Mongolia in the "Age of the Market": Pastoral Land-use and the
Development Discourse', in *Markets and Moralities. Ethnographies of
Postsocialism*, eds R. Mandel and C. Humphrey, Oxford and New York: Berg,
191–210.

Southgate, C. and D. Hulme 2000. 'Uncommon Property: The Scramble for
Wetland in Southern Kenya', in *African Enclosures? The Social Dynamics of
Wetlands in Drylands*, eds P. Woodhouse, H. Bernstein and D. Hulme, Oxford:
James Currey; Trenton: Africa World Press; Cape Town: David Philip; Nairobi:
EEP, 73–117.

Swain, N. 1996. 'Getting Land in Central Europe', in *After Socialism. Land Reform
and Social Change in Eastern Europe*, ed. R. Abrahams, Providence and Oxford:
Berghahn Books, 193–215.

Thompson, E.P. 1993. *Customs in Common.* New York: The New Press.

Toulmin, C. and J. Quan, eds 2000. *Evolving Land Rights, Policy and Tenure in
Africa.* London: DFID/IIED/NRI.

van Donge, J.K. 1999. 'Law and Order as a Development Issue: Land Conflicts and
the Creation of Social Order in Southern Malawi', *The Journal of Development
Studies* 36(2): 48–70.

Verdery, K. 1994. 'The Elasticity of Land: Problems of Property Restitution in
Transylvania', *Slavic Review* 53(4): 1071–109.

—— 1999. 'Fuzzy Property: Rights, Power, and Identity in Transylvania's
Decollectivization', in *Uncertain Transition: Ethnographies of Change in the Post-
socialist World*, eds M. Burawoy and K. Verdery, Lanham, Boulder, New York,
Oxford: Rowan and Littlefield, 53–81.

Woodhouse, Ph., P. Trench and M.D.M. Tessougué 2000. 'A Very Decentralized
Development. Exploiting a New Wetland in the Sourou Valley, Mali', in *African
Enclosures? The Social Dynamics of Wetlands in Drylands*, eds Ph. Woodhouse,
H. Bernstein and D. Hulme, Oxford: James Currey; Trenton: Africa World
Press; Cape Town: David Philip; Nairobi: EEP, 29–72.

Worby, E. 2001. 'A Redivided Land? New Agrarian Conflicts and Questions in
Zimbabwe', *Journal of Agrarian Change* 1(4): 475–509.

Chapter 5

Land as Asset, Land as Liability:
Property Politics in Rural Central and Eastern Europe*

Thomas Sikor

Post-socialist land reforms have offered many people in Central and Eastern Europe the opportunity to become land owners. People have readily seized on the opportunity, lodging formal claims on land. They expend significant effort to recoup historical land holdings, acquire new parcels, and influence land privatisation processes. They invoke various social and moral values to justify their claims on land against competing claims, to influence allocation procedures, and to win court cases. Once they have received land titles, they struggle to translate the newly acquired legal rights into practice, fighting the constraints on machinery services, input supplies, output marketing, and land markets. People expend all this effort because they consider land an important asset, for the material and symbolic values derived from land ownership.

Yet land ownership has also brought along various legal obligations, to which the new land owners are held responsible. Land titles carry not only rights but also obligations. My particular concern in this paper is with the obligations originating from concerns for environmental protection. Environmental concerns have found their way into land legislation, because agriculture influences the rural environment in many ways. Agricultural practices not only produce food and fibre but also condition the rural environment. Agriculture shapes cultural landscapes

* This paper has benefited greatly from comments by Keebet von Benda-Beckmann and the participants of the property conference in Halle. It would not have been possible without the field work conducted by Krysztof Krukowski, Veronika Krumalova, Tomas Ratinger and Adam Wasilewski. I want to thank them for their cooperation and enthusiasm over the course of our research. The research has been conducted under a grant from the European Commission (Contract No. QLK5–1999–01611) to the Division of Resource Economics at Humboldt University, Berlin (Prof. Konrad Hagedorn).

and modifies the distribution of valuable flora and fauna, to name just two environmental amenities affected by agricultural practices. In consequence, post-socialist reforms tie people's newly acquired rights on agricultural land to the general obligation to preserve valuable environmental amenities.[1]

Central and Eastern European governments have chosen a regulatory approach to put the environmental obligations of land owners into practice (Howarth 1998; Sikor forthcoming). They subject land owners to specific duties and restrict their options in land management in order to protect the rural environment. Specialised government units, often the agricultural agencies, set environmental standards to be met by agricultural producers. The units also have the mandate to enforce the standards through a variety of measures, including penalties for environmental offenses. For example, agricultural agencies may require producers to perform certain land management practices for the protection of valuable flora. The producers face the threat of penalties if their practices do not comply with the regulations. Regulation, therefore, has become the primary mode of environmental protection in agriculture.

In this paper, I take a closer look at rural property relations in Central and Eastern Europe to understand how environmental regulation is played out in practice. By property, I refer to the 'bundle of rights and obligations' associated with an object (von Benda-Beckmann et al. in this volume). I speak of a 'bundle of rights and obligations' to reflect the many kinds of relationships concerning land and its use. In agriculture in particular, it is important to employ such a nuanced notion of landed property, because of the many functions of agricultural land use. For example, agriculture in a particular region may not only produce a range of agricultural crops, but also contribute to clean drinking water, provide habitats for endangered bird species, maintain the cultural landscape, and absorb atmospheric carbondioxide. The specific practices employed by agricultural producers determine the contributions of agriculture to these multiple functions. Seemingly minor changes in land management practices can have significant impacts on the rural environment. Agricultural practices, therefore, continuously redefine the contributions of agriculture to environmental protection. Correspondingly, environmental regulations include a long series of very concrete and detailed duties and restrictions in land management.

I use this framework to examine two empirical cases from the Czech Republic and Poland. The cases deal with typical rural environmental problems in the region: biodiversity conservation and protection of peri-urban open space. Farmers in both cases not only produce marketable products but also provide environmental amenities. The case studies provide valuable insights into the dynamics of rural property at three of the four 'layers' delineated by von Benda-Beckmann et al. in the introduction of this volume: the material and symbolic reactions of local actors to legal obligations as manifested in concrete agricultural practices; the dynamics of actual property relations, with particular attention to the obligations connected with land rights; and changes in environmental regulations applicable to agriculture. In fact, the cases suggest that people's reactions to environmental regulations not only re-work actual property relations but also produce emerging new sets of regulation different from those originally legislated.

The paper begins with a review of the literature on post-socialist property relations in Central and Eastern Europe. The literature review helps me identify three concrete questions that guide the subsequent analysis of the two empirical cases. The case analyses inform a more general discussion of land management practices, rural property relations, and environmental regulation. The paper concludes with alternative interpretations of the observed property dynamics.

Land as a Post-socialist Asset

What emerges from the literature on post-socialist property is a general consensus that actual property relations are significantly different from legislation. They have been different from the outset of land reforms due to the negotiation of legal procedures at the local level (de Waal 1995; Hann 1996; Verdery 1996: 159–64, 1998; Kaneff 1998). Political struggles accompany the restitution and distribution of legal land titles among various social actors. Villagers, village communities, urban residents, agricultural managers, ethnic groups and entrepreneurs compete with each other about control over land. Local negotiation results in distributions of land titles that deviate from those envisioned in legal texts, as broader political and social relations shape actual property relations.

Variation in the distribution of land titles is associated with the existence of multiple justifications for claims on land, or 'ideologies of land ownership' (Verdery 1996: 163). People make variable claims on land by asserting the primacy of individual entitlement and just desert, historical justice and kinship, collective work and entitlement, or the efficiency of 'the market'. These justifications go beyond narrow notions of land ownership. People react to the notions of private property, smallholder agriculture, and capitalist individualism embedded in property reforms by asserting competing values associated with land, production and entitlement (Verdery 1998: 166; 1999: 65–75; Giordano and Kostova 2002: 75, 79; Lampland 2002: 41). For example, Bulgarian and Russian villagers contest the notion of land as a source of individual wealth by emphasising the importance of land as a source for communal funds, as basis for collective enterprise, and as a resource to feed the local population (Humphrey 1995: 45; Kaneff 1995: 32, 1996: 111; Hivon 1998: 48). Romanian villagers assert a collective entitlement to a granary built by them under socialist agriculture (Verdery 1998: 166, 1999: 65–75). Elderly Hungarian villagers display a strong emotional attachment to particular plots, as a way to re-establish identities and conserve family bonds (Hann 1993: 310, 313).

As a result, not only is the distribution of legal titles different from legal provisions, but the new rights are often limited in practice. Serious contextual constraints limit the exercise of land rights, beginning with practical problems encountered in identifying the location of one's land (Verdery 1998: 163–65). Once people have identified their land, they face tremendous problems to turn their legal rights into tangible economic benefits. Agricultural producers have difficulty to access the necessary machinery, obtain agricultural credit, and purchase inputs (Verdery 1998: 173–78, 1999: 59–65; Zbierski-Salameh 1999: 194–98). They encounter product markets controlled by a few buyers and urban speculators (Zbierski-Salameh 1999: 198–202; Giordano and Kostova 2002: 87–88). The sale of land is often not an attractive option either, as land legislation prohibits sales to outsiders and constrains demands for land in other ways (Hann 1996: 36). Many smallholders, therefore, have little choice but to lease out their land to various types of agricultural associations and private entrepreneurs, in return for meagre lease payments (Verdery 1999; Giordano and Kostova 2002: 82). These constraints led Hann to conclude that:

> there are many persons and families in Hungary today for whom the current rhetoric about widening choice and extending property rights must seem a sick joke: … they cannot become entrepreneurial farmers because they lack the basic capital resources, and their social rights are being whittled away all the time (Hann 1993: 313).

The local agents of post-socialist governments play an active role in the negotiation of property. They staff the privatisation and liquidation councils that are in charge of privatising land and other assets at the local level. They seek to bend the decisions of those councils in favour of their own personal interests, the directives sent down by the central government, and the interests of various social actors. For example, accusations of power abuses by members of the councils are numerous in the Romanian village studied by Verdery (1996: 160–61). Villagers in Bulgaria resent the control exerted by the central government over the councils and their decisions (Kaneff 1996: 89–92). A liquidation council in Romania bends the rules to auction a collective granary off to the successor organisation of the agricultural cooperative (Verdery 1999: 65–75). Local government agents also play an active role in land relations after the initial privatisation. In Albania's mountains, local officials look away from apparent discrepancies between actual land relations and the legislation in case of agricultural land, but try to enforce legal regulations over forests (de Waal 2004). In the lowlands, Albanian officials display little interest in settling land conflicts, as the promise for permanent resolution and land titles is a useful tactic in election campaigns (ibid.). Finally, local government officials may decide to go private, utilising their skills and networks developed under socialism for private ventures (Humphrey 1995: 56; Giordano and Kostova 2002: 82–86; Lampland 2002: 43–44).

David Stark (1996) suggests an additional dimension to the politics of property in post-socialist Central and Eastern Europe. The political struggles are not confined to negotiations about the rights to property objects, but they also extend to associated obligations. Stark finds 'recombinant property' in Hungarian industry, 'recombinant' in the sense that the privatised property objects present new combinations of rights and obligations. Just as described above for rural areas, local negotiations shape the distribution of assets under Hungary's enterprise restructuring programme. The negotiations do not terminate at the question about who gets what object, however. Industrial managers negotiate the very nature of the objects to be privatised, as they combine rights and obligations in surprising new ways. They are quite successful in separating control over assets (buildings, machines, etc.) from responsibilities for liabilities (primarily financial debts). By this process the managers succeed in pushing the responsibilities onto the central state, turning private into government obligations. The managers' actions define obligations away from rights, constructing the assets to be privatised. The nature of property objects as assets or liabilities, therefore, is not given but established during the privatisation process. Managers' practices shape actual property relations in Hungarian industry, with national policy eventually following suit and legalising the changed property situation.

In the following analysis, I want to use Stark's insights to examine how rural people have reacted to environmental obligations. Stark's attention to rights *and* obligations appears useful for my purposes, because land is the object of multiple rights and obligations. Some of these obligations originate from environmental regulations, making agricultural producers liable for 'environmental debts' similar to the financial debts afflicting Hungarian industry. My inquiry, therefore, is guided by three questions. First, how do agricultural practices comply with the obligations imposed by environmental regulations? Or, in other words, are agricultural producers able to circumvent environmental obligations? Second, to what degree do land owners and agricultural producers share the environmental concerns motivating the obligations? What values do local people invoke in addition or in opposition to environmental protection? And third, what role do post-socialist governments play in the negotiation of environmental obligations? Do local officials implement and enforce the regulations enacted by national governments?

The Cases

I examine these questions through two case studies from contemporary Central and Eastern Europe, one on biodiversity conservation in the Czech Republic and the other one on the preservation of open space in Poland. The cases are chosen to facilitate insights into the social dynamics underlying common environmental problems in rural Central and Eastern Europe (Sikor 2004). I begin with the Czech case, as it nicely illustrates the symbolic struggles that accompany the implementation of environmental regulation.[2]

Biodiversity Conservation in Bílé Karpati, Czech Republic

Extensive livestock husbandry has nurtured rare orchid species in the White Carpathians for centuries.[3] To preserve the orchids, the Czech government established the Protected Landscape Area *Bílé Karpati* in 1980. In the early 1990s, land in and around the Protected Landscape

Area was restituted to its historical owners and their heirs. Thousands of small land owners received legal titles to often miniscule plots. The titles granted them ownership rights over the land, but the 1992 Law on the Protection of Agricultural Land also obliged them to follow good agricultural practice, in particular 'proper' grassland management. The administration of the Protected Landscape Area translated that to mean that agricultural producers in the core zone did not have permission to intensify grassland management by use of chemical fertilisers and pesticides. Nor did the administration allow them to abandon the management of the meadows. Land owners, or their tenants, had to perform the practices needed to prevent encroachment by bushes.[4]

Yet local land owners and producers showed little inclination to follow the regulations imposed by the park administration. In the 1990s, many producers ignored the obligation to perform 'proper' grassland management, applying chemical fertilisers and neglecting the duty to mow the meadows at certain times. A few land owners even abandoned agricultural production all together, letting bushes encroach on the meadows and suppressing the orchids. Land owners and producers were not inclined to follow the management prescriptions by the Protected Landscape Area office because of the perceived negative effects on grassland productivity. They did not risk any negative sanctions, as the administration of the Protected Landscape Area was at a loss to enforce the regulations. The few officers working in the administration saw themselves unable to deal with the large number of land owners. Targeting agricultural producers was also not an option. Around 60 percent of land owners did not have a written lease for their land, which made it extremely difficult to identify the producers on specific parcels. The administration, therefore, shied away from levying fines on non-compliant land owners and producers. Instead, it sought to motivate compliance with the regulations through awareness campaigns and educational outreach programmes.

Land owners, producers, and the administration of the Protected Landscape Area invoked different values to justify their actions. The officers of the Protected Landscape Area voiced the notion embedded in the legislation that land owners are subject to certain duties in land management as a way to preserve environmental amenities. For them, land rights came with the obligation to comply with environmental regulation. The officers pointed at the special value of the protected orchids and understood their mission as to conserve the orchids through proper practices in extensive grassland management. In contrast, land owners and producers argued that land restitution should not only involve the restitution of legal title. They demanded the restitution of all rights on the land in their historical extent, as remembered and portrayed by them. Their argument of historical justice denied the legitimacy of restrictions, such as the prohibition to utilise chemical fertiliser and pesticide, and obligations, such as the requirement to perform grassland management. Land owners and producers demanded financial compensation if the state imposed restrictions on land use.[5]

The local struggles around property took a sudden turn in 1997, when the Czech government initiated a subsidy programme for grassland management similar to the agri-environmental schemes of the European Union. Land owners and producers in the Protected Landscape Area have since been eligible for annual payments in exchange for grassland management. They are no longer required to provide environmental amenities for free but are now entitled to receive financial compensation for the costs incurred in the provision of biodiversity. Land owners and producers have gained what Bromley and Hodge (1990: 199) call 'presumptive entitlements in the policy arena'. The policy entitlements imply a radical change in the distribution of benefits and costs associated with land management. The Czech government now pays for land management practices performed by agricultural producers on a voluntary basis, practices that were legally required without compensation in the past. The subsidy programme, therefore, redefines the rights and obligations associated with land ownership. Land ownership has now become a source of claims on public funds, turning the regulatory regime in *Bílé Karpati* upside down.

The subsidy programme has shifted the terms of debate in the White Carpathians. In particular, three government units have repositioned themselves in reaction to the new regulatory regime and the newly available funds. The programme has strengthened the position of the Agricultural Agency, which is in charge of implementation. Being the regional office of the Ministry of Agriculture, the Agency emphasises agrarian interests. The new funds help the Agency work towards its goal to achieve 'commercially viable' farms. The Agency applies financial criteria, such as minimum area and livestock density, to target the programme to 'commercially viable' farmers. Programme participation is voluntary and open to producers independently of their location inside or outside the Protected Landscape Area. The environmental goals of the subsidy programme generally receive short thrift. The Agency shows little commitment to enforce the environmental conditions attached to programme participation. It did not conduct any monitoring of compliance until 2001. When the aerial inspection conducted in that year revealed non-compliance by programme participants on around 20 percent of the contracted land, the Agency refrained from any sanction beyond the request to violators to return the payment received for the area in violation.

The administration of *Bílé Karpati* deplores this lack of linkages between payments and compliance with environmental regulations. The officers call for a reorientation of the payments towards environmental goals, targeting the payments to the more valuable land for orchids, monitoring compliance in a more stringent way, and finding ways to enforce compliance. They want a close linkage between producers' rights to payments and their obligation to perform environmental services. The officers' possibilities to influence programme implementation are limited, however, as the park administration does not have any formal role in programme implementation.

In addition to these agrarian and environmental moralities, a third value 'rural development' has emerged. The local government authorities and a local NGO assert the goal of broader local development, including agriculture, ecotourism and other economic sectors. They resent the programme focus on large farmers and its neglect of economic and social problems in the White Carpathians, such as unemployment and out-migration. For them, the problem of biodiversity conservation is tied to the broader economic and social viability of rural life in the region. All three government units, therefore, embrace the subsidy programme as a means to serve larger goals but assert competing visions of a desirable future. The local authorities demand attention to local development in reaction to the agrarian and environmental values promoted by local branches of national authorities.

Preservation of Open Space in Piaseczno, Poland

The tension between local and wider interests is also a key theme in this case. The concrete issue is that residential development absorbs a rapidly growing portion of agricultural land in Piaseczno County at the outskirts of Warsaw.[6] Agricultural land in the county shrunk at an annual rate of around 2 percent between 1995 and 2000. The county government has plans to zone another 30 percent for residential development in the coming years. Urbanisation makes open space in Piaseczno County increasingly scarce, diminishing the recreational value of the land, not only for local residents, but also the inhabitants of the larger region. Residents of Warsaw and neighbouring counties lose the opportunity to enjoy the cultural landscape of Piaseczno, characterised by a mixture of old growth forests, wetlands, swamps and agricultural fields.

Powerful interests drive residential development in the county. Local land owners have a strong interest in conversion from agriculture to house plots. Most have operated small family farms for decades, even under Socialism. Nevertheless, today they increasingly envision a future outside agriculture and are eager to 'cash in' on the newly acquired right to sell their land granted by the Land Law.[7] Land owners' interests meet those of the broader local population, including long-time rural residents and recent migrants from Warsaw. Many express a dominant concern for economic development, even though some people display some interest in a liveable natural environment. People expect the inflow of new residents to bring about an increase in employment opportunities, local businesses, and physical and social infrastructure. The associated loss of rural landscape and open space is not a matter of serious concern. The county government, in turn, has taken advantage of decentralisation to promote local development.[8] The 1994 Act on Spatial Development has given the county government the primary authority over spatial planning, which it has employed to serve the local interests in economic development. In fact, its active promotion of local interests has gained it a good reputation among the local population. Land conversion, therefore, is driven by a local alliance of land owners eager to 'cash in' on their newly acquired rights, a broader rural society primarily oriented towards economic progress, and a county government understanding economic development as its primary mandate.

The local alliance faces a regulatory framework that asserts central authority over land conversion for the protection of open space. Land owners have received more extensive land rights under the new Land Law, yet the rights have been connected to certain obligations. One of these obligations is the requirement that land use conforms with the land use category designated by the government. Land owners are not allowed to change the use of the land at their liking. Any conversion of agricultural land to other uses not covered by the government's spatial plan requires approval by the Ministry of Agriculture, even if it is a tiny plot of 1,000 square meters only. Yet in practice, land owners have an easy time converting plots that have not been designated for residential development in the master plan. The required permit for conversion from the Ministry of Agriculture is a mere formality. Land holders usually receive the required permit without any complication. Without any representation at the county level, the Ministry lacks the capacity to subject the large number of requests to any serious check for environmental impacts.

The county government, in turn, displays no interest in helping the Ministry enforce the regulations on land conversion. Being elected by the local population, the county government acts in favour of local interests. Land owners are well entrenched in local politics and county decisions. In addition, the county government itself has a stake in land conversion, because of the nature of the revenue-sharing arrangements between local and central government. Land conversion bolsters the financial resources available to the county government, as it is entitled to retain all revenues from the real estate tax. Also, the county government's share in overall personal income tax returns increases when the local population grows. In Piaseczno, residential development boosted the returns from real estate tax by more than seven times between 1994 and 2000. The revenues derived from the tax almost doubled their contribution to overall county revenues in the same period.

Another element of the regulatory framework governing land conversion is the supervisory mandate given to the central government over the county spatial plans. Central authorities can institute restrictions on allowable land designations and designate protected areas. They have made extensive use of this possibility in Piaseczno, declaring about two thirds of the county's total land as protected landscapes or landscape parks. The county government is legally bound to the land use regulations instituted by the central government when it develops spatial plans. It has to submit its spatial plans to the central government for approval.

The legal framework has little significance in practice. County planning does not follow the directions set out in the regulations. Though the county government may emphasise broader interests in spatial planning, economic growth takes overarching priority when the master plan reaches the county council. Local financial interests originating from land owners and rooted in state budgetary regulations exert direct influence on decision making in the county council. Land conversion is also a primary means of revenue generation for the county government, as discussed above. As a consequence, county master plans have in the past designated areas for residential development that directly violated the principles set out in central government regulations, as county officials are ready to admit. County decision making follows the logic of real estate market, as a way to maximise county tax revenues, the financial returns to land for farmers, and the interest of broader rural society in economic development. Cultural landscapes and open space get lost in the process.

Central authorities do not have the capacity to exercise their mandate of oversight. The required approval by the Ministry of Agriculture resembles more a rubber stamp process than a serious exercise of central supervision. The Ministry has no means to evaluate the compliance of the master plan with central directives, as it lacks the most basic information about the county. If the Ministry should raise concerns, county governments have an easy time to fend off the concerns due to their superior access to information. There has not been any case yet when a master plan was subjected to Ministerial authority. Land owners, therefore, are able to ignore the obligations connected to land rights, with active support from the county government. The actions of the land owners and county government dissociate rights from obligations, putting the goal of local development in opposition to and above the environmental goal motivating the national regulation.

The Contested Nature of Land as an Asset

The case studies suggest that actual obligations are radically different from those put into legislation for the protection of environmental amenities. Land owners and agricultural producers have ignored the legal obligations connected with the newly acquired land rights. Producers in *Bílé Karpati* did not comply with the grassland management regulations enacted for the conservation of valuable orchids in the 1990s. Land owners in Piaseczno have circumvented the obligation for land use to conform with the land classification decided by the government. Land owners and agricultural producers, therefore, have reworked the combination of rights and obligations found in the legislation through their concrete land management practices. They have successfully dissociated rights from obligations. Their practices form more general patterns, reconfiguring actual property relations.

Given the reconfigurations of actual property relations, rural privatisation has amounted to a much more radical assault on landed property than envisioned by privatisation laws. Actual property relations in land have shifted further towards private control than foreseen in land

and environmental legislation. Land owners have been quick to assert the newly acquired rights to land. Agricultural producers employ practices that serve their private objectives of generating cash revenues and meeting subsistence requirements. The eagerness to assert the new rights is juxtaposed by various strategies to ignore and circumvent the obligations and restrictions connected with the rights. Where agricultural producers provide the desired environmental amenities, they do that on a voluntary basis and in return for 'presumptive policy entitlements'. Governments find themselves paying for land management practices that were originally assigned to land owners as a legal obligation.

Local contestants invoke different values to justify their reworking of property relations. Czech restituants portray their resistance against land use duties as a struggle for historical justice. They demand the restitution of land rights in their remembered historical extent, refuting the 'new' restrictions motivated by biodiversity conservation. When the government's agenda changes, though, the restituants and other local residents quickly add an argument emphasising local development. Asserting the primacy of local interests, they react to a government agenda that prioritises national and international interests in biodiversity conservation. In local people's claims, land is not so much a source of biodiversity but an asset to be used for local economic development. Polish land owners profess to a similar concern for local economic progress. In their case land becomes an asset to be mined for local development, which is seen as being in opposition to the preservation of open space. Local people therefore react to environmental legislation and programmes not only through material struggles but also by way of symbolic contestations. They couch local struggles against obligations in terms of social justice and local development, countering the government's emphasis on environmental goals.

What is at stake, I surmise, is the very nature of land as an asset. People seek ways to enhance the material and symbolic values derived from control over land. Compliance with environmental regulations tends to affect the profitability of agricultural production and price of land negatively. Land owners and agricultural producers react by ignoring legal obligations, as a way to secure the value of land as a productive resource, source of income, and basis of social security. They may even abandon agriculture or forego claims on marginal land, as happened in *Bílé Karpati*, if anticipated costs caused by the obligations outweigh expected benefits derived from the rights. Land owners and agricultural producers also contest the environmental goals that serve as justification for the obligations connected with rights. They invoke competing moralities and visions of a desirable future that emphasise concerns of local development and social justice. Asserting these moralities and visions they seek to influence the grounds that legitimate the concrete rights and obligations associated with land ownership, hence shape the control over material and symbolic resources derived from land ownership.

The obligations connected with land rights may turn land into a liability. Land is not an asset by nature, but land becomes an asset – or a liability – through the specific rights and obligations connected with land ownership in practice. In reaction, people assert rights to land against competing claims and various contextual constraints on the exercise of the rights (Hann 1993; Verdery 1998, 1999). But it is not only competing claims and contextual constraints that threaten to diminish the value of land to the new owners. One also needs to consider the obligations connected with land rights and their potential to reduce or even erase the material and symbolic benefits of land ownership. People react to the obligations through hidden forms of non-compliance and open protest. They seek to dissociate land rights from obligations, defining the nature of land as an asset. It is the balance of rights *and* obligations, in relation to dominant moralities and visions, that makes land an asset or a liability.

These negotiations are influenced by the 'state of the post-socialist state' (cf. Sturgeon and Sikor 2004). The struggles over rights and obligations are interwoven with the condition of the post-socialist state in at least three ways. First, the nature of government authority, in particular government control over property, influences the contestations of rights and obligations (Howarth 1998). What matters in this regard is not only the capacity of governments to enforce regulations, but also their will to do so, or to recognise the sets of regulations emerging from people's concrete practices. Second, governmental actors differ in their alignment with competing interests. These agricultural, environmental and rural development interests differentiate governments and divide different branches of governments. Third, the distribution of government authority between national and local levels influences the negotiations of rights and obligations. The comparison between the Czech and Polish cases is illustrative here, as government authority is highly centralised in *Bílé Karpati* but decentralised in Piaseczno.

Just as the values associated with land are multiple, there are various source of obligations imposed on land owners. My account has focused on the obligations originating from environmental regulations, as environmental concerns are a major justification of duties imposed on the new land owners. Environmental goals are also at the forefront of current rural policy debates within the European Union and, by implication, the negotiations about accession to the European Union.[9] There are obviously other sources of liability. For example, agricultural producers are typically required to maintain the productive potential of land. Land titles in Romania are connected with the duty to actually work the land (Verdery 1998: 171, 1999: 57). The new managers of agricultural enterprises in Hungary are held legally responsible for the debt burdens accumulated by those in the socialist period (Lampland 2002: 43–44).[10]

Moving beyond Central and Eastern Europe, Deborah James (this volume) provides interesting cases from South Africa that highlight the negotiation of the concrete rights and duties associated with land ownership in the privatisation processes. Although the setting is different, the dynamics underlying land privatisation are similar. Just as in Central and Eastern Europe, South Africans are eager to get land rights, for the material and symbolic values derived from land ownership. They find out in the process that the value of land titles is not given but depends on the concrete combination of actual rights and obligations associated with the title. As James points out, the obligations connected with land ownership actually threaten to alienate land from its new owners. People therefore employ various material and symbolic strategies to strengthen their rights and reduce connected obligations. They assert moralities that are quite different from those used by the state to justify land privatisation. Like the new land owners in *Bílé Karpati*, South African land recipients justify their visions with reference to a social memory of past rights and obligations, in their case that of the state welfarism promoted by the apartheid regime. James also indicates that people's struggles are related to the condition of the post-apartheid state. The nature of land as an asset is tied to the actions of local chiefs, new and old political elites, and local state authorities.

Conclusion: 'Recombinant Property' and Prospects for an Environmental Bail-out

The dynamics I describe in this paper demonstrate striking similarities with the 'recombinant property' discussed by Stark (1996) in Hungarian industry. Social actors contest the legal assignment of rights and obligations through material and symbolic struggles. They successfully define obligations away from rights, forming new assets out of rights and obligations. In the process, they invoke values and visions that counter the goal proclaimed by the central government. Their reactions lead to a stark discrepancy between actual property relations and the original regulations, which governments eventually resolve by redesigning regulations in accordance with property relations.

Following Stark, I surmise that the discrepancy between legislation and practice goes beyond the mediation of legislation commonly encountered at the local level. Suggestions of a 'gap between the new laws and reality' (Abrahams 1996: 9) fall short of capturing the dynamics of rural property in rural Central and Eastern Europe. Similarly, it does not suffice to explain the gap between legislation and practices with reference to contextual constraints on the fulfilment of obligations, such as lack of government enforcement capacity. Instead, people's practices not only refashion property relations but also influence state regulation. People's reactions to the property legislation are forming new sets of regulations that eventually find recognition in legislation. These reconfigurations of rural property are possible because the larger political-economic and cultural transformations have left a 'social vacuum' in post-socialist Central and Eastern Europe. The radical nature of the larger transformations combines with the massive assault on property relations to throw the most basic social rules and values associated with land up into the air (Burawoy and Verdery 1999; Sturgeon and Sikor 2004).

There are several possible interpretations for these property dynamics. One may conclude that the remaking of property relations is part of a special Central and Eastern European route to capitalism (cf. Staniszkis 1991). The emphasis on privatisation and weakness of post-socialist governments imply a (temporary?) loss of environmental amenities. Once the economy and political order have stabilised, public interests may motivate more attention to environmental protection again. The question is, however, how easily future environmental efforts can overcome the sets of regulations that are being currently established.[11] Alternatively, one may juxtapose the gains derived from the adaptability of 'recombinant property' with the losses due to the lack of accountability (cf. Stark 1996). Continuous negotiation of property relations and environmental regulations facilitates the flexibility required for the formation of diverse paths of agrarian change and rural development. In this way, the flexibility may serve the search for rural development options at a time when rural people find themselves in radically new conditions. The trade-off is obvious. My account highlights problems of accountability, in particular to regional, national, and international interests in the rural environment.

A third interpretation highlights the distributive aspects of rural property dynamics. Post-socialist land reforms and subsequent environmental regulations impose obligations on land owners and agricultural producers that limit the material and symbolic values derived from agricultural land. The new land owners and agricultural producers end up shouldering responsibility for environmental protection. In contrast, the emerging sets of regulations shift the financial responsibility for environmental protection to governments. Where agricultural producers provide environmental amenities, they only do so if they receive sufficient compensation from government coffers. What is perhaps in the making here is nothing less than an environmental bail-out, with governments taking over the financial responsibility for environmental protection. Bolstered by the pending access to the European Union's agricultural budget, Central and Eastern European governments may just be ready to do exactly that.

Notes

1. My discussion here simplifies and homogenises legislation that is much more complex and variable in practice. Yet I expect this condensed discussion to be useful for clarifying more general problems involved in the implementation of environmental legislation, the purpose of this paper.
2. I want to stress the exploratory nature of the research. There are obvious limitations to the research, above all the scant attention paid to the historical antecedents of contemporary property relations and social actors' concrete strategies and motivations. Yet I surmise that the evidence presented here highlights important dynamics of property in rural Central and Eastern Europe.
3. See Ratinger et al. (2003) and Ratinger and Krumalova (2002) for more detailed discussions of this case.
4. Land restitution has led to a busy reorganisation of land holdings in *Bílé Karpati*, as many land owners have rented the newly acquired plots to agricultural producers. The following discussion does not distinguish between land owners' and producers' rights and obligations in the case of rented land. It would be important to investigate how land owners and farmers negotiate the distribution of benefits and responsibilities, for example by looking at rental agreements and payments. But this is beyond the scope of the paper.
5. National legislation had opened the door for such conflicting arguments, by keeping the definition of land owners' duties rather vague. For example, the

1989 Land Law and 1992 Law on the Protection of Agricultural Land require land owners to perform 'proper' grassland management. Yet what practices does 'proper' grassland management involve? Another example is the duty to 'maintain fertility'. What measure should one use for soil fertility? In reference to what period should fertility be maintained?

6. See Wasilewski and Sikor (2003) and Wasilewski and Krukowski (2004) for more detailed discussions of this case.

7. One hectare of land designated for residential development sells for app. 600,000 Zloty, as demand by residents of nearby Warsaw is high. The amount vastly exceeds the average annual income of 2,000 Zloty per capita derived from agricultural production on the same land.

8. Since the 1990 Act on Local Self-Government, the county council has been directly elected by the local population and enjoys significant legal authority over public matters in the county.

9. Environmental concerns motivate an increasing share of payments to agricultural producers in the European Union. Environmental subsidies currently account for around 15 percent of total subsidies, their share being on the rise. Their significance varies between regions and producers, however. Environmental subsidies are especially important for producers on marginal land. Many small land owners in Central and Eastern Europe therefore attribute high importance to the expected payments, as suggested by anecdotal evidence. For example, smallholders in *Bílé Karpati* retain their land in the expectation of the subsidies brought about by accession to the European Union, as those might drive up land prices.

10. One may even argue that land privatisation generates new liabilities in a more general sense as land privatisation is connected with the dissolution of collectives and termination of social services (Kaneff 1995: 32; Abrahams 1996: 12).

11. See the chapter by Edella Schlager in this volume for an example of how difficult it is to change actual property relations.

References

Abrahams, R. 1996. 'Some Thoughts on Recent Land Reforms in Eastern Europe', in *After Socialism: Land Reform and Social Change in Eastern Europe*, ed. R. Abrahams, Oxford: Berghahn Books, 1–22.

Bromley, D.W. and I. Hodge 1990. 'Private Property Rights and Presumptive Policy Entitlements: Reconsidering the Premises of Rural Policy', *European Review of Agricultural Economics* 17: 197–214.

Burawoy, M. and K. Verdery. 1999. 'Introduction', in *Uncertain Transition: Ethnographies of Change in the Postsocialist World*, eds M. Burawoy and K. Verdery, Lanham: Rowman & Littlefield Publishers, 1–17.

de Waal, C. 1995. 'Decollectivisation and Total Scarcity in High Albania', *Cambridge Anthropology* 18(1): 1–22.

—— 2004. 'Postsocialist Property Rights and Wrongs in Albania: An Ethnography of Agrarian Change', *Conservation and Society* 2(1): 19–50.

Giordano, C. and D. Kostova 2002. 'The Social Production of Mistrust', in *Postsocialism: Ideals, Ideologies and Practices in Eurasia*, ed. C.M. Hann, London and New York: Routledge, 74–91.

Hann, C.M. 1993. 'From Production to Property: Decollectivization and the Family-Land Relationship in Contemporary Hungary', *Man* 28(2): 299–320.

——— 1996. 'Land Tenure and Citizenship in Tazlar', in *After Socialism: Land Reform and Social Change in Eastern Europe*, ed. R. Abrahams, Oxford: Berghahn Books, 23–49.

Hivon, M. 1998. 'The Bullied Farmer: Social Pressure as a Survival Strategy?', in *Surviving Post-Socialism: Local Strategies and Regional Responses in Eastern Europe and the Former Soviet Union*, eds S. Bridger and F. Pine, London: Routledge, 33–51.

Howarth, W. 1998. 'Property Rights, Regulation and Environmental Protection: Some Anglo-Romanian Contrasts', in *Property Relations: Renewing the Anthropological Tradition*, ed. C.M. Hann, Cambridge: Cambridge University Press, 181–200.

Humphrey, C. 1995. 'The Politics of Privatization in Provincial Russia: Popular Opinions Amid the Dilemmas of the Early 1990s', *Cambridge Anthropology* 18(1): 40–61.

Kaneff, D. 1995. 'Developing Rural Bulgaria', *Cambridge Anthropology* 18(2): 23–34.

——— 1996. 'Responses to "Democratic" Land Reforms in a Bulgarian Village', in *After Socialism: Land Reform and Social Change in Eastern Europe*, ed. R. Abrahams, Oxford: Berghahn Books, 85–114.

——— 1998. 'When "Land" Becomes "Territory": Land Privatisation and Ethnicity in Rural Bulgaria', in *Surviving Post-Socialism: Local Strategies and Regional Responses in Eastern Europe and the Former Soviet Union*, eds S. Bridger and F. Pine, London: Routledge, 16–32.

Lampland, M. 2002. 'The Advantages of Being Collectivized: Cooperative Farm Managers in the Postsocialist Economy', in *Postsocialism: Ideals, Ideologies and Practices in Eurasia*, ed. C.M. Hann, London and New York: Routledge, 31–56.

Ratinger, T. and V. Krumalova, 2002. *Provision of Environmental Goods on Potentially Abandoned Land – The White Carpathians Protected Landscape Area*. CEESA Discussion Paper 6, Humboldt University Berlin.

Ratinger, T., V. Krumalova and J. Prazan 2002. *Institutional Options for the Conservation of Biodiversity: Evidence from the Czech Republic*. CEESA Discussion Paper 21, Humboldt University Berlin.

Sikor, T. 2004. 'The Commons in Transition: Agrarian and Environmental Change in Eastern Europe', *Environmental Management* 34(2): 270–80.

Staniszkis, J. 1991. '"Political Capitalism" in Poland', *East European Politics and Society* 5(1): 127–41.

Stark, D. 1996. 'Recombinant Property in Eastern European Capitalism', *American Journal of Sociology* 101(4): 993–1027.

Sturgeon, J. and T. Sikor, 2004. 'Postsocialist Property Relations – Variations on Fuzziness', *Conservation and Society* 2(1): 1–16.

Verdery, K. 1996. *What was Socialism? And what Comes Next?* Princeton, NJ: Princeton University Press.

—— 1998. 'Property and Power in Transylvania's Decollectivization', in *Property Relations: Renewing the Anthropological Tradition*, ed. C.M. Hann, Cambridge: Cambridge University Press, 160–80.

—— 1999. 'Fuzzy Property: Rights, Power, and Identity in Transylvania's Decollectivization', in *Uncertain Transition: Ethnographies of Change in the Postsocialist World*, eds M. Burawoy and K. Verdery, Lanham: Rowman & Littlefield Publishers, 53–81.

Wasilewski, A., and Krukowski 2004. 'Land Conversion for Sub-urban Housing: A Study of Urbanization around Warsaw and Olsztyn, Poland', *Environmental Management* 34(2): 291–303.

Wasilewski, A. and T. Sikor 2003. *Institutional Options for the Protection of Open Space: Evidence from Poland.* CEESA Discussion Paper 16, Humboldt University Berlin.

Zbierski-Salameh, S. 1999. 'Polish Peasants in the "Valley of Transition": Responses to Postsocialist Reform', in *Uncertain Transition: Ethnographies of Change in the Postsocialist World*, eds M. Burawoy and K. Verdery, Lanham: Rowman & Littlefield Publishers, 189–222.

Chapter 6
Property, Labour Relations and Social Obligations in Russia's Privatised Farm Enterprises

Oane Visser

Market oriented land reform and farm privatisation was started in Russia in the early 1990s, with two broad goals.[1] First, these property reforms were seen as the solution to the inefficiency of the Soviet farms (World Bank 1992). Second, the reforms were intended to empower the rural population, by making them landowners and giving them influence as shareholders in their farm enterprise (World Bank 1992). It is widely acknowledged that the economic effects of these radical legal property changes have been disappointing (Humphrey 1998; Spoor and Visser 2001, 2004). In the 1990s the production on the farm enterprises (the large-scale successors of the *kolkhozes* and *sovkhozes*) declined by about 65 percent and the labour productivity went down also.[2] The issue of empowerment of the rural population has received less attention, but in this contribution, I show that changes in this area were also insignificant.

Distinguishing different layers of property following the von Benda-Beckmanns (F. and K. von Benda Beckmann and Wiber, this volume), I will show that reforms failed to realise both objectives, as legal reforms (the categorical property changes) did not lead to significant change in concretised property relations at the farm level. The property reforms did not empower workers enough as shareholders to become really responsible for farm matters, and to sanction management for rent seeking. On the other hand reforms also did not lead to a farm management with enough control over (and interest in) property and labour issues, to enforce far-reaching farm restructuring (although managers often have enough power over farm property to enrich themselves).

I contend that farm workers have received quite a lot of rights formally (they became shareholders in farm assets through property shares, and became landowners through land shares). But in practice these are mostly empty rights as the institutions such as courts, cadastres and markets, as well as information are lacking to make these rights valuable. Furthermore, the object of property is unclear as the shares represent some parcel of land (or asset) somewhere on the farm, which is not physically demarcated. As a consequence, farm workers do not feel themselves owners of farm land and assets, and do not feel responsible for farm property.

Furthermore, in many farms a process of disempowerment of workers is taking place. Farm managers and local authorities have kept land de facto centralised within their large farm enterprises, and are sometimes concentrating land personally in their hands. An authoritarian, paternalistic style of leadership has remained (or deepened). However, this has not led to such effective management control over labour and property so as to make farm restructuring possible.

This chapter focuses on the management-worker relationship as the most important social and economic relation within the farm.[3] I show that the new property relation (management versus shareholders/landowners) has little impact on the (daily) interaction between management and workers. Instead, the relation between management and worker has remained basically a labour relationship (employer-employee). To explain this, I discuss not only the property reforms, but even more importantly, the context of wider social and economic relations in which the property relations are historically embedded (especially the farm-community relations, and relations of exchange in the wider economy). This chapter shows that the manager-worker relation is characterised by mutual dependencies and moral obligations.

I conclude that the limited changes in property and labour relations (despite wide changes in legal property structures) are to some extent a result of the design and implementation of reforms. The property reforms were a compromise of two goals: egalitarian distribution and empowerment on one hand, and economic efficiency and effective management on the other. Furthermore, the implementation of reforms was very cumbersome. However, the most important reason for the slow change in concretised property and labour relations is that reformers have underestimated the extent to which property relations are interwoven with other social and economic relations formed during the Soviet era, and the extent to which they can be lifted out of this wider context.

Privatisation and the Property Relations in the Soviet Farm

In the Soviet period, all agricultural land was owned by the state and used by the *kolkhozes* and *sovkhozes*.[4] The farm assets were state property in *sovkhozes*, and were formally owned by members in the case of *kolkhozes*. The formal membership of the *kolkhoz* had little meaning in practice. Workers could not take out assets and their formal influence on farm issues was extremely limited. However, each rural household with a member working on a *kolkhoz* or *sovkhoz* had use rights to a small subsidiary plot of a maximum of a quarter of a hectare, and was also allowed to have some private livestock. Produce from the private plot was mainly for their own consumption, but could also be sold in the market. In the late 1980s, during Gorbachev's *perestroika*, the size limits on subsidiary plots were abolished and left up to local authorities and farm enterprises. Private initiative was further stimulated by the introduction of lease contracts for land and livestock.

Large-scale privatisation started in Russia after the fall of the Soviet Union. The first phase took place from 1991 to 1993. The *kolkhozes* and *sovkhozes* were mostly converted into independent enterprises (joint stock companies, limited liability companies, cooperatives) and state land was handed over to them. In the second phase, from 1993 to the mid-1990s, land and farm property was handed over to the farm workers in the form of paper shares. Employees generally lease these land shares to the farm enterprise. As owners of a land share they are in principle able to use the land parcels as they see fit, for example, hire it out to another farm. Farm workers can also use these land shares to start a private (peasant) farm, but few have taken the risk to do so. The main obstacles are the lack of all-round agricultural knowledge among most farm workers, difficult access to credit (Visser 2003c), and the lack of crucial personal contacts with directors of purchasing firms and processors (Spoor and Visser 2004). Probably the most important reason why farmers do not embark on independent private farming is the specific (informal) property relations that existed within the farm enterprise (Visser 2003a).

The boundaries between agricultural enterprises and household enterprises (the subsidiary plot, including private livestock) were vague. Households could let their livestock graze on the collective meadows. Employees used tractors of the enterprise to plough their plots and informally received fodder for their private livestock. It was a public secret that farm employees obtained part of the inputs for their own enterprises by stealing it from the collective farm. Further, *kolkhozes* often marketed surplus production (above the plan) through the household enterprises to hide actual production figures and evade higher production quota in the future. Apart from resources that the enterprise offered to its members, semi-legal or illegal goods flowed towards the household sector. In brief, the blurred boundaries of *kolkhoz* and household property enabled a symbiosis between collective farm and household enterprises.

Thus, any farm workers who under current circumstances take out their share and establish a private farm, deprive themselves of crucial (informal) access to former collective property. Furthermore, they largely cut themselves off from the vital social services provided by the larger enterprise (see below). The formation of private farms largely stagnated in the mid-1990s, and the contribution of these farms in terms of production and employment is very limited. In addition to land shares, employees received paper shares in the assets of the larger enterprise, as shareholders. Despite these rights they do not feel they are owners, and mostly do not receive any dividends. To explain why workers have not been empowered and have not become real owners, I investigate in more detail the rights that farm workers have received. Given the above, this chapter concentrates on the property relations within large-scale farm enterprises (the heirs of the *kolkhozes* and *sovkhozes)* and their link to the private (subsidiary) plots.

Failed Empowerment of Farm Workers

Under current conditions, the bundle of rights attached to Russian farmland is quite inclusive. Employee-shareholders can use their land share to start an independent private farm or to extend their subsidiary plot. Furthermore they can give away, inherit, hire out or sell their land. Although farm workers have a lot of rights connected to their land shares, the object of these rights is unclear. Contrary to land reform in central Europe (Verdery 2003), land was not physically distributed in

Russia (and most CIS countries). The land shares in Russia are basically paper shares, which represent some plot of land (of on average five to twelve hectares) somewhere on the farm enterprise. The landowners (farm workers) do not know where their land shares are located. When they want to convert their land share into a physical plot to work or to transfer, the general assembly of shareholders (in practice the management) decides what parcel of land is assigned. In this way, the management has considerable power over the property of the employees, as it can give a farm worker a centrally located fertile parcel, or an outlying parcel of bad quality.

The rights attached to property shares (the shares in farm assets, like machinery and buildings) are more circumscribed, and depend on the legal form of the farm enterprise. Shareholders in open joint stock companies are allowed to sell their shares to both outsiders and insiders. However, less than 5 percent of the farm enterprises have this legal form. On the other side of the spectrum of legal forms, in cooperatives (which still are the predominant organisational form), farm workers cannot transfer their property rights at all. The object of property shares is even less clear than with land shares. Farm workers, who took out their property share to start a private farm when the farm enterprise was privatised, often received a tractor and other machinery. However, generally the farm enterprises' constituent documents stipulate that farm workers starting a private farm later, can only receive a sum of money in accordance with the value of their property share. Often the farm management did not index the value of a property share as was legally required. Due to inflation such property shares have now become virtually worthless.

Taking into account that farm workers have no pre-socialist memory of ownership and that the property objects are so unclear, it is not surprising that they do not feel like owners. Farm workers have little knowledge about their rights and many easily had those rights stripped away as farm directors set out to keep collectives together, to avoid time-demanding legal procedures or to increase their power. Many workers were persuaded by farm directors to invest their shares in the farm enterprises for next to nothing. About half of all the land shares are used by farm enterprises without legal formalities for lease or investment (Uzun 1999). Farm workers rarely receive compensation for land rent in cash or in dividends on property shares. Mostly, farm workers receive some in-kind compensation that is determined yearly by the farm management without underlying contracts or negotiations. 'As everyone leases their share into the collective and dividends seem remarkably like the fodder, straw and grain that the collective gives out anyway, on the surface everything seems to operate as if the shares did not exist' (Humphrey 1998: 472). In sum, the object of property of both land and property shares is quite unclear, and with regard to property shares the right to transfer them is generally very limited, thus limiting the power of the shareholders.

Laws are sufficiently vague or badly enforced to offer managers opportunities to constrain the power of workers as shareholders. Formally, the highest democratic body, the general assembly of share-holders and employees, has considerable power over developments in the farm enterprises. Moreover, it has the power to dismiss a farm man-ager. In reality, the role of the assembly is minor. According to the law on cooperatives, farm management can turn worker-shareholders into non-voting members as a penalty for breaches of labour rules. Managers often use this law to their own advantage. Nearly half of the worker-shareholders have lost their right to vote. Furthermore, many farm workers did not receive a property share document at all, as stipulated by the law (Uzun 1999). Farm enterprises' constitutional documents sel-dom set limitations on the rights of the management. Sometimes direc-tors have assigned themselves the exclusive right to determine financial and productive decisions, without the permission of the shareholders.

Such rights are against the law, but only the director and a narrow cir-cle of office personnel know the laws well. As a consequence, directors can use and circumvent laws to their own advantage if local authorities close their eyes to such practices. For the majority of shareholders, the only source of information about legal regulations is the general assem-bly, which is led by the director (Uzun 1999). Thus, farm management virtually has a monopoly over knowledge of legal issues. Lindner (2002: 79) describes how an old woman in his case study enterprise came up to the chairman to inherit the share of her late husband, as stipulated by the federal law. The chairman refused her request by saying that such a law existed, but that their own farm laws ranked higher.

The insignificant power of worker-shareholders, caused by unclear property rights, cumbersome implementation and enforcement of the law, and lack of information on legal procedures, is further weakened by the malfunctioning or lack of institutions like courts and cadastres. The registration of land rights is problematic and the independence of the courts is questionable. As Duma deputy Viktor Pokhmelkin stated recently, in most cases where rural inhabitants have tried to defend their property against farm managers and/or authorities, courts have decided in favour of the local elite. The control of local and regional authorities over land transactions and property issues is quite strong, as the land code leaves a lot of power over practical implementation to these authorities. Finally, there is little demand for land in the regions outside the fertile areas of central and southern Russia. Even if all institutions for free land transactions were in place, workers are tied to the farm management, as the local farm enterprise is often the only actor interested in their land.

All these factors (weak property conception, cumbersome implementation, lack of information on legal issues, as well as lack of institutions and markets) create an environment in which relations of dependence persist (as will be elaborated on below) and directors can hold on to (and abuse) their power. As the power of workers as shareholders and landowners is very limited, the relation between management and workers has remained in essence an employer-employee relation.

Further Blurring of Farm Property and the Decline of Responsibility

As the rights of farm workers have remained largely meaningless and their influence is very limited, it is no surprise that an increase of individual responsibility has not materialised. In fact the categorical property changes have had little impact on the concretised property relations that existed within the *kolkhozes* and *sovkhozes*. This is most visible when we take a closer look at the property relations between farm enterprise and household enterprises. The discussion of these property relations points out that it is important to look at the whole set of (especially informal) property rights that farm workers hold to understand their actions, and subsequently the relationship between management and workers.

During and after privatisation, farm workers expanded their household enterprises. Private production has become necessary as a supplement to (or substitute for) wages. Farm wages, already low during communism, were not on par with the rocketing prices of consumer goods. Furthermore, wages were not paid for months on end and employees mostly received a large part of their wages in kind. As mentioned above,

official restrictions on private plot production by the government were
lifted. Thus most farm workers doubled the size of their plots from the
former maximum size of 0.25 to 0.50 hectare. But I found also several
farm workers who had hired extra land and had plots up to five hectares.
Furthermore, private livestock herds had increased.[5] The increased production is still primarily for self-subsistence, but sales have also
increased.

For such an expansion of their private enterprises, farm employees
have needed a continued (or increased) flow of resources from the larger
enterprise. Some managers have tried to limit the outflow of resources to
the private enterprises, as they came to realise how costly these transfers
were under conditions of increasing costs of fuel, seeds and electricity.
Especially they attempted to limit the transfers of fodder to private
herds, with free fodder transfer reduced, and farm workers required to
buy fodder at prices somewhat below the market price. However, as
these limits were set on fodder for private use, the illegal flow to the
households increased. It is widely observed that the stealing of enterprise
resources has become a more widespread phenomenon since 1991
(Nikulin 2003; Visser 2003a).

Thus, the privatisation of the *kolkhozes* and *sovkhozes* and turning the
employees into shareholders rarely translated into better care for the
property of the larger enterprise. On the contrary, the heirs of the
kolkhozes and *sovkhozes* are first of all seen as prey, a fertile ground for
informal activities. As a consequence, the dispersion and degradation of
larger enterprise property has accelerated. Workers try to channel larger
enterprise resources as much as possible to their private operations. The
symbiosis between larger (collective) and smaller (private) enterprises
has become more and more detrimental to the continued existence of the
former.

The majority of nearly a hundred farm workers that I interviewed stated that farm work has become less intensive since the start of reforms.
Especially in highly unprofitable enterprises, discipline has deteriorated
sharply (Visser 2003a). Farm managers and workers complained that
alcoholism has become more widespread. In sum, privatisation has coincided with a further blurring of the boundaries between large farm enterprises and household property, and a further scavenging of large enterprise property. Although farm managers try to guard large enterprise
property it is certainly not always because of their concern for the common good, but because they try to aquire this property for themselves in

other ways. Farm directors, for instance, try to concentrate shares in their own hands, or they do not register part of the acreage and sell produce from these fields for their own profit under the table.

Authoritarian Farm Leadership and Weak Labour Discipline

It is understandable that individual workers have become de-motivated as wages have declined or are largely paid out in kind, dividends are rarely paid out and their influence as shareholders is extremely limited. The managers have de facto kept land centralised, constraining the influence of shareholders, and sometimes seeing the farm as their own property. Thus farm managers have an incentive to increase discipline and guard larger farm enterprise property against theft and irresponsible treatment by farm workers. Based on a survey in several regions, Uzun (1998) suggests that the small number of enterprises that chose a legal form where all control is in the hands of the manager, perform better than those where farm workers have formal voting rights.[6] It has also been argued that the short-term consumption interests of workers predominates and is causing long-term investments to decline (World Bank 1992: 20). Perhaps control by the management, although not preferable in terms of equity and empowerment of workers, is more conducive to effective farm restructuring? Will it lead to a better protection and use of farm property?

During the Soviet period agricultural enterprises were characterised by a strong hierarchy. The power of the farm directors was considerable, but circumscribed and controlled by the hierarchical structures of the party and the state planning apparatus. With the demise of the communist system, party officials disappeared and the control of the state over local and regional authorities and the farm directors weakened. In the daily functioning of the farm enterprise, managers generally have maintained an authoritarian style of leadership, a pattern that ethnographic studies on Russian farm enterprises has confirmed (Nikulin 2003), or in some cases has illustrated to have deepened (Allina-Pisano 2002: 301). Some studies even speak about quasi-feudal or hacienda-like relations (Nikulin 2003). Farm directors generally give their farm workers and foremen little room for expression of their own initiative and use the daily *planerka* (plan-meeting) to control labour effort. Practically none of the farm enterprises I visited have devolved decision-making power towards sub-divisions or work brigades. If decentralisation takes place it is not initiated by the management, but mostly occurs through a sponta- neous process in weak enterprises (Visser 2003a). Farm workers are not used to any formal influence on decision making and as a rule see a strong leader as an advantage. A statement by a villager in the Moscow region was echoed in many conversations: 'where you see a strong farm leader there is progress, where such a leader is lacking, there is *bardak* (chaos)' (see also Miller and Heady 2003: 267–68).

However, despite continued (or increased) authoritarian power, it has been shown that farm managers generally have not been able to enforce discipline and care for the property of the larger enterprise. Farm man- agers do not quickly lay off employees to increase labour productivity. Even alcoholism and stealing seldom lead to dismissal since farm work- ers are usually allowed a chance to be 'decoded' (receiving a medical treatment that makes it nearly impossible to stand alcohol for several months) before dismissal is considered. Stealing or destruction of farm property also does not mean dismissal. Miller and Heady (2003) describe the case of a milkmaid who set a barn on fire when she was drunk, but still continued to work for the larger enterprise.

I turn now to a deeper investigation of the labour relations within the farm enterprise in order to explain why managers have not enforced a more strict property and labour regime. I begin with a brief discussion of labour relations as they existed in the Soviet enterprise, using new insights from recent ethnographies on the (post)-soviet industrial enter- prise.

Labour Relations in the Soviet Enterprise

The enterprise in the planned economy was fundamentally different from the Western enterprise. The prosperity of a Soviet enterprise did not depend on its efficiency but on successful negotiations by the direc- tor for favourable production quotas and sufficient inputs (Clarke 1993). The lack of incentives to make production more efficient led to the familiar shortcomings of the planning system; labour hoarding, ineffi- cient use of inputs, low quality products, neglect of maintenance and of repair. The resulting shortages of inputs stimulated the managers of enterprises to horde excessive stocks of inputs whenever possible, and this further exacerbated the problem of shortages in the economy. The combination of strict deadlines for plan fulfilment and irregular inputs led to an uneven rhythm of production, with periods of little activity and hectic rush periods. This uneven rhythm of production and strict planning requirements underlay the considerable power supposedly enjoyed by the workers collective.

The enterprise management depended on the cooperation of the workers to meet the production quota, for example, on their willingness to improvise when supplies were irregular, and to work overtime during rush hours. But the management had little power to dismiss workers, as regulations for dismissal were very strict and there was a shortage of labour in society due to the labour hoarding that all enterprises practised in order to cope with rush periods. Also, management had little formal means to stimulate workers positively, as payment of bonuses was impossible due to the communist principle of equal payment. Aside from that, performance related payment was not very effective in the Soviet system, as the performance of a unit of workers depended more on the supply of goods and on the functioning of ancillary units within the enterprise (such as repair services), than on its own labour input (Clarke 1993: 19). As a consequence, there were few incentives for workers to increase production. Moreover, the refusal to pay bonuses could lead to endless disputes over the responsibility for any failure. In practice, management ensured that workers received a regular wage, more or less regardless of performance. Piece-rate and bonus systems were essentially 'a discretionary payment system, through which workers could be penalised or favoured, but it could not be used to regulate the collective effort' (Clarke 1993: 20).

Although management had little control over the labour process, there is little justification for concluding that it had little power vis-à-vis the workers. There was a paradoxical situation; Soviet workers were powerful, in that managers were unable to impose labour discipline and had to make concessions to enlist their cooperation, but they were weak in that they were atomised and had no means of collective resistance (Clarke 1993: 16). Managers could persuade workers to fulfil the production quota only through informal bargaining. In such negotiations, the social entitlements that were connected to farm enterprise membership played an important role. Resources and services for the private plots were an important token in informal bargaining. As farm wages were (and still are) low, many farm workers depended partially on their private plot. It was through the provision of collective farm resources (such as fodder, manure, and help from tractor drivers) to the household enterprises that farm managers could motivate employees to work harder during rush periods. Furthermore, the formal collective social services such as education, holidays, electricity, that farm enterprises provided (see below), were complemented by more informal mechanisms of paternalistic responsibility vis-à-vis the workers. For example, farm staff assisted workers stricken by disease or helped them to defray the costs of life-cycle ceremonies. The management-worker relation in the Soviet farm enterprise can be described as a patron-client relation, and (as will be shown further on) this is still true for contemporary heirs to the collective socialist enterprise.

Labour Relations as a Constraint on Restructuring

The power of the farm directors over their enterprises has been maintained or has increased during the 1990s. But despite the disappearance of the plan economy, their actual control over the production process is still limited. How is this possible?

First, although the shortage economy (Kornai 1980) has ended, and all kinds of inputs are available, farms still face shortages simply because they lack the finances to buy them. In fact, shortages have become much more problematic. As was discussed earlier, prices of inputs have risen much more than the farm gate prices. In regions with strong support by regional authorities in agriculture, farms receive in-kind credit to buy essential inputs. Authorities provide farms with fuel, spare parts and seeds. Farms pay back the debts through obligatory delivery to parastatal food purchasing organisations. But as the system depends on the deteriorating finances of regional authorities, the supply of inputs is rarely timely. For example, sometimes farm enterprises receive credit for inputs after the sowing period has finished.

Because of the insecurity of timely inputs and the insufficiency of inputs and machinery, managers still depend strongly on the improvisation skills of the workers, with the result that workers still have a strong influence over the production process. The irregularity of inputs and the bad state of machinery, combined with the huge size of the farms, makes monitoring of the labour process extremely difficult. To illustrate this point, I take a closer look at the example of machinery.

In all farms that I visited, the state of machinery had undergone a sharp deterioration. Some farms survived the economic decline by selling productive livestock, machinery and equipment, in other cases machinery deteriorated because of lack of responsibility by employees, or due to lack of spare parts and finances. A farm accountant of an unprofitable farm in Pskov noted: 'the normal time to write off a *Belarus* tractor is eleven years. We are forced to use them for twenty years already'. At another farm I was told that one of the tractors was thirty years old. Even the stronger farms lack the finances to buy new machinery. The director of a profitable farm in Rostov stated: 'our equipment is very old. Within two years the enterprise needs to buy new equipment, or we cannot harvest at all'.

During the communist period, agricultural institutes calculated the productivity of tractors and combines for all kinds of crops, in order to assist the planning apparatus and the farm specialists to plan and control production. Farm specialists still use these norms. However, due to the bad state of machinery farm workers are not able to harvest as many hectares of crops per hour as the norms prescribe. A farm worker of a profitable enterprise in Rostov told me: 'It is like we are back in the Stone Age. You should have seen how we did the harvest. Tractors drive for one 100 metres and they break down. They drive another 100 metres and they stop again, and so on.' Tractor drivers are generally very creative in fixing these breakdowns in the field, but planning the harvest or production effectively becomes all but impossible. In such a situation the calculated production norms become a kind of theoretical ideal, with little reference to the daily practice of production. Furthermore, monitoring the performance of workers becomes unrealistic because of the bad state of machinery. How can a manager know if a tractor driver was indeed busy repairing his tractor out in the field, or simply sat down with a colleague because he was not motivated to work?

A second reason why farm managers are not able to enforce discipline is because they hesitate to dismiss workers. Farm directors confided that they found it difficult to replace fired workers. At one level, such remarks are surprising given the high level of unemployment in rural areas. Nearly a third of the population in the Russian countryside is currently unemployed. However, in rural areas (especially in the outlying districts) young people have migrated to the city and the old, least entrepreneurial people remain. What the managers mean when they say that finding employees is problematic, is that it is difficult to find experienced or reliable, hardworking personnel. What Clarke (1993) observed about the Soviet enterprise is still true for the post-Soviet farm. Management largely depends on a small core of experienced hardworking members, who keep the enterprise going when inputs are not on time or machinery breaks down. A chairman of a farm enterprise in the Rostov region with over 300 employees stated: 'There is a core of about ten to twelve farm workers, who in fact keep the whole enterprise going'. An agronomist on another farm in Rostov remarked: 'I consider reliable only about 10 percent of the farm workers'.

It is difficult for farm enterprises to attract reliable, new workers, especially skilled 'core workers' like mechanics and tractor drivers. Livestock workers are particularly difficult to find. Unlike crop production, livestock farming requires constant, daily care. If cows are not taken care of for a day, health problems may quickly arise. Thus managers are afraid to fire undisciplined workers because they might not find another (experienced) employee. As Russian sociologist, Koznova (1999: 212) observed: 'it happens that the enterprise fires a drunkard, and takes an even worse person instead'. As a result of continuing (or reinforced) labour shortages, the power of (core) workers over the production process has not diminished, but continues or has even increased.

There is still another reason why it is difficult for managers to impose more discipline and to dismiss undisciplined workers, which is connected to the interwoveness of the farm enterprise and the village. In the next section, I examine this link between the farm enterprise and the wider rural community relations.

Farm Enterprise and Village Community

It is understandable that directors find it difficult to increase discipline or productivity, and to lay off workers (even when they can find others), as dismissal means that workers are also cut off from the social services in the village. Soviet enterprises (especially farm enterprises) were not only economic units but also took care of the welfare of workers. While in the cities basic public welfare functions were provided by the state, in villages virtually all social functions were shouldered by the farm enterprise. Collectives provided villages with running water, gas, and even arranged the construction of apartments. Furthermore, *kolkhozes* and *sovkhozes* provided all kinds of social and cultural services. They financed local schools, kindergartens, libraries, and the 'house of culture'. Strong collective farms even organised vacations for employees and youth camps for the village youth. Collective farms were not just economic units, but 'total social institutions' (Humphrey 1998), providing 'workfare' or welfare intimately connected to work.

Reformers wanted collectives to throw off these social functions, and hand them over to the municipality. The argument was that only in this way could farms concentrate effectively on production and become market-oriented, profit-seeking enterprises. However, in most cases the municipality has only a coordination function, with hardly any finances. In fact, farm enterprises still form the centre of rural communities (Nikulin 2003; Visser 2003b; Peters this volume). Because of their poor finances, municipalities refuse to take over obligations of the farm enterprises, and some profitable collective farms decided to maintain the social services themselves, fearing that transfer to the municipality would lead to their degradation or disappearance. The local administration I visited in Rostov resided in two small rooms in the large central building of the most successful farm enterprise in the municipality. This is symbolic of the dependent position of most municipal administrations in relation to farm enterprises.

Farm workers thus not only lose their job, but also most of their access to social facilities when they are dismissed. Other non-agricultural jobs are virtually non-existent in rural areas. Also, households still depend strongly on the resources of the local farm enterprise for the production on their private farms. Managers of the larger enterprise are fully aware that dismissal of farm workers has far reaching consequences for all aspects of the life of their families.

Furthermore, directors of farm enterprises are more socially engaged with their employees than directors in urban enterprises, as they live together with them in the same village and know about their personal difficulties. The main agronomist on a farm in Rostov told me: 'it is true that we could do the work with less people. But how could I fire these people? I would send their children and wives into poverty'. Some directors who responded to the survey carried out in Rostov and Pskov gave less priority to increasing profitability or increasing production than they did to keeping intact their collective.

There is another, more fundamental, problem with the reformer advice that farm enterprises should throw off social functions and follow only economic goals. It supposes a clear distinction between economic and social considerations, assuming that provided that managers would focus on economic motivations, the enterprise would blossom. In reality, the distinction between social and economic is difficult to make, because the units 'farm enterprise' and 'village or community' are so densely interwoven. Most Russian villagers work in the local farm enterprise, and if they are not employed there, they are still linked to the enterprise as shareholders or because their relatives work there.

As a consequence, the social considerations that urge a manager to keep workers despite production decline may be in fact 'economically' quite rational. Farm directors may fear that dismissals lead to social disorder in the village, which in turn may threaten the farm. In a survey in Saratov region managers stated that they could not consider firing employees, because theft by dismissed workers would be more difficult to control than theft by employees (Amelina 2002: 282). The boundaries between farm enterprise and village are still ill-defined, and managers expect that fired workers continue to be a cost to the enterprise. Moreover, if fired workers cannot access collective property anymore themselves, they most likely will try to obtain these resources through their relatives or friends who still work at the enterprise. As the territory of farms is so huge, it is all but impossible to protect them from theft.

Conclusions

The effects of property reform on both economic performance and the empowerment of the rural population until now have proven to be less influential than many reformers expected or hoped for at the beginning of the 1990s. In terms of empowerment of the rural population, the results were disappointing despite an egalitarian distribution of property. The value of property farm workers received is very limited, as the objects of property (land and farm assets) are very abstract. Farm workers do not know what kind of parcel their land shares represent. Farm managers have considerable power, as they can decide in practice what kind of plot farm workers receive, if they want to take land out of the larger enterprise to rent, sell or use themselves. The paper shares in farm property are even more abstract to the workers. The power of farm workers (as shareholders and landowners) is further reduced, through the vagueness of reform laws and the cumbersome enforcement of legislation. Many farm managers have not (fully) implemented legislation (such a giving out titles to land, or setting up lease contracts), because it takes too much time, or because they want to curtail the rights of farm workers. Just as important for the limited effect of property reform on empowerment, is the difficulty for farm workers to access information on legal procedures, the weak development of institutions (like courts, cadastres) required for the transfer and protection of private property, and the rudimentary state of land markets.

In sum, the rights of farm workers are virtually meaningless and workers have little formal influence on farm issues. Thus, it is not surprising that farm workers do not feel more responsible for farm property. Moreover, benefits still bear little relation to their labour performance, as dividends are rarely paid out. Work bonuses are mostly paid on a farm-wide basis, thus given the hundreds of workers the individual performance of one person makes little difference. The lack of responsibility of the workers for the farm enterprise in which they are now shareholders can only be wholly understood by looking at the whole set of (formal and informal) rights they hold. Apart from their stake in the farm enterprise, workers also maintain their right to an (enlarged) household plot, which they really feel is their property. Farm workers have concentrated on expanding their household production, supported by the informal rights to resources from the farm enterprise (such as fodder).

As the relation shareholder/landowner versus management has little meaning in practice, the manager worker relation has remained basically a labour relation, in which the manager acts as the employer (and often de facto owner), and farm workers are simply treated as employees. The labour relation has remained authoritarian or has become even more authoritarian. Farm managers generally have a strong control on both general farm and formal property issues. Most assemblies vote unanimously for the legal organisational form that the farm director proposes. Open opposition of worker-shareholders to the management, especially in a collective form, is rare.

However, this does not mean that farm managers have effective control over the concretised property relations (and labour relations). As in the Soviet period, the effective control of management on the production process is very limited. The Soviet paradox of workers who were powerful, in that managers were unable to impose labour discipline and had to make concessions to enlist their cooperation, but weak in the sense of formal power, is replicated in the post-Soviet environment. That this mechanism can still be observed widely does not mean that we deal with a simple persistence of old routines, out of conservatism or resistance to restructuring. Following Verdery, I think we should be cautious not to place excessive emphasis on legacies and path dependency in describing continuity in post-socialist phenomena. In the case of the Russian farm enterprises, 'what might look like legacies are better seen as responses to quite contemporary processes' (Verdery 2003: 11). The economy of shortage persists as the foundation of the above-mentioned paradox, but in a new vein and based on new processes. Nowadays central planning as the underlying cause of the economy of shortage has disappeared, but the current uncertain market economy has created new shortages of inputs and labour.

It has been shown that management does not have enough control to impose a strong property regime. Managers were seldom able to stop the outflow of collective enterprise resources to the household enterprises, which was a typical feature of the informal property practices in the *kolkhozes* and *sovkhozes*. When farm managers tried to introduce a more strict property regime, for instance through a limitation of the (informal) entitlements of workers to farm enterprise resources like fodder, it had little effect. Farm workers, who expanded their plots and livestock holdings to supplement their minimal wage, had a strong need for fodder. A limitation of the rights to farm resources led to increased pilfering of collective enterprise property, with even more destructive consequences.

When farm managers were able to stop the degradation and outflow of the property of the larger enterprise, it was not through a change in property relations, but primarily through a change in the labour regime. Farm enterprises that were able to curtail the outflow did so by introducing a labour regime consisting of two parallel measures. First, they enforced required work hours/time at the collective enterprise. In most enterprises, farm workers shirk from labour on the farm in order to work on their own plots, taking a long lunch break to feed their animals, and leaving their formal workplace around three or four o'clock. In surveys, the majority of farm workers stated that their work on the collective enterprise had become less intensive. As a consequence of stricter labour-hours regimes, workers had less time to work on their private endeavours, and had to reduce the livestock number or size of private plots. As a consequence their demand for fodder and other farm resources declined. Second, these enterprises offered their workers higher wages than in surrounding enterprises. As a result, workers depended less on their private plot for income, and the need for household production and the required resources from the farm enterprise declined.

Farm restructuring is difficult also, because the boundaries between farm enterprise and the village community are blurred. Property and labour relations within the enterprises are interwoven with community relations, such as being neighbours or relatives. Agricultural reforms were characterised by the belief that property reform in itself could turn *kolkhozes* and *sovkhozes* from social-economic units into market-oriented enterprises. Reforms aimed at changing the official, categorical structure of property relations into a legally simpler (economic) configuration. Although farm enterprises had to transfer social services to the municipality, the reformers did not provide local authorities with the (financial) means to take over these obligations. Framed in another way, the attention of reformers focused mainly on the *rights* associated with ownership, while insufficient attention was paid to the (social) *obligations*. Verdery (2003) and Kandiyoti (2003) present cases where land is even turned into a negative asset through privatisation, as the risks and obligations transferred to owners outweigh the rights and benefits. These obligations can also consist of environmental taxes, as in the case of Czech farms (Sikor, this volume).

Social responsibility, economic motivations and power considerations cannot easily be separated from each other. The social motivation of managers not to fire undisciplined workers may in fact be quite economic, as the resulting social disorder in the village could also negatively affect the farm enterprise. Furthermore, even if the formal social services like schools and hospital are handed over to the municipality, directors have an incentive to continue providing paternalistic social help to workers as well as resources to their private endeavours. Through these forms of paternalistic support directors maintain power in the delicate negotiations with the workers with respect to the labour process (Nikulin 2003).

As was stated earlier, farm workers have not been empowered nor have they become more responsible, due to the lack of a whole range of conditions required for property rights to be of any value. The formal property reforms have also not enabled the farm managers to implement a stricter property and labour regime, as this would mean a radical change of the existing social-economic relations, and the resulting threat of social disorder and the undermining of their own power base as manager. Thus, this chapter illustrates how property reformers have overestimated the extent to which reforms in formal property by themselves can induce changes in property practices and labour relations at the farm level.

Notes

1. I use 'privatisation' as it is the commonly used term to describe the conversion of *kolkhozes* and *sovkhozes* into independent farm enterprises such as joint-stock companies. However, it is highly questionable whether we can really speak of privatisation, as it did not lead to individual private, but to corporate private ownership (basically still collective ownership).

2. The difference between *kolkhozes* (collective farm enterprises) and *sovkhozes* (state farm enterprises) was largely formal. Before the start of privatisation, both *kolkhozes* and *sovkhozes* were about 8,000 ha large, and had several hundreds of employees. The privatised successors of the *kolkhozes* and *sovkhozes* mostly remained as large as before, while the number of employees decreased by half. This decline is not the result of dismissals, but of the flight of (young) workers that look for better paid jobs (see further on in this chapter). After a strong decline in the first half of the 1990s, the production in the farm enterprises increased after 1998, but production and productivity are still below the 1991 level (Spoor and Visser 2004).
3. This chapter is based on fieldwork in 2001 and 2002 in three regions; Pskov (north-western Russia), Moscow (central Russia), and Rostov in the south. The research consisted of interviews, observations and a survey among 200 workers and managers in forty-six farm enterprises, and was made possible by a grant of the Netherlands Foundation for Scientific Research (NWO-42512009).
4. For more on property relations in the pre-Soviet agriculture see Kingston-Mann, this volume.
5. The expansion of household enterprises in terms of land and livestock took place largely in the early 1990s. The share of households in total agricultural production increased from 25 to more than 55 percent in the 1990s, but declined somewhat in the late 1990s and early 2000s, as production in the larger enterprises began to increase again.
6. But we should not confuse cause and effect here. I contend that such large enterprises most likely do not perform better because they are manager-controlled, but rather that the managers in strong enterprises had a larger incentive to take full control over, and responsibility for, the continued operation of the enterprise.

References

Allina-Pisano, J. 2002. 'Reorganisation and its Discontents: A Case Study in Voronezh Oblast', in *Rural Reform in Post-Soviet Russia*, eds D.J. O'Brien and S.K. Wegren, Washington: Woodrow Wilson Center Press, 298–324.

Amelina, M. 2002. 'What Turns the Kolkhoz into a Firm? Regional Policies and the Elasticity of Budget Constraint', in *Rural Reform in Post-Soviet Russia*, eds D.J. O'Brien and S.K. Wegren, Washington: Woodrow Wilson Centre Press, 264–97.

Clarke, S. 1993. 'The Contradictions of "State Socialism"', in *What About the Workers? Workers and the Transition to Capitalism in Russia*, eds S. Clarke, P. Fairbrother, M. Burawoy and P. Krotov, London, New York: Verso, 1–26.

Humphrey, C. 1998. *Marx Went Away, But Karl Stayed Behind*. Ann Arbor: University of Michigan Press.

Kandiyoti, D. 2003. 'Pathways of Farm Restructuring in Uzbekistan: Pressures and Outcomes', in *Transition, Institutions and the Rural Sector*, ed. M. Spoor, New York, Oxford: Lexington Books, Rowman and Littlefield Publishers, 143–62.

Kornai, J. 1980. *Economics of Shortage*. Amsterdam: North-Holland.

Koznova, I.E. 1999. 'Gor'koe Maslo Reform: Ob Preobrazovaniyakh na
     Vologodskoi Zemle', in *Krestyanovedenie 3. Teoriya, Istoriya, Sovremennost'*, eds
     T. Shanin and V. Danilov, Moscow: MSSES/Intercenter, 200–27.
Lindner, P. 2002. 'Reproduction Circles of Poverty and Wealth in Rural Areas of
     Russia', *Sociological Research* 41 (6): 69–84.
Miller Gambold, L.L. and P. Heady 2003. 'Cooperation, Power and Community:
     Economy and Ideology in the Russian Countryside', in *The Postsocialist
     Agrarian Question. Property Relations and the Rural Condition*, eds C.M. Hann
     and the 'Property relations' group, Münster: LIT, 257–93.
Nikulin, A. 2003. 'The Kuban Kolkhoz between a Holding and a Hacienda.
     Contradictions of Post-Soviet Rural Development', *Focaal* 41: 161–76.
Spoor, M. and O. Visser. 2001, 'The State of Agrarian Reform in the Former Soviet
     Union', *Europe-Asia Studies* 53(6): 885–901.
————— 2004. 'Restructuring Postponed? Russian Large Farm Enterprises Coping
     with the Market', *Journal of Peasant Studies* 32(4): 31, (3–4): 515–51.
Uzun, V.Y. 1998. *Reformirovanie Sel'skokhozyastvennykh Predpriyatii; Sotsial'no
     Ekonomicheskii Analiz (1994–1997)*. Moscow: VIAPI and Rosagrofond.
————— 1999. 'Privatization of Land and Farm Restructuring: Ideas, Mechanisms,
     Results, Problems', in *Farm Profitability Sustainability, and Restructuring in
     Russia*, ed. Institute for Economy in Transition, Moscow: Analytical Centre
     Agrifood Economy of IET, 36–50.
Verdery, K. 2003. *The Vanishing Hectare. Property and Value in Postsocialist
     Transylvania*. Ithaca, London: Cornell University Press.
Visser, O. 2003a. 'Farm Restructuring, Property Relations and Household
     Strategies in Rural Russia', in *Transition, Institutions and the Rural Sector*, ed.
     M. Spoor, New York, Oxford: Lexington Books, Rowman and Littlefield
     Publishers, 83–102.
————— 2003b. 'Family, Community and the Decline of the Former *Kolkhozi* in
     Russia', in *Distinct Inheritances. Property, Family and Community in a Changing
     Europe*, eds P. Heady and H. Grandits, Münster: LIT Verlag, 313–28.
————— 2003c. 'Property and Post-Communist Poverty. Can the Mystery of Capital
     be Exported to the Post-Soviet Countryside?', *Focaal* 41: 197–201.
World Bank 1992. *Food and Agricultural Policy Reforms in the Former USSR. An
     Agenda for the Transition*. Washington, D.C.: World Bank.

Chapter 7

Cooperative Property at the Limit

John R. Eidson

Ideological Ambivalence as Minimal 'Legal Pluralism'

Given the central and controversial status of property in political philosophy, law, economy and society, it is probably inevitable that anthropological analyses of property relations often contain a strong dose of cultural criticism. For reasons illuminated by Pauline Peters in her contribution to this volume, this is especially true of the recent literature on developments in post-colonial and post-socialist settings, where anthropologist have to contend with those peddling privatisation as the cure to all economic and societal woes. All too often, it seems, the programmes that are supposed to promote political stability and spur economic growth are based on oversimplified notions of both the collective property arrangements that are being replaced – 'traditional' or socialist, as the case may be – and the private property arrangements that are supposed to replace them. Hence the attempt to correct ideologically tinged analyses of property relations by showing that neither individual property nor collective property exist in pure form (F. and K. von Benda-Beckmann, this volume).

Arguably, however, the debunking of ideological notions of individual and collective property, or private and public property, is not a perfectly commutative exercise. When we expose public aspects of private property – by pointing to limitations of the owner's prerogatives inherent in zoning law, for example – we qualify the ideology of private property without addressing issues of legality or illegality. But when we expose the private appropriation of public or collective property, we must leave the realm of property rights per se and enter into a gray area stretching between the use and abuse of property. Socialist regimes seem to have been especially attuned to this asymmetry, apparently because determining the proper use of public property was central to social engineering and the maintenance of power.

In this chapter, I explore struggles over the definition, distribution, and use of cooperative property, a variety of socialist property, in the agrarian sector of the German Democratic Republic (GDR). My approach is based largely on the model provided by Caroline Humphrey (1998) in her seminal study of collective farms in the Soviet Union – specifically, in her analysis of collective property in terms of a 'hierarchy of rights held in practice' (ibid.: 118). My emphasis falls, however, on a complication that Humphrey acknowledges but does not discuss in detail. In her comments on property relations on the collective farm, she posits a kind of continuum extending from formal rules to de facto rights and various forms of manipulation and violation. At what point, however, does the exercise of de facto rights become the violation of de jure rights? In clarifying any given case, a number of factors would have to be taken into account, including the status of those involved, their attitudes and intentions, conventional thresholds for bending the rules, and so on. Especially in systems governed less by laws than by administrative decrees, which are subject to frequent revision, there will be many instances, however, when it is difficult to achieve consensus on where exactly to draw the line (Verdery 2003: 48–49). For this reason, it seems necessary to suggest that, in discussing property rights, we must also take into account actual or perceived abuses.

Surely, however, there will be some kind of overarching framework, whether political, legal or ideological, that allows actors in particular settings to resolve issues of gaining access to means of production and disposing of products, at least in most cases. Was this not true for socialist agriculture in the Soviet Bloc as well? At least in the countries that tended toward Stalinist or post-Stalinist orthodoxy, such as the GDR, the answer to this question was yes and no. And the name behind this ambivalent answer is 'Lenin's cooperative plan', the subject of the next section.

Following the discussion of the von Benda-Beckmanns (1999) regarding the various 'layers' or aspects of property relations, we may regard Lenin's cooperative plan as a property ideology, which must be considered in its complex interrelation with the legal, social and practical aspects of property, if we are to arrive at an adequate understanding of it.

Distinguishing among ideological, legal, social and practical aspects of property relations is, however, not enough, unless we also point out that each aspect may be characterised by a kind of indeterminacy that has far reaching implications. This point is especially obvious under conditions of legal pluralism, where two or more overarching frameworks provide alternative bases for establishing multidimensional relations among persons with respect to valuable goods (F. and K. von Benda-Beckmann 1999). But it may also be pertinent for the analysis of political systems in which we would not normally expect to discover legal pluralism. In some cases, it seems, property laws or property ideologies may function less as a blueprint for consistent policy formation than a language for articulating alternative approaches and justifying alternative practices. Cooperative property under socialism was just such a case.

Lenin's Cooperative Plan – a Socialist Myth?

'Abolition of private property' – that, in the famous phrase of Marx and Engels, is 'the theory of the Communists' in sum.[1] Under the conditions of industrial capitalism, they reasoned, the means of production would come increasingly under the control of a powerful but ever dwindling class of owners, until they were finally seized by the ever growing mass of oppressed and impoverished labourers. But what of countries such as Russia, which were still largely agrarian? Were these countries ripe for revolution? And, if so, would the private property or communal arrangements and personal allotments of millions of peasants have to be abolished as well?

One of Lenin's main objectives in *The Development of Capitalism in Russia* (1899) was to demonstrate that the peasants did not really constitute an exception to Marxist theory. In the Russian countryside, he argued, industrialisation was already resulting in the concentration of wealth in the hands of estate owners and wealthy peasants (kulaks) and in the increasing exploitation of the poor peasantry (Lenin 1899). Given their somewhat larger holdings, many middle peasants might hope to join the ranks of the kulaks, though, in Lenin's view, they were actually destined to suffer the same fate as the poor peasantry. With proper guidance, however, even the middle peasants would become convinced that their place was at the side of the revolutionary class, the proletariat. Thus, conditions were favourable for the formation of the 'Alliance of the Workers and the Peasants', the centrepiece of the revolutionary social order in the Soviet Union (Ponomarjow et al. 1960: 542–43).

It is evident, however, that the peasants continued to be the more problematic member of the Alliance. In the official *History of the Communist Party of the Soviet Union,* 'guiding the millions of farms tended by small peasants … along the path to socialism' is described as 'the most difficult historical task facing the socialist revolution' in Russia, following 'the seizure of power by the working class' (Ponomarjow et al. 1960: 592). But even the problem presented by the 'habits, routines … and consciousness of the peasants' had a solution (Ponomarjow et al. 1960: 585). In the celebratory language of the official party history, this solution is described as 'the ingenious cooperative plan of Lenin', which provided a formula for 'the transition from the small private peasant holdings to socialist agriculture on a large-scale' (Ponomarjow et al. 1960: 521, 592).

Those who seek Lenin's cooperative plan in the writings of Lenin himself will seek in vain. Lenin wrote about the peasants and the extension of the revolution to the countryside at many points in his vast corpus of works, and he took up the question of rural cooperatives in some short and suggestive essays in the last years of his life (e.g., Lenin 1923; see also Kingston-Mann 1983). Nowhere, however, does he present a detailed plan for the collectivisation of agricultural production, as it was carried out in his name in the Soviet Union, and in most of the countries that later came under Soviet influence (Pryor 1992). Rather, Lenin's so-called cooperative plan emerged from debates among Bolsheviks during the 1920s regarding the significance of his last writings for determining the relative status of trading and producer cooperatives in the new socialist state. As Edward H. Carr and Robert W. Davies explain, the debates were resolved at the close of the decade when Stalin declared that Lenin's article of 1923 applied to 'all forms of cooperatives, both in their lower (supply, marketing) and in their higher (kolkhozy) forms,' and was especially relevant to 'the kolkhozy of our period' (Carr and Davies 1969: 924, citing a quotation from Stalin). 'Thereafter,' Carr and Davies continue, '"Lenin's co-operative plan" was unconditionally identified with the policy of collectivisation.'

Following Stalin's decisive intervention, party historians fleshed out Lenin's scattered statements on the peasantry and rural cooperatives and, in this way, constructed what Carr and Davies (1969: 924, footnote 6) refer to as the 'myth' of Lenin's cooperative plan. After the Second World

War, this myth was transposed to the countries within the Soviet sphere of influence through the agency of the corresponding Marxist-Leninist parties.[2]

In the following, I examine Lenin's cooperative plan, its application in East Germany, and its results from three different angles: as a legal or political norm, as a social historical datum, and as subjective experience. First, I review the normative version of Lenin's cooperative plan, as articulated by an expert on the law of socialist cooperative farms. Second, I provide a brief sketch of the implementation of agricultural policy from 1945 to 1989. And, third, I draw on interviews with farmers and agricultural functionaries in order to show how they reflect upon their experiences of corresponding crises in property relations during the socialist era. By combining these three approaches to cooperative farms and cooperative property in the GDR, I hope to provide a multidimensional framework for analysing rural property relations under conditions of 'actually existing socialism'. I argue not only that rural property relations exhibited multiple layers or aspects but that each layer or aspect displayed a characteristic ambivalence that must be taken into consideration if we want to understand what property could have been and what it became.

The Socialist Theory of Agricultural Cooperatives

In the political, economic and legal theory of the GDR (and other states within the Soviet sphere of influence), the distinction between 'lower' and 'higher' forms, which Stalin employed to distinguish trader and producer cooperatives, was raised to a central logical principle. Thus, in *Grundriss des LPG-Rechts* (1959), an 'Outline of the Law of Socialist Cooperative Farms', the East German authority Rainer Arlt distinguishes between private enterprises and socialist enterprises and among various forms of socialist enterprises in these same terms.

Arlt's analysis of the broader context of socialist agricultural production corresponds closely to the general guidelines provided by Lenin. The countryside is viewed as a battlefield in the larger class struggle. Once the owners of large estates have been eliminated through the confiscation of their land, the agrarian bourgeoisie remains as the principle advocate of the exploitative system based on private property. The rural poor, it is assumed, will be most sympathetic to the socialist cause, but many small peasants and especially the middle peasants will have to be convinced that socialist policies are in their best interests. In order to persuade the small and middle peasants to join the forces of progress and social justice, socialist policy makers must lead them through 'a long series of gradual transitions', first offering them institutional arrangements that are the 'simplest, easiest, and most accessible' to them (Lenin, quoted in Arlt 1959: 37).[3] These transitional forms are potentially contradictory, insofar as they represent a step in the direction of socialism but still contain aspects of capitalism. The assumption is, however, that contradictions within mixed forms will be resolved, once the superiority of 'higher' forms over 'lower' forms is demonstrated in practice. Then, the residue of earlier, 'lower' forms, which, as long as they exist, continue to represent a kind of irritation, can be cast aside.

Lenin's cooperative plan is, Arlt insists, universally applicable, but it does have to be adjusted to variable historical circumstances. In Russia, for example, agricultural land was nationalised following the October Revolution of 1917, but the same measures were not taken in Central and Eastern Europe following the Second World War. Rather, once the owners of large estates had been dispossessed, agricultural land that did not exceed a certain maximum number of hectares remained in the hands of private owners. Since the countries of Central and Eastern Europe had achieved a higher stage of capitalist development than Russia had, the peasants of those countries had stronger 'traditions of private property' (Arlt 1959: 359).

> Our republic has ... three different types of agricultural cooperatives ... which are understandable and accessible to our farmers. The working farmer, who previously had managed an individual enterprise, may decide according to his interests whether and to what extent he would like to take part in the agricultural production that is characteristic of each. The transition from a system of individual enterprises to a system of developed cooperative enterprises will be facilitated by a number of stages (Arlt 1959: 67).

The reference in this quotation is to the *Landwirtschaftliche Produktionsgenossenschaft* (LPG), or socialist agricultural cooperative, which came in three different forms called Type I, Type II and Type III.[4] In fact, these varieties of agricultural cooperative were not uniquely German; rather, they corresponded more or less to Soviet prototypes such as the commune, artel, TOZ and kolkhoz (Humphrey 1998: 145).

In the 'lowest' form, the LPG Type I, members pool their arable land and raise crops together but keep animals privately in their own barns.

The LPG Type II (which occurred quite infrequently in the GDR) is an intermediary form involving the extension of cooperative usage not only to arable land but also to forests, beasts of burden and farm machinery, while leaving private animal husbandry intact. The LPG Type III is the 'highest' form, in which land, animals, machinery, and even farm buildings are pooled. The goal of socialist policy at the end of the 1950s is, we learn, first, to induce independent farmers to found or join one of three types of LPG, then, to encourage members of Type I and Type II cooperatives either to transform their enterprise into the 'highest' form or to merge with an already existing LPG Type III – as in the processes of amalgamation that are known from the history of collectivisation in the Soviet Union (Humphrey 1998: 140–41).

For all three types of LPG, the basic structure and the mode of operation are prescribed in the model statutes, which are based on Soviet prototypes (Arlt 1959: 56; Wädekin 1982: 64). The highest instance of LPG governance is supposed to be the assembly of members, which arrives at decisions according to the principle of 'intra-cooperative democracy' (Arlt 1959: 56, 92–94). One of the first responsibilities of the full assembly is to elect a chairperson and the members of an executive committee, who are then responsible for managing cooperative properties, including capital assets, accounts, agricultural products and liquid assets. The purpose of the LPG is, however, to fulfill goals prescribed by the party-state, including the annual plan for agricultural production and corresponding social policies, such as overcoming inequality among LPG members and assimilating their lifestyle to urban standards. This would seem to suggest that there were definite limits to intra-cooperative democracy, but Arlt denies this. In the LPG, there is no contradiction between state directives and self-government, because, 'in socialism, for the first time in human history, the goals of societal production correspond to the personal interests of all producers, the members of society' (Arlt 1959: 455). Apparent contradictions to this general rule are, in Arlt's analysis, attributed to 'certain capitalist ideas and petit bourgeois tendencies among isolated members of the cooperative' (Arlt 1959: 52).

Even the 'highest' form of cooperative farm, the LPG Type III, is 'lower' than the state farm, because it is still characterised by the 'peculiar situation' of incorporating privately owned land (Arlt 1959: 356). Upon admitting new landowning members, the chairman of the LPG Type III is required to keep a record of the location, size and quality of the land brought into the cooperative. For his or her part, the new member is required, upon entry, to contribute his or her farming inventory, to surrender control over use rights for his or her land, and to pay an *Inventarbeitrag* (inventory contribution), which amounts to at least 500 marks per hectare of contributed land (and which, under certain circumstances, could be over 3,000 marks per hectare).[5]

The primary basis for calculating the monetary compensation of cooperative farm members is the quality and quantity of their actual work, which is measured in *Arbeitseinheiten* (work units). As Arlt notes with some embarrassment, however, landowners in the LPG have the right to receive at least a portion of their compensation in payments called *Bodenanteile* (land shares), which vary depending on the amount and quality of the land contributed. According to the corresponding model statutes, landowners in the LPG Type I receive at least 60 percent of their pay for work units and at most 40 percent of their pay for land shares; and landowners in the LPG Type III receive at least 80 percent of their pay for work units and at most 20 percent for land shares. In his *Grundriss*, Arlt (1959: 365–67) takes pains to explain that land shares are not 'absolute rent' in Marx's sense. Moreover, land shares are a transitory phenomenon, which will later be eliminated. In the meantime, their deleterious effects in promoting inequality among cooperative farm members can be counteracted by instituting corresponding privileges for those without land. For example, upon entry into the LPG, landless members are entitled to nominal ownership of a portion of those state-owned or state-managed lands that are included in the acreage of most socialist cooperatives, so that they too can receive land shares (Arlt 1959: 47, 445).

Arlt insists that there is a fundamental difference separating socialist cooperatives from cooperatives in the capitalist world. Under socialism, cooperative property is not *Miteigentum der Mitglieder*, or property held in common by members (Arlt 1959: 257). Inventory contributions are not converted into shares, and members are not co-owners. Rather, the LPG is a legal person with the status of a legal subject in the sense of civil law, which allows for the 'independent exercise of the property owner's authority' (Arlt 1959: 257). Officially, it is this legal person, not the collected members, who owns the assets that are acquired, in one way or another, by the cooperative farm. The one exception is, of course, the land, which is owned privately or by the state, though the LPG enjoys exclusive use rights (Arlt 1959: 365).

Agricultural Policy in the Soviet Zone and the GDR

At the end of the Second World War, East Germany was devastated by war, overrun by ethnic German refugees from Eastern Europe, and occupied by Soviet forces.[6] This was the setting for the land reform, which was proposed by German Communist Party members in the newly reformed provincial parliaments at the instigation of Soviet authorities (Bauerkämper 2002: 68–122).

The expropriation of all agricultural enterprises with over one hundred hectares of land and the redistribution of acreage to refugees, agricultural labourers, workers and poor farmers had the effect of creating a clientele, called the *Neubauern* (new farmers), from whom authorities expected support for their next action, namely, the concerted campaign against the *Großbauern* (owners of large farms). Pressure was exerted on the owners of large farms (those with over twenty hectares) through the manipulation of tax rates, delivery quotas, access to farming machinery, and prices for factors of production. These measures had negative effects on agricultural production, but they were remarkably effective politically, inducing 5,000 East German 'kulaks' (10 percent of the total) to flee to West Germany between 1950 to 1952 (Bauerkämper 2002: 139–44).

The official plan to promote the foundation of LPG, or cooperative farms, as part of a larger program for the *Aufbau des Sozialismus* (Construction of Socialism), was announced in 1952. Thereafter, the party-state induced members of rural populations to found new cooperatives or to join existing cooperatives – once again, by manipulating delivery quotas, access to factors of production, subsidies, and tax and debt relief. Most of the early cooperative farms were founded by new farmers, who may be viewed as clients of the party-state; but even for this group 'the decisive factor was not the attractiveness of the cooperative farm but dire necessity', that is, their inability to survive on their own (Bauerkämper 2002: 440). Throughout the 1950s, the majority of private farmers retained their independence for as long as possible, looking with condescension and scorn upon the inefficient agricultural cooperatives (Eidson 1998; Bauerkämper 2002: 409–91).

Despite the difficult conditions and the frequent antagonism in villages, private farms and cooperative farms coexisted for several years. There were even suggestions from within the Socialist Unity Party to maintain this dual agrarian structure indefinitely. Especially

symptomatic was the case of Kurt Vieweg, director of the Institute for
Agricultural Economics in the German Academy of Agricultural Science,
who proposed in 1956 that the GDR foster both a private sector and a
state and cooperative sector in agricultural production. Vieweg was
censured for 'counterrevolutionary tendencies' and expelled from his
office and from the party in 1957. After fleeing to West Germany, Vieweg
returned to the GDR in 1958 and was arrested and convicted on charges
of espionage and 'fleeing the republic'. He was condemned to twelve
years in prison, of which he served six (Bauerkämper 2002: 176–81).

The Vieweg affair coincided with the decision of party and government
authorities to launch a final drive for the full collectivisation of
agricultural production. By April 1960, when practically all farmers had
been convinced or compelled to join one LPG or another, the government
announced that full collectivisation had been achieved. When, however,
formerly independent farmers had no choice but to enter into the LPG,
they usually took the path of least resistance by forming small groups of
acquaintances and founding the 'lower' form of cooperative, the LPG
Type I, which allowed them to keep their cattle and continue animal
husbandry privately. In essence, the Type I cooperatives became a way of
fulfilling norms for obligatory deliveries of crops to the state, while still
producing enough surplus fodder for privately owned pigs and milk
cows, with which farmers could earn good money at the established
outlets for agricultural produce (Bauerkämper 2002: 184–92).

At first, 'full collectivisation' often meant that single villages were
divided between one LPG Type III and one or more LPG Type I. Under
these conditions, policy makers and agricultural administrators wasted
no time in exerting the familiar economic pressures on 'lower' forms of
agricultural cooperatives, in an effort to induce them to merge with
'higher' forms. Simultaneously, in the context of the so-called New
Economic System (1963–1967), the LPG Type III were given economic
incentives and granted greater discretion in fulfilling the plan
(Bauerkämper 2002: 196). The result was that most Type I cooperatives
had merged with an established Type III cooperative by the end of the
1960s, though a few held out until the mid-1970s. By this time, however,
the integrity of the Type III cooperatives was being challenged by the
next phase of development.

Writing in the late 1950s, Arlt still expected that the LPG, which was
based in large part on privately owned land, would give way to the state
farm, based on state-owned land (Arlt 1959: 50, 253). We now know,

however, that this was not the case. In 1987, nearly 80 percent of the East German enterprises for agriculture, forestry and fishing were in the cooperative sector, while only about 20 percent were in the state sector.[7] Still, the industrialisation and specialisation of agricultural production, beginning in the 1960s, served to increase the distance between property owners and their land, from which they had already been alienated in the process of collectivisation.

Once the cooperatives in individual villages had been joined together in a single LPG Type III, the next step was to detach the divisions for crop production from the LPG of neighbouring villages and join them together in a larger inter-village unit. By 1975, such units became the basis for the founding of a new type of cooperative farm, an LPG-P (LPG for crop production), which then became the centre of a larger 'unit of cooperation.'[8] The cooperating partners of the LPG for crop production were the successors to the local LPG Type III, which became LPG-T (LPG for animal husbandry), usually specialising either in dairy farming or in raising pigs (Küster 2002: 75–79).

Today's commentators are critical of the gigantism of socialist planning in the agrarian sector, but planners seem to have been convinced of the scientific and progressive character of their policies (Bauerkämper 2002: 194–205). Simultaneously, however, the industrialisation of agricultural production had the effect of levelling differences between landowning and landless members of socialist enterprises. The land shares, which had still provided a 'material basis' for 'potential social conflict' and, hence, had constituted 'elements of class struggle' within the cooperative farm (Arlt 1959: 51), fell by the wayside with the dissolution of the LPG Type III and the founding of the specialised LPG-P and LPG-T (Arlt 1988). A further effect of the industrialisation and specialisation of agricultural production was the centralisation of administrative authority both within the new enterprises and in larger administrative agencies. As a result, intra-cooperative democracy suffered. How farmers responded to these developments is the subject of the next section.

Farmers' Responses to Crises in Property Relations

In her study of the Karl Marx Collective in the Buryat ASSR, Humphrey (1998: 227) argues against explaining the behaviour of farm members in terms of strategies that they develop in the pursuit of their own interests.

Instead, she insists, analysis of behaviour must be firmly embedded in the institutional structures in which farm members were active, particularly the collective farm, the party, and the local administrative unit: 'It is the organisation of the Soviet political economy which calls forth semi-legal "strategies", not the other way round.' This reminder about the importance of the social context in behavioural analysis may be overstated, however, especially for those investigating socialist regimes with a much shorter history of collectivisation. In East Germany, most founding members of the LPG had previously been involved in private agriculture, and their experiences were still fresh in their memories. What is more, East German farmers were very much aware that their situation differed radically from that of West German counterparts, who provided a kind of alternative model reinforcing memories of private farming. Finally, the leeway provided by Lenin's cooperative plan forced all of those involved in agricultural planning or production to reduce the ambiguity in one way or another. Therefore, it seems reasonable to attribute strategies to farmers and functionaries, insofar as their behaviour can be understood to have corresponded simultaneously to aspects of Lenin's cooperative plan and to extra-socialist motives, which had correlates in pre-socialist memories or West German models.

In this section, I provide illustrations of such strategies with reference to the specialisation of agricultural production in the 1970s, which was still of great concern to the interview partners with whom we spoke during an ethnographic and social historical project set in Northwest Saxony.[9] While the data in question are drawn from a single field site in a country characterised by considerable regional diversity, this site may be regarded as representative, at least for the points under discussion, due to the levelling effects of the postwar land reform.[10] I quote from only two interview partners, but these two have been chosen from a much larger pool to convey the differences and convergences in the viewpoints of informants who varied by social origin, generation, gender and party membership. The descriptions and interpretations of the two men quoted below have often been corroborated by other interview partners, who are not quoted here, and by farmers from other regions who are quoted in the secondary literature.[11]

Socialist-era developments in Breunsdorf, a village of about 600 souls, corresponded to the general description given above. Since there was no large estate in the village, hardly any land was redistributed during the postwar land reform. Then, however, with few exceptions, the farmers with over twenty hectares of land abandoned their farms and fled to West Germany in the early 1950s. In 1953, an LPG Type III was founded by new farmers and agricultural labourers, but the owners of small to medium-sized family farms opposed collectivisation and did not join the LPG until 1960, when they founded two new LPG Type I. By 1970, the members of the two LPG Type I had merged with the LPG Type III, which was chaired by a member of the ruling socialist party from a farming family in a different village in the region. Under the leadership of their socialist chairman, the members of the Breunsdorf cooperative farm prospered, resisting participation in cooperative arrangements with other LPGs in the region for as long as possible. By 1978, however, the Breunsdorf cooperative had become an LPG-T specializing in milk production, which was linked to an LPG-P in a unit of cooperation centered in Stolpen, a village six kilometers to the west.

'In the beginning' said Lothar Arnold, referring to the year 1969, when he became LPG chairman in Breunsdorf, 'there was some friction over the inventory contributions, but after one year ... most members concentrated fully on production and helped the LPG move forward'.[12] Our interviews with other former members of the LPG confirm this general description. Some of the leading members of the LPG Type I, who came from local farming families, were incorporated into the management of the Type III cooperative; and some of their sons and daughters were encouraged to study agronomy or accounting, then to return to positions in production or administration in the LPG. Whether or not LPG members from farming families occupied management positions, however, they often belonged to the productive core of the cooperative farm.

In this context, there developed a conflict of interest that cannot be described in neutral terms. Some may have viewed it as a conflict between the public mission of the LPG and the private interests of its members; and others may have viewed it as a conflict over the very definition of the LPG's public mission. I am not referring to the classic tension between devoting time and resources to work on the cooperative farm or on the private allotment, which is so well-known from the secondary literature on socialist agriculture (Humphrey 1998: 289–99). While such tensions did arise in the GDR, the private allotments were established and sanctioned parts of agricultural production, upon which the party-state came to rely for significant percentages of certain products (Eckart 1983). My example touches instead on the status of the LPG itself – on the struggle over the control of the LPG, the attempts of various interested parties to establish it either as a more or less autonomous enterprise serving the combined interests of its members or as a dependent component in the larger system of industrialised and centrally controlled agriculture.

Our interview partners agree that the period lasting from the mid-1960s to the mid-1970s was an era of relative autonomy, commitment, and even entrepreneurship within the LPG Type III (Eidson and Milligan 2003). In contrast, the process of specialisation in the 1970s is said to have deprived cooperative farm members of room to manoeuvre within the LPG. Our interview partners are convinced that this was intentional, and statements made by Arlt in his *Grundriss des LPG-Rechts* regarding the need to guard against 'capitalist tendencies' within the collective farms, suggest that this was indeed so (Arlt 1959: 441).

The first voice to be heard is that of Georg Preissler, the son of an established farming family, who first went away to study agronomy, then returned to take over a mid-level management position in the LPG Type III. He gives expression to a new degree of acceptance of collectivised agriculture as a fact of life in the GDR, even among those, who, like most people from local farming families, were not members of the Socialist Unity Party. His statement also indicates that there was a sense of common purpose within the LPG, which was not based on socialist convictions but on the shared perception that the cooperative farm belonged to its members, who, therefore, had the right to benefit from its successful operation.

Georg Preissler (agronomist, born 1951):[13] 'The members of the LPG Type III were, for the most part, all employees, unless someone had a position of responsibility or leadership ... It didn't matter whether you'd contributed land, been a founding member of the LPG, or whether you'd just joined at age eighteen or nineteen ... What mattered was that, as a new member, you carried out your work conscientiously, just like everyone else, and didn't say, "Well, I'm done for today, and I want to go home" ... It was different than a state-owned enterprise, because the sense that "this belongs to us" was stronger. If, at the end of the year, we had produced a surplus, then a supplemental salary could be paid out ... And this produced a different attitude toward work in the agricultural cooperative. There really *was* a cooperative spirit, but not enough, I'd say, since it came from the state.'

In the next passage, it is striking that even the LPG chairman, a Socialist Unity Party member, explains the motives of cooperative farm members not in official phraseology but in terms of their desire to increase their own monetary rewards. This quotation gives evidence of a general entrepreneurial attitude underlying behaviour in the LPG Type III, which was subsequently dampened by the changes accompanying industrialisation and specialisation. It also provides support for Preissler's suggestion that LPG members had developed a new attitude toward cooperative property, one which differed from earlier notions of private ownership but which still did not correspond to official definitions.

> **Lothar Arnold (LPG chairman, born 1932):** 'In 1960, things started to look up for agriculture, until 1972 or 1973, when there was a trend toward specialisation. Then there was another big shakeup ... Up to then, we had always had animal husbandry and crop production together. And when we had crops that we didn't need to sell to the state, we could put them into animal husbandry to upgrade the quality. We made money that way. But then the state needed the fodder ... for the big cattle stalls and pig sties. That only worked if they took produce away from the farmers and put it into the industrialised farming enterprises.'

Addressing these same issues, the farmer's son expands upon the chairman's statement regarding profit-oriented activities in the cooperative farm by emphasising the plasticity of the phrase 'crops that we didn't need to sell to the state.' His description of past practices clearly indicates that crops that the LPG owed to the state were sometimes intentionally withheld in order to use them for purposes that were more profitable for cooperative farm members. Once again, this statement is embedded in a kind of 'before and after' scenario, in which the relative autonomy of the LPG Type III is contrasted with the increase in centralised control that accompanied industrialisation and specialisation. The farmer's son takes for granted that the separation of crop production and animal husbandry represented a conscious attempt on the part of state authorities to deprive cooperative farm members of the degree of autonomy that they still retained – an interpretation that was repeated to me by other informants as well, including former party members.

> **Georg Preissler (LPG agronomist):** 'In a cooperative where animal and plant production were together, the state requirements played a secondary role. You could still do pretty much what you thought was right. If the state said, "You have to deliver 100,000 tons of sugar beets", but you didn't have enough beets for fodder, then you took some sugar beets, dumped them on the edge of the field, and covered them up with dirt. Later, in the winter, the beets were fed to the cows in order to get more milk and to make money with the milk. The farmers didn't really care if there was any sugar in the shops or not. They said,

"First our cattle have to be fed, and then we'll make our delivery to the state."
But with the separation of animal husbandry and crop production, they really
had leverage on us, since each enterprise was legally autonomous and did its
finances independently ... It was a matter of state direction, in order to
introduce a form of control into the cooperatives.'

In the final passages quoted in this chapter, the LPG chairman provides
an analysis of the motivation of cooperative farm members, including
especially those who used to be independent farmers, as he himself had
been. This was linked, he argues, to their freedom to manage the
productive and financial affairs of the cooperative in a way that promoted
both the enterprise and their own well being. Changing regulations for
managing LPG finances and for compensating LPG members, which
accompanied the trend toward industrialisation, specialisation and
centralisation, are invoked in order to explain the general malaise that
spread among cooperative farmers, beginning in the late 1970s.

> **Lothar Arnold (LPG chairman):** 'During the first years, when the LPG
> couldn't yet achieve a positive balance, the state didn't exert any influence ...
> with regard to how much they were paying their members. The members'
> assembly, the executive committee could decide: We need such and such
> percent for making investments, such and such for repairs ... Either we add it
> to the reserves ... or ... supplemental salaries will be higher at the end of the
> year. And there was always pressure from individual members to earn as many
> work units as possible – since this was the basis of our wages – and to produce
> as cheaply as possible, so that there would be as much as possible left over at the
> end of the year [to pay a bonus salary] ... This is the same principle as in
> capitalist agricultural production today. Then, ... in the second half of the
> 1970s, this was systematically diminished, so that the cooperative farmers
> could be organised more or less like other workers ... It was prescribed by the
> state how many thousand marks you were allowed to earn on average per
> cooperative farmer, ... regardless of whether the farm was profitable or not ...
> And because of this the whole interest of the formerly independent farmers
> [who were now in the LPG] was systematically destroyed.'

Speaking in 1994, four years after the demise of the GDR, the LPG
chairman compares the way he ran the LPG Type III with the forms of
operation typical under capitalism. Nevertheless, the chairman was a
party member and an important figure in the party's county organisation.
Other portions of our interview with him, which are not included here,
give convincing evidence of his commitment to socialism and of his belief
that the policies that destroyed the LPG Type III had 'nothing to do with
socialism'. In his view, socialist policy makers destroyed a form of
cooperative agricultural that he regarded as socialist – or at least socialist

enough. Thus, the chairman's attitudes toward socialism appear to be contradictory, but the contradiction may lie within socialism itself. As we learned from Arlt (1959: 92–94), intra-cooperative democracy was supposed to be one of the hallmarks of cooperative farms under socialism, but, as the chairman, Lothar Arnold, indicates, it eventually fell victim to administrative centralisation: 'In the end, there were about two members' assemblies per year. That didn't have anything to do with socialist agriculture anymore'.

Conclusions

Lenin's cooperative plan was supposed to facilitate the gradual transition from capitalist to socialist agriculture by incorporating apparently contradictory aspects, while arranging them sequentially in a series of 'lower' and 'higher' developmental stages. One sequence led from private property to cooperative property; another led from 'lower' types of cooperative farms to 'higher' types; yet another led from petit bourgeois consciousness to the socialist personality, and so on (Humphrey 1998: 93; Verdery 2003: 52).

The logical integrity of Lenin's cooperative plan, not to mention its practicality, depended on a whole series of assumptions. It was assumed that a system based on pubic property was superior to one based on private property, that its superiority would be evident to everyone involved, and that, therefore, private property would eventually fall by the wayside on the road to the socialist future. This apparent faith in the rightness and inevitability of socialist goals was linked to two further fictions: first, that the party-state could count on the voluntary participation of peasants or farmers in socialist programmes; and, second, that cooperative farms could be granted self-government and would still comply willingly with the dictates of central planners. Consideration of these assumptions helps us to understand why LPG law admitted private property at one level, while invalidating it at another; why it called for the self-government of cooperative farm members, while contextualising it in a way that amounted to an evisceration; why it demanded that farmers join the cooperative 'voluntarily', bringing their assets with them, without, however, receiving any shares in it; and why it made landowning members eligible for a special form of remuneration, then extended this form of remuneration to landless members and, finally, did away with it altogether.

Once the validity of the assumptions underlying Lenin's cooperative plan were challenged, either in the subjective responses of coerced farmers or by declines in productivity, the logical edifice upon which it was built collapsed, leaving only a bundle of contradictions (Humphrey 1998: 434). At different times and in various contexts, different actors came to terms with these contradictions in different ways. But if Lenin's cooperative plan and the policies it supposedly inspired can be understood to represent a series of logical or actual alternatives – in the form of developmental stages or changing policy initiatives – then it is clear that cooperative farmers often had distinct preferences. When, for example, our interview partners talked about *the* LPG, it often turned out that they were referring to a particular phase in its historical development, namely, the heyday of the LPG Type III in the 1960s and early 1970s. This applies not only to the case study in my field site. An East German historian who investigated a series of LPG cooperatives just outside of Berlin reports that, 'among the interviewees, the reigning opinion was that "the best years were between 1965 and 1975"' (Nehrig 2000: 216). The many LPG members throughout East Germany who held this opinion – and that included most of those who thought of themselves and were seen by others as 'real farmers' – regarded the developments of the mid- to late 1970s as a mistake and even as an exception to the general rule of their experience. This was true for those who supported the socialist government, those who opposed it, and those who were indifferent to it.

The example provided by Lothar Arnold, the LPG chairman in Breunsdorf, is especially telling, because it shows that socialism's advocates could use aspects of socialist theory to argue against socialist policy. Thus, Arnold criticised the dissolution of the LPG Type III and the transition to the specialised LPG in regional units of cooperation with reference to intra-cooperative democracy, which he regarded as a central principle of socialist agriculture.

A close reading of the interview passages quoted above indicates that intra-cooperative democracy is best understood as one aspect of a larger complex. It was intra-cooperative democracy, or the best possible approximation of it, that made it possible for LPG members to participate, at least to some degree, in decisions affecting production, investment and remuneration. It was these factors taken together that gave members 'the sense that "this belongs to us"' (Preissler), at least before they were 'systematically diminished … in the second half of the

1970s' (Arnold). This explains the bitterness with which our interview partners described how 'the whole LPG was torn apart' when specialisation required the separation of crop production and animal husbandry.[14] 'We resisted for as long as we could', Arnold explained, 'but the state pushed it through.' There is a 'we' in these statements that refers to the people who thought the LPG belonged to them, despite Arlt's (1959: 257) claim that the LPG as a legal person was distinct from its membership. This was one possible understanding of cooperative property among the range of options opened up by Lenin's cooperative plan, and it was the one to which many cooperative farmers subscribed.

What are the implications of these reflections for our understanding of cooperative property as one variety of property under particular historical and political circumstances? First, we must supplement Humphrey's (1998: 118) notion of property rights in the socialist cooperative or collective farms as a 'hierarchy of rights held in practice'. As Humphrey (1998: 434) herself notes, local understandings and practices did not correspond exactly to legal definitions, because legal definitions were ideologically formulated and there were 'inconsistencies in the ideology itself'. This, she continues, gave rise to 'instructions or stated aims which ... [were] ... either contradictory or confusing'. In this case, however, it is not enough simply to invoke 'de facto rights', since, as is evident once more in Humphrey's (1998: 219–21) own exposition, the boundary between de facto rights and perceived violations could not always be determined.

Approaches to cooperative property – and perhaps also to other forms of property – that emphasise property rights, without also taking account of regular and therefore predictable ways in which they are violated (or might be thought to be violated) are inadequate, because they leave out a realm of ambivalence that is constitutive of the actual and routine ways in which people gain access to and exploit resources. Given their fundamental ambivalence, property relations in the East German agrarian sector might be said to have been negotiable – at least sometimes, under some conditions, and to some degree (see Lund 2002). Policies were often modified or even reversed, and the responses of the producers were also variable. During some phases in the historical development of the agrarian sector, there was more freedom to manoeuvre within the cooperative farms, and these periods played a central role in the self-understanding of the cooperative farmers. Clearly, however, property relations in East Germany's agrarian sector were negotiable only to a limited degree (see Peters 2002). Speaking very generally, it might be said that the ambivalence inherent in Lenin's cooperative plan and in the corresponding laws and policies often provoked crises, which were then resolved in favour of supposedly 'higher' forms. These 'higher' forms were, in turn, consistent with the trend toward mechanisation and central control. In conclusion, I shall explain briefly why I am still convinced that we should expand our scope to include the full range of associations evoked by ambivalent ideological precepts and jural strictures, rather than restricting it to those aspects that have been selected in the exercise of political power.

The reform legislation of June 1990 required the dissolution or the transformation of the LPG within a year (Küster 2002: 84–125). Thereafter, thousands of new enterprises of various types were founded, but many observers were surprised by the dearth of new private enterprises. Indeed, the dominant trend was the founding of cooperatives or corporations, many of which could be understood as successors to the cooperative farms of the socialist era. The point of departure in the founding of new enterprises was, of course, the last stage of development under socialism, namely, the units of cooperation, made up of an LPG for crop production and one or more LPG for animal husbandry; and from this starting point, many new arrangements were possible (Küster 2002: 157–215). Nevertheless, many members of the former socialist cooperatives made the same decision that was made in Stolpen and Breunsdorf, the villages in my case study, where the specialised LPG for crop production and animal husbandry were joined together to form a new cooperative, which corresponded to the strictures of federal law, while bearing a strong resemblance to the LPG Type III of 1960s and early 1970s. Many in my field site and elsewhere have described the founding of new cooperatives as an attempt to return to the type of LPG that was torn apart in the 1970s by the policies of industrialisation, specialisation and centralisation. But this attempted return was problematic for at least two reasons: first, because circumstances had changed so dramatically and, second, because people were trying to reconstruct a form that may have never existed. By that I mean simply that reproducing the old LPG Type III is more complicated than it might first appear, given the contestation surrounding that type of enterprise, even in its heyday. In attempting to reconstruct the LPG Type III, the cooperative farmers of the new era inevitably referred not only to what it was but also to what it should have been and what they had tried to make it. For these reasons and others, it is sometimes necessary, in theorising property relations, to go beyond 'hierarchies of rights', not simply to de facto powers but, at least occasionally, to a kind of 'neither nor' space of alternative ideals, organisational forms, and practices, which stand in an ambivalent relationship to the established order and represent a potential for transformation to an order of another kind.

Notes

1. The quotation is from the *Manifesto of the Communist Party* (1848, 1888), which is reprinted in Tucker (1972: 335–62; see especially p. 346).
2. On the basis of previously inaccessible archival materials, scholars have recently criticised oversimplified notions of 'Sovietisation', insisting instead on the contingency and variability of developments in the various 'peoples' republics' of Central and Eastern Europe (see Bauerkämper 2002: 22–35). Critical reflection on Sovietisation teaches some important lessons about the complexity of events and the necessity for multi-causal explanations, but it cannot obscure the remarkable consistency in many policies throughout the Soviet Bloc, despite the considerable range of variation and the well-known exceptions. Agriculture is a case in point, as, after the Second World War, the countries in question proceeded, if at different times, with varying tempos, and to different degrees, through a series of stages that were first manifested in the Soviet Union after the First World War (Wädekin 1982; Pryor 1992).
3. All translations from German-language texts are my responsibility. I translate the German term *Bauer* sometimes as 'peasant' but usually as 'farmer', since, following the liberal reforms of the nineteenth century, most independent agricultural producers in Saxony had become small businessmen or businesswomen, who participated in the market economy.
4. I use the acronym LPG for both the singular and plural forms of the term. The literal translation of *Landwirtschaftliche Produktionsgenossenschaft* is 'agricultural production cooperative'. Some writers choose to call this kind of enterprise a 'collective farm', in order to underline its difference from the producer cooperatives that exist in market economies (e.g., Verdery 2003: 42 note a). My preferred translation remains closer to the original term, while still marking the difference between cooperatives under socialism and capitalism.
5. Depending upon the estimated worth of the assets of a particular LPG, entering landowning members were required to supplement the minimal inventory contribution with a further payment, sometimes called a *Fondsausgleich*, or assets adjustment (Eidson and Milligan 2003: 53).
6. An estimated 12 million ethnic German refugees from Eastern Europe settled in either East or West Germany. In 1947, refugees made up almost one quarter of the population of the Soviet Zone (Bauerkämper 2002: 236–37).
7. See Pryor (1992: 19), where data comparing the percentage of land in the state and cooperative sectors are given for Bulgaria, East Germany, Hungary, Poland, Romania, the USSR and Yugoslavia. Neither Poland nor Yugoslavia had

significant amounts of land in either sector. Of the remaining countries, only Hungary had more land in the state sector than in the cooperative sector, and only Bulgaria had a higher percentage of land in the cooperative sector than did East Germany.

8. On the Soviet precedent for the development of 'cooperation' in the East German agrarian sector, see Humphrey 1998: 137 ff.

9. Since 1994, I have carried out fieldwork intermittently in the Southern Region of Leipzig with support from the Sächsisches Landesamt für Archäologie, the Sächsisches Staatsministerium für Bildung und Kunst, the Institut für Kulturwissenschaften of the Universität Leipzig, the Zentrum für Höhere Studien, also of the Universität Leipzig, and the Max Planck Institute for Social Anthropology. Most of the interviews of 1994 were conducted with residents of Breunsdorf by Hans-Jürgen Ketzer, a member of our research team. Ketzer is also responsible for most of the early transcriptions. In 2001, I began with a new phase of fieldwork in the same general area, supplementing the focus on Breunsdorf with a broader survey of the 'unit of cooperation' into which Breunsdorf was integrated in the late 1970s.

10. The most dramatic regional difference in East Germany was between the East Elbian and West Elbian territories, which, before the land reform, were characterised by large estates and by small to medium-sized family farms, respectively. The postwar land reform involved the dissolution of large estates and the distribution of the farmland among numerous small farmers. As a result, patterns of ownership in the two regions were, prior to collectivisation, less extremely variable than they had been before the land reform.

11. Publications that include quotations from interviews with former cooperative farmers include Eidson (1998), Laschewski (1998), Küster (2002), and Eidson and Milligan (2003). Comparing the statements in these publications results in a remarkably consistent picture.

12. Our interview with Lothar Arnold was conducted in Neukieritzsch on 19 July 1994. This and all other personal names in this chapter are pseudonyms.

13. We spoke with Preissler in Neukieritzsch on 7 August 1994.

14. Interview with Andreas Grunewald in Neukieritzsch-Breunsdorf on 12 August 1994.

References

Arlt, R. 1959. *Grundriss des LPG-Rechts*. Berlin: VEB Deutscher Zentralverlag.
——— 1988. *Theoretische Grundfragen des LPG- und Agrarrechts*. Berlin: Staatsverlag der Deutschen Demokratischen Republik.
Bauerkämper, A. 2002. *Ländliche Gesellschaft in der kommunistischen Diktatur: Zwangsmodernisierung und Tradition in Brandenburg 1945–1963*. Köln: Böhlau.
Benda-Beckmann, F. von and K. von Benda-Beckmann 1999. 'A Functional Analysis of Property Rights, with Special Reference to Indonesia', in *Land and Natural Resources in Southeast Asia and Oceania*, eds T. van Meijl and F. von Benda-Beckmann, London and New York: Kegan Paul International, 15–56.

Carr, E.H. and R.W. Davies 1969. *Foundations of a Planned Economy, 1926–1929*. New York: Macmillan.

Eckart, K. 1983. 'Die Bedeutung der privaten Anbauflächen für die Versorgung der Bevölkerung in der DDR', *Deutschland Archiv* 4: 415–20.

Eidson, J.R. 1998. 'Der lange Abschied: Breunsdorfer Bauern berichten über Landwirtschaft, Kohle und dörfliches Leben der letzten 50 Jahre', *Sächsische Heimatblätter* 44(2): 99–110.

Eidson, J.R. and G. Milligan 2003. 'Cooperative Entrepreneurs? Collectivization and Privatization of Agriculture in Two East German Regions', in *The Postsocialist Agrarian Question*, eds C.M. Hann and the 'Property Relations Group', Münster: LIT Verlag, 47–92.

Humphrey, C. 1998. *Marx Went Away But Karl Stayed Behind*. (Revised edition of The Karl Marx Collective, 1983). Ann Arbor: University of Michigan Press.

Kingston-Mann, E. 1983. *Lenin and the Problem of Marxist Peasant Revolution*. New York, Oxford: Oxford University Press.

Küster, K. 2002. *Die ostdeutschen Landwirte und die Wende: Die Entwicklung der ostdeutschen Landwirtschaftsstrukturen ab 1989 am Beispiel Thüringen*. Kassel: Kassel University Press.

Laschewski, L. 1998. *Von der LPG zur Agrargenossenschaft: Untersuchungen zur Transformation genossenschaftlich organisierter Agrarunternehmen in Ostdeutschland*. Berlin: edition sigma.

Lenin, V.I. [1923] 1975. 'On Cooperation', in *The Lenin Anthology*, ed. R.C. Tucker, New York: W.W. Norton & Co, 707–14.

—— [1899] 1977. *The Development of Capitalism in Russia: The Process of the Formation of a Home Market for Large-scale Industry*. Moscow: Progress Publishers.

Lund, C. 2002. 'Negotiating Property Institutions: On the Symbiosis of Property and Authority in Africa', in *Negotiating Property in Africa*, eds K. Juul and C. Lund, Portsmouth, New Hampshire: Heinemann, 11–43.

Nehring, C. 2000. 'Das Leben auf dem Lande: die Genossenschaften (LPG)', in *Befremdlich anders: Leben in der DDR*, ed. E. Badstübner, Berlin: Dietz, 195–218.

Peters, P.E. 2002. 'The Limits of Negotiability: Security, Equity and Class Formation in Africa's Land Systems', in *Negotiating Property in Africa*, eds K. Juul and C. Lund, Portsmouth, New Hampshire: Heinemann, 45–66.

Ponomarjow, B.N. et al. (author collective) 1960. *Geschichte der Kommunistischen Partei der Sowjetunion*. Berlin: Dietz Verlag.

Pryor, F.L. 1992. *The Red and the Green: The Rise and Fall of Collectivized Agriculture in Marxist Regimes*. Princeton: Princeton University Press.

Tucker, R.C., ed. 1972. *The Marx-Engels Reader*. New York: W.W. Norton & Co.

Verdery, K. 2003. *The Vanishing Hectare: Property and Value in Postsocialist Transylvania*. Ithaca: Cornell University Press.

Wädekin, K.-E. 1982. *Agrarian Policies in Communist Europe: A Critical Introduction*. Edited by E.M. Jacobs. Totowa, New Jersey: Allanheld, Osmun & Co.

Chapter 8

Who Owns the Fisheries? Changing Views of Property and Its Redistribution in Post-colonial Maori Society

Toon van Meijl

In recent years the New Zealand government has developed a rather progressive policy to redress the grievances of the country's indigenous population, the Maori, about the dispossession of their land and natural resources in the nineteenth century. It has signed several compensation settlements with Maori tribal organisations that have entailed the return of significant sections of lands and natural resources as well as monetary payments. The settlement process, however, is rather controversial for two reasons. First, the government negotiates settlements only with tribal organisations, whereas 80 percent of the Maori population is currently living in urban environments in which tribal connections have lost a great deal of meaning. There is a growing awareness in New Zealand that somehow this group needs to be included in the settlement process as well. Second, the sociopolitical organisation of Maori society has changed radically since the nineteenth century, which raises the question of the representation for descendants of the Maori who were originally dispossessed. This question is preceded by the more fundamental question about the nature of property rights in the nineteenth century. Who used to own the land and other resources: extended families, sub-tribes, tribes, or super-tribes? Subsequently, the issue of who are the rightful heirs of the original owners may be addressed.

This paper will investigate these questions through an analysis of the most complicated claim that concerns Maori property rights to the fisheries. In 1992 the government signed a compensation agreement about Maori fisheries with a delegation of four tribal chiefs that claimed to have a mandate on behalf of 'all Maori'. This agreement, however, has so far not been implemented, because it has been disputed from two different angles. Urban groupings have been arguing that it is unlawful that the deal is signed exclusively with tribal organisations, thus effectively dispossessing all pan-tribal Maori. The main issue at stake in this dispute concerns the question: what is a tribe? The second type of dispute revolves around the question whether the benefits should be distributed on a per capita basis, which is to the advantage of tribes that are made up of large numbers of people living on relatively small territories, or on the basis of the 'traditional' rights to fish the sea off tribal land areas, which privileges tribes with a huge coastline but only a limited number of beneficiaries. The main issue at stake in this debate is the point of departure for the negotiations: historical justice based on the restitution of property rights that were dispossessed in the nineteenth century or social justice on the basis of contemporary concerns about Maori poverty.

The political debate about balancing historical versus social justice and the related debate about the embeddedness of property rights in Maori sociopolitical organisation both past and present, makes the dispute about the distribution of fishing quotas in contemporary Maori society rather messy. In this paper an attempt will be made to clarify the complex nature of the dispute through a focus on the systemic nature of property as a 'bundle of rights' (F. and K. von Benda-Beckmann 1999; see also F. and K. von Benda Beckmann and Wiber in the introduction to this volume). Property rights are understood as a multidimensional web of linkages between categorical and concretised property relationships, each with a specific position in equally complex property practices. The practice of property has furthermore changed under the impact of colonialism and is therefore different in past and present. As a consequence, any solution to political disputes about property rights in Maori society is necessarily a complicated compromise between categorical and concretised property relationships in the past *and* present. And like any compromise, this may in fact create new problems. In addition, it should be considered that over the past two decades this complex debate about Maori property rights has been compounded with regard to the fisheries following the introduction of a quota system that in fact changed the properties of the fishery. Since this debate about the dynamics of Maori property rights to fish is dominated by the interpretation of the Treaty of Waitangi, originally signed in 1840

between the first British Governor of New Zealand and a large number of
Maori chiefs, a brief excursion into colonial history is inevitable.

Colonisation

Some 1000 years ago Maori people sailed in canoes from Eastern
Polynesia to the islands of New Zealand, where they settled over a period
of several centuries. Over the years they multiplied and formed a society
with a complex structure of sociopolitical organisation. In anthropology,
consensus has emerged that the *hapuu*, usually translated as 'sub-tribe',
was the central unit of the Maori tribal structure. A sub-tribe defined
itself by descent from an apical, often eponymous ancestor, and was made
up of a group of kin that occupied a common territory and lived together
in a communal settlement. Sub-tribes, in turn, comprised a collection of
extended families or *whaanau*, while several sub-tribes made up a group
linked together by descent from a relatively remote founding ancestor.
Groups at this level were called *iwi* (literally 'bone' or 'people'), a term
that is nowadays usually translated as 'tribe', which is misleading to the
extent that it suggests that it was the core of the sociopolitical organisation
of which all other units of organisation were derived. The composition of
tribes was rather disjointed and flexible and *iwi* probably did not develop
as corporate groups until in the nineteenth century (Webster 1997). The
highest level of the tribal organisation was formed by the 'canoe' or *waka*,
which was made up of various tribes that had all emerged from ancestors
who had reached the shores of New Zealand on the same canoe. However,
no form of political or economic cooperation existed between tribes until
the beginning of the nineteenth century, when European settlement
began (Ballara 1998).

The intensification of contact between Maori and European colonists,
mainly from Britain, prompted the Colonial Office in London to
intervene. A governor was assigned to secure sovereignty for Britain,
preferably by means of a treaty with the Maori people. On 6 February
1840, exactly one week after his arrival, Governor Hobson signed a treaty
with a number of Maori chiefs in Waitangi (Orange 1987). The debate
about the Treaty of Waitangi is complicated since there are significant
differences between the English version and the Maori translation that
was signed by most Maori chiefs.

The Treaty is made up of three articles. In the First Article the
English version states that the chiefs ceded 'all the rights and powers of

Sovereignty', but the Maori version does not use the nearest equivalent to sovereignty, i.e., *mana*, but *kawanatanga*, a transliteration of 'governorship' improvised by the missionaries. In the Second Article the English version guaranteed the Maori 'the full exclusive and undisturbed possession of their Lands and Estates Forests Fisheries and other properties'. According to Kawharu's (1989: 319-20) translation, the Maori version of this clause confirmed to the indigenous people 'the unqualified exercise of their chieftainship over their lands over their villages and over their treasures all'. The Third Article conferred 'royal protection (to the Natives of New Zealand) and ... all the Rights and Privileges of British Subjects'. This article appears less contentious, but was politically compromised by the ultimate goal of British colonisation: the amalgamation of the Maori people.

The immediate impact of the Treaty on colonial relationships must not be exaggerated. Not until the mid-1850s did it become apparent that the agreement signed at Waitangi had opened up the avenue for the arrival of growing numbers of European settlers. This increased the pressure on the land and made Maori people more reluctant to share their country with the Pakeha, the 'foreigners'. Ultimately, the interaction between Maori and Europeans became rather hostile, degenerating into a war in 1860. Following a series of battles, one and a quarter million acres of land were confiscated in 1864. Outside the confiscated areas, New Zealand was brought under colonial control through the individualisation of customary land titles (Kawharu 1977).

In the 1870s, the Maori people massively had recourse to the law in order to settle their grievances over breaches of the Treaty, but found that it no longer offered them protection. In a leading case in 1877 Chief Judge James Prendergast regarded 'the pact known as the "Treaty of Waitangi"... as a simple nullity' for '(n)o body politic existed capable of making cession of sovereignty, nor could the thing itself exist'.[1] This ruling dismissed any Maori rights based on the Treaty and set a precedent for all legal cases with which Maori attempted to secure redress through the courts until 1987.

Steps toward Decolonisation

In the 1960s the political climate in New Zealand changed under the impact of the black civil rights movement in the United States. The Maori intensified their struggle for the recognition of the Treaty of Waitangi

(Walker 1990). In 1975 the government responded with the Treaty of Waitangi Act which established the Waitangi Tribunal (Sorrenson 1989). Section 6 of the act allowed any Maori to submit a claim to the Tribunal on grounds of being 'prejudicially affected' by any policy or practice of the Crown that was 'inconsistent with the principles of the Treaty'. The most important limitation of the act, however, was that 'anything done or omitted before the commencement of (the) Act' was excluded from the Tribunal's jurisdiction. Maori could not therefore submit claims about their large-scale dispossession in the nineteenth century. In addition, it must be noted that the Tribunal itself had no power to redress grievances, only to make recommendations to the government.

In 1985 the newly elected Labour government led by the charismatic David Lange amended the Treaty of Waitangi Act and provided for the extension of the Tribunal's jurisdiction back from 1975 to 6 February 1840 when the Treaty was signed. This clause opened up an important avenue for Maori people to seek redress for past grievances. Towards the end of the 1980s some 600 claims had been submitted to the Waitangi Tribunal, most of which had been sparked off by the government policy of corporatisation, which involved a gigantic transfer of lands and resources held in Crown ownership to semi-private State Owned Enterprises. The Court of Appeal ruled on 29 June 1987, that such transfer of assets to State Owned Enterprises would be unlawful without considering whether the transfer of assets would be inconsistent with the Treaty of Waitangi. It was the first time in New Zealand history that the legality of the Treaty was recognised.

The recognition of the Treaty made it legally and politically inevitable to redress violations that had occurred in the past. In the 1990s the New Zealand government made a beginning with the settlement of Maori grievances about the loss of their property. The first major Treaty settlement dealt with Maori claims over fisheries and was signed in 1992. This settlement has demonstrated, however, that unambiguous strategies for settling Maori grievances are not available as various Maori groups have since been engaged in a vigorous debate about the implementation of the settlement. Indeed, the debate about Maori fisheries has grown into an exemplary case of changing properties of property relationships.

The Fisheries Settlement

Like all Polynesian people, Maori were a maritime and fishing people. Fisheries were therefore mentioned explicitly among the proprietary interests of the Maori protected by the Treaty of Waitangi. The prevailing British view in the nineteenth century was still that the sea and its fish were not private property, which implied that they were considered open to all New Zealanders, Maori and Pakeha alike, but Maori have continued to consider New Zealand fisheries as belonging to them.

In 1986 the legal situation changed dramatically. A Maori fisherman, Tom Te Weehi, appealed his conviction of gathering undersized *paua* (a species of shell fish) in the District Court. He claimed that at the time of committing the alleged offence he was exercising a customary fishing right, protected by section 88 (2) of the Fisheries Act 1983, which provides that 'nothing in this act shall affect any Maori fishing right'. Considering the implications of this Act, the High Court judge rejected the restrictive approach to Maori customary fishing rights expressed in earlier judicial decisions, and accepted the view that customary rights based on aboriginal title continue after a change of sovereignty (Hackshaw 1989: 115–16; McHugh 1991: 130–31). The ruling by Justice Williamson represented a revolutionary reversal of judicial attitudes towards Maori fisheries.

The Te Weehi case also returned the political initiative to Maori people at a moment when the New Zealand government was left bewildered with the unexpected impact of their decision to backdate the jurisdiction of the Waitangi Tribunal. Notably it encouraged them to challenge the quota system that the New Zealand government had introduced under the 1983 Fisheries Act in order to protect the fish resources in the country's inshore and offshore waters. Some regulation had become inevitable since certain species of fish were facing extinction following the extension of New Zealand's economic fishing zone to the 200 mile limit in 1977. The fishing quota system, however, was controversial since it transformed traditional common use-rights in fish into privately owned, divisible commodities (compare Helgason and Pálsson 1997). The unprecedented property interests in commercial fishing were labelled Individual Transferable Quotas (ITQs) and their allocation was based on reported catches over the previous years. In consequence, the system also changed the properties of property rights to fish as it favoured large commercial operators, while the livelihoods of Maori fishermen were threatened as many did not have a history of substantial catches sufficient to qualify them for quota. Within a few years the number of Maori fishermen was reduced by more than 50 percent as almost 1,800 were not given quota (Walker 1990: 274).

Two initiatives were taken to challenge government policy regarding fisheries. In the Far North of the North Island of New Zealand, where almost 600 fishermen were phased out, the Muriwhenua tribes collectively filed a claim with the Waitangi Tribunal in 1985, arguing that the government had failed to gain their permission to create a property right to fish resources from which they were effectively excluded, while the Second Article of the Treaty of Waitangi explicitly guaranteed them their 'full exclusive and undisturbed possession' (Norman 1989). The Muriwhenua people presented a mass of compelling evidence to the Waitangi Tribunal, including claims to fishing their coastal waters as far out as thirty-two kilometers (Waitangi Tribunal 1988). The tribes clearly considered fishing grounds their property, and successfully argued that they had never relinquished them to the Crown. In September 1987 the claimants from the Far North obtained an interim ruling from the chairman of the Waitangi Tribunal, which provided the High Court with sufficient arguments to issue an injunction to the implementation of the quota management system in the northern region (Walker 1990: 275).

Parallel to the strategy of the Muriwhenua tribes operating primarily through the Waitangi Tribunal, the New Zealand Maori Council along with the large tribes of Tainui and Ngai Tahu lodged an application for an injunction directly with the High Court. This law suit also ended in a victory for Maori as the injunction granted to Muriwhenua was extended to the trade in fishing quota throughout New Zealand. Subsequently, a joint working party of Crown officials and four Maori representatives was set up to negotiate a settlement. The Maori delegation included the chairman of the New Zealand Maori Council and the tribal leaders of Muriwhenua, Tainui and Ngai Tahu. The Maori delegates were given a mandate at a national *hui*, a traditional gathering, at which initially the view was taken that the Treaty of Waitangi entitled Maori to 100 percent of the fishing quota. Later the Maori representatives were instructed to refuse any settlement of less than 50 percent of the fisheries (Ward 1999: 46).

In view of the political climate the government was not unwilling to seek a settlement, but the resulting Maori Fisheries Act 1989 granted only 10 percent of the fisheries quota to be held in trust, plus NZ$ 10 million to develop the Maori fishing industry. Obviously, this was unsatisfactory to Maori. Litigation regarding the distribution of fishing quota did not stop, while negotiations for a better settlement were also pursued.

The continuation of litigation and negotiations notwithstanding, in 1990 a Maori Fisheries Commission was appointed by the government to manage the assets returned to Maori ownership in 1989; this Commission was later renamed the Treaty of Waitangi Fisheries Commission (or *Te Ohu Kai Moana*, 'the seafood group') and the resources transferred initially were later labelled the pre-settlement assets. Te Ohu Kai Moana was made up again by the chairman of the New Zealand Maori Council and three delegates of Muriwhenua, Tainui and Ngai Tahu; the latter two were this time represented by their highest chiefs.

In 1992, after a major fishing company put 50 percent of its holdings on the market, Te Ohu Kai Moana managed to reach another agreement about a further transfer of fisheries with the Minister in charge of Treaty negotiations, Douglas Graham. The Crown bought and transferred to the Maori Fisheries Commisson, 50 percent of the shares of Sealord Products Limited at a cost of NZ$ 150 million. Since Sealord held about 26 percent of the total national fish quota, the interest transferred to Te Ohu Kai Moana amounted to 13 percent of commercial fishing quota, later referred to as post-settlement assets. By the end of 1992, along with the 10 percent of quota awarded in 1989, Te Ohu Kai Moana held approximately 23 percent of the total national fishing quota. At that time, the total assets of Te Ohu Kai Moana were estimated at a value of approximately NZ$ 400 million (Moon 1998).

The Sealord Deal was until then the largest settlement that had ever been signed between the New Zealand government and the Maori people, and yet it was extremely controversial from the outset. Many Maori were angry about the clause that made the deal binding on all Maori people, regardless of the question whether they had authorised the Deed of Settlement. In addition, the representativeness of the four Maori delegates on the Maori Fisheries Commission was frequently disputed. Notwithstanding these objections, the core of the agreement was upheld, although one additional concession was granted. Treaty of Waitangi rights covering fishing for personal or tribal consumption were retained and even new *mahinga kai* reserves ('traditional fishing grounds') were designated around the coast before the settlement was embodied into the Treaty of Waitangi (Fisheries Claims) Settlement Act 1992 (Ward 1999: 47).

After the fisheries settlement had passed into law, controversy surrounding the deal did not lessen. New Zealanders of European origin accused the government of introducing racist rules by establishing recreational fishing areas which were not accessible to the majority of the New Zealand population. At the same time, a number of Maori groups continued to challenge the binding force of the settlement in New Zealand courts and before the Waitangi Tribunal, without success. The Waitangi Tribunal concluded that there was a mandate for the settlement, provided the Treaty was not compromised, but this precisely was the overriding concern of the Maori groupings opposing the settlement (Walker 1994).

Tribes in Past and Present

In the mid-1990s the terms of the debate about the fisheries shifted from the principles of the settlement to the distribution of the settlement. The 1989 Act had ordered the commission to retain and manage the fisheries for the benefit of 'all Maori', but the 1992 Act instructed the commission to allocate the pre-settlement assets to its beneficiaries and to retain management only of Sealord shares. Although the 1992 Act also refers occasionally to the beneficiaries as 'all Maori', Maori tribes had obtained new prominence in the political arena of New Zealand and were therefore in a position to specify the distribution of the fisheries settlement to their advantage.

In the second half of the 1980s the Labour government introduced new economic policies to restructure the ailing economy. Government assets and enterprises were sold, and government departments were eliminated or downsized (Fleras 1991). The reorganisation of the government also affected the Department of Maori Affairs, which was almost completely devolved to tribal organisations or *iwi* authorities that were recognised under the Runanga Iwi Act 1990. This Act created a subnational structure of governance that linked the state to tribal organisations. Economic development programmes and social services were no longer provided by the centralised Department of Maori Affairs, but by tribal organisations. As a result, tribal organisations regained recognition and status at a time when Maori society was becoming more and more pan-tribal following the urbanisation of the Maori in the twentieth century (Van Meijl 1997). Some statistical data may clarify this.

By the end of the twentieth century the Maori made up about 15 percent of the New Zealand population totaling close to four million people. More than 80 percent of all Maori are living in urban areas, and less than 20 percent of the total Maori population is fluent in the Maori language. In addition, it is significant that nearly 30 percent of all self-identified urbanised Maori cannot or will not identify with any tribal organisation, *iwi* or *hapuu* (Statistics New Zealand 1998). Over the past twenty years this figure has been relatively stable, which is particularly telling in view of the political reconstitution of tribes in New Zealand and the long-term trend of increasing numbers of Maori acknowledging Maori descent and identifying ethnically as Maori (Cheater and Hopa 1997). These opposing tendencies of detribalisation and ethnic reidentification have also been noted by Maori academics, who even argue that unofficially at least 50 percent of all Maori do not maintain any active connections with their tribal organisations (Durie 1998, Walker 1996).

The ambiguous demographic profile of the Maori population also influenced the discussion about the distribution of the fisheries after the Sealord deal had been sealed. Although the Runanga Iwi Act had been repealed by the National Government immediately after re-election in 1990, it left a legacy of a strong centralised structure of tribal organisations which had a far-reaching influence on the debate about Treaty claims and settlements, including the fisheries, at least until the mid-1990s. The struggle about the distribution of the fisheries became therefore a continuation of the struggle to qualify as *iwi* brought about by the introduction of the Runanga Iwi Act. Here it must be reiterated that *iwi* is generally translated as 'tribe', whereas the literal meaning is 'bone' or 'people'. Against this background a profound controversy emerged regarding whether the fisheries should be distributed among tribal organisation or among 'all Maori', including pan-tribal organisations (Levine 2002).

Initially the terms of the debate were formulated by Te Ohu Kai Moana, whose viewpoint was fairly straightforward: the fisheries have been dispossessed from Maori tribes, and should therefore be returned to tribal ownership. There was no discussion about the meaning of the term *iwi*, which in the opinion of the fisheries commission referred exclusively to traditional tribes. The main characteristics of *iwi* were summed up as: sharing descent from ancestors; comprising a number of *hapuu* or sub-tribes; having a number of *marae* or traditional ceremonial centres, usually including an ancestral meeting-house; belonging historically to a *takiwa* or territory; and, finally, having an existence that has traditionally been acknowledged by other *iwi*. This definition of *iwi* has recently been deconstructed by the New Zealand anthropologist Steven Webster (2002:

350-52), who has argued that *iwi* nor *hapuu* are generally not nearly as stable as the Maori representatives of Te Ohu Kai Moana, all tribal chiefs, would like to establish. Maori society has traditionally had an extremely flexible kinship system, characterised by ambilineal descent and ambilateral affiliation, which also explain the waxing and waning of tribes over time. Accordingly, the number of *iwi* has increased and decreased throughout colonial history (Ballara 1998).

The recent redoubling of *iwi* nicely illustrates that *iwi*, unlike *hapuu*, which constitute the core groups of the Maori kinship system, may rise and decline opportunistically in response to changing sociopolitical and economic conditions (Webster 2002: 358). Te Ohu Kai Moana, however, simply brushed aside the foundational differences between *hapuu* and *iwi* by extending the constitutive principle of descent lines from lower ranking *hapuu* to higher ranking *iwi*. Thus, it imposed simultaneously an unprecedented hierarchical subordination of *hapuu* to *iwi* on the basis of a kinship ideology that concealed the sociopolitical and economic motivation of this strategy, in this case the distribution of the fisheries assets.

The irony of the influential position of Te Ohu Kai Moana, too, is that its model of the structure of Maori sociopolitical organisation is rooted in anthropological accounts drawn up in the beginning of the twentieth century, notably by the famous Raymond Firth (1959 [1929]), who, in turn, based his interpretations on the impressive corpus of ethnographic data that were collected by the legendary Elsdon Best towards the end of the nineteenth century (e.g., Best 1941 [1924]). This intellectual pedigree of the essentialist construction of Maori tribal organisations relied on by Te Ohu Kai Moana also betrays the legacy of the structural-functionalist tradition of academic research (see also Van Meijl 1995). In consequence, it may be argued that the proposal of the fisheries commission to allocate the fisheries assets exclusively to *iwi* is not primarily grounded in a vision of tribes as survivals of the past. Te Ohu Kai Moana is no longer concerned with a representation of the historic past, but only with a stereotypical representation of contemporary ideas about the past. In their worldview, *iwi* have become a simulacrum of the past, a copy of a copy, or a reconstructed simulation of the past as it was imagined by the informants of Elsdon Best (Barcham 2000: 147). Following Barthes (1957) it could also be argued that the tension around the position of Maori tribes in present-day New Zealand is brought about by the increasing discrepancy between their denotation, which has remained unchanged, and the connotations they evoke, which are indeed unprecedented.

The essentialised meaning of tribe in contemporary discourses in New Zealand compounds the debate about the realisation of historical and social justice for the Maori since it does not take into account that Maori property relationships have changed fundamentally in the course of colonial history. The persistent neglect of the transformation of concretised property relations is particularly acute since the property category of Maori fisheries has also been changed through the introduction of the quota system. The creation of new property categories and the changes in concretised property relations, however, are barely taken into consideration in the debate about the distribution of fishing quota which is dominated by contemporary transformations of historical tribes that have a vested interest in creating continuity by leaving old concepts untouched, in spite of their new meanings.

The resulting pastiche of historic styles in contemporary New Zealand exemplifies the inevitable influence of postmodernity on post-colonial Maori society, which itself follows from a weakening of historicity that is associated with a dramatic transformation of sociocultural conditions in the colonial era. Notwithstanding any historical explanation, the new construction of Te Ohu Kai Moana's image of the tribe or their simulacrum of traditional sociopolitical organisation has become Real (in the Lacanian sense of hyperreal, that is more than real) in contemporary New Zealand. It cannot be surprising, then, that the political dispute about the distribution of fishing quota revolved initially about the Maori concept of 'tribe', *iwi*.

Iwi versus *Iwi*

The first political confrontation over the definition of the concept of *iwi* and its implications for the distribution of the fisheries settlement did not involve pan-tribal groupings, but took place solely among tribes. Although the organisations favouring an exclusive allocation of fisheries assets to tribes had been branded as '*iwi* fundamentalists' (Levine and Henare 1994), even they could not agree on the criteria for making the allocations. Two opposing positions dominated the debate, causing roughly a division between southern and northern tribes. The southern Ngai Tahu tribes, supported by east coast North Island tribes, argued for allocation of quotas on the basis of the Maori dictum *mana whenua mana moana*: the right to fish the sea off their tribal land area. This position was clearly motivated by the long coastlines of these tribes who were relatively small in numbers. The opposite applied to their opponents, who were large in numbers but living on smaller territories with a shorter coastline. Hence they argued for allocations to be made on a per capita basis. Their arguments for this position was also grounded in tradition: they claimed that in the past only inshore fisheries had belonged to tribes and sub-tribes, but that deep sea fisheries had been shared among tribes without consideration for the length of their coastline (Webster 2002: 354). Since the historical evidence for this point is rather thin, there was little doubt that this position was also motivated by contemporary concerns.

This divergence over the ownership of fisheries among tribes raised the question whether *iwi* constituted the appropriate channel for the government policy to return some of the resources that had been dispossessed in the past. As soon as these doubts began to arise, the tribal fundamentalists closed ranks and reached a compromise, based both on traditional fishing areas and on tribal numbers. The inshore quota were proposed to be distributed according to *mana whenua mana moana*, while the deep sea quota were proposed to be distributed 50 percent on the basis of *mana whenua mana moana*, and 50 percent on the basis of population numbers. This compromise, however, was never implemented since it was challenged on the part of both some tribal organisations and pan-tribal organisations.

The proposed allocation of 50 percent of all deep sea quota to the northern tribes was interpreted as being to their advantage, since only 20 percent of these were caught in their territorial waters. The northern tribes, however, were far more populous than the southern tribes. Ngai Tahu, for example, is one of the smallest Maori tribes in terms of population numbers but still it claimed almost the entire coastline of the South Island. The compromise about the distribution of the fisheries outlined above entitled them to almost 15 percent of all quota (Webster 2002: 358), yet this was still unacceptable to them since they argued their case purely on the basis of property rights. Tipene O'Regan, chief of the Ngai Tahu tribe on the South Island and chairperson of Te Ohu Kai Moana simply argued 'We do not want other people's assets, neither do we want them to have our Treaty assets' (O'Regan 1995: 92).

Thus, Ngai Tahu substantiated its position in the debate about the distribution of fisheries on the basis of Article II of the Treaty of Waitangi: their property rights had been violated and this breach of the

Treaty was to be redressed simply by restitution of resources that had been dispossessed in the past. During the conference of which this paper was a part, Hann described the goal of this strategy as 'historical justice', while Lashley (2000) introduced the term 'reparative justice'. This restricted interpretation of the Treaty focusing merely on Article II was contentious since it did not take into account the obligation of the Crown to provide social justice to all Maori for violation of Article III offering 'all the Rights and Privileges of British Subjects'. In view of the abominable socioeconomic indicators of the Maori population, the vast majority of whom are trapped into a vicious circle of poverty (Statistics New Zealand 1998), there can be no doubt that this obligation has also been breached. The New Zealand government is therefore required not only to provide historical or reparative justice to settle breaches of Article II, but also to provide redress for breaches of Article III by redistributing traditional resources among all Maori people, tribally affiliated and non-affiliated. Lashley (2000) has described this strategy aiming at social justice as 'distributive justice'. The main issue in this context is undoubtedly the need to find the right balance between historical justice and social justice (see also James, this volume), which will also become clear from the specific dispute between so-called 'traditional' tribes and pan-tribal organisations.

Tribal Organisations against Pan-tribal Organisations

The dispute about the need to provide social or distributive justice alongside historical or reparative justice has played a prominent role in the debate between the tribal organisations represented by Te Ohu Kai Moana and urban Maori authorities that were also seeking a share of the settlement. Over the past fifty years many urban groupings have established themselves as incorporations or trusts, for which they have to meet the same formal economic criteria as tribal organisations that were recognised under the Runanga Iwi Act or that were later recognised by Te Ohu Kai Moana (Maaka 1994). In their deliberations with the fisheries commission they argued that 80 percent of all Maori live in urban areas and that most are not living in their original tribal districts. In their view, urban Maori who were not living in their tribal 'homes' had to be included in the distribution of the fisheries since the settlement had referred not only to *iwi* but also to 'all Maori'. Their claim was further substantiated with reference to the shocking statistics of the Maori underclass in urban centres in New Zealand. Webster (2002: 355), however, has correctly criticised the stereotypical dichotomy in this respect: most tribal chiefs live in cities, while rural communities also suffer from urban problems associated with unemployment, drug abuse and high crime rates. This argument therefore moved to the background of their court case, which focused mainly on the notion of *iwi*, 'tribe' and/or 'people'.

In 1995 urban Maori authorities filed their case in the High Court, aiming at preventing the implementation of the policy proposal of Te Ohu Kai Moana to allocate fisheries assets exclusively to *iwi*. The claim proved too complex for the High Court, which avoided a decision and passed the case on to the Court of Appeal. In May 1996 the British Lord Robin Cooke of Thorndon eventually rendered the famous judgment in the Court of Appeal in which it was emphasised that the original Deed of Settlement was not for the benefit of selected groups of tribal Maori only. Instead, he argued that the Sealord deal should be considered a pan-Maori settlement of fisheries claims. His decision revolved around the meaning of the word *iwi*, which in his opinion referred to 'the Queen's subjects already living on the land and others yet to come' (Lashley 2000: 41). He defined *iwi* as 'nation people' and not as 'tribe'; he considered the concept of *hapuu* the correct Maori equivalent of both 'tribe' and 'sub-tribe' (ibid.). In consequence, Cooke ruled that the fisheries settlement was ultimately for the benefit of all Maori, including urban Maori, even if they have no coastline. Thus, the Court of Appeal established a precedent by giving *iwi* status to urban Maori people with no tribal affiliations.

Needless to say, this historic decision of the Court of Appeal was welcomed by pan-tribal communities, particularly since in their view it also opened up the avenue to health, educational and social contracts with the government that were previously denied to pan-tribal groupings because they did not have the status of tribal organisation. Pan-tribal leaders made clear that they did not want the valuable fishing quota, but that they instead wanted cash and a slice of shares held by Te Ohu Kai Moana. The chief executive of the Maori authority of west Auckland, Te Whanau o Waipareira Trust, even stated provocatively: 'The last thing urban Maori want to do is go fishing ...' (*New Zealand News* 1996, 2515: 23).

The *iwi* fundamentalists were, not surprisingly, agitated and annoyed about the landmark decision of the Court of Appeal to grant urban Maori the status of tribal authority and chose to take the case to the Privy Council in London, the highest legal body of the judicial system in the commonwealth nation of New Zealand. Their case centred on the definition and the interpretation of the concept of *iwi* in the ruling of the Court of Appeal. The tribal organisations argued that from a traditional Maori perspective the word *iwi* not only includes all lower ranking sectors of society, such as extended families (*whaanau*) and sub-tribes (*hapuu*), but also individual Maori without any tribal affiliation, even including those who are unable to identify their tribal affiliation (*New Zealand News* 1996, 2545: 33). Pan-tribal groupings, on the other hand, argued that they were reluctant to become dependent on tribal organisations, which they expected to privilege tribal communities in the distribution of the fishery settlement and to target the implementation of development programmes on their own, tribal relations.

In January 1997 the Privy Council invalidated the decision of the Court of Appeal on legal grounds, stating that its description of *iwi* was outside the bounds of the appeal it had considered. In consequence, the Privy Council argued it had no option but to refer the case back to the High Court. The five Lords of the Privy Council formulated specific questions for the High Court judge to consider, relating to whether the distribution of fisheries assets should go solely to *iwi* and/or bodies representing *iwi*, and, if so, did *iwi* mean only traditional Maori tribes (*New Zealand News* 1997, 2552: 3)?

In the High Court the urban Maori authorities argued again that early references to tribes, such as in the Treaty of Waitangi, involved *hapuu* instead of *iwi*, that many *iwi* were not constituted until the nineteenth century, that the earliest *iwi* were irregular and non-territorial formations usually united on an ad hoc basis, and, finally, that *iwi* were commonly defined arbitrarily by those in power, not on the basis of kinship or descent, but for political and economic expediency. *Iwi* fundamentalists, on the other hand, reiterated their position that all Maori could trace their descent from the founding ancestor of an *iwi*. Furthermore, their case was grounded in the outdated structural-functionalist, segmentary model of sociopolitical hierarchy, in which extended families and *hapuu* were subordinated to *iwi*, holding collective customary property rights to all subordinate – *whaanau* and *hapuu* – sectors of *iwi* territory and waters.

In another historic judgment on this case, Justice Paterson (1998: 82) ruled that all Maori fisheries assets can only be allocated to *iwi* or bodies representing *iwi*. He further ruled that in terms of the allocations of these assets, only 'traditional' Maori tribes qualified as *iwi*. Although his judgment was clear, Paterson seemed ambiguous when he emphasised that in his opinion Te Ohu Kai Moana did have a duty to ensure that the fisheries' settlement catered adequately for all beneficiaries, including Maori members of urban Maori authorities, because, as he argued, 'urbanisation of Maori has made it very difficult for many Maori to retain active tribal links' (ibid.: 35).

The ambiguity in Paterson's judgment and the references to the urban profile of the Maori population induced urban Maori authorities again to appeal the decision. Justice Paterson's indications of inequality among the Maori population also entailed that henceforth claims of poverty reinforced the case of the urban Maori authorities. According to Webster (1998), however, these probably reflected increasing differences of social class among the Maori population at large. In the 1990s, 11 percent of Maori became more impoverished, but at the same time the small proportion of a relatively prosperous, mostly tribal elite increased from 3.4 percent to 7.7 percent of the Maori population (Lashley 2000: 45-46). Among this group was probably the membership of Te Ohu Kai Moana and some of its beneficiaries, who received almost NZ$ 5 million in fees between 1993 and 1999. Over the years, the chairperson of the fisheries commission was even paid a total of NZ$ 2.1 million in fees for managing the fisheries (*New Zealand Herald*, 17 May 2003). In this context, Elisabeth Rata (2000) has coined the oxymoron 'neotribal capitalism'.

In October 1999 the New Zealand Court of Appeal upheld Justice Paterson's interpretation of *iwi*. Interestingly, however, two of the five Appeal Court judges were dissenters with respect to the decision, supporting the urban view that the commission was not required to allocate solely to *iwi* (*New Zealand News*, 27 October 1999: 6). The split decision of the Court of Appeal provided the pan-tribal groups with sufficient inspiration to take the case to the Privy Council again, but in the ultimate judgment on this case, at least for the time being, it unanimously dismissed the appeal and upheld the decisions of the New Zealand courts that the fisheries must be allocated to *iwi*, and that *iwi* means 'traditional' tribes (Berry 2001). To uphold the suspense surrounding this case the Privy Council did add that in view of the appeals and cross-appeals in New Zealand courts perhaps the Minister of Fisheries would find political reasons to review the settlement in consultation with Maori leaders and ensure that in spite of the exclusive allocation of assets to *iwi*, 'all Maori' would benefit.

The conclusion to be drawn from this judgment on the Maori fisheries is that the urban Maori authorities have been the legal losers of this controversial case, but at the same time they seem to have booked a political victory, testified both by the ruling of Judge Paterson and by the final suggestion of the Privy Council to reconsider the foundations of the settlement signed in 1992. This political progression has been endorsed by a landmark ruling of the Waitangi Tribunal in 1998, giving one of the main claimant urban Maori authorities, Te Whanau o Waipareira Trust, negotiating status with the government as '*iwi*' (Waitangi Tribunal 1998). In their claim to the Tribunal the group from west Auckland had argued: 'Waipareira is not an *iwi* but is *iwi*' (ibid.: 6), and the Tribunal accepted that '(t)oday, "*iwi*" can mean either the people of a place or a large tribe composed of several dispersed groups' (ibid.: 18). This report of the Waitangi Tribunal resulted in some social welfare programmes for pan-tribal Maori communities in Auckland, while in the fisheries debate it also necessitated the formulation of a new proposal for the distribution of the settlement assets that acknowledges pan-tribal interests.

When the Labour Party was able to form the new government after the elections in 1999 it reorganised Te Ohu Kai Moana and appointed several new commissioners who are not unsympathetic towards urban Maori interests. In 2000 the chairman of the commission, formerly the chief of the main South Island tribe, was also replaced by a younger Maori leader with affiliations to the northern Muriwhenua tribes, a Harvard degree and some business experience. After a long round of new consultations with all tribal and pan-tribal groupings he submitted a new proposal for the distribution of fisheries to the Minister of Fisheries in May 2003.

The proposal contains a model for the allocation of fisheries assets, key features of which are that all inshore quota will be allocated to *iwi* using a coastline formula, while all deep sea quota will be allocated to *iwi* through a 75 percent *iwi* population and a 25 percent *iwi* coastline formula (*mana whenua mana moana*). In addition, the commission is proposing to allocate NZ$ 20.7 million to *iwi* using an *iwi* population formula, while at the same time a NZ$ 20 million trust will be established to support Maori, including those who do not know or choose not to associate with their *iwi* (*New Zealand Herald*, 7 April 2003). At present, the market value of Te Ohu Kai Moana's holdings has increased to approximately NZ$ 700 million, amounting to control of about one-third of New Zealand's commercial fisheries.

After eleven years of heated legal and verbal arguments, this proposal is now supported by 93.1 percent of *iwi* representing 96.7 percent of *iwi*-affiliated Maori (Reed 2003). It continues to be controversial for many northern tribes, however, arguing that the South Island's Ngai Tahu will receive more than NZ$ 86 million, while North Island's Ngapuhi, for example, with more than three times the population of the South Island *iwi*, will receive not more than NZ$ 22 million (ibid.). Most tribal organisations, however, have accepted that after the protracted litigation in the 1990s a better distribution formula is not likely, let alone that consensus be reached. The South Island tribe, however, continued its objections against the current proposal as a further violation of their property rights guaranteed under Article II of the Treaty of Waitangi. In June 2003 they filed a claim in the High Court for judicial review against the Minister of Fisheries after he formally accepted the latest proposal of Te Ohu Kai Moana (*New Zealand Herald*, 9 June 2003), but in November they lost their battle against the proposed fisheries allocation model (Chapple 2003). At the moment, only pan-tribal groupings continue to advocate for more than the NZ$ 20 million earmarked for them in the current proposal. In the latest allocation model Maori who live distanced and removed from their *iwi* receive less than 3 percent, whereas most Maori nowadays live in cities and for them tribal connections have little meaning. Not surprisingly, therefore, they have also initiated a last ditch court action to stop the distribution of Maori fisheries assets.[2] Thus, tribal and pan-tribal groupings continue to contest each other's basis of authority over the distribution of the funds, resources and compensation settlements devolved by government to Maori management and ownership.

Concluding Remarks

The dramatic dispute about the distribution of fish resources in post-colonial Maori society disproves the popular saying that big fish eat small fish, since it demonstrates that small fish also eat big fish, while most fish do not eat any other fish at all. The protracted deadlock in the dispute about the distribution of fishing quota in contemporary Maori society follows from the ambiguity surrounding notions of eligibility to historical and contemporary ownership, compounded recently by the changing properties of Maori property rights to fish resources following the introduction of a quota system. There is no disagreement that all Maori should benefit from the new government policies to redress legitimate Maori grievances about the dispossession of their lands and natural resources, including fisheries, in the nineteenth century. The problem is only how to achieve justice in a fair and equitable manner (Barcham 1998; Bourassa and Strong 2000; Van Meijl and Goldsmith 2003). Maori property rights are not disputed in principle, but the question of how to restore them in practice cannot be answered without ambivalence (Maaka and Fleras 2000).

The ambiguity of political reality in contemporary Maori society is not simply the result of colonial history, but predates the arrival of Europeans in New Zealand. Maori society was characterised by an inherently flexible sociopolitical structure. Kinship was organised by ambilineal descent and ambilaterial affiliation, while leadership was guided primarily by primogeniture, usually in the male line, but this principle was simultaneously complemented by achievement. As a corollary, Maori individuals always had the option to change their position within society, either by affiliating to another kinship line or to improve their ranking within the political hierarchy. The structure of relationships within Maori sociopolitical organisation may not have changed fundamentally in the colonial period. The transformation of the context of Maori society since the colonisation of New Zealand has only widened the range of options for Maori individuals, which makes the contemporary situation even more complex.

The dispossession of the Maori in the nineteenth century and the large-scale urbanisation of Maori in the twentieth century have resulted in a situation in which more than 80 percent of Maori are living in urban environments. The implication of the migration of many Maori for the sociopolitical organisation of their society has been, first, that Maori claims to multiple affiliations or membership to more than one tribe have multiplied and, second, that large numbers of Maori have lost affiliation to their descent lines. At present, 70 percent of all Maori are not living within their own tribal district and almost 30 percent of all Maori are no longer familiar with their tribal affiliations. This situation makes it very complicated to redress the grievances of all Maori people.

The complexity of the social and political organisation of contemporary Maori society is not reflected in the legal frameworks of New Zealand. The legal situation in New Zealand is also complex but for different reasons, while its implementation is based on an objectified and therefore simplified interpretation of the complexity in Maori society and the historical changes that have taken place therein. New Zealand law regarding the position of the country's indigenous population has changed dramatically since the recent recognition of a Treaty that was signed more than 160 years ago. This occurred in the same decade as the government made the political mistake of introducing fishing quota without contemplating the necessity to provide compensation to Maori people for the dispossession of their fisheries, which were protected explicitly by the Treaty of Waitangi. The compelling connection between these political developments in the 1980s made it inevitable for the powers that be in New Zealand to establish justice for past wrongs.

Successive governments in New Zealand have since opted for a strategy of historical or reparative justice by returning lands and natural resources to so-called 'traditional' tribal organisations. Their essentialist interpretation of sociopolitical organisation in Maori society of the nineteenth century, however, is rooted in the structural-functionalist tradition of research dating from the beginning of the twentieth century, in which the characteristic flexibility of Maori society was subordinated in a segmentary model of structural hierarchy. This relatively unambiguous framework for the interpretation of sociopolitical relationships within Maori society can never do justice to the inherent ambiguity of contemporary Maori society that has even been reinforced by colonial history. The changes in Maori property relationships are perforce to be taken into account lest the creation of historical justice leads to new forms of social injustice within Maori society.

The current strategy to establish justice aims principally at providing reparation for property rights that were taken unfairly and unlawfully. In terms of the Treaty of Waitangi government policies are grounded mainly in Article II, but the Crown is also obliged to redress the violation of Article III of the Treaty, which guaranteed all Maori households and individuals the benefits and privileges of citizenship. The New Zealand academic Andrew Sharp (1997 [1990]: 36) has described the strategy of historical or reparative justice therefore as a 'form of conservative justice'. Reparative justice is problematic to the extent that it presents itself as reactionary justice by focusing exclusively on historical conditions, without taking into account the transformation of the past or the dynamics of the present. A strategy of historical or reparative justice, therefore, is to be complemented by a strategy of social or distributive justice to provide compensation for breaches of Article III to all Maori, tribal and pan-tribal, in both rural and urban environments. The ultimate challenge is to create an inter-temporal balance between historical and social justice.

Note

1. *Wi Parata v. The Bishop of Wellington and the Attorney General* (1877) 3 N.Z. Jur (N.S.) SC 72.
2. After 14 years of litigation, the last proposal for the distribution of Maori fishing quota that is mentioned above was finally included in the Maori Fisheries Act in 2004. It will probably be implemented as of the year 2006.

References

Ballara, A. 1998. *Iwi: The Dynamics of Maaori Tribal Organisation from c. 1769 to c. 1945.* Wellington: Victoria University Press.

Barcham, M. 1998. 'The Challenge of Urban Maori: Reconciling Conceptions of Indigeneity and Social Change', *Pacific Viewpoint* 39(3): 303–14.

—— 2000. '(De)Constructing the Politics of Indigeneity', in *Political Theory and the Rights of Indigenous Peoples*, eds D. Ivison, P. Patton and W. Sanders, Cambridge: Cambridge University Press, 137–51.

Barthes, R. 1957. *Mythologies.* Paris: Éditions du Seuil.

Benda-Beckmann, F. von and K. von Benda-Beckmann 1999. 'A Functional Analysis of Property Rights, with Special Reference to Indonesia', in *Property Rights and Economic Development: Land and Natural Resources in Southeast Asia and Oceania*, eds T. van Meijl and F. von Benda-Beckmann, London/New York: Kegan Paul International, 15–56.

Berry, R. 2001. 'Setback for Urban Maori', *New Zealand Herald*, 3 July 2001.

Best, E. 1941 [1924]. *The Maori.* Wellington: The Polynesian Society, Memoirs of the Polynesian Society, vol. V.

Bourassa, S.C. and A.L. Strong 2000. 'Restitution of Fishing Rights to Maori: Representation, Social Justice and Community Development', *Pacific Viewpoint* 41(2): 155–75.

Chapple, I. 2003. 'Ngai Tahu Loses Battle over Fisheries Allocation Model', *New Zealand Herald*, 7 November 2003.

Cheater, A. and N. Hopa 1997. 'Representing Identity', in *After Writing Culture: Epistemology and Praxis in Contemporary Anthropology*, eds A. James, J. Hockey and A. Dawson, London/New York: Routledge, 208–23.

Durie, M. 1998. *Te Mana, Te Kaawanatanga: The Politics of Maaori Self-Determination.* Auckland: Oxford University Press.

Firth, R. 1959 [1929]. *Economics of the New Zealand Maori.* Wellington: Government Printer, Shearer.

Fleras, A. 1991. '"Tuku Rangatiratanga": Devolution in Iwi-Government Relations', in *Nga Take; Ethnic Relations and Racism in Aotearoa/New Zealand*, eds P. Spoonley, D. Pearson and C. Macpherson, Palmerston North: Dunmore, 171–93.

Hackshaw, F. 1989. 'Nineteenth Century Notions of Aboriginal Title and their Influence on the Interpretation of the Treaty of Waitangi', in *Waitangi: Maori and Pakeha Perspectives of the Treaty of Waitangi*, ed. I.D. Kawharu, Auckland: Oxford University Press, 92–120.

Helgason, A. and G. Pálsson 1997. 'Contested Commodities: The Moral Landscape of Modernist Regimes', *The Journal of the Royal Anthropological Institute* 3(3): 451–71.

Kawharu, I.H. 1977. *Maori Land Tenure: Studies of a Changing Institution*. Oxford: Oxford University Press.

——— , ed. 1989. *Waitangi: Maori and Pakeha Perspectives of the Treaty of Waitangi*. Auckland: Oxford University Press.

Lashley, M.E. 2000. 'Implementing Treaty Settlements via Indigenous Institutions: Social Justice and Detribalisation in New Zealand', *The Contemporary Pacific* 12(1): 1–55.

Levine, H. 2002. 'The Maori Iwi – Contested Meanings in Contemporary Aotearoa/New Zealand', in *Politics of Indigeneity in the South Pacific: Recent Problems of Identity in Oceania*, eds E. Kolig and H. Mückler, Hamburg: Lit Verlag, 73–83.

Levine, H. and M. Henare 1994. 'Mana Maori Motuhake: Maori Self-determination', *Pacific Viewpoint* 35(2): 193–210.

Maaka, R. 1994. 'The New Tribe: Conflicts and Continuities in the Social Organization of Urban Maori', *The Contemporary Pacific* 6(2): 311–36.

Maaka, R. and A. Fleras 2000. 'Engaging with Indigeneity: Tino Rangatiratanga in Aotearoa', in *Political Theory and the Rights of Indigenous Peoples*, eds D. Ivison, P. Patton and W. Sanders, Cambridge: Cambridge University Press, 89–109.

McHugh, P. 1991. *The Maori Magna Carta: New Zealand Law and the Treaty of Waitangi*. Auckland: Oxford University Press.

Meijl, T. van 1995. 'Maori Socio-Political Organization in Pre- and Proto-History; On the Evolution of Post-Colonial Constructs', *Oceania* 65(4): 304–22.

——— 1997. 'The Re-emergence of Maori Chiefs; "Devolution" as a Strategy to Maintain Tribal Authority', in *Chiefs Today; Traditional Pacific Leadership and the Postcolonial State*, eds G.M. White and L. Lindstrom, Stanford: Stanford University Press, 84–107.

Meijl, T. van and M. Goldsmith 2003. 'Introduction: Recognition, Redistribution and Reconciliation in Postcolonial Settler Nation-States', *The Journal of the Polynesian Society* 112(3): 205–18. (Special Issue on 'Postcolonial Dilemmas: Reappraising Justice and Identity in New Zealand and Australia', eds T. van Meijl and M. Goldsmith).

Moon, P. 1998. 'The Creation of the "Sealord Deal"', *The Journal of the Polynesian Society* 107(2): 145–74.

New Zealand Herald 2003. 'Fisheries Commission Sends Proposal to Iwi', 7 April 2003.

——— 2003. 'Hodgson Gives Nod to $700m Fishery Model', 9 June 2003.

New Zealand News 1996. 'Urban Maori Win Share of Fisheries', 8 May 1996, 2515: 23.

——— 1996. 'Language a Barrier in Historic Hearing', 4 December 1996, 2545: 33.

—— 1997a. 'Urban Maori Decision Overruled', 22 January 1997, 2552: 3.

—— 1997b. 'Urban Maori Claim Rejected', 27 October 1997, page 6

Norman, W. 1989. 'The Muriwhenua Claim', in *Waitangi: Maori and Pakeha Perspectives of the Treaty of Waitangi*, ed. I.D. Kawharu, Auckland: Oxford University Press, 180–210.

O'Regan, T. 1995. 'A Ngai Tahu Perspective on Some Treaty Questions', in *Treaty Settlements: The Unfinished Business*, ed. G. McLay, Wellington: New Zealand Institute of Advanced Legal Studies and Victoria University of Wellington Law Review, 88–104.

Orange, C. 1987. *The Treaty of Waitangi*. Wellington: Allen & Unwin/Port Nicholson.

Paterson, B.J. 1998. *Maori Fisheries Case: Decision on Preliminary Question Remitted by Privy Council*. Auckland: High Court, 4 August 1998.

Rata, E. 2000. *A Political Economy of Neotribal Capitalism*. Lanham: Lexington.

Reed, G. 2003. 'Reeling in the Decades', *New Zealand Herald*, 17 May 2003.

Sharp, A. 1997 [1990]. *Justice and the Maori: The Philosophy and Practice of Maori Claims in New Zealand since the 1970s*. Auckland: Oxford University Press.

Sorrenson, M.P.K. 1989. 'Towards a Radical Reinterpretation of New Zealand History: The Role of the Waitangi Tribunal', in *Waitangi: Maori and Pakeha Perspectives of the Treaty of Waitangi*, ed. I.D. Kawharu, Auckland: Oxford University Press, 158–78.

Statistics New Zealand 1998. *New Zealand Now: Maori*. Wellington: Statistics New Zealand (Te Tari Tatau).

Waitangi Tribunal 1988. *Muriwhenua Fishing Report* (Wai–22). Wellington: Waitangi Tribunal.

—— 1998. *Te Whanau o Waipareira Report* (Wai 414). Wellington: GP Publications.

Walker, R. 1990. *Ka Whawhai Tonu Matou: Struggle without End*. Auckland: Penguin.

—— 1994. 'Maori Issues', *The Contemporary Pacific* 6(1): 183–85.

—— 1996. *Ngaa Pepa a Ranginui: The Walker Papers*. Auckland: Penguin.

Ward, A. 1999. *An Unsettled History: Treaty Claims in New Zealand Today*. Wellington: Bridget Williams.

Webster, S. 1997. 'Maori Hapuu and their History', *The Australian Journal of Anthropology* 8(3): 307–35.

—— 1998. *Patrons of Maori Culture: Power, Theory and Ideology in the Maori Renaissance*. Dunedin: Otago University Press.

—— 2002. 'Maori Retribalization and Treaty Rights to the New Zealand Fisheries', *The Contemporary Pacific* 14(2): 341–76.

Chapter 9

How Communal is Communal and Whose Communal is It? Lessons from Minangkabau*

Franz and Keebet von Benda-Beckmann

Introduction

In most literature on property, communal property figures as one of the four major categories, besides private individual ownership, state ownership and open access. These categories are building stones in the construction of theoretical propositions concerning the evolution of property rights and of the relationships between property types and their economic and/or ecological significance.[1] 'Communal' or 'common' property is perhaps the most general and most misleading concept pervading interpretations of property systems, academic theories and policies. It has had mainly negative economic and civilisational connotations ever since the nineteenth century. Individual private ownership was taken as an important indicator of social and legal evolution as well as the backbone of capitalist economic progress. Communal property rights, by contrast, were dismissed as a sign of backwardness and economic inefficiency, as an obstacle to economic development and commercial production. This applied both to 'primitive communism' and to twentieth century socialist property in communist states. Government policies inspired and legitimated by such theories were directed against communal property, especially with respect to productive resources. Only in very recent times has communal property gained some respectability, but this is limited to its assumed usefulness for sustainable resource management and nature protection.

* We thank Chris Hann, Jacqueline Knörr and Melanie Wiber for their thoughtful comments. For a long and detailed version see F. and K. von Benda-Beckmann 2004.

Theories and policies based on these assumptions have not been very successful.[2] A basic reason is that the category is not well suited as a descriptive device or as a basis for theories or policies. For example, communal property may comprise different kinds of rights, as in ownership to complexes of inherited lineage property, village commons, state land, or the inheritance of mankind. Furthermore, it comprises a wide variety of collectives, ranging from a few individuals, to larger groups, entire villages, the state, and even 'mankind'.[3] And the rights of the members of such collectives, and the resultant complex combinations of possible groups vary considerably. Moreover, communal or common property was mainly theorised at the level of categorical property rights, that is abstract categories and general rule sets that define generalised types of property objects, holders and the relationships between them.[4] Little attention was given to the nature and distribution of concrete property relations that connect actual property objects and holders. Moreover, other functions of property, such as its significance for social security, the continuity of social groups and as the source of political power were not considered.

Assuming more or less uniform intrinsic functions for such a broad category is not warranted. As we shall demonstrate with the example of the Minangkabau of West Sumatra, very different coexisting types of communal property may undergo radically different developments, while the economic function they obtain is more a result of government misrepresentation and regulation than of intrinsic characteristics of the property rights per se.

Minangkabau matrilineal and economic organisation puzzled nineteenth- and early twentieth-century observers, travellers, scientists and civil servants, who were thinking in evolutionist terms. If communal stood for an evolutionary 'early' and therefore backward mode of social (property) organisation, matrilineal relations were doubly backward, given their 'unnatural' neglect of the father-children relationship. Yet the 'matriarchal' Minangkabau were obviously much more 'advanced' culturally, economically and technologically than many patrilineal communities the Dutch encountered elsewhere in the Indonesian archipelago. Moreover, they were devout Muslims. How could these seemingly contradictory principles of social organisation and inheritance patterns be reconciled?

Minangkabau is also interesting because it has two rather distinct forms of communal property. One is the inherited property of matrilineages (*pusako*) that comprises both immaterial and material goods, notably irrigated rice fields. The other form is *ulayat*, or village commons, the part of the village territory that was not used for sedentary agriculture and that fell under the control of the village council or the heads of the village's matriclans. Both property forms became embedded in different ways in the plural legal system and subject to different struggles between villagers, state agencies and proponents of Islam.

We shall first deal with the complex of *pusako* property and inheritance and discuss how categorical and concretised relationships to *pusako* have been influenced by the struggle over inheritance, the incorporation into the state administration and social and economic changes. Then we shall turn to the village commons for a similar analysis. The history of various Minangkabau property forms shows interesting differential continuities and discontinuities in both categorical and concretised property rights. We demonstrate that a remarkable continuity in categorical property relations and of the basic principles of matrilineal organisation, can coexist with quite different constellations of concretised property relationships, in which conjugal and patrifiliative relationships play a considerable role. This helps us to understand why the disappearance or breakdown of matriliny in Minangkabau, predicted for the past hundred years, has not occurred (Schrieke 1955; Maretin 1961). Our discussion will also help to clarify current legal and political debates over the place of communal property in Minangkabau, debates that do not sufficiently distinguish between quite different sets of rights to *pusako* and *ulayat*.

The *pusako* Complex

The Minangkabau were organised in localised matriclans, consisting of matrilineages headed by a titled lineage head (*panghulu*). The council of the lineage heads of the founding matrilineages formed the government of rather autonomous villages (*nagari*). Villages were endogamous, post-marital residence being uxorilocal. In *adat*[5] law and philosophy, the lineage members form a social, political and economic unit. They are 'one' in many respects. They are descended from 'one womb'. They share the leadership of one lineage head, the hereditary title of their lineage and their common material property, their *harato pusako*. This lineage property-people complex is a constituent unit in the economic and political constitution of Minangkabau villages.

External Unity and Internal Differentiation

The category of inherited property (*pusako*) comprises material and immaterial goods, the most important of which are the titles of lineage heads, immovable goods, especially irrigated rice fields and lineage houses, and movables such as ceremonial clothes and jewellery. What in external relations is conceived of and treated as common or shared, is internally a highly differentiated property complex. Different kinds of inherited property are distinguished according to who originally acquired it, and the means by which it had been acquired. Subgroups thus have different rights to parts of the property. First and foremost is the property that the ancestors of the lineage members created through their cultivation of the jungle, which descends and is to be shared in continuity through the generations by all lineage members who can trace their matrilineal descent from these ancestors. This property, also called 'high *pusako*', is distributed as primary allocation (*ganggam bauntuek*) to sublineages identified by the eldest female and in principle is held and transmitted within this specific sublineage for perpetuity. Primary allocations revert to the whole lineage only if the sublineage 'dies out', that is, when the women in the group have no more female descendants to continue the descent line. High *pusako* can be subject to redistribution if the demographic and economic developments of the sublineages make redistribution desirable. Such attempts to reallocate *pusako* regularly led to serious conflicts between sublineages and often resulted in lineage splits. A second internal differentiation of property rights is the result of the inheritance of property that has been self-acquired (*harato pancaharian*) by one of the lineage members, and which subsequently accrues to the inherited property of the members of their sublineage. In lineages that have incorporated strangers from other villages or descendants of former slaves, there is a third differentiating mechanism. Their rights to those parts of the *pusako* awarded to them remain conditional on their proper behaviour towards the original lineage, and they have no claims to the lineage *pusako* of those who trace their descent from the common matrilineal ancestress. Male lineage members can be given parts of the lineage property at or after marriage to support their conjugal family. Such property, however, would in principle revert to the lineage after their death.

In all matters of external relationships and political authority, the people-property complex is treated as 'one' and is represented by the lineage head in transactions and disputes. Decisions about external transactions, such as pawning of *pusako* rice fields, or group internal allocation and inheritance of rights to *pusako* have to be taken by processes of common deliberation of all adult lineage members. In these processes the responsible mother's brother, the lineage and sublineage head has to take care that these processes are followed. The senior woman who controls the *pusako* rice-land also has an important say in these processes.[6]

Communalising and Individualising Mechanisms: The Pusakoisation of Pancaharian and the Pancaharianisation of Pusako

Lineage members had considerable freedom over their self-acquired property as long as such dealings involved normal economic exchanges. But they could not permanently give it away to non-lineage members, the classical case being a father wanting to give property to his children. Such transactions would require the consent of all lineage members. Self-acquired property was destined to become inherited property, and the future heirs would have to consent to any transfer which threatened their future inheritance. In Minangkabau conceptualisation, self-acquired property therefore was often referred to as 'low *pusako*' during the property-holder's lifetime and thus was treated as if it had already been inherited. It was 'inherited property in chrysalis state' (Willinck 1909: 584). The *pusako* system is thus predominantly conceived in diachronic terms. For any holder of a right to *pusako* property, the term implies past and future inheritance according to matrilineal rules.

The main function of *pusako* was to provide economic resources for the subsequent generations of lineage members. Permanent alienation was prohibited; only temporary transfers through pawning and donation were recognised. Pawned property could always be redeemed. In principle, the whole (sub)lineage should redeem pawned *pusako*, the individuals or subgroups contributing equally. In that case, the property would retain full *pusako* status and primary allocation rights to it would be distributed to the sublineages. If, however, the group as a whole did not want to redeem a rice field, individual members of the *pusako* holding group could do so. While the redeemed property retained its residual status as *pusako* of the whole group, the right to economically exploit the rice fields was treated as self-acquired property for the person or sublineage that had redeemed it. After death, such *pancaharian*ised rights to *pusako* property would form a separate *pusako* complex for the redeemer's heirs.

Other group members, however, could at any time pay their share of the redemption costs and thus acquire a share in the land.

Challenges to the *pusako* System

The *pusako* system has been challenged for a number of reasons and by various influences, including: Islam, the colonial government and later the Indonesian government. In addition, socioeconomic factors also put pressure on the system.

Changing Inheritance and Islamic Law

Islamic law was a competitor to property *adat* well before colonisation.[7] For the proponents of true Islam, the *pusako* system with its dominant matrilineal principles for structuring political authority over people, resources and succession was a heathen practice and therefore prohibited for Muslims. Matrilineal rules of inheritance were in flagrant contradiction to the rules of Islamic inheritance law with its strong patrilineal bias. But the property struggles and negotiations between Islamic and *adat* leaders changed in intensity over time. The fiercest struggle took place in the beginning of the nineteenth century during the Padri war, in which orthodox Islamic leaders attempted to establish a theocracy in Minangkabau. This war led to the Dutch intervention and the incorporation of Minangkabau into the colony of the Dutch East Indies. The Dutch colonial government supported the *adat* proponents against the orthodox Islamic movement as they thought that the latter would present a greater danger to colonial rule. They built their indirect rule on the basis of the *nagari-pusako* system, and recognised and maintained the *adat pusako* as the valid property law in Minangkabau.

The front line of Islamic attack was on the inheritance of self-acquired property. It was a double attack against the communal nature of kin property and against the limitations of individual freedom over self-acquired property. The main bone of contention was men bequeathing property by gifts or testament to their children. Islamic pressure was aimed at transforming inheritance rules from the matrilineal to the Islamic system. The classical conflict in matrilineal societies between a man's children and his matrilineal nephews and nieces thus was exacerbated by Islamic law. It was also fuelled by social and economic changes. The new educational system and migration had led to changing patterns of residence and closer social and economic bonds between spouses and their children. Social and economic authority began to gradually shift away from the mother's brother to the parents, with a resulting desire to transmit properties that were used in the conjugal family within it. This development was supported by Dutch administrators and judges, in whose eyes the matrilineal inheritance was 'unnatural' anyway. Inheritance law and practice for self-acquired property gradually changed. An important development was the recognition in the 1930s that a man could bequeath his self-acquired property by gift or testament to his children without the consent of his matrilineal relatives. In practice, the children and the matrilineal relatives usually worked out some form of compromise about the inheritance of self-acquired property. Depending on the quality of family relations this could be a friendly process but it could also result in serious and protracted disputes before village authorities or the state courts (K. von Benda-Beckmann 1981, 1985).

After Independence, two major meetings were held in which religious and *adat* leaders, university academics, judges, and local politicians participated.[8] They agreed that *pusako* property should remain governed by matrilineal rules of inheritance. Property self-acquired during marriage was to be divided by half between the surviving spouse and the heirs. The latter would inherit according to Islamic inheritance law. In line with Islamic inheritance law, a person would be allowed to make a testament for up to one third of the self-acquired property (Naim 1968: 243). These meetings and their conclusions attempted to undermine the conceptual and temporal logic of the *pusako* system by redefining self-acquired property, including self-acquired property in the traditional sense, and property received by gift (*hibah*) and testament. Self-acquired property would retain its status after inheritance. It would continue to be inherited according to Islamic law and not become low *pusako* property as it would in *adat*. There would be no more growth of *pusako*.

These far reaching consequences have not emerged as expected. Today, it is a generally accepted practice that children inherit at least the major part of self-acquired property from their father. When inherited, whether by a man's children or his matrilineal heirs, it will become *pusako* for the heirs' respective sublineages. However, it still is a major issue in legal political debates whether this is done according to Islamic law or according to new *adat* law. Contrary to the conclusions of the 1952 and 1968 meetings, in 1968 the Supreme Court validated the change in intestate inheritance of self-acquired property as 'new *adat* law'.[9] Among ordinary people opinions are divided, but most people consider the change as changed *adat* and not as a replacement of *adat* by Islamic law. And even those who consider 'the inheritance by the children' as due to, or in accordance with Islamic law, do not bequeath property to all Islamic heirs.

Administrative and Judicial Transformation of the *pusako* System

The general principles and rules of the categorical *adat pusako* system have remained dominant for allocation, use and distribution of *pusako*. However, the (post-)colonial administration and courts made several attempts to change the system.

Standardisation and the Dissociation of Political and Property Units

One of the first major interventions was that the Dutch prohibited the establishment of new positions of lineage head in the 1880s.[10] This led to a gradual dissociation of the *panghulu* headed lineages and the emergence of sublineages, which became largely autonomous in *pusako* affairs. They had their own representative in property affairs (the mother's brother who is the head of the heirs, *mamak kepala waris*) without the official status of lineage head. A *panghulu* headed linage could comprise one or more of such sublineages. Although in village practice lineage splits continued and new *panghulu* titles were established, the status of such new groups and their relations to the sublineages became increasingly ambiguous, an ambiguity which continues into the present time.

This intervention affected mainly the external status of lineages and sublineages and the composition of subunits within lineages. For the major part of the nineteenth century the Dutch had little interest in internal lineage affairs, so long as they delivered coffee to Dutch marketing agencies under the policy of forced coffee production. This changed dramatically after the first decade of the twentieth century for a number of interrelated reasons. When the system of forced coffee production was abolished and a tax system was introduced, smaller and more coherent social groups with a clear representative were required. Besides, the *pusako* system became more important to the colonial government as it saw the *pusako* based rice economy as the basis for subsistence and restricted local trade (Kahn 1993). This invoked more systematic exploration and systematisation of Minangkabau *adat* by Dutch administrators and scholars of the *Adat* Law School.

The colonial administration introduced two important changes. First, lineage property was reinterpreted as communal or family ownership with the help of the interpretative schemes of Dutch common ownership and the distinction between public and private law. *Pusako* was interpreted as family ownership, located in the domain of private law. The family (lineage) was a legal community with common property and common administration. This external unity was translated into the internal structure of the group. The group internal rights of primary allocation (*ganggam bauntuek*) and the separate pool of inherited self-acquired property were suppressed and replaced with the notions of equal shares of all members in the pool of communally owned property (Adatrechtbundel 1910–1955, 6: 179). Secondly, the authority of the lineage and sublineage heads in external property affairs was strengthened. This reflected the Dutch desire to have one person responsible for the *pusako* complex also in non-tax affairs. The representative could now pawn *pusako* without the consent or acknowledgement of his matrilineal relatives in the cases allowed for in *adat* (Guyt 1936; F. and K. von Benda-Beckmann 1985: 264). In the courts and in villages the limitations for pawning were also loosened. 'Modern needs' such as paying school fees or paying for the costs of the pilgrimage were increasingly recognised as legitimate reasons for pawning. And the conditions under which the last members of an extinct lineage could sell *pusako* were softened.

However, these instances of Minangkabau 'lawyers' folk law' were not generally followed in the village or in disputing processes within the village and remained largely confined to cases brought to courts.[11] What was decided in court was often 're-*adat*ised' in village politics (K. von Benda-Beckmann 1985). But the reinterpretations increased the ambiguities of the *pusako* system and opened up new strategic avenues for manipulating claims in the courts.[12]

The Basic Agrarian Law and the Push for the Conversion of Property Rights

Fifteen years after Independence, the Basic Agrarian Law of 1960 introduced a powerful alternative to the *pusako* system. Its aim was to promote individualisation of communal lands by introducing individual titles and demanding conversion of *adat* land rights into the legal categories of the Law that were largely modelled after Dutch law. The most important category, *hak milik*, more or less corresponded to the notion of ownership. *Pusako* land of a lineage could be registered as one property right, but there was no provision for the registration of communally held land with all its differentiation.

The system of registration has been rather unsuccessful so far in West Sumatra. Despite recurring exhortations by the provincial government, programmes for cheap and efficient registration (PRONA) and a World Bank Project giving special attention to the registration of communal land, the programme has largely remained an 'empty dream castle'.[13] Besides the rather bureaucratic, time-consuming and often corrupt registration practices that are mainly held responsible for this failure, we think that a major reason lies in the nature of the Minangkabau property system and in the ways villagers interpret and compare this with the likely consequences of registration. Registering the whole property of a (sub)lineage would be extremely difficult and lead to innumerable conflicts. If it is only registered in the name of the group representative, people are afraid of loosing their rights. Moreover, people fear that with registration, land would obtain ownership status and would then be inheritable by the children of men. These concerns are certainly realistic, for in cases of registration, the land is often treated as freely disposable and inheritable by the children. Very little land with *pusako* status has been registered in rural areas. The little land that has been registered concerns specific plots of land, usually for houses.

Economic Change and Changing Concretised Property Relationships

*Pusako*isation of self-acquired property and the restrictions on transfers create the image of an ever-expanding *pusako* complex through the continuous addition of self-acquired property. But under the umbrella of lineage property, a variety of concretised rights to parts of that property could exist, changing over time through redistribution, pawning, redemption and inheritance. Pawning and redemption were the primary mechanism through which concretised rights to *pusako* could be temporarily and provisionally withdrawn from the normal allocation within the lineage under the control of the elder women and the lineage head. Such cases seem to have occurred on a rather grand scale already in the 1880s (F. von Benda-Beckmann 1979: 289). Increasing monetisation of the economy through the system of forced coffee cultivation and limited possibilities to invest money outside the village infused money into pawning and redemption cycles. Over time, new needs for cash and new ways of earning money through wage labour, trade and the cultivation of cash crops, in the private and public salaried job sector, and remittances from migrants enhanced investment in land (Naim 1974; F. von Benda-Beckmann 1979: 291; Kato 1982; Biezeveld 2002). To avoid problems with inheritance, Minangkabau men preferred to pawn or redeem land 'for their wife and children'. Pawning and redemption became a dominant way of getting access to land, as uncultivated land had become ever scarcer, especially in the densely populated core areas of Minangkabau. This process has been fraught with frequent and heated conflicts, especially after the inheritance rules for self-acquired property changed in the 1960s. When use rights to individually redeemed *pusako* property are inherited, they now cross the boundaries of a lineage.[14]

Through these mechanisms much agricultural land rotated and a market for individualised temporary rights to *pusako* developed. The flow of property from a man's matrilineage to his conjugal family also strengthened the bonds within the conjugal family at the expense of the multiplex relationships within the matrilineage. Within the matrilineage, most property is held by small lineage segments. The older mechanism of primary allocation thereby lost importance, because the stock of *pusako* common for all members has decreased. The authority of group heads and older women over *pusako* has been weakened as a result.

Ulayat
The Right of Avail, Sovereignty and State Domain

Ulayat denotes village land or territory and comprises land, forest, water, minerals and grazing land. Village land was mostly under the sociopolitical control of the village government, but it could also be distributed among the founding clans of the villages, and then administered by the heads of the clans (Holleman 1981: 137). *Ulayat* was mainly used for collecting forest products or grazing. It also served as a reserve for the expansion of agriculture or horticulture. Village land could thus become converted into irrigated rice fields or permanent tree gardens. Over time, it became inherited lineage property for the original cultivator's descendants. *Ulayat* was usually freely accessible to the members of the village or clan respectively. It could not be alienated. Temporary access and withdrawal rights could be given to non-residents against a fee of recognition. The Dutch called this right of sociopolitical control *beschikkingsrecht*, right of disposition or right of avail (Holleman 1981: 287, 431).

Early nineteenth century agrarian legislation in the Dutch East Indies had more or less recognised all land rights of the local population, including the rights of avail. But in a gradual process starting when forced cultivation of market crops was abandoned, and founding European plantations and agribusiness was encouraged, these rights were systematically reduced. Rights held by the state were also held to be important for legitimating mineral extraction and forest exploitation and conservation. The Domain Declaration of Sumatra's West Coast of 1874 declared land, for which 'ownership' could not be proven, to be the domain of the state (Logemann and Ter Haar 1927: 106). It created considerable legal uncertainty and became an important issue in legal-political debates.[15] The major question was whether the resources subject to the communities' right of avail could be taken over by the state and reallocated to public or private companies, or whether the land had to be officially expropriated with compensation for the communities. In the colonial administrators' view, expropriation and compensation were regarded as matters of private law rights. In their opinion, the rights of avail did not conform to the criteria of private law ownership. Consequently, these were not regarded as 'rights' but as mere 'interests', subject to the state's political consideration of the 'common good', i.e., capitalist economic development by European entrepreneurs. Since each piece of land needed to have an owner in the colonial legal logic, it was considered 'inevitable that the state became the owner of that land given the absence of any other owner' ('s Jacob 1945). In the dominant colonial interpretation the right of avail was regarded as a purely public right of the village government. Such public rights had been superseded and absorbed by the new, overriding public rights emanating from the state's sovereignty. Opponents of this view argued that such interpretations could not be sustained since they were based on a fundamental misunderstanding of the nature of *adat* rights. These rights, they pointed out, could not simply be understood in terms of mutually exclusive public or private rights. Rather, the right of avail had both public and private character and therefore fell under the protection clause of the Domain Declarations.

Despite heated legal debate, the *adat* rights over village land continued in practice to be widely recognised in West Sumatra. The Domain

Declaration for Sumatra's West Coast was even called the 'secret' declaration because the government for some time did not dare publicise the text or put it into practice for fear of popular uprisings. Unless there were overwhelming economic interests at stake, the government refrained from asserting its rights. Where land or forest concessions were given to outsiders, agreement with village governments was sought. The number of Dutch plantations created in this way, however, was relatively small. In the less densely populated regions more concessions were given to plantations, mostly in the form of a long lease (*erfpacht*) for seventy-five years (see Oki 1977: 111, 114; Kahn 1993: 202–19). In the late nineteenth century, there emerged something of a plantation belt with migrant labour from Java. Exploration permits and mining concessions for coal, gold, silver, zinc, copper, lead and tin were granted to Dutch firms, usually also for a period of seventy-five years.

The Dutch forest reserve policy had a greater practical impact on *ulayat*. It was meant to protect forests from uncontrolled timber extraction but also to provide cheap timber for public works. In 1923, 35 percent of the total area of Minangkabau was forest reserve. Resentment against these measures by Minangkabau villagers and leaders grew, because it diminished their possibilities to bring new land under cultivation. In the central parts of West Sumatra demographic developments had necessitated expanding rice areas into forests that were declared protected by the forestry department, fuelling the Communist uprising in 1925–26. As a result, the Commission investigating the uprisings issued a regulation that the government and European companies exploiting timber were to pay 25 percent of the timber value to the concerned villages (Oki 1977: 114–16; Kahn 1993: 220 ff.).

After Indonesia's independence the legal situation changed only gradually, and the state operated on the same legal and political logic as its colonial predecessor, handing out titles as it deemed fit. The Basic Agrarian Law of 1960 professed to be based upon *adat* law. The right of avail (*hak ulayat*) was recognised in a rather ambiguous way, subject to the state's regulatory control and the 'common interest'. The legal basis for concessions was broadened by Presidential Decree 32 of 1979 on the conversion of 'Western rights' into state land. This Decree stated that all land leased to Dutch plantations would fall back to the state as state land after expiration of the lease; the status as *adat* land was erased. Forestry legislation imposed ever more restrictions on the use of forest, while the area under their control widened, deepening the conflicts with *ulayat* claims. During the last twenty years of the Suharto regime his family members and loyal political supporters liberally received timber, mining and agricultural concessions, leases and ownership titles. These titles encroached upon both state forestry and *ulayat* land. Claims of local populations were usually disregarded.[16] The result is a situation fraught with uncertainty and with resentment against the old regime, but also against village leaders who were accused of having privately profited from these transactions.

Developments since 'Reformasi'

The demise of the Suharto regime and the ensuing new political freedom in Indonesia led to a number of changes, including general calls for more regional autonomy and claims for greater recognition of *adat* rights to village resources. This led to a policy of decentralisation with more rights and obligations for districts and villages. In West Sumatra this has been accompanied by a restructuring of village government that has evoked a region-wide debate about the position of traditional leaders and control over *ulayat* (see F. and K. von Benda-Beckmann 2001). While villages had received their entire income from the central government, the *ulayat* issue had been dormant. But when the central government cut back on services, villages were forced to seek other sources of revenue, and *ulayat* moved to centre stage. *Ulayat* no longer was an issue of the past, but one on which the future seemed to rest.

Responding to increasing local pressure, in 1999 the central government issued a ministerial regulation concerning the recognition of village land, in order to resolve the problems of *ulayat* land within *adat* law communities.[17] The regulation was heavily criticised because it only recognises *ulayat* land that 'continues to be held as in the past by the *nagari*, where *ulayat* land still exists in reality, and where the relationships between *adat* law community and *ulayat* have not been severed in the course of time' (see Syahmunir 2000; F. and K. von Benda-Beckmann 2001). It would thus validate all actions with respect to *ulayat* taken by the government in the past, including the legal transfer of former Dutch plantations to the state. In response to protests the West Sumatran provincial government has now proposed a draft regulation restating the disputed regulation of the ministerial regulation of 1999. This is unacceptable to those such as the Association of Adat Village Councils, who demand the reversion of land with expired state leases and use rights to the former *ulayat* status. Not surprisingly, this demand in turn is unacceptable to the central ministry and the provincial government. In 2005 the issue was still unresolved.

Apart from these legal politics there are other attempts to bring *ulayat* resources back under village or clan control. In the past, fear of repression had kept the local population from filing complaints, but now open conflicts, court proceedings and negotiations about forest areas, plantations, water resources, and sub-soil resources such as the coal, sand and gravel have emerged.[18] Sometimes the villagers' intention is to regain full control over the land to be able to exploit it. More often, however, negotiations are aimed at regaining a say in the use of the resource, or getting some benefits out of it. *Ulayat* rights then are used to levy taxes. Some land and village markets have been restored to villages by the district administration, and some clans have successfully reclaimed (some of) their land or negotiated a share in the profits made by enterprises exploiting natural resources on the village territory. Influential migrants in Jakarta and elsewhere also play an important role in these struggles and help to balance the power relationships between state agencies and villagers (see Biezeveld 2002). Nevertheless, despite these first successes, it is difficult to predict the eventual outcomes, defeats, victories and compromises of these struggles.

Struggles over *ulayat* resources not only concern the relationship between villages and the state. Due to the decentralisation policy, there is an increased focus on *adat* law and on village resources in the new village organisation. This has given new life to internal village struggles. The 1979 Law on Local Government and the 1983 division of villages (*nagari*) into small administrative villages (*desa*), had meant that the *nagari* ceased to be an official administrative unit. However, in 1983 the Provincial Regulation 13 recognised the *nagari* as an 'adat law community' and acknowledged the Village Adat Council as the institution representing this community with the task of managing the riches of the *nagari* (mainly *ulayat* resources) and of settling the disputes on *adat* matters. With the 2000 regulation on village government in which the *nagari* were reinstalled as state local government units, this 1983 regulation was repealed. It is an open question who now has such control, the mayor as the head of the official *nagari* government, or the Village Adat Council as holder of traditional *adat* authority. According to a circular letter of the governor, final control should be with the village government, which should administer it jointly with the Village Adat Council. Actual practice varies. In some villages, the authority over village resources has

been officially handed over by the chairman of the Village Adat Council
to the village government. In other villages compromises between the
two are negotiated. But many mayors have difficulties getting their hands
on the resources still controlled by the *adat* elders or the Village Adat
Council. The issue is further complicated, since there is also *ulayat* of
clans and lineages, which is not under village control. It is not always
clear who the legitimate claimant is: the village government, the Village
Adat Council, the head of one particular clan, all lineage heads within the
clan, or even one particular lineage. In the last case, outside investors
would have to negotiate directly with the representatives of the clan or
lineage, bypassing the *nagari* government or the Village Adat Council.
This is likely to spark off new conflicts about interpretation and actual
control over the nature and holders of *ulayat* rights. Every little victory
against the state thus tends to lead to new, internal village struggles over
the distribution of the land and resources.

Conclusions

The two different forms of communal property in Minangkabau
highlight some of the fundamental problems that have plagued debates
about common property.

Communal is Not Communal

As the history of *ulayat* and *pusako* shows, communal property can mean
very different categories of property relationships even within the same
society. Moreover, in both cases, the legal status as communal property
(*ulayat, pusako*) does not adequately characterise the bundle of rights
people have to that property. Communal property constructions are
mixtures of individual and group rights. Thirdly, looking at property as
layered structures, we have seen that the way concretised rights to actual
ulayat and *pusako* resources are distributed cannot be inferred from the
categorical bundles of rights. Under the category of *pusako* as communal
property, a wide variety of actual exploitation rights can exist, held by
larger and smaller groups, married couples and individuals. To *ulayat*,
too, a variety of actual concretised rights may pertain: no rights in the case
of unused resources, rights of exploitation according to *adat*, and licences
and use rights according to national legislation. Discussing 'communal
rights' as more or less homogeneous and theorising over how people are
likely to deal with property under a 'common property' regime, without

detailing the kind of communal property and the very different possible constellations of concretised rights, does not make much sense.[19]

Misinterpreting adat Categories

The two main property categories of Minangkabau *adat* in the *adat* law literature were misinterpreted. The colonial interpretations of *pusako* as family ownership or of *pancaharian* as individual ownership did not greatly trouble the Minangkabau themselves. While *pusako* was subject to strategic interpretations in trying to adapt it to colonial economic policies, at least the government recognised *pusako* resources as the property of the Minangkabau. Ordinary people were confronted with these misinterpretations only when dealing with government institutions, such as courts, and later with the land registration and extension services. Dutch misinterpretations of *ulayat* had far wider implications, because they legitimated the state appropriation of rights over an enormous resource complex and the actual loss of access. Land of economic value was 'privatised' through leases and concessions to planters and mining and logging companies, often with inadequate compensation to local communities.

Misinterpretations of *adat* categories also contributed to confusion over the analysis of social and economic change in Minangkabau. The interpretation of self-acquired property as individual ownership led Schrieke (1955) to diagnose an imminent breakdown of the matrilineal system, due to ever increasing individualisation of land rights and inheritance of such rights by a man's children.[20] He based his conclusion on the breakdown of the matrilineal system largely on the fact that nearly all land had been pawned and thus converted into self-acquired property. Assuming that such property, like Dutch ownership, would retain its legal status after inheritance and redemption, he concluded that the stock of *pusako* was dwindling away. Schrieke and Maretin even spoke of a transition from matrilineal to patrilineal inheritance, especially when self-acquired property of a man fell to the children. They first of all overlooked the fact that pawned *pusako* could be redeemed with the residual *pusako* rights becoming full rights again. Secondly, they overlooked the fact that self-acquired property would become *pusako* for this person's heirs and henceforth be inherited matrilineally within the *pusako* pool.[21]

So there were mechanisms to reproduce the matrilineal principle in kinship, property and inheritance law. The categorical system was sufficiently flexible to accommodate quite different patterns of actual property relationships, in terms of the amount of property resources held under classical *pusako* allocation principles or under individualised and monetised *pancaharian* rights, and in terms of the actual person(s) and groups holding these rights.

Our analysis of this misinterpretation of property rights thus illustrates at least two important points. First, misinterpretations are an eminently political issue. They served very different economic and political purposes depending on the type of communal property. Second, the example of Minangkabau shows how problematic it is to extend conclusions drawn from changes in concrete relationships to changes at the categorical level, and vice versa.

Property and Economic Development

The Minangkabau example suggests that there is no inherent economic function of communal property. We have shown that the two types of Minangkabau communal property have undergone very different developments in the economic history of West Sumatra, and that their economic significance has differed as well. The assumption that communal property is unsuitable for economic development is certainly not supported by the Minangkabau example. The function of *pusako* for the social security and continuity of lineages has always been strong, but mainly related to the non-alienability of the *pusako* stock. The internal differentiation of rights within a *pusako* complex allows for much flexibility and economic, market oriented initiative. The great economic changes that have occurred took place not because of changes at the level of categorical property rules, but as a result of changes in concretised property relationships, notably the increase of pawning of *pusako* land and production on a household basis. In the past, economic stagnation was primarily due to restrictive policies of the government that suffocated economic initiatives in rice production in order to boost coffee production and protect (colonial) entrepreneurs. It was not a result of the *pusako* structure itself. Most Minangkabau today farm on a household basis and this, too, is entirely compatible with the internal differentiation of the *pusako* structure. Indeed, some of the most advanced farms are on *pusako* land. There are few Minangkabau farmers who favour abolition of the *pusako* system because it hinders economic development.

Ulayat, on the other hand, never had the chance to prove its potential for economic growth. The Minangkabau regarded its function as a reserve for future needs as more important than short-term economic exploitation. The colonial government then assumed control over large resource areas and passed these 'waste lands' on to European entrepreneurs. In addition, forestry policies put severe restrictions on the use of forest reserves. Under decentralisation, villages are now starting to economically exploit newly restored *ulayat* resources. It is still too early to decide in which ways economic development can be supported under these new exploitation patterns.

Struggles Over Rights – Struggles Over Law

Struggles over communal property are usually treated as reflecting the opposition between communal and individual *rights*. But as our examples show, they may also concern struggles over which *law* is applicable, that is, about the wider normative, ideological and political systems of which property rights are a part. That property rights are 'embedded' in a wider set of social relationships has become generally acknowledged, but the degree of embeddedness in legal systems deserves much more attention (see also Peters in this volume). This is particularly important in plural legal systems where the communal property rights that are being contested are usually based in local, ethnic or territorial laws that are more or less traditional, more or less customary. By contrast, individual private ownership rights, promoted or rejected as the main alternative, are based in state law. Our examples show that struggles over communal property in important ways have been struggles over which law – *adat*, state or Islam – is the valid frame of reference for determining legitimate categories of property-holders, objects, rights, and the rules governing appropriation, allocation, transfers and inheritance. The struggle over property and inheritance are often as *pars pro toto*, the question whose law and whose decision-making authority should prevail.

In the current literature on land rights in Minangkabau and Indonesia in general, with its focus on *ulayat*, these legal struggles over communal land are reduced to the relationship between *adat* and the state. Debates about the recognition of *adat* rights and registration of communal land are a case in point. While discussing communal property, they address *ulayat* only; the arguments do not hold for *pusako*.[22] Islamic law is largely absent in these discussions (see for example Fitzpatrick 1999; Haverfield 1999). This makes sense for *ulayat* rights, for the colonial past and for the current struggles in the context of decentralisation: Islamic law cannot provide a basis to legitimise claims to natural resources on village territory. But it does not make sense when *pusako* is presented only as *adat* law in a struggle with state law. This leaves out the ongoing tensions and struggles with Islamic law. Islamic law remains invisible in land rights issues, because that struggle seems to be over 'inheritance' only, not about landed property. But Minangkabau property law must be seen in its temporal dimension, including inheritance. Systematic application of Islamic law would put a stop to the *pusako*isation of *pancaharian*, and would withdraw resources from the *pusako* complex. But we have seen that Islamic influences in *adat* have not fundamentally undermined the *pusako* logic and that Islamic law has not replaced *adat* inheritance rules.

The Minangkabau examples show the importance of looking at property regimes as embedded in larger social, economic and political developments, but also in wider legal structures. But this embeddedness, too, may play out very differently for different types of communal property. Ignoring that fact has meant that theories and policies based on a simplistic assumption about communal property has led to many policy failures. Treating 'communal rights' as a more or less homogeneous category and theorising over how people are likely to deal with property under a 'common property' regime, without detailing the kind of communal property and the very different possible constellations of concretised rights, is bound to fail.

Notes

1. There is an immense literature on these issues. See for example F. and K. von Benda-Beckmann 1999; F. and K. von Benda-Beckmann and Wiber, this volume. On changes in socialist states, see Hann et al. 2003.
2. See for example Bruce and Mighot-Adholla 1994; Van Meijl and F. von Benda-Beckmann 1999. See also Peters, Kingston-Mann, James and the introductory chapter by F. and K. von Benda-Beckmann and Wiber in this volume.
3. In the older evolutionist discussions in the nineteenth and early twentieth century, the core meaning of communal property was property held by kinship, descent groups or tribes. Under the influence of the common property discussions following Hardin's (1968) 'tragedy of the commons', the core meaning of communal property has shifted to the commons, the latest version being the global commons.
4. On the distinction between categorical and concretised property relations, see F. and K. von Benda-Beckmann and Wiber, this volume.
5. *Adat* in the most general sense means 'the way of life'. It is sometimes translated as customs.
6. See Willinck 1909; Tanner 1970; F. von Benda-Beckmann 1979; K. von Benda-Beckmann 1981.

7. On the changing relation between *adat* and Islam in Minangkabau see Abdullah 1966; Naim 1968; F. and K. von Benda-Beckmann 1988.
8. See Prins 1953; Naim 1968; Tanner 1970; F. von Benda-Beckmann 1979.
9. Only in very rare instances are such disputes brought to and judged by the Religious Courts. While the jurisdiction of the Religious (State) Courts has been expanded in the 1980s to comprise disputes over inheritance, gifts and testaments, our research shows that between the 1970s and now there has been no change. The research is being carried out in cooperation with Andalas University in Padang. We gratefully acknowledge the help and stimulating suggestions of Aziz Saleh, Alfan Miko, Erwin, Syahmunir, Syofyan Thalib, Narullah nan Tuo, Takdir Rahmadi, and Tasman.
10. Already during the 1850s, the Dutch tried to introduce registration of *pusako* in terms of Dutch notions of onwnership, (see F. von Benda-Beckmann 1979: 210 and 318 ff; K. von Benda-Beckmann 1990).
11. See F. von Benda-Beckmann 1979, K. von Benda-Beckmann 1981 and F. and K. von Benda-Beckmann 1985. See also Vollenhoven 1909. For similar transformations in other colonial legal systems, see Clammer 1973; Chanock 1985; Woodman 1987. As in Minangkabau, such transformations should not be generalised into 'the' customary law.
12. Women had particular difficulties claiming their rights against (sub)lineage members, see K. von Benda-Beckmann 1981.
13. See for registration programmes F. von Benda-Beckmann 1986; World Bank 1994; Haverfield 1999: 57; Slaats 1999, 2000: 44.
14. Tanner 1970; F. von Benda-Beckmann 1979; K. von Benda-Beckmann 1981.
15. Van Vollenhoven (1919) and later Logemann and Ter Haar (1927) were exceedingly critical of colonial legal policies. Protest also came from Dutch administrators, including the governor of Sumatra's West Coast, Ballot and even the Dutch Minister for the Colonies. See further AB 11 (1912: 88), AB 35 (1936: 223–30); Oki (1977: 105–10); F. von Benda-Beckmann (1979); Manan (1984: 186); Burns (1989: 36); Kahn (1993: 189–212). 's Jacob (1945) gives the most systematic exposition and justification of the state policies.
16. In 1997, 606,863 ha of village land were in the hands of plantations against a area of 113,600 ha in 1926. Between 1990 and 1999 the area for oil plantations more than quadrupled, see Kahn (1993: 202ff); *Suara Rakyat* (2001).
17. From 1994 till 1999 the World Bank carried out an ambitious project to revise and improve the agrarian legal system in which the status of the communal lands was to be explored. See Slaats (1999, 2000).
18. See F. and K. von Benda-Beckmann (2001). In Padang *adat* elders claimed back a school building from the government (*Padang Ekspres* 26 August 2002). And in Ombilin people have started to mine coal on their *ulayat* land.
19. The coexistence of large tracts of lineage land and common village lands declared state domain is also frequent in former colonies in Africa. See also Peters in this volume.
20. See for example Schrieke 1955: 710, similarly Maretin 1961; Kahn 1980. For a critical analysis, see F. von Benda-Beckmann 1979; F. and K. von Benda-Beckmann 1985.

21. Later research in the same region showed that most property was *pusako* (Adatrechtbundels (1910–1955) 41: 392; Oki 1977: 126).
22. When Haverfield (1999: 69), for example, states that the acknowledgement of *adat* rights is one of the greatest challenges for the state, or when she discusses how state definitions of state land and state forest relate to *adat* rights (1999: 62), she has *ulayat* and not *pusako* in mind. See also Fitzpatrick (1999). The fact that discourses in West Sumatra themselves are often framed mainly in terms of *hak ulayat*, but distinguish between *ulayat* of the village, of clans, and of lineages, makes the discussion more complicated: *Ulayat kaum* is often identical with the *pusako* of a lineage. See Naim (1968). In the discussions about recognition of *adat* rights, it is overlooked that the official law in state courts pertaining to *pusako* property, pawnings and inheritance is *adat* law.

References

Abdullah, T. 1966. 'Adat and Islam; an Examination of Conflict in Minangkabau', *Indonesia* 2: 124.

Adatrechtbundels (AB) 1910–1955. Bezorgd door de Commissie voor het Adatrecht en uitgegeven door het Koninklijk Instituut voor Taal-, Land- en Volkenkunde, The Hague: Martinus Nijhoff.

Benda-Beckmann, F. von. 1979. *Property in Social Continuity: Continuity and Change in the Maintenance of Property Relationships through Time in Minangkabau.* West Sumatra, The Hague: Martinus Nijhoff.

——— 1986. 'Leegstaande Luchtkastelen: Over de Pathologie van Grondenrechtshervormingen in Ontwikkelingslanden', in *Recht in ontwikkeling – Tien agrarisch-rechtelijke opstellen*, eds W. Brussaard et al., Deventer: Kluwer, 91–109.

Benda-Beckmann, F. von and K. von Benda-Beckmann 1985. 'Transformation and Change in Minangkabau', in *Change and Continuity in Minangkabau*, eds L. Thomas and F. von Benda-Beckmann, Athens: Ohio University Monographs in International Studies, 235–78.

——— 1988. 'Adat and Religion in Minangkabau and Ambon', in *Time Past, Time Present, Time Future*, eds H. Claessen and D. Moyer, Dordrecht: Foris, 195–212.

——— 1999. 'A Functional Analysis of Property Rights, with Special Reference to Indonesia', in *Property Rights and Economic Development: Land and Natural Resources in Southeast Asia and Oceania*, eds T. van Meijl and F. von Benda-Beckmann, London and New York: Kegan Paul International, 15–55.

——— 2001. 'Actualising History for Binding the Future: Decentralisation in Minangkabau', in *Resonances and Dissonances in Development: Actors, Networks and Cultural Repertoires*, eds P. Hebinck and G. Verschoor, Assen: van Gorcum, 33–47.

——— 2004. 'Struggles over Communal Property Rights and Law in Minangkabau, West Sumatra', working paper of the Max Planck Institute for Social Anthropology, Halle/Saale, Germany.

Benda-Beckmann, K. von 1981. 'Forum Shopping and Shopping Forums; Dispute Processing in a Minangkabau Village', *Journal of Legal Pluralism* 19: 117–59.

———— 1985. 'The Social Significance of Minangkabau State Court Decisions', *Journal of Legal Pluralism* 23: 1–68.

———— 1990. 'Development, Law and Gender-Skewing: An Examination of the Impact of Development on the Socio-Legal Position of Indonesian Women, with Special Reference to Minangkabau', *Journal of Legal Pluralism* 30/31: 87–120.

Biezeveld, R. 2002. *Between Individualism and Mutual Help: Social Security and Natural Resources in a Minangkabau Village*. Delft: Eburon.

Bruce, J.W. and S.E. Migot-Adholla, eds 1994. *Searching for Land Tenure Security in Africa*. Dubuque: Kendall-Hunt.

Burns, P. 1989. 'The Myth of Adat', *Journal of Legal Pluralism* 28: 1–127.

Chanock, M. 1985. *Law, Custom and Social Order: The Colonial Experience in Malawi and Zambia*. Cambridge: Cambridge University Press.

Clammer, J. 1973. 'Colonialism and the Perception of Tradition in Fiji', in *Anthropology and the Colonial Encounter*, ed. T. Asad, Atlantic Highlands: Humanities Press, 199–220.

Fitzpatrick, D. 1999. 'Beyond Dualism: Land Acquisition and Law in Indonesia', in *Indonesia: Law and Society*, ed. T. Lindsey, Annandale: The Federation Press, 74–96.

Guyt, H. 1936. *Grondverpanding in Minangkabau*. Bandung: A.C. Nix.

Hann, C.M. and Property Relations Group 2003. *The Postsocialist Agrarian Question: Property Relations and the Rural Condition*. Münster: LIT Verlag (Halle Studies in the Anthropology of Eurasia, no. 1).

Hardin, G. 1968. 'The Tragedy of the Commons', *Science* 162: 1234–48.

Haverfield, R. 1999. 'Hak Ulayat and the State: Land Reform in Indonesia', in *Indonesia: Law and Society*, ed. T. Lindsey, Annandale: The Federation Press, 42–73.

Holleman J.F., ed. 1981. *Van Vollenhoven on Indonesian Adat Law*. Translation Series Koninklijk Instituut voor Taal-, Land- en Volkenkunde, The Hague: Martinus Nijhoff.

's Jacob, E.H. 1945. *Landsdomein en Adatrecht*. Utrecht: Kemink en Zoon.

Kahn, J.S. 1980. *Minangkabau Social Formations. Indonesian Peasants and the World-Economy*. Cambridge: Cambridge University Press.

———— 1993. *Constituting the Minangkabau: Peasants, Culture, and Modernity in Colonial Indonesia*. Providence/Oxford: Berg.

Kato, T. 1982. *Matriliny and Migration. Evolving Minangkabau Traditions in Indonesia*. Ithaca, London: Cornell University Press.

Logemann, J.H.A. and B. Ter Haar 1927. 'Het Beschikkingsrecht der Indonesische Rechtsgemeenschappen', offprint from *Indisch Tijdschrift voor het Recht* 125: 347–464.

Manan, I. 1984. 'A Traditional Elite in Continuity and Change: The Chiefs of the Matrilineal Lineages of the Minangkabau of West Sumatra, Indonesia', Ph.D. thesis, Urbana-Champaign: University of Illinois.

Maretin, J.V. 1961. 'Disappearance of Matriclan Survivals in Minangkabau Family and Marriage Relations', *Bijdragen tot de Taal-, Land- en Volkenkunde* 117: 168–95.

Meijl, T. van and F. von Benda-Beckmann, eds 1999. *Property Rights and Economic Development: Land and Natural Resources in Southeast Asia and Oceania.* London: Kegan Paul International.

Naim, M., ed. 1968. *Menggali Hukum Tanah dan Hukum Waris Minangkabau.* Padang: Centre for Minangkabau Studies.

——— 1974. 'Merantau; Minangkabau Voluntary Migration', Ph.D. thesis, University of Singapore.

Oki, A. 1977. 'Social Change in the West Sumatran Village: 1908–1945', Ph.D. thesis, Canberra: Australian National University.

Padang Ekspres, 26 August 2002.

Prins, J. 1953. 'Rondom de Oude Strijdvraag van Minangkabau', *Indonesië* 7: 320–29.

Schrieke, B. 1955. 'The Causes and Effects of Communism on the West Coast of Sumatra', in *Indonesian Sociological Studies*, ed. B. Schrieke, The Hague, Bandung: W. van Hoeve, part 1, 83–166.

Slaats, H. 1999. 'Land Titling and Customary Rights: Comparing Land Registration Projects in Thailand and Indonesia', in *Property Rights and Economic Development: Land and Natural Resources in Southeast Asia and Oceania*, eds T. van Meijl and F. von Benda-Beckmann, London: Kegan Paul, 88–109.

——— 2000. 'Aardverschuivingen in het Indonesische Denken over Grondenrecht', *Recht der Werkelijkheid* 1: 41–68.

Suara Rakyat, 2001, no. 2, 14.

Syahmunir, A.M. 2000. 'Fungsi dan peranan fungsional adat dalam pelaksanaan peraturan pemerintah 24–1997 tentang pendaftaran tanah di Sumatera Barat', paper presented at a workshop on tanah ulayat. Padang, 23–24 October 2000. Padang: Universitas Andalas.

Tanner, N. 1970. 'Disputing and the Genesis of Legal Principles; Examples from Minangkabau', *South Western Journal of Antropology* 26: 375–401.

Vollenhoven, C. van 1909. *Miskenningen van het Adatrecht.* Leiden: E.J. Brill.

——— 1919. *De Indonesiër en zijn Grond.* Leiden: E.J. Brill.

Willinck, G.D. 1909. *Het Rechtsleven bij de Minangkabausche Maleiërs.* Leiden: E.J. Brill.

Woodman, G.R. 1987. 'How State Courts Create Customary Law in Ghana and Nigeria', in *Indigenous Law and the State*, eds B.W. Morse and G.R. Woodman, Dordrecht: Foris, 181–220.

World Bank 1994. *Staff Appraisal Report: Indonesia – Land Administration Project.* Washington D.C.: World Bank, Agriculture Operations Division, Country Department III, East Asia and Pacific Region.

Chapter 10

Moving Borders and Invisible Boundaries:

a Force Field Approach to Property Relations in the Commons of a Mexican *ejido*

Monique Nuijten and David Lorenzo

Introduction

This chapter presents an analysis of property relations in the common lands of an *ejido* in Western Mexico. In contrast to the arable land, which was immediately divided into individual plots, the mountainous lands that *ejidos* received during the Mexican land reform remained under communal regimes of governance. In many cases no formal regulation for the use of these commons was made. In the study that is presented in this chapter, we examine what happened with these common lands in one *ejido*, La Canoa, in Western Mexico. We show how property relations developed over time in a situation where no explicit rules were ever formulated.

Property relations in the commons in La Canoa are analysed in relation to changing productive relations with the land, sociopolitical divisions in the village, and the transformation of national legal institutions and government programmes for the *ejido* sector. Among other things, attention is paid to the effects of the new Agrarian Law of 1992. It is shown how in different historical periods, distinct categories of villagers establish or contest rights and claims to land in the commons in a variety of ways.

First we present the theoretical approach used in this study, which is based on the idea that the daily practices around the access, distribution and use of land develop within a wider force field. This is followed by a short history of the *ejido* system in Mexico and an introduction of the *ejido*, La Canoa.[1] Then the development of land property relations in the commons is analysed in detail.[2]

Conceptual Approach: Force Fields, Organising Practices and Discursive Modes

Following the notions developed by Franz and Keebet von Benda-Beckmann and Melanie Wiber in this volume, we see property as a bundle of rights and relationships between persons with respect to valuable goods, whether material or immaterial. In addition, we follow the four elements that according to them comprise property relationships, including: the social units that hold property rights and obligations; the construction of valuables as property objects; the relationships in terms of rights and obligations; and the temporal dimension of property relationships. We find their idea that property relations become expressed in different sets of social phenomena, cultural ideals, ideology, legal institutions and actual social relationships very useful. Finally, we agree with their distinction between categorical property relations and concretised property relations, being the difference between the abstract legal framework and the *real practices*.

We take this analytical framework a step further by using a practice-force field approach to property relations (Nuijten 2003a). A practice approach focuses on concretised practices of access to and use of land within a sociopolitical and historical perspective. It is argued that these practices are based on a complex set of rights and obligations embedded within the wider social-political fabric, the force field. In this approach one looks at regularities that develop over time as well as at conflicts and fields of tension. Certain practices can become established over time but without a 'centre of control' that 'manages' these practices on the basis of 'fixed localised rules'. Much attention is paid here to the way in which people claim rights to land and express themselves about categories of villagers with different rights and obligations, in other words to the discursive modes in which the bundle of rights and obligations are framed.

In this approach, a *force field* is defined as a field of power and struggle between different social actors with respect to certain resources and around which forms of dominance, contention and resistance develop, as well as certain regularities and forms of ordering. These forms of ordering refer to the many 'rules of the game' we experience in everyday life, but which are often not formalised. Hence, in this view the patterning of organising practices is not necessarily the result of a normative agreement, but of the forces at play within the field.

This concept of force field resembles Bourdieu's notion of a field that has its own logic, rules and regularities which are not explicit and which make it resemble the playing of games (Bourdieu and Wacquant 1992: 94–115). In Bourdieu's field, agents and institutions constantly struggle, according to the regularities and the rules constitutive of this space to appropriate the specific products at stake in the game.[3] In the same way as Moore (1973), Bourdieu talks about the possible autonomy of fields. He argues that some fields may be more autonomous than others in terms of being capable of imposing their own logic. In our view, this idea of the relative autonomy of fields is problematic, as fields are unbounded entities that are in continuous flux. We do agree with both authors, however, that some practices are much more regularised and patterned than others. In other words, concretised property relations concerning the use and distribution of land can become so patterned that one can rightly speak about a system of property rules. Yet, in many other situations not much regularity can be found and great diversity and 'unexpected' practices are more 'the rule' than the 'exception to the rule'. For example, in La Canoa, concretised property relations around arable land developed into a well-established form of individual private property that is sold and transferred without problems. However, with respect to the common lands in La Canoa we will see that no such generally accepted property relations developed. Property relations in the commons are much more characterised by flux and change. A practice-force field approach helps one to refrain from reification of the formal law, as well as 'customary law'. It also makes it possible to analyse the weight of different kinds of sociopolitical networks, the influence of law and procedures, and the role of state bureaucracy. Finally, it shows that rights and obligations around property relations can become established over time, without a centre of control or regulation based upon a system of agreed upon rules.

Another assumption of the practice-force field approach is that the cohering of force fields around certain resources and the resulting forms of ordering, are accompanied by the unfolding of sociopolitical categories with differing positions and interests. This explains that the patterning of organising practices and the accompanying forms of domination and struggle are related to active dialogues, self-reflection, irony, and the production of multiple meanings through imagination and the work of interpretation. These dialogues reflect a continuous active engagement of social actors with the world around them in general and with land (or other resources) in particular. For that reason, the discursive modes in which people express claims, complaints and duties around land is central to any analysis of property relations.

The History of the Commons in the Mexican *ejido*

In Mexico *ejidos* were established during the land reform period between 1917 and 1992. Apart from the parcelled agricultural land, the *ejidos* received urban land, dry pasturelands and woodlands for collective use. The common lands generally formed the major part of the *ejido*, with an average of almost 77 percent of the total area the *ejido* received (Reyes et al. 1974: 458). At the beginning of the 1990s there were approximately 28,000 *ejidos*, occupying more than half of Mexico's arable land and including over 3 million *ejidatarios*.[4] According to the Agrarian Law, the general assembly of the *ejido*, which includes all *ejidatarios*, is the highest *ejido* authority at the local level. Every three years the assembly elects the executive committee of the *ejido*, which is responsible for the daily administration of *ejido* affairs. The president of this committee is the *ejido* commissioner.

The Mexican Agrarian Law allowed the division of the arable land into individual plots and also allowed the *ejidatarios* to choose their own heir for this land. According to the law the mountainous common lands could not be divided and had to remain in common use. The general *ejido* assembly had to develop a regulation for the use of the commons and the executive committee of the *ejido* had to supervise the exploitation and report irregularities.

The main characteristics of the *ejido* regime were not changed till 1992 when article twenty-seven of the Mexican Constitution and the Agrarian Law were radically transformed. The most important elements of the new Agrarian Law in comparison with the old Federal Agrarian Reform Law are the following. Firstly, the Mexican agrarian reform has come to its end. Secondly, the *ejido* form of land tenure will continue to exist, but *ejidatarios* are now allowed to sell, buy, rent, or lease their individual arable plots, activities that were all forbidden under the old Agrarian Reform Law. Thirdly, the law opens the possibility for *ejidatarios* to work in association with private enterprises (stockholding companies) and individual investors. Under certain conditions, the *ejido* common lands may now be rented out to commercial enterprises. Also the use of the commons as collateral for loans is allowed, as well as the division of the commons into plots for individual use. The sale of plots in the commons is still prohibited.

La Canoa is a small hamlet of 837 inhabitants in the valley of Autlán in Jalisco[5] that in 1938 received land to establish its own *ejido* as part of the Mexican land reform (see Map 10.1). In 1942 the *ejido* received a small extension grant. At present the *ejido* possesses approximately 450 hectares arable land and 1800 hectares of lands in the mountains. The arable land was immediately divided into individual plots, while the mountainous land remained 'common lands'.

In the dry area the predominant crop was maize which was cultivated in the rainy season from May to November. During the 1960s, half of the arable *ejido* land of La Canoa fell within a newly developed irrigation district. Recently the remaining area has been incorporated in the extension of this irrigation system and all the lowlands are now irrigated. The dominant crop in the irrigated zone is sugarcane. In the same way as in other *ejidos* throughout Mexico, the possession of individual arable plots in the *ejido* gradually turned into a form of private property (see Nuijten 1997). It even became a commodity with a price attached to it. An active land market developed and between 1942 and 1993, twenty-nine plots or parts of plots were sold in La Canoa (Nuijten 2003a).

At the establishment of the *ejido* almost every household received an arable plot, but with population growth over the years, most families in the village became landless. The village grew from 258 in 1921[6] to 837 in 1990 and today 138 of the 196 households in the village do not have access to an arable *ejido* plot.[7] Besides working as day labourers on the fields of others, or at jobs in the sugarcane refinery or in the service sector in Autlán, migration to the United States has been an important source of income for landless as well as *ejidatario* families.

This growing group of landless families in the village are called *avecindados* (residents) and the common *ejido* lands have always been an important resource for them. Although officially the commons belongs to the *ejidatarios*, these official owners did not complain if *avecindados* collected fruits and vegetables or hunted there, as the land is steep and stony. According to the season, the commons may be used for collecting fruits (*pitayas, tunas*) and vegetables (*nopales, guamuchiles*), for hunting,

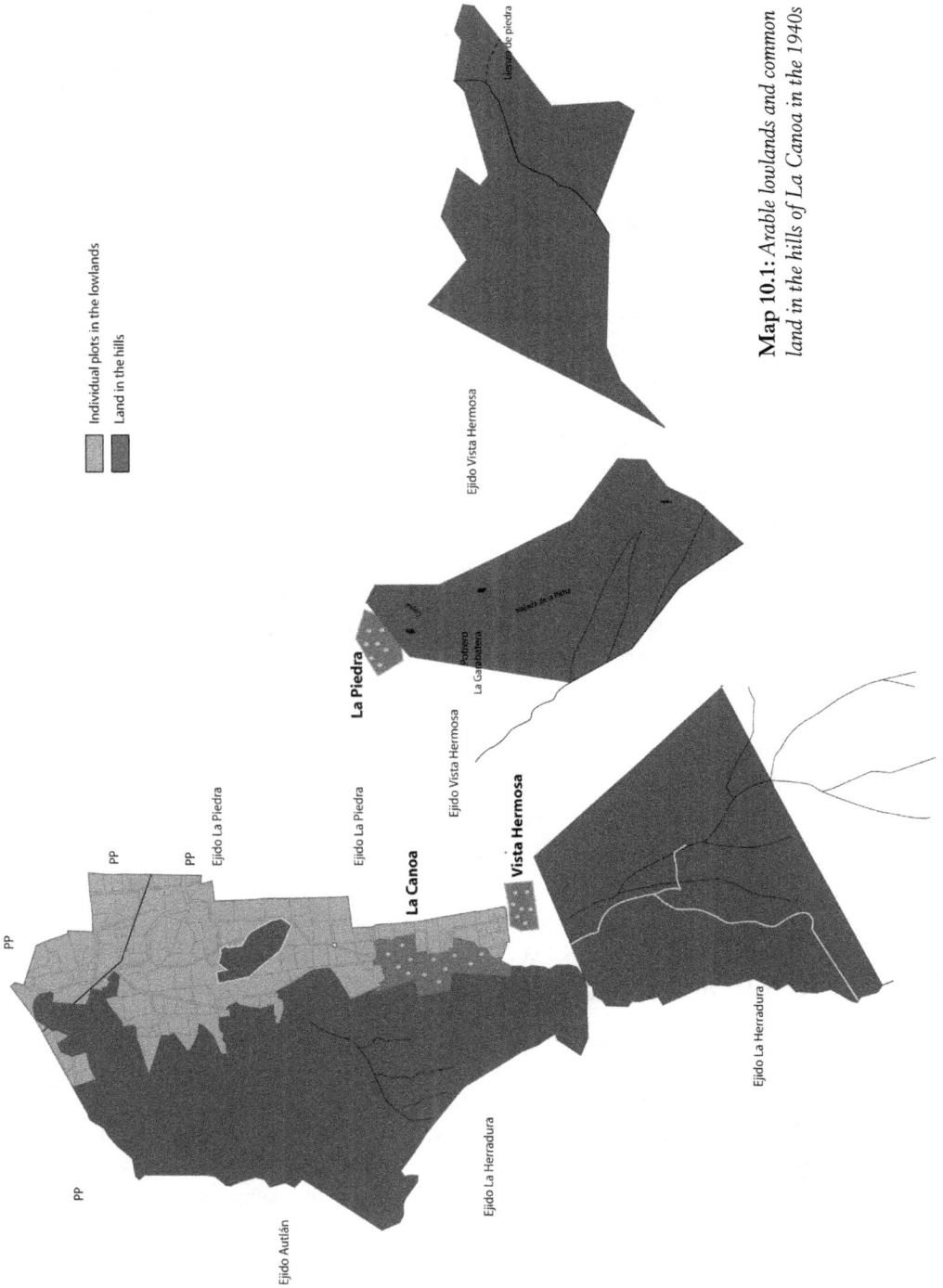

Individual plots in the lowlands

Land in the hills

Lienzo de piedra

Ejido Vista Hermosa

La Piedra

Potrero
La Garrabatera

Majada de la Peña

Ejido Vista Hermosa

Vista Hermosa

PP

PP

PP

Ejido La Piedra

Ejido La Piedra

La Canoa

Ejido Vista Hermosa

PP

Ejido Autlán

Ejido La Herradura

Ejido La Herradura

Map 10.1: *Arable lowlands and common land in the hills of La Canoa in the 1940s*

gathering firewood, and for the herding of cattle. The herding of cattle is especially favourable in the humid parts of the commons, where people have built water reservoirs. Although the official legal name of this part of the *ejido* is *tierra de uso común* (land of communal use), people never use this term but always talk about *los esquilmos, los coamiles* or *el cerro* (general names for these mountainous areas). *Esquilmos* are common fields, whether sown with grasses or of natural vegetation, that are used for the herding of cattle. *Coamil* refers to a specific form of agriculture in the hills in which slopes are deforested, burnt and sown with a *coa*, the only agricultural tool of use in these parts.

Because of the limited economic value of the land and the 'remoteness' – in terms of access rather than physical distance – the commons are a sort of 'frontier area'. It is not always easy to find out what exactly is going on there and much happens outside the 'public view'. An interesting phenomenon is that *ejidatarios* have to consult with the *avecindados* when they wish to resolve issues related to the commons, such as boundaries with other *ejidos*. The *avecindados* have either worked there for themselves or as labourers for the *ejidatarios*. This has led to the paradoxical situation that *avecindados* have much more knowledge of the hills than *ejidatarios,* the official owners of the commons.

In La Canoa, an official regulation for use of the commons was never made. Today a large part of the commons has been fenced by the *ejido* and the pasture here is rented every year to a neighbouring *ejido*, thus serving as an important source of revenue for the *ejido*. Other parts of the commons are rented to a neighbouring *ejido* for the cultivation of maize, and in exchange, the cultivators leave the corn stalks for La Canoa cattle. Yet another part of the commons is enclosed and used for the collective herding of cattle of the *ejidatarios* of La Canoa. Finally, there are many individual plots in the commons, which are also enclosed (see Map 10.2).

The Relation Between Land Use Patterns in the Commons and the Wider Economy

Here we present a historical analysis of land use patterns in the commons and how these were shaped by wider socioeconomic processes. Villagers refer to the period shortly after the establishment of the *ejido* by saying: 'In the past, the hills were free' (*el cerro era libre*). Although everybody realised that the land officially belonged to the *ejido*, the use of these extensive areas for hunting and gathering was to a large extent 'free' and

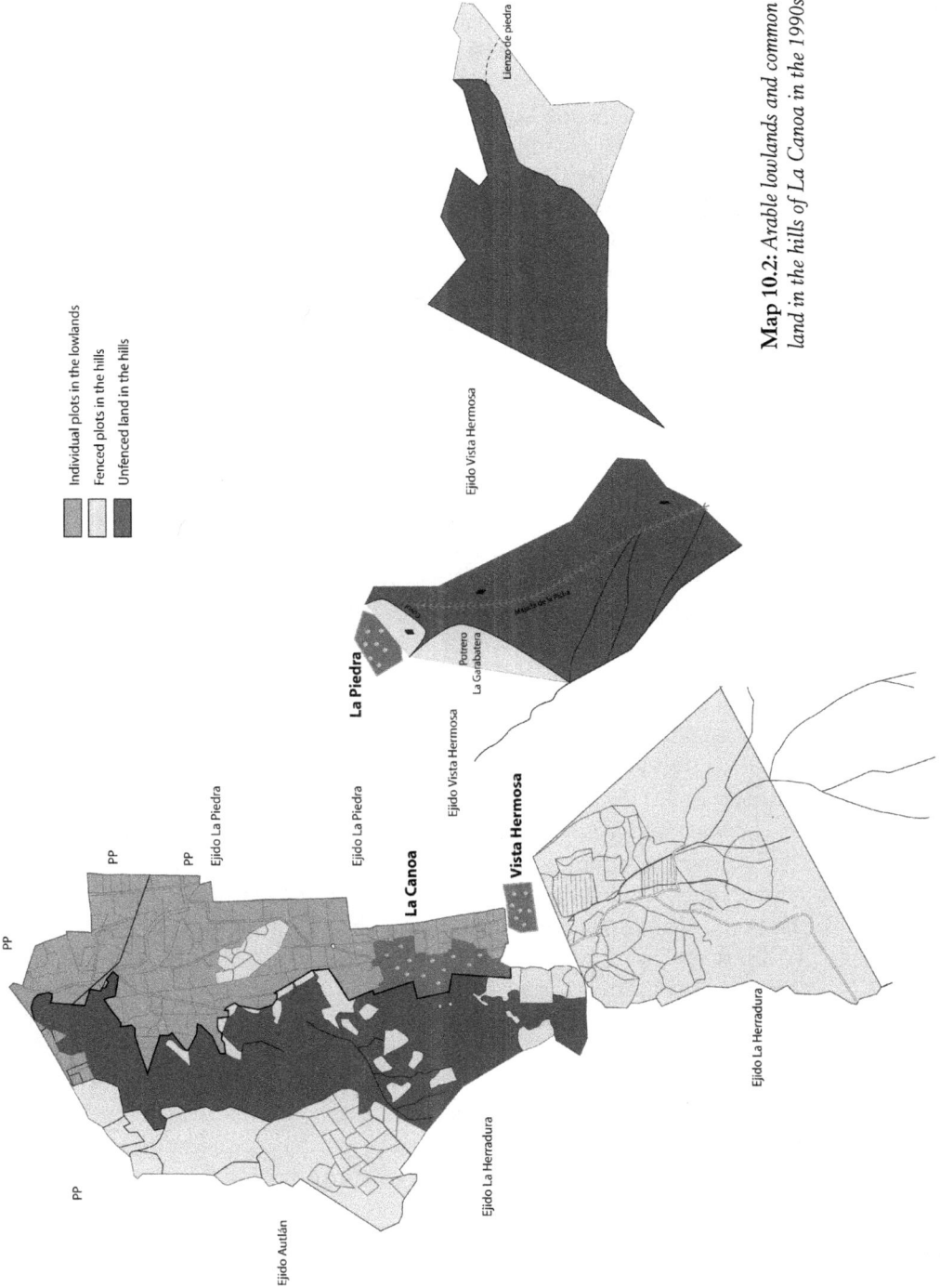

Map 10.2: *Arable lowlands and common land in the hills of La Canoa in the 1990s*

'invisible' to the public eye. In these years, *ejidatarios* used the hills mostly for herding cattle. Extensive animal husbandry in the mountains and cultivation of maize on the lowlands during the rainy season were complementary activities. The animals came down from the mountains when the plots in the lowlands had been harvested. In this way the corn stalks could be used as fodder for cattle during the dry period when there was a scarcity of natural pasture in the hills.

The situation changed at the beginning of the 1960s when half of the arable land of La Canoa received irrigation from a government system. This meant that *ejidatarios* with irrigated land could cultivate their lands during the whole year. Hence the cattle that came down from the hills in the dry period could now only use the leftovers of the remaining rainfed plots. This development put an end to the complementarity of maize production in the lowlands and animal husbandry in the commons. Extensive animal husbandry became less profitable but remained an important activity in the commons.

Because of the growing pressure on the land 'below', the agricultural frontier moved to the hills, the only land that remained open for exploitation. Despite the limitations of the steep terrains and many stones, the land is fertile, has a better precipitation pattern and less risks of crop disease. Because of the higher altitude it also has important advantages for the cultivation of maize, the basic ingredient of the rural diet. These favourable conditions stimulated *coamil* agriculture, and both landless families and *ejidatarios* now practiced *it*. *Ejidatarios* often cultivate maize on the *coamil* as a form of spreading agricultural risk. But there are also *ejidatarios* who think the *coamil* is much too labour-intensive and show no interest in working on the hills.

The *coamiles* are cultivated during the rainy period, during which time the cattle are returning to the hills. In contrast to the cultivation of the rainfed plots in the lowlands, *coamil* agriculture is thus incompatible with the practice of extensive animal husbandry. That explains why in the 1970s, the villagers began to enclose plots in the hills in order to protect the maize against damage by cattle. After the maize harvest, the leftovers on the *coamiles* can be sold as fodder, thus allowing extensive animal husbandry and *coamil* cultivation to partially complement each other.

In the 1980s, the hills began to be used for clandestine activities such as the cultivation of marihuana (*mota*) and poppies. This illicit cultivation was widespread in Mexico at that time, especially in the more isolated common lands. Gledhill (1997: 10) argues that this production of drugs in rural areas was an alternative and profitable use for land that formerly had been used for pastoral production but that had become unprofitable as a result of the crisis in the agricultural sector. In La Canoa there were many marihuana and poppies fields, in the lowlands as well as in the hills. When government control became more severe, the crops moved higher and higher into the hills. Opiates were cultivated as a mixed crop with maize and in the open spaces of the woods. At the beginning of the 1990s, the eradication of marihuana was followed by a return to maize cultivation in the hills. An analysis of the *ejido* sector (Davis et al. 1999: 2) reveals that access to the commons was one factor that positively affected domestic economies between 1994 and 1997. Many landless families improved their living standard when remittances from migration helped finance fences for the *coamiles*. For the landless families in La Canoa, access to a *coamil* meant an important difference for family survival.

When the government dropped the guaranteed price as part of the Free Trade Agreement with the United States and Canada, the market for maize took a downturn, resulting in the abandonment of maize in the hills and a reconversion into pasture. While sowing pasture was more profitable and less risky, animal husbandry quickly became unprofitable as well with the free trade agreement for cattle coming into force at the beginning of 2003. Another problem for animal husbandry is that all the lowlands in La Canoa are now irrigated and maize has been replaced by sugarcane. Cattle can no longer use the maize leftovers on the rainfed land. Most cattle owners have sold their cattle and there are few cattle in the hills at present. As maize production has also become unprofitable many *coamiles* in the commons are useless. This leads to the strange situation that today many plots in the commons are enclosed but abandoned.

Different Categories of Villagers and the Construction of Valuables as Property Objects

In order to understand the development of property relations in the commons of La Canoa, we have to take the sociopolitical differences in the village into account as well as the transformation in productive patterns. As was mentioned in the beginning of the chapter, property relations become expressed in actual social relationships. In La Canoa it is obvious that existing social and economic relationships to a large extent directed the development of property relations. For example, at the start of the *ejido*, the poor and the landless were not explicitly excluded from the use of the commons but they did not have the cattle to make use of it. As Brouwer (1992) has shown for the common lands in Portugal, so-called 'open access' is not necessarily most important for the poor and landless. It is the rich people, especially the cattle owners who can benefit most. In this way, even though they were said to be 'free', the commons accentuated the existing economic and social differences.

During the 1960s a change in land use occurred with the irrigation of part of the lowlands. During this period, many landless villagers were given permission to clean a part of the commons for an individual *coamil* on the condition that they would leave the corn stalks for the cattle. Despite this, some rich *ejidatarios* resisted the development as they needed the landless as workers on their plots and for looking after their cattle. Thus, they attempted to deny their workers the right to a *coamil*, for fear that they would loose their labourers, as is illustrated in the following example.

Felipe is an *avecindado* of La Canoa who received a *coamil* twenty-three years ago. Felipe came to live in La Canoa when he married the daughter of an *ejidatario* in the village. He had no land and worked for the other *ejidatarios*. He was the fixed worker of Ricardo, one of the richest and most powerful men in the village. When Ricardo was *ejido* commissioner, Felipe asked him permission to take a *coamil* in the commons. However, Ricardo said that he did not want to give him a *coamil*, because then he would loose Felipe as his fixed worker.

> Felipe: He feared that I would only be interested in working my own coamil then. So then I waited for him to the leave the position of commissioner and then asked the next commissioner, Marcos, for a coamil. Marcos asked permission at the *ejido* assembly. At that occasion, he asked a coamil for three of us. Not all *ejidatarios* agreed with it. If it was not for José, I doubt that we would have gotten a coamil. Some started asking why the *ejido* should give me a coamil as I am not an ejidatario, nor the son of an ejidatario. José said; this man wants a plot to work it himself, let's give him a plot. One of the *ejidatarios* who most opposed to it was Eusebio. He said: remember that many of our sons live abroad. One day they will return. Then there will be no more land left for them. Then all land will have been taken. José responded: do you really think that when our migrated sons return they will go and move stones in these damned hills! These men want their plot to work it. Finally, the other *ejidatarios* agreed and we received a plot.

As no explicit rules existed in the *ejido* about rights of *avecindados* to plots in the commons, these requests were obviously prone to negotiations and different interests. In the case of Felipe, we see that the landless were sometimes denied access to land in the commons because they were needed as labourers on the land of the richer *ejidatarios*.

A similar development in which the poor were indirectly excluded, occurred in the 1970s when in order to keep cattle from damaging the sown fields, strong fences had to be made around the *coamiles*. The poles were not a problem as there were many available from clearing the hills. The wire, however, had to be bought and some used remittances from the U.S.A. for this purpose. For *avecindados,* fencing money was their biggest limitation in getting a piece of land. This means that again the *ejidatarios* were the ones who could profit most from the hills. Again the socioeconomic differences in the village are accentuated, not because the poor could not get formal access to the commons, but because they did not have the money to fence their plots and protect the land from the cattle. This was clearly expressed by the *avecindado* Guillermo:

> The *ejidatarios* appropiated land by taking the law into their own hands [a la ley del tigre] because they have money. The miserables [los jodidos] … with what can they take? They don't have money to enclose. Whereas the others [*ejidatarios*] just go, see, make their calculation and buy the wire for the fences.

So, access to the commons was limited by the resources people had with which to enclose. This has also been described for other communities in the region (Gerritsen 2001). As a consequence, many landless villagers did not ask for land and the distribution of land in the commons among villagers is very unequal. In 2003 60 percent of the individual plots in the commons were in the hands of *ejidatarios* (Lorenzo 2003). So we see that *avecindados* were not excluded from the commons on the basis of formal rules that denied their rights to access, but on the basis of other factors such as having no cattle that could make use of the common lands, the lack of money to enclose a plot and the influence of the rich *ejidatarios* who were afraid of losing their labour.

This phenomenon of direct and indirect exclusion is especially painful for the *avecindados,* as they tend to be sons of *ejidatarios* who did not inherit any land from their father. Hence, the *coamil* is their only remaining link with the land. It remains a poor substitute, for they possess the land only as a loan from the *ejido* and they are excluded from the *ejido* community. In this way they are second-rate peasants. Still it makes it possible for them to continue a 'peasant way of life'.

This 'peasant way of life' and the related importance of land in the rural Mexican setting has several reasons (Nuijten 2001). Obviously, land is important for providing some basic food security. In addition, the production of one's own maize has a strong cultural significance. Yet, most of all, the possession of *ejido* land is related to the agrarian struggle at the beginning of the twentieth century. Several people lost their lives in the fight against the *hacendados*. The *ejidatarios* today claim that they are directly related to this heroic past while at the same time they argue that the landless villagers did not play a role in the struggle for land and the establishment of the *ejido*. This explains the strong value attached to the possession of land in the Mexican context. As González argues: 'in the rural environment almost the only way to stand out, to be taken seriously, to become a respectable and respected person is to be the owner of arable and pastoral lands' (1988: 56, authors' translation).

Many *avecindados* consider their plot in the commons as the last opportunity to be recognised in the future as full members of the community, that is to say as *ejidatarios*. Their hope is based on the fact that in the past some people have become *ejidatario* on the basis of a *coamil* in the hills. The *avecindados* would like very much to become part of the core group from which they now are excluded. As Hann points out, property is linked to a vast field of cultural and social relations within which collective identities are made (Hann 1998: 5). In La Canoa possession of land in the commons involves sociopolitical relationships in which different identities are defined and different types of claims can be asserted. Although less than the arable *ejido* land, the common lands also have a strong symbolic significance. This land is especially important for the *avecindados* who have not inherited arable *ejido* plots.

Practices of Access and the Development of Property Rights

As mentioned above, no regulation controls use of land in the commons in La Canoa. The only national rule, to which local people frequently refer, is the rule that the *ejido* is the formal owner of the commons. Although no specific rules exist about individal use of land in the commons, over the years certain practices developed. However, much variety exists in these practices and it would be inaccurate to talk in terms of established and generally accepted practices that have turned into a system of local property rules.

The procedure by which people got access to commons land differed. The formal procedure, for *ejidatarios* as well as *avecindados*, was to ask permission at the general assembly of *ejidatarios*, the highest *ejido* authority. However, in most cases permission was asked of the *ejido* commissioner who then decided on his own. There were no local rules on which the commissioner could base his decision and most of the time people were given permission to use the land. When people were given permission by the assembly or by the commissioner, it was quite common that they enclosed more land than was officially allowed. There were also *ejidatarios* who never asked permission for the land that they enclosed. The *avecindados*, however, always asked permission. Officially the *ejido* only lends such people the land so that they can cultivate it for several years and then return it to the *ejido*.

Such permissions were normally oral agreements not formally registered. Only in a few cases were acts drawn up. Yet, no copies of these acts were given to the people concerned and as the *ejido* archive is very incomplete, many of these acts are now lost. Thus it is very confusing as to who gave permission for what. For example, it happened sometimes that an *ejidatario* or an *avecindado* said that commissioner Romero gave him permission to take land in the commons, while commissioner Romero denied this and said that probably it had been commissioner Paz. In his turn, commissioner Paz denied everything.

As was mentioned, the division into plots in the hills began in the early 1970s, when the agricultural frontier moved upland and people started cultivating *coamiles*. Enclosure of plots was officially forbidden by law, however, locally it was accepted and from the moment people enclosed a plot, they had to pay tax to the *ejido*.[8] The tax is a fixed amount per hectare per year for *ejidatarios* as well as for *avecindados*. *Ejidatarios* and *avecindados* pay the same amount per hectare but it is quite common that the *ejidatarios* pay for less hectares than they really have, whereas the *avecindados* pay for more. The *avecindados* do not resist this as the tax is a small amount of money and may prevent problems with the *ejido*. The tax payment has turned into a symbolic form of official recognition of the right to use a specific parcel of commons land. In the case of conflicts these receipts make it possible to show that use rights were recognised by the *ejido*. On the other hand, if the *ejido* treasurer does not accept the tax payment this means that you are in trouble. As the *avecindados* feel insecure in their possession of the *coamiles*, for them both the payment of the tax and the receipts are especially important. In contrast, many *ejidatarios* forget to pay entirely.

There are other indirect ways through which the *avecindados* feel strengthened in certain property rights and through which they experience a form of recognition of their position. For example, in 1993 the Mexican government introduced the PROCAMPO subsidy programme for agricultural producers. People receive subsidy for a variety of crops, including maize and pasture. A significant difference in comparison to former subsidy programmes in the agricultural sector is that this subsidy is also given for production in the hills, so that *coamiles* with maize and *esquilmos* sown with pasture receive a subsidy per hectare in the same way as plots in the lowlands. Another difference is that the subsidy is not for the owner of the land, but for the person who cultivates the land, irrespective whether he/she is an *ejidatario* or *avecindado*. For the *avecindados* this has enormous significance as for the first time in history they are to a certain extent officially recognised in their use of a plot in the commons. One of the unintended consequences of this subsidy programme is that it has strengthened *avecindados* claims to land. Further, plots in the commons with a subsidy attached to it immediately rise in value as a commodity.

People who have been cultivating their *coamil* for many years feel that they have developed certain individual property rights to this land, and it has become common practice that *coamiles* are passed on to children as a form of inheritance. *Coamiles* are also exchanged and even sold. By national law all these transactions are forbidden, but the *ejidatarios* differ in their opinion about these practices and there is no general agreement. Sales among *ejidatarios* are generally respected, but sales which involve *avecindados* are much more criticised. Sales to outsiders are generally not accepted and the few times that it has happened, they were cancelled by the *ejido*. In order to be on the safe side, sales are often formalised through a notary and in the presence of witnesses. Although the documents mention the price of the land, in reality *coamiles* are hardly ever transferred for money but always for goods, such as a truck, several cattle or sheep.

Even though all sale of land in the commons is officially illegal, any sale by *ejidatarios* has a higher legal security than that by the *avecindados*. For that reason the price of a *coamil* sold by *ejidatarios* is higher than if one is bought from an *avecindado*. In the price, people take into account that in the future sales by *ejidatarios* will be respected, whereas the sale by *avecindados* might well be cancelled. Antonio Romero who bought *coamiles* from *ejidatarios*, as well as from *avecindados* explains the situation in the following way: 'Since the 1970s when people started enclosing, 11 plots have been sold and 19 have been passed over as inheritance'. Antonio: '*Ejidatarios* as well as non-*ejidatarios* have sold me land. In case the *ejido* decides to divide the land among *ejidatarios*, they will have to give me the land that belongs to the one from whom I bought the land. Obviously I will claim that land as I bought it. In case of the ones who are not ejidatario the situation is more complicated, but these *coamiles* are also cheaper'. The inheritance of *coamiles* is generally accepted for *ejidatarios* as well as for *avecindados*. *Ejidatarios* never criticise the *avecindados* if a widow or a son continue to work the land of a deceased man, as is shown in the following interview with an *avecindado*:

> Da: What would you do to make sure that your *coamil* would stay within the family the day you would pass away?
>
> Fe: During my life I would leave a document, signed by a notary and two witnesses with the name of the son whom I would leave the land to.
>
> Da: Would you not ask permission from somebody from the directive committee of the *ejido*?
>
> Fe: No. I have made sure that when I die somebody of my family will take care of the continuation of the tax payment.
>
> Da: Are you so sure that they will continue to receive the tax?
>
> Fe: Until now they have done so …

Persons who have bought land in the commons feel that they have private property rights over these plots. In fact, *ejidatarios* as well as *avecindados* have bought *coamiles*. There may be several reasons to buy a *coamil* instead of asking permission to clear a plot, including: the plot is already cleared; permission does not have to be obtained from the *ejido*; or the presence of water. Whereas many *ejidatarios* say that officially these people cannot claim any property rights, opinions differ and the buyers obviously see this in a very different way.

Differences in interests and opinions exist not only between *ejidatarios* and *avecindados*, but also among *ejidatarios* themselves. For example, an issue that many *ejidatarios* consider to be a serious problem is that some *ejidatarios* have taken and fenced enormous parts of the commons and rent the pasture for their own benefit. Some rent the pasture lands for two hundred thousand pesos (67 USD) per hectare to cattle owners, while the *ejido* only charges the symbolic tax of one thousand pesos (0.33 USD) per hectare. Thus, the usurpers make a profit at the expense of the *ejido*.

To a certain extent land in the commons has been privatised and commoditised. Yet, the practices that have developed are not clear-cut and rights are not the same for everybody. Although there is no general agreement on these issues, many *ejidatarios* accept the inheritance of land in the commons by *avecindados*, but not the sale of plots. The sale of plots among *ejidatarios* is more generally but by no means universally accepted.

Struggles around the Commons and the Discursive Framing of Property Rights

Despite the abundance of land in the hills, and the fact that much of it is not used anymore, the *ejidatarios* always express their preoccupation with the fact that there is hardly any land left. Many *ejidatarios* fear that soon there will be no land available anymore for themselves or their children. The changes of the Agrarian Law in 1992 stirred up these local discussions. In fact, the new Agrarian Law and the accompanying PROCEDE programme (aimed at measuring and registering *ejido* lands) had more influence on local discussions about the commons than on the arable land. For the arable land, the new Agrarian Law was an adaptation to reality, as arable land had in practice already become individual private property in most *ejidos* throughout Mexico. However, for the *ejido* common lands new rules were introduced. For example, the new Agrarian Law allows the *ejido* to divide the common lands into individual plots. Many *ejidatarios* say that this is the moment to take land back from the *avecindados* and to divide the commons in equal parts among all *ejidatarios*. Obviously, this is a highly sensitive issue. *Ejidatarios* who possess large extensions in the commons are very much against these plans, as are *avecindados* and people who have bought a *coamil*. For the time being these have only been plans and threats and no concrete action has been undertaken. One reason may be that the new Agrarian Law still prohibits the sale of plots in the commons.

There are several reasons to prevent the *ejido* from taking concrete action against the *avencindados*. In the first place, the *ejidatarios* are very divided on the issue and among *ejidatarios* themselves much more serious conflicts are going on. In the second place, the value of the *coamil* is low and not comparable to the value of arable plots in the lowlands. Thirdly, many *ejidatarios* are close relatives of *avecindados*. They may be their brothers or sons. So, although the *ejidatarios* may be annoyed that the commons are 'invaded' by families who do not have formal rights to this land, denying their brothers and sons is another issue. Still, a lot of verbal fighting and claim-making goes on with respect to the commons plots.

According to most *ejidatarios*, the central categorisation with respect to property rights in the commons is the degree of relatedness to an *ejidatario* - whether the son of an *ejidatario* or 'being nothing' (*no es nada*) and unrelated through kinship. The further the kinship distance, therefore, between a person and an *ejidatario*, the less rights he/she can claim to land.

The landless people in their turn recognise that the *ejido* only lent them the land and that the *ejido* remains the 'real owner'. At the same time they feel that they have developed certain rights to 'their' *coamil* or *esquilmo*, and are very angry with what they call the selfish and egoistic attitude of the *ejidatarios*, who are better off and yet claim lands that landless families have been working for many years. One example is the case of José Luís. He is a man in his sixties who arrived in La Canoa in 1954 to visit an uncle. There was much work in cotton production at that time and José Luís found work and stayed. The *ejido* lent him and his wife a *coamil* in the commons. Today José Luís sells sweets and *raspados* (ice) at a table in the centre of the village. He is a nice quiet man, who is respected by everybody. However, when he talks about his *coamil*, a fighting spirit emerges. José Luís explained to me in 1993:

> The comunidad [*ejido*] wants to take away the *coamiles* from us. In the times that we received the land, there was much land above which they did not use; they lent it to us; as long as we cultivated it, we could keep it. They lent me 1,5 hectares. Afterwards I took more. I possess two hectares now. I have been working this plot for fifteen years now. Three years ago, the *ejidatarios* started talking about taking the *coamiles* back. The government does not allow them to take it away from us; it is not mine but ... if they really want to take it away they can. But all the people with a coamil agreed, that we won't let this happen. We will go to Guadalajara or to Mexico City. The *ejidatarios* have more than enough land and should not take the *coamiles* away from us.

José Luís passed away, but in 2003 we talked to his son Héctor who expresses the same spirit,

> Hé: We [referring to his family] have worked this plot for more than twenty years. We were born in this village and are Mexicans, we have right to a plot of land whether the *ejidatarios* like it or not. In this village there is much envy... It is the Tunny!
>
> Da: Can you explain what you mean by Tunny, others also have used this term.
>
> Hé: the Tunny is a very fat lady who cannot eat more because she is full, but she does not let others eat who are hungry. Now they want to take the land away from us ...

However, the non-*ejidatarios* are very careful with expressing these feelings in public as they realise that their position is one of dependence; officially the control rests with the *ejidatarios*.

It is interesting to note that divisions exist among the landless families themselves; landless sons of *ejidatarios* claim that they have more rights to land in the commons than landless people in the village who are not even related to *ejidatarios*. Some sons of *ejidatarios* even argue that they have more rights than the *ejidatarios*, as they see themselves as the first generation of men for whom there was no arable land available and who were thus excluded from the *ejido*. They feel abandoned by the *ejidatarios* who only think in their own interest. For example, Gerardo Lagos, who himself is a landless son of an *ejidatario* said the following when he was discussing the problems of the commons with several men:

> It's a scandal that everybody is taking land wherever he likes, without taking into account the people who really need it; the sons of the *ejidatarios*! I myself am the son of an ejidatario and it hurts me to see how people with much cattle go to the hills and fence some terrains without consulting anybody. I will go to the hills and take some land myself as well. Let them accuse me in an *ejido* meeting. Then I will talk against the abusers. What we need is another revolution! I know of people who are not *ejidatarios*, nor sons of *ejidatarios* and they give them land in the hills!

Thus, some groups claim to have more rights to the commons than others and they use a language of differing rights. The *ejidatarios* use a language which is based on the Agrarian Law that states that the commons belong to the *ejido* and not to the village. In their turn, the non-*ejidatarios* use a language of moral rights and local recognition to claim rights to their *coamil*. So, while the agricultural frontier moved up into the hills, the frontier that never changed was that between the village and the *ejido*, between the *avecindados* and the *ejidatarios* (Lorenzo 2003).

Conclusion: Practices and Property Relations in a 'frontier area'

In this chapter the development of property relations in the commons have been discussed in a situation where no formal property rules exist other than that the *ejido* is the official owner of 1800 hectares of land in the hills. It was shown how and why in different periods of time the common lands signified distinct types of property objects for different categories of villagers. At the start of the *ejido*, the commons were considered to be 'free' in the sense that all villagers could make use of it. However, at that time poor *ejidatarios* and landless *avecinados* did not have animals to make use of the natural pasture. The poor and landless were not denied rights to land in the commons but they were not in the position to exercise those rights as were the rich *ejidatarios* in the village who owned large herds of cattle. This illustrates that property rights are closely linked to other social and economic conditions.

With the growing scarcity of arable lowlands, the commons became attractive for agriculture in the form of *coamiles*. Here we clearly see the changing meaning of land as property object. Land in the commons was no longer seen only as valuable in the form of grazing lands, but was also valued for the cultivation of maize. This raised the value of land in the commons as property object. Many landless *avecindados* were given permission to take a plot in the commons for a *coamil*, but again there were other factors at play that limited them exercising these rights. First of all, some of the richer *ejidatarios* did not want to loose the landless as labourers on their arable lands. In several cases *avecindados* who asked permission to clear a plot in the commons were denied these rights. Another limit on their access to *coamiles* was that they did not have the money to pay for fences necessary to protect the crop from damage by cattle.

At a later stage when the *avecindados* became more prosperous, many of them asked and received permission to enclose lands in the commons. Yet, as the *ejido* is the official owner of the commons, accepting these rights always implied entering into a domain of negotiation with the *ejido*. For example, they had to make sure not to bother the *ejidatarios* in any way and to be seen as quiet and responsible villagers. 'Troublemakers' were not given access or their plots were taken away from them. So, for the *avecindados* property in the commons entail a bundle of rights and obligations with the *ejidatarios*, in which they lose a certain independence and have to exercise care in their other village activities.

As many *ejidatarios* and *avecindados* have used their plots in the commons for many years consecutively, a new set of property relations has come into being. Gradually, people have started to develop private property rights over their land and the privatisation and commoditisation of plots in the commons has partly become institutionalised. This is shown by the fact that many plots in the commons have been inherited, exchanged between individual persons and even sold. Another phenomenon is that some of the richer *ejidatarios* have appropiated and fenced enormous extensions of common lands. Yet, these more recent practices have not turned into generally accepted property relations. On the contrary, they have led to much local tension and heated debates take place in the village about who has what type of rights to land in the commons, about who can be property holders and what these property rights entail.

Different discursive framing of rights reflects sociopolitical divisions in the village (see also Peters, Van Meijl and James, this volume, for similar arguments). The point is that property relations are embedded in wider fields of social relationships. For example, many *ejidatarios* would like to take the land away from the rich *ejidatarios* who have appropiated hundreds of hectares. Officially the *ejido* assembly as highest authority is authorised to do so. But taking land away from the rich involves messy and difficult sociopolitical processes which would normally have high social costs. In a different way social relationships play a crucial role in the discussion around the plots kept by the *avecindados*. Many *ejidatarios* would like to take the land in the commons away from the *avecindados* and distribute the land equally among all *ejidatarios*. These *ejidatarios* refer to the fact that they are the 'real owners' of the commons and that *avecindados* only have access as long as the *ejidatarios* give them permission. Although formally this is perfectly true, all *avecindados* are in one way or another related to the *ejidatarios*; as friends, neighbours or relatives. These people have perhaps no formal rights but certainly can claim certain 'moral' property rights to the land. These moral claims are strengthened by the fact that during many years the *ejido* received their tax payments for the land. So, practices around tax payment which developed a long time ago when no tensions around the commons existed, are used today to claim certain rights to the land. So far, the *aveindados* have not been evicted from the commons but they have to suffer humiliations and constant threats of eviction. Government programmes and changes in official state law indirectly influence these struggles. The PROCAMPO subsidy programme supported the *avecindados* in claiming certain rights by providing them subisidies for their *coamiles*. In contrast, the new Agrarian Law of 1992 stirred up emotions against the *avecindados* as the *ejido* is now given the formal right to divide the commons into individual plots. Many *ejidatarios* see this as the right moment to 'clear up' the common land and divide it in equal parts among all *ejidatarios*.

It would be tempting to analyse changing property relations in the commons of La Canoa in terms of a lineal relation between population growth and available land, implying that because of the growing scarcity of cultivable land people increasingly started using the commons. The increased use of the commons would then explain the growing tension in the village with respect to property relations in the commons. This analysis, however, would be seriously flawed and would not explain why continuous struggles exist over land that is not much used anymore. This phenomenon can only be explained by taking the ideological and cultural dimensions into account that affect social relationships in the village and that are reflected in the construction of land as a valuable property object, even when it is not used for productive ends. Most importantly, land in the *ejido* has ideological significance related to the historical significance of the agrarian reform in the first half of the twentieth century. This history is part of the value of land as property object. It explains why the attitude of *ejidatarios* and *avecindados* towards land cannot be reduced to an economic rational choice model. This historical significance also suggests that a change in official property rules will not automatically result in the expected changes in resource management (Spiertz and Wiber 1996: 1). This is precisely what many policy makers, who only stress the economic function of land and use a very limited notion of land tenure, do not recognise (Nuijten 2003b).

In fact, one could argue that the fight around the commons land is less about the economic value of the land than about 'the fear of exclusion', of 'not belonging' to the core community (*ejido*). For the *avecindados*, the issue of exclusion is linked to the notion of being a 'second-rate citizen' and thus not having received an individual arable *ejido* plot. A *coamil* is a form of substitution. In their turn, *ejidatarios* fear that they are losing control over resources that formally belonged to them. Even if they do not use the hills at the moment, they fear the prospect of losing the land in the future. One could see it as the image of the limited/extinguishable good. Even if you yourself do not need it at the moment, you fear that other people might then use it and develop claims and rights to something that you or your children may need in the future. Thus the fierce fights around the commons, while there is still much land left unemployed, and while there is no scarcity of land. This leads to the paradox that in a situation of apparent abundant land, severe emotional struggles take place centred on the commons. Hence, the problem with the commons is not one of overuse, but of privatisation and exclusion (Rifkin 2000). For *ejidatarios* as well as *avecindados*, the struggle concerns the right not to be excluded from access to a valuable with strong ideological meaning.

Finally, we argue that a better understanding of property relations in their respective force fields is crucial for the debates about the management of natural resources. A large part of Mexican forest and pasture resources can be found in the common *ejido* lands. In La Canoa, the *ejido,* as a local institution, has been responsible for the commons management since the creation of their *ejido* in 1938. Many studies on sustainable development formulate solutions for the maintenance and use of common lands in terms of returning responsibility for the management of natural resources to local communities (Ghai and Vivian 1992; Berkes 1995). The basic underlying idea is the assumption that an institution exists with certain rules with respect to land tenure, centralised decision-making organs and procedures for conflict resolution. Yet, as the situation in La Canoa has shown, property relations tend to be incredibly more complex and demand a much more sophisticated frameworks of analysis.

Notes

1. The first part of the research was conducted in the *ejido* La Canoa and several government agencies from 1991 to mid 1995. This research was financed by WOTRO (the Netherlands Foundation for the Advancement of Tropical Research). The continuation of the research project between 2000 and 2006 is financed by the KNAW (the Netherlands Academy of Arts and Sciences).
2. We thank Juan Ayala for drawing the maps.
3. The coherence, ruling and regularities that may be observed in a given state of the field, or even its apparent orientation toward a common function, emanate from conflict and competition, and not from some kind of immanent self-development of the structure. The field is the locus of relations of force and not only of meaning. A difference between Bourdieu's approach and ours is that we do not focus on different types of capital in society at large but instead focus on the field of force around specific resources in a defined and reduced context.
4. INEGI 1988, Encuesta Nacional Agropuecuario Ejidal, 1988, volume I: Resumen general.
5. INEGI 1991, XI Censo General de Población y Vivienda, 1990. Jalisco. Resultados definitivos. Datos por Localidad (Integración Territorial).
6. Departamento de Estadística Nacional, 1926.
7. Figure of 1993.
8. In 2003 there were 126 fenced plots in the commons of La Canoa.

References

Berkes, F. 1995. 'Community-Based Management and Co-Management as Tools for Empowerment', in *Empowerment: Towards Sustainable Development,* eds N. Singh and V. Titi, London: Zed Books, 138–46.

Bourdieu, P. and L. Wacquant 1992. *An Invitation to Reflexive Sociology*. Chicago: University of Chicago Press.

Brouwer, R. 1992. 'The Commons in Portugal: A Story of Static Representations and Dynamic Social Processes', in *Law as a Resource in Agrarian Struggles*, eds F. von Benda-Beckmann and M. van der Velde, Wageningen Agricultural University, 127–48.

Davis, B., A. de Janvry, E. Sadoulet and T. Deihl 1999. 'An Analysis of Poverty in the Mexican *Ejido* Sector', paper presented to the workshop 'Land in Latin America: New context, New Claims, New Concepts', organized by CERES, WAU and CEDLA, Amsterdam, 26–27 May 1999.

Gerritsen, P.R.W. 2001. 'Estilos agrarios en la comunidad indígena de Cuzalapa en la Reserva de la Biosfera Sierra de Manantlán, en Jalisco y Colima.', in *Historia ambiental de la ganadería en México*, ed. L. Hernández, Xalapa: Instituto de Ecología/IRD, 176–85.

Ghai, D. and J. Vivian, eds 1992. *Grassroots Environmental Action: People's Participation in Sustainable Development*. London: Routledge for UNRISD.

Gledhill, J. 1997. 'Fantasy and Reality in Restructuring Mexico's Land Reform', paper presented at the annual meeting of the Society for Latin American Studies, St Andrews, Scotland.

González, L. 1988. 'Lugares Comunes Acerca de lo Rural', in *Las Sociedades Rurales Hoy*, ed. J. Zepeda, Zamora: Colegio de Michoacán, CONACYT, 51–61.

Hann, C.M., ed. 1998. *Property Relations; Renewing the Anthropological Tradition*. Cambridge: Cambridge University Press.

INEGI 1988. 'Encuesta Nacional Agropecuaria Ejidal, 1988', vol. I, Aguascalientes: INEGI.

INEGI 1991. 'XI Censo General de Población y Vivienda, 1990', Agualscalientes: INEGI.

Lorenzo, D. 2003. 'Yo tambien quiero tener! Como las personas organizan el acceso y uso a los terrenos comunales en un *ejido* mexicano', Masters thesis, University of Wageningen.

Moore, S.F. 1973. 'Law and Social Change: The Semi-autonomous Social Fields as an Appropriate Subject of Study', *Law and Society Review* 7: 719–46.

Nuijten, M. 1997. 'Agrarian Reform and the *ejido* in Mexico; Illegality within the Framework of the Law', *Law and Anthropology* 9: 72–104.

——— 2001. 'What is in the Land? The Multiple Meanings of Land in a Transnationalized Mexican Village', in *Land and Sustainable Livelihood in Latin America*, eds G. van der Haar and A. Zoomers, Amsterdam: Royal Tropical Institute, KIT Publishers, 71–92.

——— 2003a. *Power, Community and the State; the Political Anthropology of Organisation in Mexico*. London: Pluto Press.

——— 2003b. 'Family Property and the Limits of Intervention; the Article 27 Reforms and the PROCEDE Program in Mexico', *Development and Change* 34(3): 475–97.

Reyes, S., R. Stavenhagen, S. Eckstein and J. Ballesteros 1974. *Estructura agraria y desarrollo agrícola en méxico: Estudio sobre las relaciones entre la tenencia y el desarollo agrícola de México.* México: Fondo de Cultura Económica.

Rifkin, J. 2000. *The Age of Access; the New Culture of Hypercapitalism where all of Life is a Paid-for Experience.* New York: Tarcher Putnam.

Spiertz, J. and M.G. Wiber, eds 1996. *The Role of Law in Natural Resource Management.* The Hague: VUGA.

Chapter 11

'The Tragedy of the Private': Owners, Communities and the State in South Africa's Land Reform Programme

Deborah James

Introduction

The distribution of property, as many of the papers in the present volume suggest, lies at the heart of debates over equity and social justice. This is particularly true at moments of political change when former property regimes are critically scrutinised and reforms proposed. In such settings, a debate of several centuries' standing is continually replayed: between those viewing private property rights as the foundation of society's economic and civil order and those advocating the restriction of private property in order to secure it for the 'public good' (Hann 1998: 13).

A modern-day version of this dispute is being played out between participants in South Africa's post-1994 land reform programme. The state, while aiming to transform the racial profile of land ownership, is committed to achieving this through the transfer of land from one private owner to another. Critics of state land policy, including human rights lawyers and NGO activists and those whose rights they claim to defend,

The research for this paper was conducted as part of a project, funded by the U.K.'s ESRC (award reference number R000239795), entitled 'Property, community and citizenship in South Africa's Land Reform Programme'. Interviews were conducted with a range of people, including land claimants (both those with successful claims and those with claims pending) and landless people in Mpumalanga; also land activists and human rights lawyers in South Africa's urban centres. Thanks to all whom I interviewed; to Alex Xola Ngonini and Geoffrey Mphahle Nkadimeng for assistance in the field; to those who offered help and support while I was in the field – particularly Patrick Pearson, David and Jenepher James and Belinda Bozzoli; to the organisers of and participants in the Changing Properties of Property conference at the Max Planck Institute of Anthropology, Halle, Germany, for providing the opportunity to present this paper.

have reservations about this. Although it was the apartheid regime that removed millions of people from tenancies in the white areas of South Africa into the African Bantustans (Platzky and Walker 1985), it did ensure some protection to land occupiers in these Bantustans through a racially distorted form of welfarism. It is to a future in which such forms of protection will be less assured, and to the associated threat of ultimate land alienation, that emerging forces in civil society have objected. Claiming that 'we cannot buy what already belongs to us', organisations such as the Landless People's Movement demonstrate – ironically – a commitment to the apartheid model of communal landholding under the rubric of state ownership which formerly applied in the Bantustans. This clinging to older ideas about property in the face of change is reminiscent of similar patterns in post-socialist Europe.

The dispute thus counterposes two positions. One, in line with the assertion in 'The tragedy of the commons' (Hardin 1968) that resources owned in common are misused since no one takes responsibility for them, is that securing land ownership on a private and individual basis can provide certainty about rights and responsibilities. The other is that the true 'tragedy' lies in ensuring or perpetuating the private ownership of land, since this threatens either to lead to its eventual alienation from its new owners, or to make it effectively unusable by placing it under 'community' control without state support. It is anxieties about the latter which will be illustrated by case studies in this paper.

In disputes about land ownership, the new approach promoted by the state is pitted against putatively old-fashioned visions of landholding. The resulting dichotomy – between modern/private and traditional/state-owned – harks back to the apartheid era. Although the planned reforms will result in a wide variety of tenurial types, depending on whether the land in question is in the former communal areas or on the privately-owned farms of white South Africans, some land activists nonetheless express anxiety that a bipolar division looks set to be further entrenched overall. As is the case in other transforming regimes, however, the boundaries between these apparently opposed polarities are blurred (see Sikor, this volume). Neither 'traditional' nor 'modern' is quite what it may seem. The traditional models of landholding now defended by poorer landless people were less the product of pre-colonial experience than the result of apartheid's extensive planning regimes.[1] Conversely, forms of ownership now endorsed by the state, although private, transfer land to communities rather than individuals.

State planning also involves a blurring of boundaries. While the present regime is committed to privatising land, like other assets, it currently relies on a public legal/bureaucratic planning apparatus in order to achieve this. Such has been the complexity of the new frameworks generated, however, that they have in turn required the intervention of private consultants for their design and implementation. These private consultants nonetheless act on behalf of and are paid by the state. Here, as in post-socialist Europe, 'new intermediate layers emerge between private actors and government, combining private and public elements' (Sikor, this volume) which interweave in a bewildering manner. Ownership becomes so complicated that some local actors, by contrast, idealise apartheid's earlier system of custodial/state ownership.

Private ownership carries different implications for richer and poorer people respectively. For both, the promise of autonomy is tenuously counterbalanced against the dangers of operating with somewhat less state support. For poorer people – the focus of the present paper – a system of private property based on market forces has returned land to dispossessed communities, or encouraged aspirant owners to pool their resources to buy new land. The state aims to transfer ownership of farms to these groups, thus privatising responsibility for development, social services, and the adjudication of disputes. Activists point to the resulting lack of clarity on the nature of rights and responsibilities, on how disputes between communal owners are to be resolved, and on exactly who is entitled to make decisions about land use. Where communal owners do, despite such uncertainties, succeed in using landed property as loan collateral, debts incurred by individuals threaten to deprive whole groups of their land. Lobbying by NGOs has challenged the state in its intention to transfer responsibility for such lands, pointing out that it is the fully alienable nature of land entailed in unprotected ownership which renders its owners vulnerable. The role of chieftaincy is also now part of the debate. Despite the fact that chiefs were thought of as deeply compromised during the apartheid era, their obligation to protect their subjects is cited by many as a reason for retaining apartheid's 'customary'/chief-based models of landholding with state protection as a backup.

In South Africa, as in the New Zealand case described in this volume, 'ownership, in the process of constant change, has become more ambiguous than ever before' (Van Meijl, this volume). Owners must attempt to pursue the freedom of private ownership while safeguarding themselves from its vulnerability by calling for assistance from a state increasingly unwilling to supply it. They must juggle the demands of communal responsibility against the risk taking of the individual entrepreneur. This entails balancing the promises of modernity against the security of the well-trodden path.

What makes these interlinked juggling acts necessary, but what also renders them particularly difficult, is their setting in a transitional social context in which many institutional and legal apparatuses are being consciously and deliberately redesigned. The 'extraordinary degree of planning' endured by Africans during apartheid (Crush and Jeeves 1993) has required equivalent levels of planning, by state officials as well as those in the NGO sector, in order to *undo* apartheid's schemes. At the same time, the social forms of the old order – and the expectations which these engendered – have an extraordinary tenacity; in part because the elaborate designs to supplant these forms are taking so long to be realised. The aspirant black South African landowner of the early twenty-first century is like an explorer setting forth in a rickety old ship, relying on the stars for guidance because more complex technological navigational systems are still being perfected. Set against the promise of new lands to be gained is the fear of old lands lost.

Land Reform and Communal Property: Laws, Models and Precedents

The symbolic and economic implications of South Africa's land reform have been difficult to square. Arousing millennial expectations and exaggerated fears, land policies have been charged with conflicting tasks. The aim, on a symbolic level, is to restore lost citizenship and nationhood. On a practical level, land reform is counted upon to create a new and prosperous class of African farmers and to ameliorate unemployment and rural poverty. At the same time, it is expected to resolve racial tensions which it, itself, has partly created.

From the outset, the programme acknowledged the diversity of land reform's intended 'beneficiaries' – and the complex interplay of moral and economic motivations – by subdividing its intended activities into three categories: restitution, redistribution and tenure reform. In theory, this would allow for the restoration of historical property rights as well as satisfying the demands of redistributive justice. In the programme's initial conceptualisation, lands were to be returned, not to 'tribes' as in New Zealand, but to African titleholders who had lost their property during the apartheid era as a result of forced removals: both strategies excluded large-scale dispossession in the nineteenth century (Van Meijl, this volume). Negotiations by lawyers and land activists on behalf of their constituents have broadened the remit of restitution to include the holders of 'informal rights' – including some 'tribes' – as well as the holders of formal title. But restitution has, in practice, proved so cumbersome a process that many of those convinced that their claims fall within its remit have been left to satisfy their demands for land by means of redistribution. This sub-category of land reform enabled people such as tenants and farm workers to pool 'settlement grants' provided by the government and buy farms: it increasingly seemed the only effective way of transferring significant amounts of white-owned land to the historically oppressed. Finally, tenure reform aimed to safeguard the rights of residents of white farms and state land in the former homelands. It was designed to protect poor people from summary eviction by securing their existing rights, or buy alternative land on which they could live.

The programme has received inadequate funding, however, to make this combination of moral with material objectives possible (Walker 2001; Hall and Williams 2003: 104). Nonetheless, the reform and/or restoration of land has remained a fulcrum for fierce disputes: over public responsibility versus private enterprise, welfarism versus self-reliance, traditional-style leadership versus egalitarian democracy, and private property versus land as an inalienable right.

During the first few years after the 1994 election, South Africa's new 'land reformers' – both in state and NGO sectors – designed new forms of legislation to provide a legal framework for the ownership of land restored to the communities who formerly owned it. The CPA (Communal Property Association) Bill was drafted and approved by Parliament in 1995, and the CPA Act passed in 1996 (SAIRR 1995–6: 369; Klug 1996: 194–95).[2] It stipulates that each CPA must have a constitution, a system of governance such that individual members elect a committee, a means of transferring property upon the death of individual members, and the like.

Almost a decade after its original design, the CPA model has been much criticised. It is seen, on the one hand, as inadequately geared to the needs of particular kinds of communities for particular kinds of ownership, but on the other as attempting to cater for these kinds of special needs in a paternalistic way. Where one set of commentators calls it a land reform 'product, ... ill-matched with the real needs and capacities of the rural poor' and criticises it for assuming too much in the way of experience and leadership on the part of rural leaders, another view disparages it for assuming that African people are different from other property owners in being inherently 'communal', and thus for stultifying all entrepreneurial initiatives.[3]

The new 'land reform' ownership model is, then, both denounced for embodying an inferior ownership specific to Africans and for being too complicated for rural Africans to understand: it is either insufficiently – or overly – different from normal ownership. It balances communal against individual, and public against private, in an uneasy combination. As a model it is not unprecedented. But it would be inaccurate to see it as rooted in African tradition. Instead, it combines diverse – even contradictory – social, political and intellectual influences.

When dispossessed African titleholders struggled to reclaim their land during the decades before 1994, they interacted with land activists who took up their cause. The dispossessed were mostly converts to mission Christianity who had bought farms jointly at the turn of the nineteenth century. Having distanced themselves from tribal forms of religion and authority, they combined peasant cultivation with labour migration before succumbing to the forced removals of grand apartheid (James 2000a; 2000b). The lawyers and activists were mainly white, middle-class, left/liberal people outraged by the inhumanity of these communities' resettlement. The dealings between these sets of actors – so different in their social origins and yet converging on this morally charged issue – produced a series of convictions concerning the nature of communal ownership: particularly, and misleadingly, concerning its egalitarian and inclusive character.

An NGO-published booklet *Botho Sechabeng/A feeling of community* (Small and Winkler 1992) [see Figure 11.1], based on interviews with African titleholders, reveals strong convictions about the moral benefits of communal ownership and a certainty that individual title would lessen 'the unity of the area by undermining the feeling of community'. Such convictions sprang, in part, from the threat or experience of resettlement. Memories of an earlier existence, sharpened by the intensity of loss, had added an extra dimension to ordinary nostalgia (see Harries 1987). The insistence on community solidarity was also partly tactical in nature (Pienaar 2000: 329). Human rights lawyer turned Land Commissioner, Durkje Gilfillan, stressed the strategic necessity for concerted community action by all claimants if they were to persuade the government to take land claims seriously. Her advice did not constitute a mere machiavellian tactic, but was informed by ideas of egalitarian community central to a vision of reform shared by many South African activists. In its idealisation of African communality, it represents a misunderstanding – perhaps derived from a dichotomy between private/individual and communal ownership which prevailed in nineteenth century Western thought – of the collective element in traditional land tenure systems (Hann 1998: 321).[4]

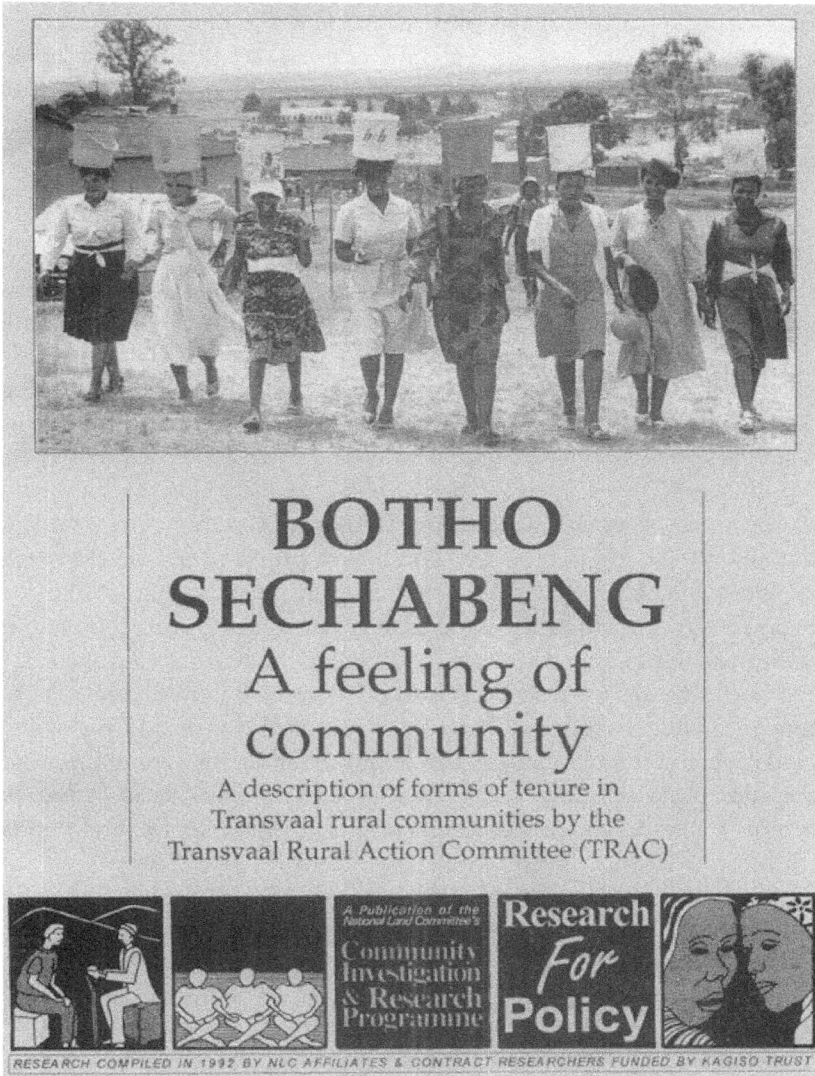

Figure 11.1: *Botho Sechabeng. A feeling of community (1992). An NGO-published booklet*

Interactions between activists and titleholders yielded other themes besides egalitarianism. Alongside the image of the harmonious community emerges the darker picture of those excluded from titleholders' lands. Such lands had, in most cases, been purchased by groups of people wanting to set themselves apart from surrounding populations, often on the grounds that they, as mission Christians, eschewed the pagan ways of their neighbours. Restitution provided an opportunity for at least some claimants to restate their opposition to sharing their territory with non-owners. Human rights lawyers such as Gilfillan, despite a commitment to ensuring equitable land access for all, became aware in the course of their work with African owners that former tenants would have to be excluded in order to avoid reinstating the chaotic situations of uncontrolled land occupancy which had developed on African–owned land during the 1960s and 1970s (Gilfillan forthcoming: 27–36). Such lawyers, helping to design the new ownership models, were mindful of the need to establish secure rights of private ownership at the same time as enshrining communal ideals. It became clear that the land hunger of these former tenants would have to be satisfied by the purchase of other farms for redistribution: a setting in which the same private/communal models were also to be applied.

Other precedents for the new ownership models likewise combined the demands of private ownership with those of communality, although initially privileging the former. These were provided by 'development experts' schooled in Third-World agriculture. Policy-makers from the World Bank, initially attempting to lead but later influenced by South African opinion, attended a series of local workshops during the early 1990s where they made proposals to liberalise agriculture and to transform land ownership. The resulting hybrid combined developers' models, a reading of Kenyan land reforms of the 1950s, and a passing acquaintance with Bundy's influential 1979 book *The Rise and Fall of the South African Peasantry.* The small family farm was initially proposed as the most efficient ownership unit, but subsequent persuasion by local land activists led to a modification of the proposal, allowing 'communities and not only individuals to acquire land' (Francis and Williams 1993: 398–99; Hall and Williams 2003).[5] Through these policy workshops, land reformers' image of 'communal property' was further shaped.

The ideological and historical basis for South Africa's new model of communal property thus stressed the value of community while suggesting the exclusivity of private ownership. One precedent – the interaction between lawyers and dispossessed titleholders – was based upon previous experiences of landownership. The other, based on a version of international development discourse, posits an intended ideal of the future. The two have become merged into a standardised framework which offers owners a limited range of fixed alternatives (LRC Cape Town 2001).[6] The prospective beneficiaries of land reform projects are all advised that they need to choose one out of the range of possible alternatives. Once the choice is made, a standard set of bureaucratic procedures follows. A constitution is drawn up and committee elections organised, the CPA or Trust is registered, and a certificate of ownership is issued. The farm will now be officially owned – and governed – by its own particular 'legal entity'.

The choice of model has changed over time. In restitution cases initiated early in the 1990s, the CPA, as an embodiment of the strong communal ethic involved in 'getting land back', was preferred and advocated by state and NGO officers alike. As time went by it was realised that CPA ownership often led to a paralysis of decision making. Prospective buyers in a recent redistribution project, through a process of extensive 'workshopping', have instead opted for a Trust-style legal entity on the grounds that it will facilitate decisive action. They opted for a later transition to communal ownership 'after land transfer, when the community has become close-knit' (Amos Mathibela, interview).

To give some idea of the contradictory nature of these newly designed legal frameworks, and how far people relate to these as overly – or just sufficiently – modern or traditional, some case studies from Mpumalanga province [see Figure 11.2] will demonstrate their operation in specific contexts.

Restitution: 'exactly what they had before'?

One case in which the interactions between restitution claimants and land activists produced an image of a strong community is that of the farm Doornkop, which in 1994 was restored to the descendents of its original titleholders, adherents of a nineteenth-century Lutheran mission. The CPA to which the land was restored is governed by an elected committee. Its members are called upon to exercise considerable expertise and judgment, in technical matters of ownership as well as political ones of representation and governance. The two areas often overlap.

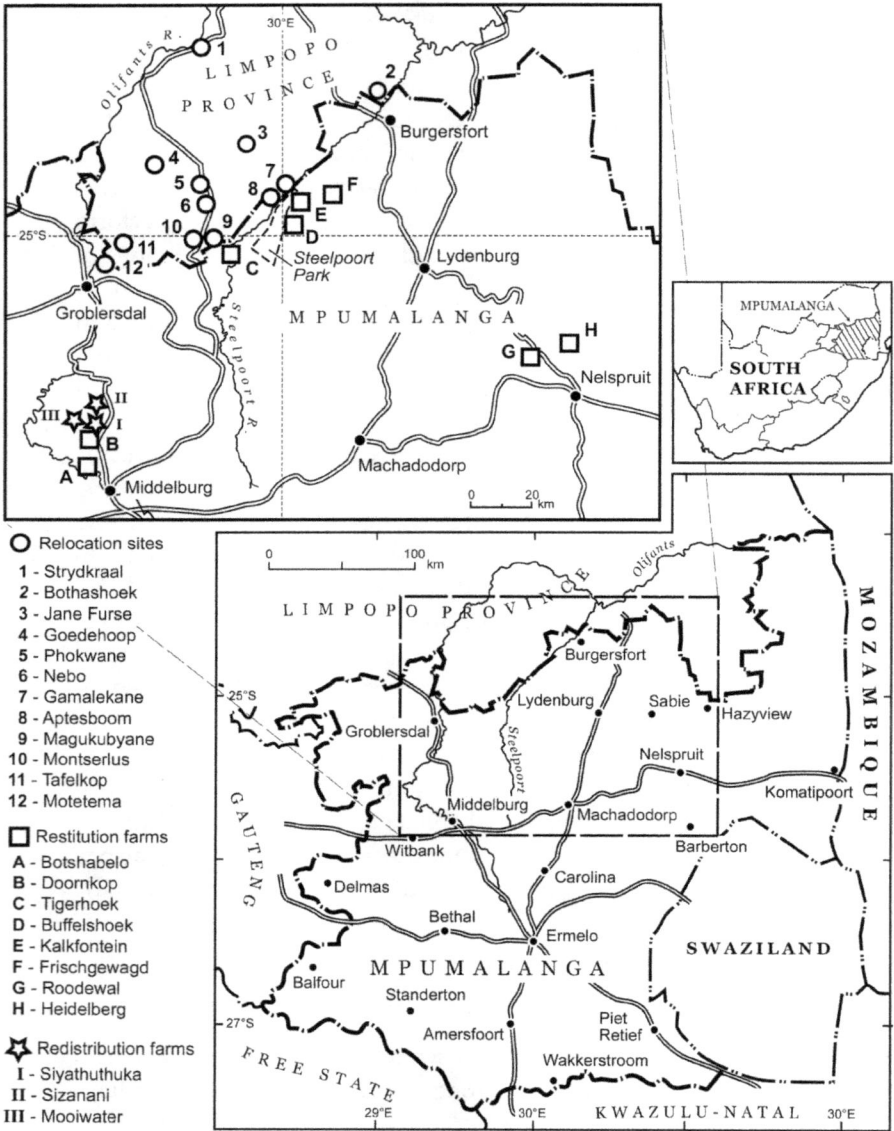

Figure 11.2: *Mpumalanga province*

What complicates the already onerous duties of this committee is the social division between it and its constituents. Socioeconomic differentiation in the community, already entrenched when the farm's occupants were forcibly removed in 1974, re-emerged after the farm's restitution in 1994 and became entrenched in leadership/rank-and-file divisions. Those resettling on the farm relied on a mostly absentee elite – whom they elected to the committee – to represent their interests. Apart from providing services like the water and residential housing, a major task for the committee was to deal with the re-emergence of tenancy on the farm. By 2001 Doornkop had been invaded by more than 100 families of shack-dwellers who claim to have lived there in the pre-removal period. Indeed, some poorer CPA members had 'sold' plots, illegally, to these 'squatters', in an attempt to augment their meagre incomes. The rest of the community was divided over whether to evict or accommodate them. The resulting crisis of leadership was exacerbated by uncertainty about exactly which land was owned by whom. Residents claimed that if they had been certain of their specific property rights from early on (a matter of ownership), they – or their representatives, the CPA committee – would have been empowered to evict the squatters on their behalf (a matter of leadership) before the problem escalated. Lack of certainty about property rights likewise caused vacillation amongst co-owners about holding other members of the CPA accountable. Had there been less uncertainty, the illegal vendor of land, himself, might have been more swiftly disciplined: 'he should lose his position – and his membership – with immediate effect. Otherwise, where are people going to get their idea of private property? If the mayor comes and explains, they do not understand. Different people say different things, and no one is clear on the Government's policies' (Amos Mathibela, interview).

Such a sense of uncertainty seems a far cry from the spirit of self-reliance which African titleholders pursued during the period of resistance against forced removals and immediately after reoccupying their land. The earlier independence of these farms, originally deriving from Christians' longstanding suspicion of outside interference from the state (James and Nkadimeng 2003), has now been augmented – but distorted – by the effects of private/communal ownership. Ironically, at a time when restored owners are orienting themselves to take up full citizenship in the broader society, these farms have become, in effect, more separate than ever.

On this point, human rights lawyers, continuing to engage in debates over communal ownership models and now willing to admit to what they see as their former mistakes, have been critical of CPAs' separation from the public realm and of the corresponding reluctance of the state to intervene in their affairs. They show how private/communal ownership induces uncertainty about the specific rights of individual members. Disputes between members, or inactive committees, may lead to the withholding of the consent which is required by the CPA constitution in order for individuals to use or transfer their land, resulting in paralysis. The remedy to this, according to lawyer Kobus Pienaar, lies in holding the state responsible, as it formerly was, 'in respect of the allocation and ongoing administration of the rights of individuals to use the land'. It also lies in a clearer initial definition of people's entitlements to specific assets: people's rights 'to various kinds of assets within the broader communally owned unit must be ensured' (Kobus Pienaar, LRC, interview). Effectively, this is a call for the individual 'sticks' in the 'bundle' of rights to be more clearly specified: for an eradication of what Verdery calls the fuzziness of property (1999).

These kinds of uncertainties, and the community conflicts which underpin but are also intensified by them, highlight the extent to which communally owned 'land reform' farms have come to be viewed as separate arenas – 'while the trust or communal property association tries to draw boundaries around itself to protect resources, it adds to the danger of creating an abnormally isolated zone' (Lund 1998) – despite their occupants' wish to exercise the citizenship rights of those in the broader society.

Based on his experience with several CPA-owned properties, Pienaar asserted that such problems would be obviated by treating land reform beneficiaries as though they were governed by society's normal legal frameworks, rather than by special forms of legislation. 'The implication of this', he said, 'would be to recognise that the state has a role to play in administering relationships, and regulating conflict, between co-owners, as much as it does between neighbours in a city context. Other property relations in society do get a lot of state support from local government, which helps to define your relationship with the street, your neighbours, the area in front of your house, and so on. There are public institutions, like the Deeds Registry, the Surveyor-General's office, which perform these functions. It is presumed that people in CPAs must take charge themselves, but no one would expect this in the case of normal individually-owned property'.[7]

The case of Doornkop shows that individual and communal aspects of ownership combine in ambiguous ways, resulting in many of the disadvantages of private ownership with few of its concomitant benefits. A model of communality, combined with inattention to the precise nature and content of property rights, has served to paralyse leaders.

In reaction, landholders have reverted to models of chiefly authority and ownership: somewhat surprisingly, given their history. Doornkop's purchasers had separated themselves geographically from the wellsprings of chiefly power in the late 1800s, and had long insisted on elected rather than traditional forms of leadership. During the 1980s and 1990s, the farm's claimants spoke scornfully of all forms of patrimonial authority. But by the early 2000s they were sufficiently disillusioned with committee-style CPA government to be idealising the chiefship in retrospect: 'We thought there would have been a chief here – if so, he would have been responsible for everything' (Eva Mankge, interview). These sentiments were echoed by a claimant at another restitution farm: 'Now we have no master. We are ruled by a hundred rats, not by one lion. There are many committees ruling us now – we prefer to be ruled by just one chief' (Simon Tshehla, interview).

A land researcher, to whom I mentioned these attitudes, agreed that there had been a general reawakening of interest in the chiefship in South Africa, largely in reaction against the putatively 'democratic' alternative, chiefs are seen as champions – 'strong people with clout, not people bogged down by bureaucracy. People think, "if only we had a strong leader"… One can relate this to the appeal of authoritarianism to the poor in other settings' (Ed Lahiff, interview).

Such sentiments, rather than being seen as a wholehearted endorsement of traditional leadership, represent a critical commentary on the opacity and ineffectiveness of CPA committees: groups of (mostly male) office holders whose deliberations and machinations are a mystery to most, who fail to deliver on numerous promises of development, and who in many cases do not even live on the restored farms but travel there infrequently from the cities where they reside and work. Similar problems, widely reported, suggest profound flaws in the assumption – enshrined in the original legislation – that communal landholding would automatically be translated into harmonious and conflict-free leadership. Instead, there is a 'breakdown of communication between the leadership and members', as well as 'inequitable allocation of assets based on self help; mismanagement; the squandering of opportunity; a disregard for internal rules'. The result has been that 'infrastructure and land are left to deteriorate' (Pienaar 2000: 327). In the face of such problems, chiefs appear to present an alternative model of ownership/leadership which contrasts favourably with government by committee.

The 'tragedy', here, appears to be that no one has sufficient authority and clout to act in the way that truly 'private' owners of land might do. Instead they revert to a misremembered past in which chiefs acted with decisiveness and authority rather than being crippled by indecision and doubt.

Redistribution: 'future oriented'?

In the new South Africa, as with other regimes focused on reforming land ownership, there has been consciousness of a need to provide distributive justice alongside reparative justice, since the latter focuses entirely on historical conditions without taking into account the dynamics of the present or the demands of the future (see Van Meijl, this volume). If restitution was a backward-looking enterprise, redistribution appeared to promise new, future-oriented ideals of community, oriented towards progressive forms of social organisation and exemplifying the best features that modern technical/legal planning could offer.

Planners have attempted to meet the challenge – along the lines outlined by Pienaar, above – by disaggregating the 'bundle' and specifying the precise content of different kinds of entitlements and obligations. Enlightened policy should, it is thought, solve the problems posed by the failure of existing projects. The case of two redistribution farms exemplifies this. One is the earlier-settled – and 'failed' – Sizanani. The other, Siyathuthuka, is presently being designed to forestall a similar 'failure'.

Sizanani has been seen by many commentators as a casualty of an early phase in the redistribution process. A system of government subsidies or grants was devised, whereby Africans could procure an amount of money, either to help with the purchase of a house, or to put towards the purchase of land. The policy was designed to ensure equity as well as to be compatible with a market-based model of land reform, but the cost of farmland purchase led people to a practice derogatorily referred to as 'rent-a-crowd'. Beneficiaries, often with nothing in common, began to pool their grants in order to buy white-owned farmland which they lacked the capacity to run.[8] Problems arising in such cases have derived from the low levels of financial redress being provided to individuals, which are really only sufficient to allow for the running of communal rather than individual farm projects. This approach was later replaced by one geared towards encouraging aspirant commercial small farmers with their own sources of matching finance, but it left numerous unsuccessful 'rent-a-crowd' projects in its wake.

Problems at Sizanani have included mismanagement, financial shortages (insufficient funds remained after purchase to initiate an 'agricultural project'), and unsustainably large numbers (determined by the purchase price rather than by commonality of interests). The purchase was initiated by a member of the new political elite in the region on behalf of a group of farm labourers who needed a place to live. When extra members were then recruited so as to be able to afford the farm, this led to the inclusion of the names of people who did not intend to participate but had been persuaded to be listed in order that their government grants be accessed.

The prospects of effective representation were slim from the outset, but were made even more remote by the group's members' lack of experience of commercial agriculture, finance or business. Although many had worked on farms, their habituation to a decades-old despotic regime as labourers for white farmers made egalitarian models of participatory democracy unfamiliar:

> The problem they have is with management. There are seven families who are working on the farm from the previous farm owner. They do have experience with farming but the previous farm owner was in the position of farm manager and they were working by instruction. But now they need a person who can manage them – and they … have this problem of not respecting any of their own members (JB Mahlangu, interview).

The remedy proposed in the case of this farm, as in that of many like it, was to appoint an outside expert with managerial and commercial farming experience to run the farm in the interim, and to share his knowledge with the new owners. In a somewhat grotesque caricature of earlier apartheid practice, the person proposed – in this as in similar cases – was the former white farm owner.

But not all CPA members were enthusiastic about accepting his help. In cahoots with a relative well-connected in the tourist industry he made proposals – while a neighbouring farmer competed for the post of manager by making counterproposals – about running the farm. Each informed the committee about the fees, generated out of future profits, they would be charging. In the face of these conflicting ideas, the recently elected CPA committee members felt bewildered and unable to assert themselves, and resentful at the promises made which, as they later said, were 'never fulfilled'. They were thus relieved when development agents from the parastatal Eskom confirmed their suspicions by telling them not to work with any white people, because 'they are going to rob us and later dispossess us of our farm. Whites are the ones who make us suffer' (Driver Ntuli, interview).

Such assurances seemed to provide a sense of security by pointing to a mutually-agreed-upon enemy, which could be blamed for the CPA's, and the farm's, misfortunes. But it remains to be seen whether Eskom's agents, who in turn plan to outsource the training of Sizanani's owners to two black-owned companies of 'service providers', are more reliable than the earlier candidates for the position of manager. What will certainly remain true for the foreseeable future is the perpetuation of the CPA's present sense of dependency. Although the representatives of Eskom and of the Department of Agriculture were shrilly insistent that Sizanani's farmer/owners must now be independent rather than continuing to rely on employment by white farmers, many of the owners felt pessimistic about being able to make an independent living on the land and were hence reluctant to relinquish their jobs as labourers on white farms, as this extract from my field diary shows:

Meeting at Sizanani, 26 January 2003

George Mahlaela (from Eskom Development Foundation): You no longer work at *makgoweng* (the place of the whites) – *makgoweng* is here, work is here. You are the farmers – you are your own bosses. Your children are your eyes and your ears, they must be involved. Do not come and tell us that your children are in town working. You must get here in time for meetings. This place belongs to you.

Female CPA member: If we start farming, who's going to pay for this? Will we be paid if we start to farm here? ... What is the government going to do? When are they going to give us water, electricity, and so on? When is electricity going to be laid on here?

George: These things will be settled by the service providers. ...
(Some people get up and start to leave. Rose Msibi gets upset.)

Rose: We want to have a general meeting every month. ... We would like to have the meeting on a week day – this will force people to attend and thus to stop their work on farms. ... People should not be working on farms here. You're your own bosses – you are like whites.

Male CPA member: If you have it in the week, some will come, and those who are working will not.

George: We could have it at 5 o'clock, or 6 o'clock, to accommodate them. (They take a vote to hold it on a weekday afternoon).

Male CPA member: (defiantly) I cannot make it in the week – I work on a farm.

(Everybody laughs).

This exchange shows the state and its agents attempting to foist the responsibilities of ownership onto beneficiaries. While employees of the state or of parastatal development agencies attempt to reshape reality by portraying Sizanani's members as independent owners responsible for their own future prosperity, the members themselves recognise that their poverty will continue to render them reliant on white farm employment and on state welfare, even though the former is dwindling and the state has shown itself increasingly unwilling to provide the latter.

The perceived failure of communal ownership and responsibility in projects such as Sizanani has led to an increasing emphasis on new models which allow for the individualisation of rights. Given that the CPA ownership model is flawed, there are increasing moves towards models of ownership which – as originally suggested by the World Bank – privilege the family farm or foreground the individual entrepreneur. But land functionaries continue to design projects for groups of 'landless' people who still feel unable to own or run properties as individuals. In Mpumalanga, as elsewhere, many of these are displaced farm labourers. There were those who early on became the beneficiaries of Sizanani. There are the 'squatters' who invaded Doornkop and settled there without any immediate prospects of a land reform project or CPA. These are the intended 'beneficiaries' of Siyathuthuka. In this case, individual ownership within the commons has been perfected – at least in theory.

Planning: Technical Solutions to Political Problems

In the process of making new plans to overcome old problems, consultants gain considerable experience at constructing 'business plans' for use on communally held lands. These plans, with their complex provisions for sub-letting of communal property and the like, made up for the failure of earlier CPA constitutions to specify individual rights to assets. Manifesting a pattern well-known in Third-World development, technical solutions were thus beginning to substitute for legal or political ones (Robertson 1984; Ferguson 1990).

In preparing to purchase a redistribution farm where squatters would be settled, the consultants drew up a business plan. It allocated resources in such a way as to avoid a 'tragedy of the commons' scenario in which a failure of responsible leadership results in wasting assets. The 'commons' here have been conceptualised as an asset, owned by the Trust, which members must lease: 'the Trust will be responsible to collect rent from each beneficiary and people operating small businesses that will then be used to maintain infrastructure and to pay for services '(Fundile Afrika 2002).

The specified grazing arrangements are similar: 'an amount of R5 to R10 per month per head is paid to the Trust for the grazing. ... The reason why a rent should be asked is that the property belongs to all the beneficiaries collectively and that those that use the grazing use the assets of other individuals; it is therefore reasonable for the advantaged to compensate the others for the use of the Trust's common assets' (Fundile Africa 2002: 11). The consultant laid out the rationale for this cooperative ownership schema, claiming that its 'somewhat autocratic' nature was necessary in the interests of sustainability.

This sophisticated model attempts to compensate, through elaborate technical specifications, for the ambiguities entrenched in the legal outlining of communal property arrangements. At the same time as guaranteeing the proper custodianship of 'the commons', it thus appears – though on a technical rather than legal level – to satisfy some of the requirements outlined earlier for a clearer initial definition of people's rights over specific assets.

This plan entailed two drawbacks, however. It conceived of rights as something earned through continuous enterprise rather than guaranteed by the state. Using a commercial model, it seemed to embody an assumption that cattle owners would be generating cash income from their enterprises, and would thus be in a position to pay rent to the Trust. In this way it seemed to be out of kilter with the priorities of most squatters, who kept cattle as a form of long-term saving but were reluctant or unable to make ongoing monthly investments such as payment for grazing. Instead of assuring the citizen's inalienable entitlements as pledged by the state, the plan proposed a model of citizenship based on post-welfarist propositions about self-sustaining individual enterprise.

A second drawback lay in the plan's misrecognition of existing social realities. In the same way that it seemed to take little account of members' incomes by failing to recognise that few were in a position to pay rent for grazing, it also ignored both their aspirations and their shortcomings on the level of managerial or organisational skills. In both these respects, the consultant's plan thus continued to fall into the trap of the communal property plans which it was attempting to transcend. Without extensive state intervention and agricultural support it was unlikely that its way of 'privatising the commons' could be put into practice.

That squatters' aspirations were being ignored had already become evident to me from several interviews: '... we don't want it. ... In fact, they have gone behind our backs. Firstly, we were told to simply register our names and we later realised that our housing grants were used without our consent to buy the farm' (Ephraim and Fanie Mabuza, interview).

Such objections, based on the communal/trusteeship model of the homelands (Murray 1992: 132 *passim*), but newly reconstituted as a form of resistance against the state's plans for private land ownership, were founded in turn on a model in which the state should be the rightful owner and custodian of land.

That there was a misrecognition of the lack of managerial and organisational skills was suggested by the father of Siyathuthuka Trust's chairman. The problem with business plans, he said, was that they were too complex for ordinary people to understand. The 'workshopping' beloved of both state and NGO practitioners in the land sector did little to improve matters: 'Now we have people driving from Pretoria, ...They talk, talk, and not a single person will ask a question. Have they understood or not? It's not that they are scared, it's that they don't understand' (Hendrik Mathibela, interview).

What made these workshops worse, he implied, was that the elaborateness of their abstract plans was matched by a failure to deliver any material, practical progress. Land for the squatters was forever being discussed at meetings but never handed over. He likened this to a meal much planned-for but never actually forthcoming: 'You can't tell people "I have made food; I'm going to give you food", from the morning till the sun goes down – people are waiting. Tomorrow when you we say "we must go and eat", they say, "there's no food"...' (ibid.).

All-in-all, he was suggesting, the designing of complex plans for commercial farming was serving only to frustrate those for whom the plans had been made. While they would have been happy to settle for a much simpler solution, the process of planning was serving to render *all* solutions equally remote and hence promoting passivity among those planned-for. His account certainly confirmed squatter shortcomings on the level of 'managerial skills', but suggested that to require such skills was inappropriate in the circumstances.

It would appear, then, that consultants' technical elaborations on the communal property theme, although seeming to promise a fine-tuning of the original crude model, were so complex as to be virtually incomprehensible to their intended recipients. Although they might, with much public support, have been realisable, it was precisely this support that was becoming increasingly rare under the new privatising regime. While much was being invested by the state to pay for consultants to *design* sophisticated property regimes, *implementing* these was generally left to communities with very little assistance or expertise. Indeed, the state's 'hands-off' approach was being justified with such statements as 'the point of land redistribution is to give a community their land, not run it for them' and the insistence that they 'have to be more accountable for their own fate'.[9] In the absence of 'post-settlement support', the assumption was that plans could be conveyed to their recipients through 'workshops'. In a manner which has been widely noted in the world of development, this embodied a presumption that more effective channels of communication would enable planners' modernising paradigm to be shared by those planned-for, and ignorance replaced by rational knowledge (Hobart 1993).

In the one-size-fits-all world of communal property, things are not as they seem. In the case of restitution communities, it was presumed that their origin in longstanding group ties would provide precedents for democratic communal ownership. Instead, members ended up crying out for a return to a traditional model based on chiefly custodianship. But this call for despotism disguised a demand for state involvement and for the continuation of apartheid's particular version – albeit a partial one – of welfarist, modernist planning. Redistribution groups, in contrast, appeared to promise a future untrammeled by communalist precedents: they provided a blank slate upon which consultants' increasingly sophisticated schemas of entrepreneurial modernity and private ownership could be drawn. Instead, and in reaction, participants longed wistfully for apartheid's model of tribal/custodial landholding. This apparently regressive vision, however, masked ideas about democratic-style modernity. Deriving from the election's promises of egalitarianism and participatory democracy, redistribution beneficiaries expressed their convictions that there should be wide consultation about future outcomes rather than allowing planners to 'go behind our backs'.

Inalienable or Alienable Land?

If landed property becomes alienable and short-term gain outweighs long-term considerations, the public aspects of property may atrophy (Hann 1998:33). It remains briefly to mention the risk to newly installed private owners of alienating land altogether.

The possibility of land loss through indebtedness has loomed like a shadow in the background of South Africa's land reform programme, threatening communal/private ownership. One such case is that of the Khomani San in the Northern Cape Province whose land was restored in the 1990s. When CPA members incurred large debts from a local white shopkeeper (the former owner of one of the farms), the debtors decided, without the necessary mandate from all committee members, to auction that farm in order to settle the debt.[10] As an interim solution, the Director-General of Land Affairs was pressed into custodianship of the CPA. In the case of the 'rural poor', then, the state has continued to intervene, partly under pressure from those in the NGO sector, in order to ensure that the gains made under land reform are not prematurely lost.[11]

It is too early in the 'new look' phase of land reform to assess whether land alienation is occurring amongst the higher-income individual owners now beginning to be favoured as beneficiaries of the programme. There are, however, suggestions that a cautious approach which combines Land Bank loans with leasing and long-term payback arrangements to former owners will safeguard at least some land redistributed to commercial African farmers. The state's increasing predilection for such schemes has, however, been criticised by those on the left who feel that it is neglecting 'the poor'. In defence of this new approach, officers point to its likelihood of greater sustainability than earlier rent-a-crowd schemes. But the history of African landownership tells us that even the middle classes, for whose identity and status landowning formed such a crucial basis, have fallen prey and might again succumb to land loss. Whether in 1890s Natal (La Hausse 2000), or during the 1930s in the Orange Free State (Murray 1992), the risk always existed that mortgage debts might be unrepayable and thus that land would be forfeit. Such owners, being reliant on sources of income other than farming, were susceptible to downturns in the economy which threatened their non-farm sources of finance, such as migrant labour, transport riding or 'shack farming' (La Hausse 2000: 161–64), or leasing land to whites who would farm it instead (Murray 1992: 98). Both cases illustrate the exceptional vulnerability of African farm owners in situations where the economic, legal and political odds were against them. Although African owners now enjoy greater favour than they did in earlier historical periods, the present setting has its own risks. Since well before the 1994 transition, the state has been unwilling to provide farmer support as it once did; indeed, many of the white farmers selling to the state for land reform have become heavily indebted since the withdrawal of such support in the late 1980s. Middle class land loss thus remains a distinct possibility.

Conclusion

The context of property-holding in South Africa is one of political transition: a context in which all models of ownership appear to be negotiable and under redesign. The change of regime presented an ideal opportunity to unbundle the complex components of the property package, selecting only the most appropriate parts and streamlining property ownership to suit a changed dispensation. To the most utopian land activists and their constituents, it seemed to promise a chance for renegotiation of some of the most fundamental inequalities in society, by combining the independence of landowning with the security of state support.

The resulting models combined private and public, modern and traditional, in unexpected ways. There is the still-resilient commitment to communal ownership by civil society activists, human rights lawyers and consultants, partly drawing on but partly being imposed upon their constituents' views. There is the co-ownership of property by better- and worse-off people, with the poor concomitantly dependent on their richer counterparts to represent them or serve as intermediaries. Different models of property thus converge and their boundaries blur.

Historical struggles and contemporary disputes over land and the way it ought – or ought not – to be owned have left their imprint upon present-day policy and practice. The past weighs heavy and leaves its imprint, enshrining a view of apparent communality which leaves in place many of the features of individual property. When the private/communal model was found to be problematic and unsuited to the demands of redistributive justice, planners attempted to refine it by specifying individual entitlements in greater detail. But the resultant models of property-holding are overly complex. They also rely on a presumption about the capacity of poor people to behave as investors and rent-payers. As a result, the poor and landless appear to be excluded as real 'beneficiaries' of land reform. Unable to benefit from private ownership, they press for protection from its dangers. They affirm apartheid's familiar model of customary landholding, which seems to promise land as an inalienable right. Resisting the state's insistence on private property, they insist on their own interpretation: that 'land cannot be bought and sold – it is for everyone'.

Notes

1. Murray (1992: 132 *passim*). Apartheid planning is described by Bank (2002), after Rabinow (1989), as embodying 'middling modernism'.
2. In contrast, its twin legislation, the often-redrafted Communal Land Rights Act, provoked major controversy concerning chiefs' role and was only passed in 2004.
3. For the first view see 'Didiza's recipe for disaster', Ben Cousins, *Mail & Guardian* 22 August 2000, 'We can't deliver the land, admits government', Sharon Hammond and Justin Arenstein, *Mail & Guardian* 21 January 1999; for the second see 'Community projects drown in ideology' Saliem Fakir, *Mail & Guardian* 1 July 1999.
4. Evidence similar to that presented in this paper has subsequently caused Gilfillan, along with others in the human rights legal fraternity, to refine their ideas on communal ownership: they now favour a model of individual rights encompassed within a broader collective (personal communication).
5. For joint analyses by World Bank and South African policy makers, see Mbongwa et al. (1996) and other articles published in van Zyl et al. (1996).
6. CPA 'is not so much one size fits all, but ... in the early examples we ... did not realise that if you do not give attention to how allocation would happen and be managed *prior* to transfer and settlement, it is very difficult if not impossible to do it *later*'(Kobus Pienaar, personal communication).
7. In his growing awareness of the problems of communal awareness Pienaar shares the attitudes of others in the human rights legal fraternity, such as Gilfillan (cited earlier). All have come to recognise a point made – independently – by 'Hann: that, although African patterns of landholding have some collectivist elements, these do not equate to communal farming à la African socialism' (Hann 1998: 321).

8. 'Land Affairs Divides and Conquers', Ann Eveleth, *Mail & Guardian*, 20 April 1999; 'Didiza's recipe for disaster' Ben Cousins, *Mail & Guardian*, 22 August 2000; similar opinions were held by Philip Mbiba, Rosalie Kingwill and Chris Mulaudzi (interviews).
9. 'Shattered dreams of the San' Yolandi Groenewald, *Mail and Guardian* 10 June 2003.
10. 'San risk losing their land' Yolandi Groenewald, *Mail and Guardian*, 15 September 2002.
11. It is possible in this case that the intervention of the state was perceived as more feasible – and more desirable – because it was a case involving indigenous people, often seen as closer to nature, more vulnerable, less likely to be able to protect themselves.

References

Bank, L. 2002., 'Xhosa in Town Revisited: From Urban Anthropology to an Anthropology of Urbanism', Ph.D. thesis, University of Cape Town, South Africa.

Bundy, C. 1979. *The Rise and Fall of the South African Peasantry*. London: Heinemann.

Crush, J. and A. Jeeves 1993. 'Transitions in the South African Countryside', *Canadian Journal of African Studies* 27(3): 352–59.

Ferguson, J. 1990. *The Anti-politics Machine: 'Development', Depoliticization and Bureaucratic Power in Lesotho*. Minneapolis and Cambridge: University of Minnesota Press and Cambridge University Press.

Francis, E. and G. Williams 1993. 'The Land Question', *Canadian Journal of African Studies* 27(3): 380–403.

Fundile Afrika 2002. *A Business Plan for the Settlement of the Siyathuthuka Trust of Doornkop*. Pretoria: mimeo.

Gilfillan, D. forthcoming. 'Common-Law and Customary Land-Rights in the Context of Section 28 of the Constitution', dissertation, University of Pretoria.

Hall, R. and G. Williams 2003. 'Land Reform in South Africa: Problems and Prospects', in *From Cape to Congo: Southern Africa's Evolving Security Architecture*, eds M. Baregu and C. Landsberg, Boulder: Lynne Reiner, 97–129.

Hann, C.M. 1998. 'Introduction: The Embeddedness of Property', in *Property Relations: Renewing the Anthropological Tradition*, Cambridge: ed. C.M. Hann, Cambridge University Press 1–47.

Hardin, G. 1968. 'The Tragedy of the Commons', *Science* 162: 1243–48.

Harries, P. 1987. 'A Forgotten Corner of the Transvaal: Reconstructing the History of a Relocated Community through Oral Testimony and Song', in *Class, Community and Conflict*, ed. B. Bozzoli, Johannesburg: Ravan Press, 93–134.

Hobart, M. 1993. 'Introduction', in *An Anthropological Critique of Development: The Growth of Ignorance*, ed. M. Hobart, London: Routledge, 1–30.

James, D. 2000a. 'Hill of Thorns: Custom, Knowledge and the Reclaiming of a Lost Land in the New South Africa', *Development and Change* 31(3): 629–49.

—— 2000b. '"After Years in the Wilderness": Development and the Discourse of Land Claims in the New South Africa', *Journal of Peasant Studies* 27(3): 142–61.

James, D. and G.M. Nkadimeng 2003. '"A Sentimental Attachment to the Neighbourhood": African Christians and Land Claims in South Africa', in *An Apartheid of Souls: Dutch Colonialism and its Aftermath in Indonesia and South Africa*, eds. D. James and A. Schrauwers, special issue of *Itinerario: European Journal of Overseas History*, XXVII(3/4): 243–62.

Klug, H. 1996. 'Bedevilling Agrarian Reform: The Impact of Past, Present and Future Legal Frameworks', in *Agricultural Land Reform in South Africa: Policies, Markets and Mechanism*, eds J. van Zyl, J. Kirsten and H. Binswanger, Cape Town: Oxford University Press, 161–98.

La Hausse de la Louvière, P. 2000. *Restless Identities: Signatures of Nationalism, Zulu Ethnicity and History in the Lives of Petros Lamula (c1881–1948) and Lymon Maling (1889–c1936)*. Pietermaritzburg: University of Natal Press.

LRC (Legal Resources Centre) Cape Town 2001. 'Draft Report on "Communal" Property Institutional Arrangements', presented at joint Department of Land Affairs/LRC Workshop.

Lund, F. 1998. 'Lessons from Riemvasmaak for Land Reform Policies and Programmes in South Africa', vol. 2, London: Programme for Land and Agrarian Studies (PLAAS), University of Western Cape and Farm Africa.

Mail and Guardian, Johannesburg, 21 January 1999; 20 April 1999; 1 July 1999; 22 August 2000; 15 September 2002; 10 June 2003.

Mbongwa, M., R. van den Brink and J. van Zyl 1996. 'Evolution of the Agrarian Structure in South Africa', in *Agricultural Land Reform in South Africa: Policies, Markets and Mechanisms*, eds J. van Zyl, J. Kirsten and H. Binswanger, Cape Town: Oxford University Press, 36–63.

Murray, C. 1992. *Black Mountain: Land, Class and Power in the Eastern Orange Free State 1880s-1980s*. Johannesburg: Witwatersrand University Press.

Pienaar, K. 2000. '"Communal" Property Arrangements: A Second Bite', in *At the Crossroads: Land and Agrarian Reform in South Africa into the Twenty-first Century*, ed. B. Cousins, Cape Town and Johannesburg: University of the Western Cape and National Land Committee, 322–39.

Platzky, L. and C. Walker 1985. *The Surplus People*. Johannesburg: Ravan Press.

Rabinow, P. 1989. *French Modern: Norms and Forms of the Social Environment*. Cambridge: MIT Press.

Robertson, A.F. 1984. *People and the State: An Anthropology of Planned Development*. Cambridge: Cambridge University Press.

Small, J. and H. Winkler 1992. *Botho Sechabeng/A Feeling of Community: A Description of Forms of Tenure in Transvaal Rural Communities*. Johannesburg: Transvaal Rural Action Committee (TRAC).

SAIRR (South African Institute of Race Relations) 1995–6. *Survey 1995–6*. Johannesburg: South African Institute of Race Relations.

van Zyl, J., J. Kirsten and H. Binswanger, eds 1996. *Agricultural Land Reform in South Africa: Policies, Markets and Mechanisms*. Cape Town: Oxford University Press.

Verdery, K. 1999. 'Fuzzy Property: Rights, Power and Identity in Transylvania's Decollectivisation', in *Uncertain Transition: Ethnographies of Change in the Postsocialist World*, eds M. Burawoy and K. Verdery, Oxford: Rowman and Littlefield, 53–82.

Walker, C. 2001. 'Relocating Restitution', *Transformation* 44: 1–16.

Chapter 12

The Folk Conceptualisation of Property and Forest-related Going Concerns in Madagascar

Frank Muttenzer

Property relations of the use and control of forest resources in Madagascar are a consequence of two kinds of pluralism. The first is a pluralism of social organisation and the forms of agency these organisations imply. It opposes direct users or producers in the village against formal economic agents such as collectors of local produce and trading firms, the forest and territorial administrations representing the state, conservation or development projects of bilateral and multilateral donors, non-governmental organisations (NGOs), and local offices of international organisations. The other kind is legal pluralism, with several independent normative orders that apply to the same situation and compete for influence. In Madagascar there are traditional, customary conceptualisations of property referring to substantive principles of equity, as well as state created forest domains and administrative territories, and newly constructed sets of rights and rights holder resulting from a partial recognition of local law by the state forest administration.

The 1996 contractual management law gives village communities that are constituted as users' associations exclusive use rights over public lands, after negotiation of local management plans with the field-level forest administration.[1] The objective of these contracts is to involve local communities and state administrators in the redefinition of property rights to reverse situations of so-called open access (Weber 1995). This policy of recognising local law is a response to mounting international concerns about tropical deforestation.[2] Under the UN Convention on Biological Diversity, Madagascar has committed to promoting environmentally sound and sustainable development in areas adjacent to protected areas, and to encouraging customary uses of biological resources in accordance with traditional cultural practices that are compatible with conservation or sustainable use requirements.[3] Adopting this Convention generated a debate in Madagascar about the causes of agricultural colonisation of forests and the measures to be taken in response by government (McConnell 2002).

Considerable scientific information goes into problem identification in deforestation and forest degradation; otherwise decision makers might doubt the necessity to take action. Public policy requires a minimal common understanding of the problem and of appropriate means to attain valued ends. Networks of professionals with recognised expertise in a particular domain and with authoritative claims to policy-relevant knowledge can be referred to as 'epistemic communities' (Haas 1992). The forest conservation epistemic community, mainly from the natural sciences, argued that demographic pressure and the traditional practice of shifting cultivation were among the main causes of deforestation. The human development epistemic community, mainly from the social sciences, pointed to open access as the major cause of human occupation in protected areas, and to the lack of administrative recognition of customary rules in adjacent zones (Weber 1995). Jointly elaborated by government and international donors, recent legislation is based on the assumption that contractual or co-management of economic concerns (conversion of forest land for agriculture, or extraction of fuel wood, timber, or other forest products) is more equitable and ecologically sustainable than centralised state control over resources.

As in many aid-dependent countries, the defenders of 'recognition' and 'pluralism' in Madagascar have been more influential than the tropical forest conservationists who called for more repression of local users. Despite the victory, the institutional diagnostic of the former was incorrect. It is true that forest resources are not open access. But use and control rights are governed by a popular conceptualisation of property, the structure of which limits the range of rules that can possibly be recognised through a contractual arrangement. Throughout this chapter, the term 'folk conceptualisation of property' is used to refer to a set of customary principles that are exempt from policy discussion because people commonly take their meanings for granted. These meanings challenge the validity of policy design principles and analytical concepts of the neo-institutionalist 'common property' epistemic community

(Bromley and Cernea 1989; Feeney et al. 1990; Schlager and Ostrom 1992; Ostrom 1990; McKean 2000).

The neo-institutionalist focus on instrumental rule change misconstrues the actual principles which underlay negotiated arrangements. Dyadic relations which regulate access to resources between cultivators and pastoralists, patrons and clients, indigenous and migrant groups are neither instances of open access nor can they be freely negotiated. Unlike the procedural design principles of self-governing commons (Ostrom 1990: 88–102), customary principles contain minimal substantive standards in the same way as natural law doctrines, 'thin' derivates of plural and otherwise incommensurate 'thick' accounts of justice (Walzer 1994). Shared minimal standards of justice not only circumscribe how legal pluralism works under conditions of organisational pluralism and vice versa. They also explain why state-recognised customary law usually fails to articulate the two pluralisms in the formal contracts between the forest administration and village user associations.

The Emergence of Property Rights in Forest-related Going Concerns

The spatial definition of forests under state law is not directly relevant for analytical purposes. From the point of view of legal practice, the unitary category of 'forest' breaks down into multiple vested interests of the groups that depend on resources and derivative products from areas the law defines as 'forested'. Forests shall here be thought of as composed of multiple autonomous going concerns (Commons 1934).[4] To understand the institutional dynamics of deforestation in Madagascar, three categories of going concerns are particularly relevant: land use conversion and extraction of non-timber forest products, charcoal manufacturing for domestic consumption in urban areas, and extraction of tropical hardwoods. Unlike forest economists who exclude land use conversion from scientific classifications of forest products, I shall consider agriculture a forest-related concern and compare its property rules with those of extracting raphia palm fibres. The illegal cultivation of cash crops in a forest reserve and the over-harvesting of raphia fibres display the same basic mechanism: both concerns are structured through reciprocal relationships between a sphere where productive flows are apportioned and a second one where economic opportunities are allotted. Although there is no space to discuss it here, I argue that the hypothesis

is also valid for other going concerns such as charcoal or timber
(Muttenzer 2001: 97–108). Property rules are variable because of
product-related or eco-geographic differences, but economic and political
structures, and issues of agency, are comparable across going concerns.

'Transactional not Cumulative' - Conceptualising Property Rights and Natural Resources

Madagascar's environmental policy, designed during the 1990s under the
influence of international development aid, reproduces in several ways
the colonial theory of public domain. Ideally, space is ordered according
to a geometric logic, from the national territory down to individual plots.
Through the institutions of state and private ownership, complete sets of
rights over each category of stocks are allocated to single right holders
who ideally manage flows based on economic rationality or other forms of
expert knowledge, producing protected areas for biological diversity,
productive forests for fuel wood and timber supplies, and private lands
for crop production. However, rural populations in Madagascar do not
reason in terms of land ownership per se, but of distribution of the income
flow from that land, based on both the fruits (differential rewards
according to effort) and the burden of labour (equal opportunity). In the
folk conceptualisation of property, security of flows takes precedence over
the spatial identification of stocks.

   Although state ownership suggests formal title and a complete set of
rights over forest lands, things are different if we look at the owner's
monopoly from a sociological perspective. Especially at the field-level of
forest administration, the reasoning of public officials appears consistent
with the folk conceptualisation of property, that is, being transactional
not cumulative. As in many parts of rural Africa, the state in Madagascar
is not able to enforce a hegemonic claim over forest domains while other
agents can and do make enforceable claims. In practice, the formally
'complete' bundle of state ownership is an incomplete set of rights
transacting with other incomplete sets. In concretised property relations
(F. and K. von Benda-Beckmann and Wiber this volume), a single bundle
of rights never contains a complete set of sticks. Each bundle has to be
built up from transactions with (at least) one other bundle to be effective.
This is illustrated by the recent work of French anthropologists who
describe access to land in Western Africa in terms of so-called 'derived
rights', arrangements premised upon distinct sets of expectations found

in reciprocal relations such that specific resource rights emerge (Le Roy 1998, 2001; Lavigne Delville et al. 2002). The primary set of expectations reflects the organisation of productive activities within the land-using unit. The secondary set of expectations reflects the present and future distribution of opportunities among economic units.

In this chapter I refer to the transactional conceptualisation of property in a broader way, not restricted to temporary access to land. A major distinction is made in all societies between rights to regulate, supervise, represent in outside relations, and allocate property on the one hand, and rights to use and exploit economically property objects on the other (F. and K. von Benda-Beckmann and Wiber this volume). Although both types of rights may refer to the same physical objects, 'rules of allotment' define these objects as stocks which have to be transformed into flows according to 'rules of apportionment' before physically entering the economic process (Gudeman 2001: 52). In order to secure the economic flow through his/her labour, a 'taker' asks a 'giver' to authorise the intended uses. In exchange, givers expect to receive a part of the revenue generated by takers. Neo-institutionalist authors make a similar distinction between rules of resource access and withdrawal on the operative level and rules of management, inclusion/exclusion and transfer on the collective choice level (Schlager and Ostrom 1992). Their distinction of levels is compatible with the folk conceptualisation where transacting bundles must be of unequal origin (inferior/superior, economic/political, indigenous/migrant). However, according to Schlager and Ostrom's conceptual analysis, operative level rights and collective choice level rights can be cumulated by single right holders, complete sets of rights constituting either public or private ownership. Thus, the more complete the bundle of rights held, the greater the holder's authority. Frequently, individuals and communities may hold less than the full set of rights, but to hold some of these rights necessarily implies the possession of others (1992: 252). But in the folk conceptualisation of property, rights are not 'cumulative' in this way. One group may for instance hold political rights (acquired through first occupancy) that secure to them the economic rights (acquired through labour) of another group, but without holding economic rights themselves. The first right does not imply the second one because their justifications (sources) are different.

During the 1990s, environmental policy and legislation in aid-dependent countries has been widely influenced by neo-institutionalist approaches (Hufty and Muttenzer 2002: 300). In her contribution to this volume, Schlager points out that government may allocate portions of water rights in a non-cumulative manner. In Madagascar, customary law is to be 'recognised' through the contractual reallocation of portions of the ownership bundle held by the forest administration. But if the state is not able to enforce a hegemonic claim while other agents can and do make enforceable claims, how does this affect the model constructed by the neo-institutionalists? Before portions of a complete bundle (state ownership) can be reallocated in such a way, state ownership must be allocated to the administration in the first place. The largely academic question of whether folk conceptualisations of property are consistent with Schlager and Ostrom's conceptual analysis suddenly becomes a policy relevant matter.

The answer to the above question is threefold. First, complete sets of rights as defined by the fiction of state and private ownership do not give an accurate description of social practices in Madagascar. In the cases I studied, incomplete sets of rights of distinct origin are balanced against one another according to principles of just transaction that are internalised by both villagers and field-level state officials. Second, the social validation of the 'roughly cumulative' bundles of rights formally created through management contracts is unlikely for this very reason. As long as the rules of contractual management are derived from a fiction of state ownership that does not exist in practice, state 'recognition' of customary law is likely to violate the substantive principles of the folk conceptualisation of property. Third, the distinction made by Schlager and Ostrom between operative level and collective choice level rules does not hinge on the assumption that complete sets are possible. Their conceptual framework remains useful if rules are consistently described in terms of cross-level transactions between unequal bundles, none of which can ever be so 'cumulative' as to contain the complete set that formally defines state or private ownership.

Cash-cropping and Land Rights in a Protected Area in Northern Madagascar

The conversion of forest lands to agricultural uses has been justly described as a major cause of biodiversity loss in Madagascar (Keck, Sharma and Feder 1994). Before the contractual management law was enacted in 1996, the phenomenon was blamed on the 'human occupation of protected areas' (Weber 1995). Although this changed after 1996, we should remember that only those forests not in protected areas are available to contractual management. And looking beyond protected areas at forests in general does little to reconcile competing interests of local livelihoods and biodiversity conservation. It may therefore be worthwhile to refocus on protected areas where the contractual recognition of customary law is of no avail. In terms of legal pluralism, we are faced with a conflicting one-to-one opposition between state legislation on protected areas and the traditional way of getting access to productive land. However, in terms of organisational pluralism, the folk conceptualisation of property in illegal cash-cropping suggests a less oppositional reality which recombines traditional custom and state law in new ways.

For example, during the last twenty-five years, migrants have partially cleared forest lands inside the Special Reserve of Manongarivo in Northern Madagascar for cultivation of subsistence crops such as mountain rice and manioc, as well as cash crops such as cocoa and coffee. Holdings are composed of primary forest relics, secondary vegetation (fallow lands) and plots bearing annual crops (rice in particular) or perennial crops such as coffee and cocoa. Inside the holding, plots are used individually. Sons at working age may cultivate the land of their fathers or else establish their own holding. Agricultural produce accrues to those who cleared the land and continue to cultivate it. Rights of occupation in a land reserve beyond the actual cultivated plots and those left in fallow is commonly recognised among family groups. Although individual holdings include significant portions of uncleared land, there are no conflicts over access to these relics of primary forest. In both natural forest relics and fallow lands, collecting forest products is not restricted to family members. Owners have the right to regulate this only if others want to withdraw products from plots already cleared for cultivation. But in practice, families are self-sufficient for such products since their holdings typically comprise up to five hectares.

Migrants temporarily work on the holdings of first occupants, both for subsistence and accumulation, before more permanently establishing themselves elsewhere later on. The social purposes of share-cropping arrangements are twofold. They allow recent migrants to gain familiarity with the community and to legitimise their presence. In addition, those already established in the area have their prior rights affirmed and increase production through additional labour. Contracts are variable as to duration and specific terms. When land is borrowed for several years, the borrower is free to cultivate any annual crops he wishes, climate and the soil quality being the only limiting factors. He cultivates either on fallow land or immediately after the owner's rice harvest, sometimes even in the undergrowth of the owner's coffee or cocoa plantations. Contracts never extend to plots of natural forest: the act of clearing the forest is the privilege of first occupants.

Terms of contract are also flexible as to the sharing of produce and monetary benefits. By contrast, there are specific requirements concerning the choice of crops and social ties between contracting partners. First occupants do not allow borrowers to plant perennial cash crops. Cash-cropping by a borrower is reported to have occurred in one case, although some argued that the land had been sold prior to cultivation. But sales of land inside the protected area are exceptional. Sales occur when migrants decide to return indefinitely to their home region, when cultivators are too old to work the land, or because of exceptional monetary needs. Contracts are written on paper and are kept by both parties, or at least by the buyers. Relatives and friends are informed first when someone intends to sell a plot. Higher bids by outsiders or less related persons have in the exceptional case, led to conflict between potential buyers. Transfers of rights in land are always conditioned by non-land-related terms, even though this is no longer a traditional situation with land rights circulating only among members of kin groups. Whether temporary or permanent, land transfers imply a relational affinity between parties. These social ties are the same for sales and temporary transfers through leases or share-cropping arrangements. There is no market for transferring land rights but only various degrees of monetarisation of social transactions that are best understood in terms of derived rights.

In a formal sense, 'derived rights' refer to the prerogatives acquired by the recipient or taker. They are temporary rights delegated by the holder of rights of first occupancy and include both traditional forms of open-ended loans and more monetarised arrangements like rental or share-cropping. Someone controlling permanent rights of access and use over farmland, in his own name or that of his family group, grants rights of use to another party on a temporary basis in accordance with specific rules (Lavigne Delville et al. 2002: 2). Recent research in West Africa views these as flexible tenure relations that allow production systems to adapt to rapid changes in economic conditions and to play a vital role in regulating local land use. For migrants, such agreements represent an important means to gain access to land (ibid.: 4). According to the authors, such agreements are not based on purely productive or monetary considerations but are both economic and social. They imply alliances and patronage between family units representing wider social units and identities (such as indigenous versus migrants). These conclusions also apply to property relations in Manongarivo, although West African lineage territorial control rights and corresponding 'chiefs' do not exist in Madagascar.[5]

The first step for a migrant wishing to acquire permanent rights to land inside the Manongarivo Special Reserve is to create share-cropping ties that oblige him to observe specific duties not only towards the host family, but to the whole community of first settlers which the host family represents in external relations. Recent migrants do not settle on their own account, but are 'filtered' into the frontier through relations with the second generation of earlier migrants who already consider themselves indigenous to the region. As it is proscribed under protected areas regulation, the colonisation of the forest is entirely controlled under customary principles. It is interesting that the same customary principles are used to interpret authorisation procedures of state forest law on lands where no such authorisations are needed. To secure resource flows from invested labour, families with rights arising from clearing the forest or representatives of the frontier community, make arrangements with both the local forest guard and the elected local government. Each year before the rice season, local producers write down a list with the names of those who intend to clear a forest plot. The list is then presented for approval to the local forest guard who makes a field visit inside the protected area to 'control' the plots to be cleared. In exchange, cultivators pay either in cash (around 5 USD per year for a family) or in kind (the equivalent in rice) at the moment of harvesting. This actually is the correct procedure (and fee) to be followed in state forests other than protected areas, the one difference being that there is no written receipt given for the payment. Elected local government officials recognise the settlements inside the protected area by assigning them the status of so-called 'cantonnements', irregular territorial subdivisions copied after the official administrative model of village neighbourhoods. Settlements inside the protected area are grouped into two such 'cantonnements'. Communal councils do not receive direct payment, but their support makes sense in terms of local electoral politics that benefit from the help of 'collectors' of the export cash crops illegally produced in the protected forest.

There is no direct link between the two procedures involving the forest and territorial administrations respectively, except that the community interlocutors are the same for both state services. Each of the 'cantonnements' is represented by a 'president' chosen from and by the families holding land inside the protected area. Although these two procedures are not 'derived rights' in the formal sense – recipients or takers acquire their rights independent of and prior to (irregular) state authorisation – the logic of reciprocity between settlers and local officials is comparable to the logic underlying the customary contracts between migrants and first occupants described above. For practical purposes (material sources of law) it does not matter whether transactions are named in a modern or a traditional legal idiom (formal sources of law). While legal orders are plural, the procedural logic defining the use of plural rules is syncretistic, rather than pluralistic. Share-cropping arrangements and petty corruption of officials are justified by similar substantive considerations, which appear in both cases to be incompatible with international pressure to protect biodiversity.[6]

Extraction and Management of Raphia Palm Fibre on the Eastern Coast

In this section, I present field work from two villages where user associations formed to implement contractual management plans for raphia palm fibre, to examine how some of the common property design principles (Ostrom 1990: 88–102) actually work in practice. The analysis of fibre extraction suggests that the procedural logic underlying its property relations is similar to the one we discovered in the protected forest case. Raphia palm fibre is a major non-timber forest product of Madagascar.[7] It represents a major source of export earnings for the country after shrimps, vanilla, coffee and lychees. The raphia palm is distributed over half of the island's surface but commercial extraction is concentrated in two zones, on the eastern coast south of Toamasina and in the western region of Mahajanga. The two villages I studied are situated in the district of Brickaville where most of the raphia resources on the eastern coast are found.

Despite growing demand from international markets, raphia fibre production is approaching a crisis, both in the quality of fibre and in the quantity exported. Stocks on the eastern coast have been decimated in recent years by over-harvesting and cyclones, leaving growing pressure on stocks from the western coast. Both the formal sector of the fibre producing chain[8] such as export firms and collectors, and many of the villagers who do the harvesting, estimate that extraction of raphia fibres may cease within ten years if no measures are taken. In 1999, the National Office for the Environment together with the Directorate General of Forests initiated a consultation process with different stakeholders that led to an action plan covering the district of Brickaville. The exporting firms and big collectors were conspicuously absent from the preparatory workshop. In 2000, local management contracts for raphia were negotiated between the Forest service and associations of harvesters in only two (Ambodiriana and Andranonamalona) of the 171 villages of the district.

Fibre extraction in these villages hardly differs from those without contractual management agreements. In the whole region, raphia leaves are harvested almost throughout the year, with the exception of months with heavy rainfall. It constitutes a complementary source of income, but villagers consider it a secondary activity, practiced alongside agriculture. Rice is cultivated twice a year on the eastern coast and in between villagers grow manioc and banana. Rice production is for subsistence but is insufficient to cover annual consumption needs, while the revenues from raphia do not compensate for resulting food expenses. Thus many of the marshlands where the palm trees grow are being converted into irrigated rice fields. Rice cultivation and fibre extraction are in spatial competition, but rice is the more valued good, both because it is the staple food and because the labour required is greater. When asked if rice fields are ever planted in association with raphia trees, villagers explained:

> The raphia growing around here belongs to all of us. However, the owner of a rice field can exclude others from harvesting because they would drop the leaves onto the rice. A rice field planted with raphia does not exist. Actually, we cut the trees when preparing the fields so that others cannot harvest the leaves. The rules of our association say that for any tree cut by someone, he must plant ten elsewhere, but the rule is not applied right now. There are some of us who destroy a hundred trees without planting a single one.

Raphia palm trees are not concentrated in a single place but are found distributed between villages. This distribution means that anywhere raphia is found is important for villagers. According to informants, it is not like agriculture where the rice fields are situated in a given place. Sometimes trees are far away, sometimes next to the village. Everyone first harvests what can be found close by. But harvesters take what they

can find, where they find it. Villagers do not particularly search for trees
with leaves ready for harvesting but rather find them as they travel. This
means that people from other regions sometimes come specifically for
raphia extraction. Villagers comment that:

> We cannot stop them. We simply tell them not to destroy the raphias. The tree
> does not die if one only harvests the leaves. It is because they take the *ovitra*
> [edible part of the tree] or the *isatra* [palm] to make *garaba* [large baskets] that
> the trees die. Since 1942 until today, we have taken the leaves from raphia and
> it has continued to grow. But later the trees were decimated because of these
> practices.

Whereas in earlier times a harvester could find between three and four
kilos of leaves in a day, after a cyclone had destroyed most adult trees
daily harvests dropped to 1.5 kilos. As there are no set areas for
harvesting, and people find leaves where they can, villagers who find full
grown leaves, harvest them immediately, taking all before going
elsewhere. It is up to every family to fit harvesting in among their daily
activities. Harvesting is complicated by the fact that it takes time. All
family members participate. While women do not climb the trees, they
extract fibre from harvested leaves, a process that requires experience
acquired over time. The fibre is then dried under the sun and bound
together for sale. It can be sold even in small quantities of half a kilogram,
although it is usual to collect larger lots before selling to a collector.

Prices are affecting current production rates. Local collectors pay
4,000 Francs Malagasy (Fmg) or about 80 cents U.S.D. per kilogram, but
exporting firms send their own collectors who will pay 4,500 Fmg,
especially in the village of Ambodiriana which is situated close to the
national road. Raphia pays well now, prices formerly being around 3,000
Fmg. Villagers expect production to rise in two or three years time, saying
that there are many young trees beginning to grow.

I have so far only mentioned the operative rules (or 'rules of
apportionment', see Gudeman 2001: 52) regulating access to trees and
withdrawal of leaves from which the fibres are then extracted. To
complete the picture, I turn now to the collective choice rules (or 'rules of
allotment', in Gudeman's terms), which regulate access to trees and
withdrawal of leaves, define holders of operational rights, and set taxation
of extraction and commercial transactions. Similar to the derived rights
observed in the protected forest case, the organisation of production and
benefit-sharing in the fibre chain results from transactions whereby
holders of collective choice rights exchange – or refuse to exchange – with

holders of operational rights.[9] For example, traditional family rights in irrigated rice fields restrict common access to palm trees that may be left standing when marshland is converted into rice fields. As one man commented:

> One always needs to ask for [the field owner's] agreement because he is sovereign on anything to be found on his property and because it can cause damage. What is strange and amusing here is that when I come on the land and I say it is mine, well, it becomes my property. Without title. In fact I can capture a lot of land carrying raphias, and then I destroy them in order to cultivate other things, and tomorrow I will go on to another field.

District level officials blame such agricultural practices for the degradation of raphia resources. Thus a major item of the contractual management plan for raphia negotiated in 2000 was to demarcate agricultural zones from those carrying the remaining raphia trees, to 'clearly establish boundaries' (Ostrom 1990: 88). But these boundaries have no practical significance as the practices did not differ before and after establishing them, nor is there a difference between villages with or without management plans in this respect. The trees to be found within the zoning plan are meant to be used only by members of the harvesters' association, but according to villagers, there are many trees harvested beyond that limit, as well as many harvesters who do not belong to the association. Although most villagers from Andranonamalona have become members of the association, those from the nearby villages are free to harvest leaves as they used to. Villagers admit: 'It creates problems, for example, those who exploit in the zone of the association and then sell it outside. Our members do not like that because it diminishes the income of the association. Even more so since those people who are not members of the association do not take care of the raphia, they destroy them ... .'

In practice, the collective choice rights over state forest lands have been unable to constrain operational rights of access to raphia trees. Another way for the administration to exercise rights over the forest domain is by temporal restriction of rights of withdrawal or by imposing minimal standards for quality of harvested leaves. A 1967 decree limits extraction and collection to a period of five to seven months between October and May. During the first republic (1960–1972), the forest administration effectively prevented extraction outside this period. But villagers explain that, at present, the harvest obtained during a campaign of six months would be insufficient because trees are scarce. Quality standards require a minimal fibre length of 1.10 metres, only full-grown leaves may be harvested and certain parts of the plant must not be harvested at all. Usually these rules are not respected either:

> We members of the association would like to see the laws on the exploitation of raphia reinforced. Taking the *isatra* in order to make the *garaba* [large baskets used to carry chickens to the market] is one of the big problems. In Antsampanana, they use thousands and thousands of *garaba*. They do not even care to sell them at night but sell them in the open daylight. There is even a house there where they stock the *garaba*. The production of lychees was not good this year but it could be better the next year.[10] So next year it would be better to apply the law more strongly for that part of the raphia used to make the *garaba*.

A second focus of the contractual management plan for raphia is community work to expand the resource base. On 1 May 2002, villagers planted 150 young trees but most have not survived the hot and dry weather. In 2003, each member was required to plant thirty young trees and to put eucalyptus around the lands planted with raphia, which most agreed to do. When I asked them how the users association's earnings are mainly spent, I found that sustainable resource management did not figure among the top priorities: 'We only use it for the construction of the school. But our wish is that we could also use it for the construction of a bridge, so that cars could come right to our village. We try to finish the school before 1 May, the children here have to walk seven kilometers to go to school.'

A third and last category of collective choice rights define fiscal rules. Government officials levy fees and local taxes in exchange for authorising the extraction or commercial use of raphia fibre and such fees are charged by the district level Forest Service. Collectors are required to apply for a collector's card that is renewable every year and specifies the territory within which fibre may be collected. Fees are also charged in proportion to the weight of fibre collected. In exchange for the fees paid, authorised collectors receive from the Forest Service a corresponding amount of stamped tickets, which are required to identify the origin of the product during transportation. When the ticket is filled in and signed by the authorised collector, it can be used by any transporter to declare the goods. Also, an export fee is paid by exporting firms in the provincial capital but the provincial government refuses to redistribute their share to district and local government levels. The management contracts generally do not devolve the right to charge an extraction fee. However, other fees are charged by the associations. Both the villages with a contractual management plan have an authorised collector among their association members and this facilitates the trading of their produce.

Association rules require these collectors to pay 15 Fmg per kilogram to the association. Either elected local governments, or the village association in the case of contractual management, levy small taxes on the trading of produce outside the locality. The total amount of fees and taxes does not exceed 150 Fmg per kilogram of fibre. It would appear that even if properly administrated, fees and taxes would not create incentives to modify the quantity and quality of raphia extracted from the zone. On the whole, it is unclear how contractual management could possibly avert the crisis of the raphia fibre production chain.

Discussion: Rules, Principles and the Politics of Recognition

The theoretical argument for the recognition of customary law is similar to Africanist doctrines that used to refer to the insecurity of 'communal tenure' to justify the appropriation of land by the colonial state (Peters 2002: 48–49). Like the colonial doctrines, the environmental policy of the 1990s takes as its starting point a situation of insecurity called 'open access', which optimally should be corrected under state law. But the property relations emerging on the agricultural frontier, or in the over-harvesting of non-timber forest products, reflect neither a lack of secure tenure nor a lack of recognition. On the contrary, unsustainable resource use patterns seem to be a consequence of the economic effectiveness and political legitimacy of folk principles whereby authorisations to withdraw forest products, cultivate land, or occupy territory, are exchanged against parts of the economic value generated through theses activities.

Legal Pluralism in the Spirit of Folk Principles: Reciprocity between Flows and Stocks

Temporary transfers of rights to withdraw forest products, cultivate a plot, or occupy forested lands to be cleared for cultivation, occur either between non-relatives, in which case the derived right organises relations between family groups, or between such groups and state services. They may also take place between individuals belonging to the same family, in which case the derived right has no bearing on external relations. Collective choice rights may therefore be variably exercised by one group alone or by several allied groups in common (Le Roy 1998: 99). Logically we must distinguish at least two bundles of rights for a transaction to be possible. Although it need not concern us here, this is true even of temporary transfers of rights inside the group, for example when a family head delegates rights to cultivate to his dependents. In any case, security of the taker's expectations related to a category of product, land or territory, depends on temporary transfers of rights derived from a *distinct* bundle having as its object the *same* type of product, land or territory (Le Roy 2001: 37). The resource base is identical for both bundles of rights, but while it is considered in terms of a flow at the operative level, collective choice level rules identify the same resource in terms of a stock.

The classificatory attribution of bundles of rights to levels does not depend on the content of rights, but on whether those rights are exercised by the taker (user) or the giver (authoriser) in a transaction concerning a given type of use. The taker's bundle may therefore contain not only rights of access and withdrawal, but any of the various types of use (access, withdrawal, management, exclusion, transfer) distinguished by neo-institutionalists (Schlager and Ostrom 1992: 250–51). The taker may well hold a complete set of rights in formal legal terms. To be able to enforce their claim by excluding other claimants from their property, they will have to have that claim authorised by a giver. State enforcement of ownership, however, may not be easily accessible in rural Madagascar. To secure their property, would-be owners and their larger groups thus have no choice other than to transact with other claimants asserting different sets of rights on the same property object.

The rules of the arrangements I have described exclude any form of accumulation by single holders of a complete set of rights. The holder of the collective choice right is never the holder of the operative right of a given type of use, although they may hold operative rights over other types of use.[11] Field-level forest administrators acting as givers of derived rights for example, authorise productive uses of takers, just as any holder of rights in stocks under title of first occupancy would do. But they do not themselves hold operative level rights over the economic flows generated through the authorised uses. Local state officials are simply entitled to counter-gift to the extent specified by principles of just transaction – or by a local law emerging on the basis of such principles – between givers and takers of derived rights.

To understand why arrangements are generated in this way rather than on the basis of complete sets, we must consider the existence of claims that are stronger than particular operative or collective choice rights. Folk legal principles reflect property rights of a different and superior kind which can be exercised not only by individuals holding particular responsibilities regarding land and resources, but by any member of the community as soon as the common good is perceived to be under threat. People will refer to a common principle when it is violated by the operative or collective choice rules of a particular arrangement. The difference between rules of particular transactions and folk principles is that the negotiation and/or imposition of particular rules are only legitimate within the scope of principles that can justify them. The immediate function of the folk conceptualisation of property is not to prescribe, but to legitimise such operative and collective choice rights as are exercised in conformity with its meaning. Constitutive principles do normally have prescriptive effects but only insofar as their meaning conflicts with a specific rule. Tacitly presupposed by discussions about the relative validity of customary or state-legal rules of particular transactions, underlying principles themselves are neither plural nor negotiable. The idea of a folk conceptualisation of property does not refer to particular 'customary' or 'modern' legal rules, idioms or systems, but to how competing rules are brought into coherence with reference to a set of substantive principles:

> According to a Malagasy saying, *izay tonga aloha tompon-tanindrazana*, he who arrives first is the owner of the land. In our community, there is not a single piece of land with title. We are still attached to traditional values. In effect, if a forefather has worked on a given plot, it is considered like a sort of delimitation of property. His descendants can then exploit it. That is how the delimitations of the land have been realised in Ambodiriana. So, if a person who does not belong to the family of the owner wants to plant, he has to arrange it himself with elders in the village in order to avoid possible social conflicts. All the lands here belong to the state but this does not mean that they do not have their owners. Generally, lands are divided among descendants. But there are those who sell a part of their land, a written agreement is then put on paper. To come into possession of the land, the foreigners have to establish the consent of village elders and of the people.

Rights in flows, or rights to a stream of income, are defined by the principle of differential rewards for labour. Fruits go to them who have applied their labour and industry, independent of whether they are forefathers or present-day migrants intending to cultivate land already owned by others. Operational level rights work like a sort of natural law. He who has cleared a piece of land may use it undisturbed by others (as long as he actually uses it). Absentee owners are penalised according to that logic because they no longer have a natural right to an income stream based on labour. In relation to post-colonial state officials, the principle of differential rewards for labour means that title, or its less formal equivalents, is granted upon proof of continued cultivation.

This implies a second principle. Differential rewards to compensate invested labour are just only when opportunities for work are equally distributed between productive units. It follows that holders of collective choice rights, that is rights in stocks, have a duty to transact with present or future holders of rights over income streams. The notion of a friendly brotherhood among those who live side by side requires first settlers to authorise migrants to cultivate ancestral land. In the case of agriculture in protected forests, migrants are holders of operational rights, authorised after the fact not by the owners of the ancestral land but by holders of rights over state-owned biodiversity. This practice had been established by public policy during the 1970s as favouring easy access to uncultivated forest land for the sake of national development. But traditionally migrants are only potential holders of operational rights given that they first need to establish the consent of first settlers before taking possession of the land.

It should be noted that neither first settlers nor field administrators of biodiversity have the right to refuse migrants, unless they first demonstrate a superior interest in the survival of their own descent group or segment of the state bureaucracy. The principle of self-conservation of going concerns justifies a giver's permanent rights over stocks that may be temporarily delegated to a taker wishing to secure rights over flows. The saying *izay tonga aloha tompon-tanindrazana* translates into an anachronism where labour and first occupancy are conflated into a single justification of acquiring rights: he who came first [to work the land] is the owner of the land-of-forefathers. In a structural reading, the concept of ancestral domain can be seen as an analogical transposition, to a higher level of organisation, of the principle of differential rewards for labour. Thus within the going concern, self-conservation is transgenerational and ensures reproduction of the group. Among going concerns, self-conservation is intragenerational and legitimises the unequal powers of coercion of several interests competing for control of the state, as in the case of cash crops against biodiversity conservation.[12]

The Folk Conceptualisation and Epistemic Claims about 'common property'

Although constitutive principles have not been completely ignored in the neo-institutionalist literature, the 'common property' epistemic community has only presented them as blueprints for formalising local custom through state law and expert knowledge. Such claims rest on a theoretically informed vision of reality and a notion of scientific validity, that in turn relies on internally formulated truth tests. As in other epistemic communities, members share a common understanding of a specific problem and a preference for a set of technical solutions. Before the 1990s, environmentalists believed that Garret Hardin's 'tragedy of the commons' metaphor captured the essence of the problem facing most common property resources. Since appropriators were viewed as being trapped in these dilemmas, it was argued that the state needed to impose a set of external rules on such settings (Hardin 1968). Twenty-two years later, social scientists interpreted Hardin's metaphor as a confusion of common property and open access (Feeney et al. 1990; see also Bromley and Cernea 1989). During the 1990s, Malthusianism has increasingly been challenged on grounds that many successfully governed common pool resources have survived for centuries. Solutions worked out by the individuals concerned were described as more successful and enduring than resource regimes imposed by central political authorities. Such wise management had supposedly changed only when forests were declared state ownership. No longer perceived as local commons with a long-term value to users, a rush ensued to harvest them before others did (Ostrom 1998: 3; McKean 2000: 35).

The appropriate means to halt deforestation logically follows from identifying the problem in this way: the recognition of robust and self-governed property regimes justifies the restitution of government appropriated forests to local users. In Madagascar, forests constitute the primary field for contractual local resource management. Legally qualified as multiple use lands in 1997, all types of forests except protected areas can in principle be transferred to local user associations. The truth tests formulated by experts to justify the recognition of common property regimes evolve around empirical criteria such as clearly defined boundaries, congruence of appropriation rules and provision rules, participation in collective choice arrangements, self-monitoring or accountability of external rule monitors, graduated sanctions, conflict resolution mechanisms, minimal rights to organise, nesting into larger organisations (Ostrom 1990: 88–102). Ostrom's objective in documenting these so-called design principles in a wide range of empirical contexts has been to 'challenge the generalizability of the conventional theory', taking into account that 'a fully articulated, reformulated theory encompassing the conventional theory as a special case does not yet exist' (Ostrom 1998: 4).

For the 'common property' theory to make valid truth claims, it should be able to specify at least some alternative accounts that it excludes. Rather than encompassing the conventional theory, it would have to specify real world conditions under which that theory is empirically false. Design principles are not specific enough to formulate truth tests that could evaluate the outcomes of a contractual 'customary law'. Neo-institutionalism describes the robustness of self-governed systems without explaining how resources are managed. Forests may be depleted or not, but it all depends on 'local institutions' (see Gibson et al. 2000). Conventional anti-democratic Malthusians make a stronger truth claim than their neo-institutionalist opponents. In Hardin's metaphor of tragedy, short term robustness of institutions is a consequence of their failure in the long term. The forest-related going concerns I described in this chapter are self-governing, robust and politically legitimate precisely because they feed on local consumption of raphia fibres and species-diverse land reserves at a rate environmentalists consider ecologically damaging.

When there is a high degree of uncertainty among bureaucrats, scientists speak out only at the latter's request. When there is also a high degree of consensus among scientists, epistemic communities may themselves seek access to governing institutions (Haas 1992: 7–16). Outcomes of aid-driven environmental legislation are difficult to predict. What is more, in a political structure characterised by authoritative coordination among aid donors but little overall control of donors over recipients, consensus among scientists becomes a functional necessity. Consensus then is a consequence, not the legitimate cause, of the funding of research programmes by international aid agencies (Muttenzer 2002: 10). But one may still disagree. Environmentalist policy research – environmental policy itself – would be a sterile exercise if consensus among scientists were its only valued end. In this chapter I have tried to show why the folk correlation between legal pluralism and organisational patterns of unsustainable resource use does not warrant a research programme based on scientific consensus about common property design principles.

The management contracts for raphia resources, for instance, restricts access to trees and limits collection to certain periods. They aim to change operational rules in order to bring down the volume of fibre extracted.

But in doing that, procedural design principles such as 'clearly defined boundaries' or 'congruence between appropriation and provision rules' (Ostrom 1990: 98–102) formally agreed in the contract between the village association and the forest service, violate the substantive principles of equal opportunity for members and non-members and of rewards for invested labour. The same would be true of management contracts on forested lands other than protected areas whose objective it is to internalise the environmental cost of forest conversion for agriculture. In practical terms, the gap between neo-institutionalist design principles and the folk conceptualisation of property is less important in cases where contractual rules do not interfere with substantive rights to basic income. Local collectors of raphia fibres comply with the duties of membership in the harvesters' association. Contractual changes of rules about benefit sharing and the restructuring of parallel production chains may be worthwhile objectives. But environmentalist 'customary law' cannot bring production down to acceptable levels because the folk conceptualisation of property excludes that possibility.

As understood by neo-institutionalists, design principles are similar to the rules of deliberative democracy, procedural not substantive. Proceduralism sets the stage for a theory/policy focus on decisions about specific rules, both at the so-called operational and collective choice levels, but ignores the structural conditions determining whether the negotiation or imposition of those rules is actually possible. The idea of procedural design principles endows Schlager and Ostrom's (1992) conceptual analysis of property-rights regimes and natural resources with the assumption that formal decisions are sufficient to cumulate operative level and collective choice level bundles in complete sets of private and public ownership. Without this unnecessary assumption, Schlager and Ostrom's model can be usefully deployed by social anthropologists committed to avoid theoretical 'cherry picking' (F. and K. von Benda-Beckmann and Wiber this volume) to describe the use of legal pluralism in 'going concerns', '(semi-)autonomous social fields', 'networks', and other shorthands for organisational pluralism.

I am aware that the resulting conceptual framework is minimalist in its critique of neo-institutionalism, compared with the pluralistic model proposed by the editors of this volume. To describe how particular rules are selected from plural legal orders (custom, state-law, contractual 'customary law') and reassembled by the agents of going concerns, I continue to use Schlager and Ostrom's distinction of levels, each level hosting a rights bundle acquired on different grounds (labour, first occupancy etc.). Existing rights are secured through transactions between bundles situated at different levels. The underlying logic of these transactions is therefore less arbitrary than neo-institutionalist proceduralism suggests. The folk conceptualisation of property cannot be designed, because according to common knowledge and practice, principles of just transaction are exempt from discussion. As I understand them, these principles are an implicit condition of any explicit agreement about, or tacit acceptance of, rules which are then referred back to either traditional custom and its contemporary equivalents, state forest law, or the 'customary law' of contractual management according to circumstance and expediency.

Notes

1. Transferable resources include trees, wild fauna and flora both aquatic and terrestrial, together with water and rangeland, falling under the state domain, with the exception of protected areas.
2. Estimations of the annual rate of deforestation in Madagascar vary between 117,000 hectares and 280,000 hectares.
3. See Articles 8 e) and 10 c) of the Convention (United Nations 1992).
4. According to J.R. Commons, 'a going concern is a joint expectation of beneficial bargaining, managerial, and rationing transactions, kept together by "working rules" and by control of the changeable strategic or "limiting" factors which are expected to control the others. When the expectations cease then the concern quits going and production stops.'(1934: 58).
5. In Madagascar, functionally equivalent prerogatives are exercised by village residential collectives themselves constituted by distinct descent groups – extended families – usually limited to four or five generations (Rarijaona 1967: 37–38).
6. The substantive principle by which would-be 'takers' acquire operational rights prior to, and independent of, later authorisation by official 'givers' may be considered a fundamental or 'natural' right to opportunities and to the fruits of labour.
7. Non-timber forest products are any usable material product including processed derivatives that are dependent on a forest environment, other than timber.
8. In rural Madagascar, small collectors are shopkeepers in villages or smalls towns who buy cash crops (vanilla, coffee, lychees) from peasant producers before selling it to big collectors or directly to exporters. They are the intermediaries in the fibre economy that harvesters depend on for small loans that are often repaid in materials. Such relations between producers and their buyers are not adequately captured through purely economic terms.

9. Given that holders of collective choice rights might refuse a transaction, rules of access to trees and withdrawal of leaves must be considered rights acquired independent of and prior to specific recognition by either customary contracts or state authorisation. In fact, a natural right to labour and to rewards for labour can be claimed by any member of the group on the basis of common principles, without the mediation of specific customary or state legal rules and authorities.

10. The *garaba* is also used to carry lychees. I was told that shortly before the opening of the lychee harvesting season, market demand for baskets rises steeply and a single person can produce up to sixty-five a day.

11. Could I not as family head control a complex of several rice fields and have individual use rights on two of them? I certainly could. But while my rights in the harvest from the two fields are acquired through labour, my rights in the complex were first acquired through its occupation by family ancestors. Each distinct type of use has to be secured through a corresponding bundle of control rights at a higher level. Family rights in the complex of several fields can secure rights in the harvest independently acquired through work on the fields. But to secure extended family rights in the complex, I must turn to the community level represented either by other family heads of the village or by the state.

12. Illegal settlers had been tolerated for twenty-five years in the Manongarivo Special Reserve, but a prolonged stay by foreign biologists eventually led the forest service to crack down on the peasants.

References

Bromley, D.W. and M.M. Cernea 1989. 'The Management of Common Property Natural Resources. Some Conceptual and Operational Fallacies', *World Bank Discussion Paper* 57, Washington: IBRD.

Commons, J.R. 1934. *Institutional Economics. Its Place in Political Economy.* New York: The Macmillan Company.

Feeney, D., F. Berkes, B.J. McCay and J.M. Acheson 1990. 'The Tragedy of the Commons: Twenty-Two Years Later', *Human Ecology* 18: 1–19.

Gibson, C., M. McKean and E. Ostrom 2000. 'Explaining Deforestation: The Role of Local Institutions', in *People and Forests: Communities, Institutions, and Governance*, eds C. Gibson, M. McKean and E. Ostrom, Cambridge: MIT Press, 1–25.

Gudeman, S. 2001. *The Anthropology of Economy.* Oxford: Blackwell.

Haas, P.M. 1992. 'Introduction: Epistemic Communities and International Policy Coordination', *International Organisation* 46(1): 1–35.

Hardin, G. 1968. 'The Tragedy of the Commons', *Science* 162: 1243–48.

Hufty, M. and F. Muttenzer 2002. 'Devoted Friends: The Implementation of the Convention on Biological Diversity in Madagascar', in *Governing Global Biodiversity*, ed. Ph. Leprestre, Aldershot: Ashgate, 279–309.

Keck, A., N.P. Sharma and G. Feder 1994. 'Population Growth, Shifting Cultivation, and Unsustainable Agricultural Development: A Case Study in Madagascar', *World Bank Discussion Paper* No. 234, Africa Technical Department Series, Washington: IBRD.

Lavigne Delville, Ph., C. Toulmin, J.-Ph. Colin and J.-P. Chauveau 2002. *Negotiating Access to Land in West Africa: A Synthesis of Findings from Research on Derived Rights to Land*. London: International Institute for Environment and Development.

Le Roy, E. 1998. 'Faire-Valoir Indirects et Droits Délégués. Premier Etat des Lieux', in *Quelles Politiques Foncières pour l'Afrique Rurale? Réconcilier Pratiques, Légitimité et Légalité*, eds. Ph. Lavigne and C. Delville, Paris: Karthala et Coopération Française, 87–100.

—— 2001. 'Actualité des Droits Dits "Coutumiers" dans les Pratiques et les Politiques Foncières en Afrique et dans l'Océan Indien à l'Orée du XXIe siècle', *Bulletin de Liaison du LAJP* 26: 34–53.

McConnell, W.J. 2002. 'Emerald Isle or Paradise Lost? Madagascar's Conservation Controversy', *Environment* 44(8): 10–22.

McKean, M. 2000. 'Common Property: What is it, What is it Good for, and What Makes it Work?', in *People and Forests: Communities, Institutions, and Governance*, eds C. Gibson, M. McKean and E. Ostrom, Cambridge: MIT Press, 27–55.

Muttenzer, F. 2001. 'La Mise en Œuvre de l'Aménagement Forestier Négocié, ou l'Introuvable Gouvernance de la Biodiversité à Madagascar', *Bulletin de Liaison du LAJP* 26: 91–129.

—— 2002. 'Local Government and the International Biodiversity Regime: Collective Bargaining over State Forests in Madagascar', paper presented at the 9th Biennial Conference of The International Association for the Study of Common Property, Sub-theme 'Globalisation, Governance and the Commons', Victoria Falls, Zimbabwe, 17–21 June.

Ostrom, E. 1990. *Governing the Commons. The Evolution of Institutions for Collective Action*. Cambridge: Cambridge University Press.

—— 1998. 'Self-Governance and Forest Resources', presentation for the International CBNRM Workshop, Washington, 10–14 May.

Peters, P.E. 2002. 'The Limits of Negotiability: Security, Equity and Class Formation in Africa's Land Systems', in *Negotiating Property in Africa*, eds K. Juul and C. Lund, Portsmouth: Heinemann, 45–66.

Rarijaona, R. 1967. *Le Concept de Propriété en Droit Foncier de Madagascar. (Etude de Sociologie Juridique)*. Paris: Cujas.

Schlager, E. and E. Ostrom 1992. 'Property-rights Regimes and Natural Resources: A Conceptual Analysis', *Land Economics* 68(9): 249–62.

United Nations 1992. *The United Nations Convention on Biological Diversity*.

Walzer, M. 1994. *Thick and Thin: Moral Argument at Home and Abroad*. Notre Dame: University of Notre Dame Press.

Weber, J. 1995. 'L'occupation Humaine des Aires Protégées à Madagascar: Diagnostic et Eléments pour une Gestion Viable', *Natures, Sciences, Sociétés* 3(2): 157–64.

Chapter 13
Property Rights, Water and Conflict in the Western U.S.

*Edella Schlager**

Introduction

Water is scarce in the western United States. Unlike states in the eastern United States, which averages between twenty and thirty-two inches of annual rainfall in Minnesota, or fourty-six and sixty-six inches in Georgia, most parts of the western U.S. average between eight and twenty inches of moisture per year (Western Regional Climate Center 2001). Such contrasting differences in rainfall are reflected in equally contrasting differences in property rights systems governing the allocation and use of water in streams and rivers. In the eastern U.S., water in rivers and streams is generally not measured, quantified and allocated. Rather, land owners adjacent to streams and rivers have rights to make reasonable use of water flowing by their land and attendant duties not to interfere with the reasonable use that other landowners make of the water (Rose 1994). In the western U.S., water is measured, quantified, allocated and transported great distances. European settlers who arrived first granted themselves the most complete and secure bundle of rights in water – largely immune to water scarcities except in times of severe and extended drought. European settlers who arrived later bore the burden of water scarcity, having their water rights satisfied, if at all, only after those who held more senior, in time, rights had appropriated their share of water.

* Prepared for the conference on 'Changing Properties of Property', Max Planck Institute for Social Anthropology, Halle, Germany, 2–4 July 2003. Research reported in this paper was supported by the National Science Foundation and U.S. Environmental Protection Agency, Grant Number R824781. Neither agency is responsible for the findings or conclusions reported herein.

Well specified and quantified rights in the water of western rivers and streams did not eliminate conflicts over water; in such a water scarce region, new and different types of conflicts emerged as new types of water were discovered, and water uses and water users changed. One of the most enduring and encompassing conflicts revolves around surface water and groundwater. Rivers and streams are often physically, or hydrologically, connected to underground water aquifers. Water seeps through river and stream beds replenishing and sustaining underground aquifers. In turn, stable water levels in aquifers sustain river and stream flows. If water is pumped from aquifers so that water tables decline, river and stream flows also decline. As pumping proceeds and water tables continue to decline, rivers and streams may dry up completely.

While the settlers of most western states adopted the 'first in time, first in right' rule, or the prior appropriation doctrine, to govern access, allocation and use of surface water, a different set of property rights were adopted to govern groundwater – the beneficial use doctrine. The beneficial use doctrine allows owners of land above an aquifer to pump as much water as they can put to beneficial use on their land. The two doctrines clash. The prior appropriation doctrine, through various strictures that have been developed, requires that surface water users not harm the water rights of other surface water users, but it does not require surface water users to take into account the consequences of their actions on groundwater pumpers. Groundwater users have little recourse if surface water users dry up a stream, lowering the water level in the aquifer and possibly drying up their wells. The same holds true for the beneficial use doctrine. Groundwater pumpers may take as much water from an aquifer as they choose as long as they do not waste it; pumpers are not required to take into account the effects of their pumping on surface water users. Surface water users have little recourse if groundwater users dry up streams by lowering the water table through pumping water from the aquifer. This latter scenario – groundwater pumping reducing or eliminating stream flows – is the more common one in the western U.S. and it often precipitates a vicious cycle. As stream flows lessen, surface water users often turn to groundwater for a supplemental supply of water, furthering the decline of the stream.[1]

Legal scholars, policy analysts, and hydrologists have long advocated the adoption of a single property rights system to govern rivers, streams and hydrologically connected groundwater aquifers in the western U.S. A single property rights system would recognise the physical reality that ground and surface water users in a watershed are drawing upon a single water source regardless of whether they divert water through a well or through a ditch. A single property rights system would force water users to take into account the effects of their actions on one another allowing for a means of settling conflicts among them.

Colorado is one of several western states that govern hydrologically connected sources of surface and groundwater by a single property rights system, the prior appropriation doctrine, just as legal scholars, policy analysts and hydrologists have advocated. Colorado's experience, however, contradicts their expectations. Rather than dampening and channelling conflict, conflict has persisted between surface water and groundwater users for the last three decades. The conflict is fueled partly by the unintended consequence of incorporating groundwater into the prior appropriation doctrine – massive volumes of groundwater have been rendered largely inaccessible. Thus, water users find themselves sitting on top of billions of cubic metres of water, while Colorado experiences its most severe drought on record, with crops wilting, lawns drying up, and cities imposing emergency water conservation measures.

How Colorado achieved this outcome and how the citizens of Colorado may extricate themselves from it requires an understanding of the interplay among the analytical levels of property as outlined by F. von Benda-Beckmann, K. von Benda-Beckmann, and Wiber (2003). They argue that a specific property rights system cannot be well understood unless the analyst takes into account 'ideologies, legal property institutions, concretised property relationships, and the social practices of creating, maintaining and changing property ...' (F. von Benda Beckmann et al. 2003: 32). This paper focuses on legal property institutions, concretised property relationships and social practices to explain the impasse between surface water users and groundwater users. It is the interaction among these different layers of social relationships that account for the inability of water users to resolve their conflicts after three decades of struggle. Because of the embeddedness of property rights in water, making what would appear to be a simple change in categorical property relations to resolve surface and groundwater conflicts would raise thorny ideological issues and would likely threaten concretised property relationships. Thus, the struggles among water users in Colorado continue.

The evolution of Colorado's water rights system will be explored in greater depth in the following section, paying careful attention to the interaction among the different analytical levels of property. Particular attention will be devoted to a single watershed, that of the South Platte River, which is the most populated and heavily developed watershed in the state. The South Platte River rises high in the Rockies just to the southwest of Denver, it briefly travels southeast and then it turns north, passing through Denver, before it turns to the northeast, cutting through some of the richest and most productive farmland in the state, before finally emptying into Nebraska. In the third section the conflict among surface water users and groundwater users will be examined. The institutional attempts to resolve the conflict will be explored and the different analytical levels will be used to explain the limited effectiveness of such attempts. In the fourth and concluding section, the analytical levels will be used to explain the multiple hurdles Colorado water users face in attempting to solve the surface water-groundwater impasse.

1859 to 1969: The Development and Institutionalisation of the 'Colorado Doctrine'

In 1859, in response to the discovery of gold in the eastern foothills of the Rocky Mountains, settlers of European descent poured into what was to become the state of Colorado. Although the gold quickly petered out, the settlers remained to mine other minerals, log timber, run cattle and farm.

Given the aridity of the region, only irrigated agriculture was viable, but the settlers, coming from the humid and water rich east, had no experience with irrigation. An 1897 article on Colorado agriculture noted that the greatest struggle that farmers faced was not harsh environmental conditions, but creating and adapting new and appropriate institutional arrangements for allocating the scarce resource of water:

> By far the most vexatious and expensive impediments to be removed have been those arising from the inapplicability of our laws and customs to the conditions prevailing within the arid region. Every instinct acquired through generations of life in a humid country seems to rebel against the methods of the irrigator and every tradition of law is in direct opposition to the proper employment of the natural waters. These instincts and traditions have had to be laboriously demolished, usually after severe struggle, and the series of contests appears a never-ending one. (cf. Hafen 1948: 122; Radosevich et al. 1976: 5–6)

The property rights tradition that farmers were familiar with was riparian law. Under riparian law, water rights resided in owners of land adjoining rivers, streams and lakes. Riparian owners were allowed to make reasonable use of the water. In practice that meant that property owners could use water only on land adjacent to the water source. Water could not be transported off the land. Also, a riparian owner's use of water could not interfere with the uses of other, riparian owners. Finally, during the rare times of water scarcity riparian owners were required to share the burden of scarcity and jointly reduce their water use (Rose 1994).

While the riparian approach was suitable for a humid, water rich setting, it was not suitable for an arid climate with modest rivers and streams, and where water scarcity was the norm. In the arid West, some of the most valuable resources, whether mineral veins or land, lay far from sources of water (Vranesh 1988: 42). In order to develop those resources, water would have to be transported away from the land adjoining the stream, something that the riparian doctrine forbids. Furthermore, the riparian practice of sharing the burden of scarcity would result in amounts of water insufficient for productive activities.

The categorical property system that water users developed came to be known as the prior appropriation system, or the Colorado Doctrine. Prior appropriation allocates water on the basis of 'first in time, first in right'. The person making the first appropriation of water from a stream holds rights to a portion of the water senior to all subsequent appropriators. The next person in time to appropriate water from that same stream holds rights to a portion of the water senior to all subsequent appropriators, but not to the first appropriator. Also, water may be transported away from the stream and used on lands hundreds of miles away. Furthermore, under the prior appropriation doctrine, if water is scarce, appropriators do not equally share in reductions, instead, the rights of senior appropriators are fully satisfied and junior appropriators are foreclosed (Vranesh 1988: 71). During a dry year, or during the driest time of a year, a junior appropriator may not receive any water whatsoever.

Frank Trelease, an expert on water law in the western U.S., has referred to the prior appropriation doctrine as a system of water that emerged from the practices of the people (Trelease 1971: 23). In Colorado, even though settlers had no experience with irrigated agriculture, a number of them had experience with the resource that first attracted them to the area – gold. The Colorado settlers adopted property rights systems that had been developed during other gold rushes (Smith 1992: 8–9). The foundational principle of those systems was first in time, first in right. Mining claims, water to work the claims, farm land and ranch land were all allocated based on first in time, first in right.

While settlers developed the property rights systems among themselves, the property rights systems were quickly written into law. In 1861, Colorado was admitted into the United States as a territory, just two years after the initial gold rush. In 1864, the territorial legislature passed a law stating that prior appropriation was the means by which water was to be allocated in the territory of Colorado (Radosevich et al. 1976: 24). In 1874, major conflict erupted between two of the largest irrigation systems in the South Platte River basin. The more senior system, located downstream of the junior system, accused the junior system of violating its water rights under the prior appropriation system. It threatened to destroy the irrigation infrastructure of the junior system as a means of enforcing its rights. A truce was negotiated between the two systems based on the prior appropriation doctrine (Abbott et al. 1994: 168). In 1876, Colorado was admitted into the Union as a state. The Colorado constitution explicitly defined prior appropriation as the means by which water would be governed. Article XVI, section six states, 'The right to divert the unappropriated waters of any natural stream to beneficial uses shall never be denied'. The Colorado Doctrine that the citizens of Colorado worked out among themselves was granted constitutional recognition and protection.

Even though the prior appropriation system was written into the state constitution, more junior in time water users disadvantaged by the system continued to contest the doctrine, searching for a more advantaged position in relation to water. More common challenges centred on the riparian doctrine as the appropriate water rights system. The riparian doctrine would allow any water user adjacent to a stream, to appropriate from the stream, regardless of time. In 1882, the Colorado Supreme Court ended such challenges by affirming prior appropriation as the means of allocating water in Colorado. The Court stated:

> [We] think the latter [appropriation] doctrine has existed from the date of the earliest appropriations of water within the boundaries of the state. The climate is dry, and the soil, when moistened only by the usual rainfall, is arid and unproductive; except in a few favored sections, artificial irrigation for agriculture is an absolute necessity. Water in the various streams thus acquires a value unknown in moister climates. Instead of being a mere incident to the soil, it rises, when appropriated, to the dignity of a distinct usufructuary estate, or right of property. It has always been the policy of the national, as well as the territorial and state governments, to encourage the diversion and use of water in this country for agriculture; and vast expenditures of time and money have been made in reclaiming and fertilizing by irrigation portions of our unproductive territory. Houses have been built, and permanent improvements made ... Deny

the doctrine of priority or superiority of right by priority of appropriation, and a great part of the value of all this property is at once destroyed. ... And we hold that, in the absence of express statutes to the contrary, the first appropriator of water from a natural stream for a beneficial purpose has, with the qualifications contained in the constitution, a prior right thereto, to the extent of appropriation. [Coffin v. Left Hand Ditch Co. (6 Colo. 443): 446–47]

Concurrently with the development of the prior appropriation doctrine, the legal system for administering it and concretised property relations among water users emerged. The prior appropriation doctrine is extraordinarily difficult to administer in practice. Prior appropriation organises water users temporally, not spatially. Water users take turns based on when they first appropriated water. Water users, however, are scattered across a watershed. Some of the most senior water users may be far downstream of many junior water users, as is the case in the South Platte River Basin. Senior water users find it difficult and costly to monitor the actions of the many junior water users upstream of them to ensure that they are not taking water out of turn and depriving the seniors of their water. Junior water users find it difficult and costly to monitor the actions of the seniors to ensure that they are not taking more water than they are entitled to, leaving less water for juniors. To make matters more complex, water users need to know how they line up in time in relation to one another so that they can better monitor one another and their own water rights, and newcomers need a mechanism by which they may develop water rights and get in line behind the water users before them in time. Finally, the opportunities for conflict are many in such a system. In an arid environment every drop of water matters and water users jostle and press to gain advantage in obtaining water.

Colorado water users moved relatively quickly from a system of self-enforcement that was rife with fights, destruction of diversion structures and canals, and occasional bloodshed, to a set of institutional arrangements controlled by water users, but manned by state officials. Water commissioners were appointed to oversee the diversion of water for specific stream and river segments. Commissioners were selected from well established, local families. They were charged with opening and closing diversion works in order to ensure that water users received only as much water as they were entitled to and only when they were entitled to it. Division engineers were appointed in each of the seven major watersheds in Colorado. Each division engineer coordinated the water commissioners within his watershed, ensuring that water rights were satisfied in their proper order across the entire watershed. The division engineers were charged with keeping public records on water rights. A state engineer was appointed to oversee the division engineers, to handle statewide issues, such as dam safety, and to represent the state in water matters. Finally, and perhaps most importantly, water users develop, modify, transfer, challenge, and enforce their water rights in water court.

It is difficult to untangle concretised property relations from these institutional arrangements. Water users relate with one another in the shadow of the water court. For instance, if an irrigation district is considering changes to its operating system that will affect how its members use water, it first consults with water users whom it believes will be affected by its actions. The irrigation district will attempt to craft its changes in ways acceptable to other water users so that when it enters water court to formalise its actions it will not confront opposition and conflict. Water courts encourage water users to work out settlements among themselves prior to entering court. If challenges to a water action emerge in court, the court will ask the parties to attempt to settle their differences, only after that has failed will a judge impose a decision. Also, water commissioners work with water users to ensure that they exercise their water rights in ways least likely to cause harm to others. Water commissioners, division engineers and water courts all work with water users to support the prior appropriation property rights system. Water rights holders are at the centre of these institutional arrangements.

The centrality of water users in the way that the prior appropriation doctrine has been defined and administered in Colorado cannot be overstated. This is particularly clear when considering the public and private divide (F. von Benda Beckmann et al., this volume). The primary role of state officials, not including water judges, is to provide information for water users and water judges. Water commissioners and division engineers keep public listings of water rights. Water commissioners keep public records of water diversions. Water judges often ask division engineers for information concerning the claims of petitioners. Water users, in conjunction with water judges, define, modify and enforce water rights.

Perhaps most telling in distinguishing the public and private divide is that the institutional arrangements that establish, administer and monitor prior appropriation rights make it very difficult for the state government of Colorado to violate or manipulate water rights. First, the prior appropriation doctrine is recognised and protected by the state constitution. As mentioned above, Article XVI, section six states, 'The right to divert the unappropriated waters of any natural stream to beneficial uses shall never be denied'. Amending the state constitution is a difficult process requiring approval of the voting citizens. Second, an independent judiciary, not elected or appointed officials, oversees the creation, revision and transfer of water rights in the context of specialised water courts. The prior appropriation doctrine constitutes a body of common law built up over 150 years, which is not easily undone by elected and appointed state officials. Third, the authority of state water officials, namely the state and division engineers and the water commissioners, is strictly limited. Only since 1965, has the state engineer been granted the power to devise and adopt regulations, a power that has been closely monitored and overseen by water users, water courts and the state supreme court. And, it has only been within the last thirty years that the state and division engineers have been allowed to have standing in water courts. Prior to that time the state could not be a party to a water case, could not protest a filing, and could not bring suit to address violations of water rights.

This complex set of arrangements came under considerable stress in the 1950s in the face of the state's worst ever sustained drought. Water users' threats to abandon the prior appropriation system occurred not as a direct result of the drought, but as a result of the widespread development and use of a new source of water, groundwater, whose use threatened to destroy existing, well established rights in surface water.

1969 to 2003: The Thirty-five Year Old Water Fight[2]

Colorado suffered a sustained drought in the 1950s. Farmers drilled wells and pumped groundwater to irrigate their crops. For instance, in 1940, in the Arkansas River Basin an estimated forty irrigation wells were in operation. By 1972, 1,477 wells pumped 256,556,000 cubic metres of water (MacDonnell 1988: 582). Noticeable effects on surface water flows appeared in the 1960s. Groundwater pumping threatened to undermine the prior appropriation system. Senior surface water rights holders were angry that their crops withered in the field while the crops of junior groundwater pumpers thrived.

Colorado courts had long recognised that tributary groundwater was appropriable water and governed by the prior appropriation system. Thus, the answer to the problem of pumping tributary groundwater seemed obvious. The groundwater pumpers' water rights are junior to those of surface water appropriators. When a senior rights holder 'calls' to have her rights satisfied, the appropriations of the most junior rights holders should cease until the senior appropriators' rights are satisfied. Wells should be shutdown.

The Colorado constitution, legislature and supreme court, however, advocated the development and use of the waters of the state to the greatest extent possible for the benefit of the citizens of the state. Foreclosing the timely use of tributary groundwater violated such intentions. Water users and government officials were reluctant to foreclose access to a major source of water.

The conflict among surface and ground water appropriators was almost as intense as the conflict between water users and the state engineer. In 1965, the Colorado legislature adopted legislation that substantially changed the authority of the state engineer. The legislation stated in part that:

> The State Engineer or his duly authorised representative shall execute and administer the laws of the state relative to the distribution of the surface waters of the state including the underground waters tributary thereto in accordance with the right of priority of appropriation, and he shall adopt such rules and regulations and issue such orders as are necessary for the performance of the foregoing duties (Radosevich et al. 1976: 138).

Never before had the State Engineer been given the power to make decisions concerning water rights. Those decisions had always been made among appropriators working with a court. When the State Engineer attempted to exercise his new rulemaking powers by regulating well pumping in the Arkansas River Basin, appropriators contested such authority in the context of the water courts. Eventually, the Colorado Supreme Court recognised the authority of the legislature to grant the State Engineer rulemaking powers, but the Court laid out a series of conditions guiding the rulemaking process (Fellhauer v. People, 167 Colo 320, 447 P.2d 986).

Each time the State Engineer attempted to devise rules to regulate well pumping in the South Platte River basin, water users challenged the rules in water court, preventing the application of the rules until all issues could be heard. Finally, after several attempts, appropriators and the State Engineer negotiated a set of rules within the context of the water court for incorporating tributary groundwater and wells within the prior appropriation system (Radosevich et al. 1976: 148; Vranesh 1988). The rules were implemented. This set a precedent for rulemaking. While the State Engineer has rulemaking authority, appropriators within the context of the water courts closely oversee that authority.

The rules permitted junior appropriators, whether of surface water or of tributary groundwater, to use water out of turn, or out of priority, by augmenting stream flow. Junior water users had to develop plans that involved determining the depletions to stream flows, or injury to the river caused by well pumping, and identifying a source of water that will be made available to the river at the time and place of injury to senior appropriators. Water users were strongly encouraged to adjudicate their augmentation plans, thereby providing for legally enforceable rights in the water that they used to augment stream flows. Water users, however, could also operate on temporary year to year plans, called substitute supply plans that were reviewed and administered by the State Engineer's office, bypassing water courts altogether, providing no opportunities for water rights holders to comment or contest such plans and their effects on the water rights of others. Rather, substitute supply plans were strictly between the state and division engineers and the well pumpers covered by the plans.

The changes to the prior appropriation system made by the rules governing groundwater pumping appear straightforward and reasonable. The prior appropriation system has long been criticised for its inflexibility. Under prior appropriation, junior water users have few options to protect their water usage during periods of the year or during years when water is limited. Allowing juniors to continue to appropriate water, even when it is not their turn, appears reasonable as long as they provide additional water supplies to satisfy the rights of senior water users. Augmentation plans provide flexibility to juniors and allow for the continued use of groundwater.

Under closer examination, however, the rules governing groundwater pumping in the South Platte Basin redrew the line between public and private, opened a new forum for administering water rights, and changed concretised property relations. First, the rules gave the state and division engineers greater authority in administering the prior appropriation doctrine. The division engineer for the South Platte Basin controlled water provided to him by junior appropriators. Furthermore, the division engineer, through substitute supply plans, and not water courts, decided how much augmentation water need be provided. Second, substitute supply plans administered by the division engineer provided a new forum for administering water rights. Junior water users could choose to pursue a formally adjudicated water augmentation plan through a water court or they could choose to create a substitute supply plan through the division engineer's office. Prior to the adoption of the groundwater pumping rules, water users had no such choice. The only forum for creating and refining water rights was water court. The new forum operated considerably differently from the water court. Participation differed significantly. In water court, all water rights holders within the watershed had standing to protest any action. With substitute supply plans, only the water user proposing the plan and the division engineer participated. Comments from other water users were not solicited. Third, as discussed below, concretised property relations began to change. No longer was conflict centred between surface water users and groundwater users. Rather conflict emerged between water users covered by substitute supply plans and water users who held surface water rights and adjudicated augmentation plans.

Well owners' associations, covering thousands of wells, formed and began to operate under substitute supply plans. It is generally acknowledged that substitute supply plans do not fully replace the water lost to rivers and streams by well pumping. In other words, substitute supply plans violate prior appropriation. Instead, the State Engineer has strategically used the water from the substitute supply plans to satisfy senior surface water rights, quieting their concerns about well pumping, and maintaining their commitment to the prior appropriation system (MacDonnell 1988: 592).

The intention of the State Engineer to strategically use water to satisfy the rights of critically situated senior rights holders was clearly demonstrated when he allowed a well owner association to pump water into the ditches of senior appropriators as a means of satisfying their rights. The effects of the pumping on the river would not be felt until the fall and winter months when no irrigation was occurring, thus not affecting other water users. A number of senior rights holders were alarmed by this turn of events. They believed that such an open and flagrant violation of the prior appropriation doctrine would eventually lead to its complete abandonment. Ultimately, all surface water rights could be satisfied by using groundwater, and well pumping could expand unabated.

Senior surface water rights holders called into question the commitment of the State Engineer to the prior appropriation doctrine. The actions of the State Engineer directly challenged prior appropriation. Eventually the State Engineer abandoned the practice of using groundwater to satisfy senior surface water rights. Nevertheless, senior rights holders continued to grumble about substitute supply plans, encouraging the State Engineer to demand greater amounts of augmentation water, but they did not challenge the plans in court. Years of adequate rainfall and the adept action by the State Engineer ensured that water users whose rights were regularly satisfied in the middle of summer prior to the widespread emergence of well pumping continued to be satisfied.

Then, in 2001, the most severe drought on record struck Colorado. The drought coincided with a Colorado Supreme Court case throwing into doubt the authority of the State Engineer to approve substitute supply plans (Empire Lodge Homeowners Association v. Movers 2001). The State Engineer initiated a rulemaking process to revise the rules governing groundwater pumping in the South Platte Basin, to bring the rules in line with the decision of the Supreme Court (Simpson 2002). The rulemaking process provided an opportunity for dissatisfied senior surface rights holders to challenge substitute supply plans.

The State Engineer filed the amended rules with the water court for the South Platte basin for approval. Senior water rights holders and well owners with adjudicated water augmentation plans protested the rules, claiming that the State Engineer lacked the authority to approve and administer water augmentation plans for wells; only a water court had such authority.[3] The water court agreed and the Colorado Supreme Court affirmed the decision. All wells operating under a substitute supply plan in the South Platte River Basin were to be shutdown. Only wells covered by a plan approved by a water court could continue to pump. The legislature and the governor provided well pumpers with a short reprieve. They passed legislation allowing wells to operate under stricter substitute supply plans until 2005. After that time all wells would have to be covered by plans approved by water court (Smith 2002).

Senior surface water rights holders used the rulemaking process to question and constrain the actions of the State Engineer. Senior water users long believed that the State Engineer used his powers to privilege junior well pumpers by weakening the prior appropriation doctrine. Senior water users have successfully limited the authority and discretion of the State Engineer, making it much more difficult for him to act against the prior appropriation doctrine and against their interests. Well owners with adjudicated water augmentation plans used the rulemaking process to constrain the actions of well owners without adjudicated plans. No longer could well owners without adjudicated plans pump water in violation of the prior appropriation doctrine and undercut the value of adjudicated plans. The prior appropriation doctrine has been affirmed once again.

Water users in the South Platte Basin appear to have come full circle from where they started in the 1960s when they first began to struggle to incorporate tributary groundwater into the prior appropriation system. Pumping of the tributary aquifer is strictly limited by the availability of surplus surface water that can be used to cover the effects of pumping on river flows. But for relatively wet years, surface water that is available in the open market is likely to be purchased by municipalities. Some of the fastest growing counties in the U.S. are in the Denver metropolitan area and cities are desperate for water to supply their rapidly expanding populations. The groundwater basin that the South Platte River is hydrologically connected to is estimated to contain approximately 9.8 billion cubic metres of water (MacDonnell 1988: 585). Most of that water is now inaccessible, not because of technological hurdles, but because of the prior appropriation doctrine.

Conclusion

Just as in the 1860s when water users struggled to replace the riparian doctrine with a property rights system more suitable for an arid environment, Colorado citizens are now confronted with how to design a property rights system that allows for greater joint use of ground and surface water supplies. To an outsider the solution seems simple. During dry years, when water is especially precious, access to groundwater should not be cut off. Instead, surface and ground water should be treated as a single source of water and all water needs should be satisfied. Surface water rights holders would have their rights satisfied through groundwater pumping and groundwater users would be allowed to continue to pump. During wet years, when surface supplies are plentiful, the system would operate as it currently does, with one exception. An aggressive programme of groundwater recharge would have to be put in place. Plentiful surface water supplies would be placed underground, both to recharge the aquifer and to provide water for the inevitable dry years to come.

Of course, such a 'simple' solution would raise a whole host of issues across the many analytical levels of property. Categorial property rights would be substantially changed. No longer would water be allocated based on seniority, rather water would be allocated on the basis of existing water rights. All would be served during wet and dry years. One of the critical issues such an approach would raise is that of limits. In the face of explosive population growth would groundwater supplies be over allocated or would the basin be managed for long term sustainability? Also, issues around transferring water rights and changing the uses to which water may be placed would have to be addressed. Would third party effects created by a proposed transfer of water rights simply be resolved by allowing additional volumes of groundwater to be pumped? Concretised property relations would also dramatically change. No longer would water users be closely tied together through the strands of time. Ties among water users would fall away. No longer would users have to wait their turn or keep a close eye on the amount of water others were using. Rather, they could take their water when they needed it. These are just a few of the many issues that would arise if surface water and groundwater were treated as a single source of water.

Just as with the prior appropriation doctrine, these issues would have to be addressed and a new set of tradeoffs among them would have to be struck. Unlike the 1860s, when water users began with a relatively clean slate, water users in the twenty-first century will have to craft their solutions in the context of an institutional setting that firmly favours senior surface water rights holders. Short of a substantial and credible threat to the water rights of seniors, such as the federal government imposing tougher clean water standards under the federal clean water act or minimum stream flow requirements to protect endangered species, senior surface water rights holders are unlikely to support substantial changes to the prior appropriation doctrine.

While it is relatively easy to design a new property rights system that would allow greater use of the groundwater aquifer, especially during times of drought, the process of restructuring relationships among rights holders is not nearly as straightforward. Property rights are embedded in a host of social, cultural, economic, and institutional structures and relationships. Loosening existing relationships so as to provide manoeuvering room to build new ones is a difficult undertaking that Colorado citizens and officials have yet to figure out.

Notes

1. The San Pedro River in southeastern Arizona provides a case in point. It is one of the last free flowing rivers in all of Arizona – it has never been dammed and it still flows almost year around. Population growth and the expansion of a military base have led to increased groundwater pumping, threatening the river. For more

than two decades, area residents have been searching for means of protecting the
river. For more information, see the Udall Center, San Pedro Basin Projects, at
www.udallcenter.arizona.edu/sanpedro/home.html.

2. See Blomquist, et al. (2004) for a more complete explication and analysis of the
    Colorado situation.
3. Why would well owners with adjudicated plans challenge the rules? As an
    attorney representing an irrigation company stated: 'We want everybody to play
    by the same rules. ... We spent $600,000 on our well augmentation plan ... We
    have to replenish every drop we use. Everyone else should, too.' (Smith 2002).

References

Abbott, C., S.J. Leonard and D. McComb 1994. *Colorado: A History of the
Centennial State*. Niwot: University Press of Colorado.

Benda-Beckmann, F. von, K. von Benda-Beckmann and M.G. Wiber 2003. 'The
Properties of Property. An Introduction to the Workshop'. Papers presented at
the Workshop *Changing Property of Property*, MPI Halle/Saale, Germany, 2–4
July 2003.

Blomquist, W., E. Schlager and T. Heikkila 2004. *Common Waters, Diverging
Streams*. Washington, D.C.: Resources for the Future Press.

Coffin v. Left Hand Ditch, Co., 6 Colo. 443 (1882).

Empire Lodge Homeowners' Association v. Moyers, 39 P.3d 1139 (2001).

Fellhauer v. People, 167 Colo. 320, 447 P.2d 986 (1968)

Hafen, L.R. 1948. *Colorado and Its People*. New York: Lewis Historical Publishing.

MacDonnell, L. 1988. 'Colorado's Law of "Underground Water": A Look at the
South Platte Basin and Beyond', *University of Colorado Law Review* 59(3):
579–625.

Radosevich, G.E., K.C. Nobe, D. Allardice and C. Kirkwood 1976. *Evolution and
Administration of Colorado Water Law: 1876–1976*. Fort Collins: Water
Resources Publications.

Rose, C. 1994. *Property and Persuasion: Essays on the History, Theory, and Rhetoric
of Ownership*. Boulder: Westview Press.

Simpson, H. 2002. 'South Platte River Basin Ground Water Rules to be Amended',
Streamlines 2(1): 1.

Smith, D. 1992. *Rocky Mountain West: Colorado, Wyoming and Montana
1859–1915*. Albuquerque: University of New Mexico Press.

Smith, J. 2002. 'A War about Water; Farmers Battle Cities for Rights to Scarce
South Platte Supply', *Rocky Mountain News*, 18 November 2002: 4A.

Trelease, F. 1971. *Federal-State Relations in Water Law. National Water Commission
Legal Study*, no. 5, Arlington: National Water Commission.

Vranesh, G. 1988. *Colorado Water Law* 1, Boulder, CO: Vranesh Publications.

Western Regional Climate Center 2001. *Precipitation Maps of the Western US*.
http://www.wrcc.dri.edu/pcpn/. (accessed October 2005).

Chapter 14
Appropriating Family Trees:
Genealogies in the Age of Genetics*

Gísli Pálsson

[T]he storage of present-day information technologies, and hence the organisation of collective memory through the use of dataprocessing machines, is not merely a technical matter but one directly bearing on legitimation, the question of the control and ownership of information being the crucial issue. (Paul Connerton 1989: How Societies Remember)

The construction of family pedigrees is a widespread commodity industry in the Euro-American context, a critical component in the mapping of genes and bodies in the era of modern biomedicine. In her ethnographic description of medical encounters in the analysis and treatment of cancer, Gibbon refers to the 'mostly hidden "technology"' involving 'the production and use of family trees' (2002: 421). For Gibbon, 'clinical family trees gain much of their "force" from being both a form of family genealogies and simultaneously a type of scientific pedigree' (2002: 433). This dual nature of genealogies, I shall argue, has potential implications for property rights. Focusing on the so-called 'Book of Icelanders', a computerised genealogical database on Icelanders, I discuss the appropriation of family trees in the era of digital informatics, genetics and biotechnology. In particular, I shall explore the contest over what kind of property family histories constitute and how access to them should be distributed. As we will see, Icelandic genealogies are both a communal property, available on the worldwide web, and a scientific or industrial commodity, in the form of an encrypted database. In their

* The research on which this article is based has been supported by the Nordic Social Science Research Fund (NOS-S), the Icelandic Science Fund, and the Research Fund of the University of Iceland. Parts of the text have appeared in Pálsson 2004 and 2006 forthcoming. I thank Charles Geisler (Cornell University), Kristín E. Harðardóttir (University of Iceland), and Melanie Wiber (University of New Brunswick) for useful comments and suggestions.

latter role genealogies have been particularly contested, as candidates for private property. The tension surrounding the use of genealogies in Icelandic biomedical projects, a tension triggered by earlier debates on access to medical records and property rights in fishing, ensured that a 'short edition' of the Book of Icelanders remained in the public domain, accessible to most Icelanders. The highly visible version of computerised genealogies publicised on the web justified the largely 'hidden' version, in Gibbon's terms, exploited in the context of private industry.

In Western discourse, the issues of possession and property have often been discussed with reference to wild animals in a state of nature. In *Moby Dick* (Ch. 88), Herman Melville discusses the problem of deciding when whales, 'loose fish' as he called them, become somebody's property or 'fast fish'. Did a whale become fast fish as soon as a whaler invested his labour in the chase or, later on, at the moment of capture? For Melville and his fellow whalers the problem of deciding what constitutes property was often a pressing one: 'after a weary and perilous chase and capture of a whale, the body may get loose from the ship by reason of a violent storm; and drifting far away to leeward, be retaken by a second whaler, who in a calm, snugly tows it alongside, without risk of life or line' (1962: 422).

In drawing the contrast between the 'weary' chase of the first whaler and the 'snugly' capture of the second, Melville seems to opt for a labour-theory of property, much like the one of John Locke (1960) which suggests that one becomes an owner of a thing by mixing one's labour with it. For Locke, in 'mixing' his or her labour with a particular resource-base, in the course of production, the appropriator claims possession over the resource. Many legal traditions emphasise one form or another of such a notion of rights over the 'fruits of labor' (Grubb 1998).

While property has more to do with relations than the essence of things (Hann 1998; Strathern 1999; F. von Benda-Beckmann, K. von Benda-Beckmann and Wiber, this volume), establishing bonds and boundaries within communities of potential property holders, the way in which one mixes one's labour with a thing must partly depend on the nature of the thing itself. As Rose has argued (1994: 269):

> property doctrine often takes at least some of its shape from the material characteristics of the 'things' over which property rights are claimed. ... [T]he physical characteristics of the resource frame the kinds of actions that human beings can take toward a given resource, and these in turn frame the 'jural relations' that people construct about their mutual uses and forbearances with respect to the resource.

For Rose, property is an unstable phenomenon, established and maintained by successful speech acts, through rhetoric and persuasion. As a result, the visual clues available to competing claimants are important for establishing property rights. In Melville's case, perhaps, the property issue is relatively straightforward. Whales are conspicuous, tangible objects – some, indeed, are the largest organisms on earth – and, after all, the process of chasing them, from the moment of sighting to the point of capture, is highly transparent and obvious to competing users if not the entire community of whalers. This article discusses a radically different case, the case of family histories and their use in gene hunting, the chasing of some of the most miniscule elements of human cells, of genes theoretically responsible for common diseases.

To the extent that genealogies represent property, they are examples of *intellectual* or *cultural* property (Brown 1998, 2003), more like the whaler's knowledge of sea currents and animal migrations than captured whales. Yet, the key questions of ownership and possession remain similar if not the same. How, exactly, does one mix one's labour with genealogies and other biomedical information? How is property established in modern biomedicine? Family histories have taken various forms, depending upon time and context. Not only has the use and visual layout of family trees taken various forms (Jacobson 1986; Klapisch-Zuber 1991, 2000; Haan 1994), they are also embedded in different cultures and property regimes, much like the living organisms we call trees (Rival 1998; Jones and Cloke 2002).

Modern biological and medical research tends to invite central questions of ownership, access and authorship (Boyle 1996; Radin 1996). In his historical study of the 'fly people' researching the fruit fly, *Drosophila*, Kohler (1994) developed the concept of 'moral economies'. For him, moral economies of science 'regulate authority relations and access to the means of production and rewards for achievements' (1994: 6). Several historians of science have followed Kohler's lead, including Rheinberger (1997) and Creager (2002). The moral economy of the fly people was characterised by reciprocity, gift relations and the absence of personal property; ideas 'that were engendered in the group's informal shoptalk were treated as a communal resource and not as personal property' (Kohler 1994: 103). As Knorr-Cetina (1999) shows, however, modern experimental science is not a unified category in this respect; the science of physics is typically communitarian while molecular biology is highly individualistic. In much recent biomedical research, the gift economy has increasingly given way to the commercial circulation of patented biological material and technological innovations. Biomedical knowledge is more and more produced within multinational companies that claim ownership of the resources they use and the knowledge and technologies they produce.

Experimental systems – the material, literary and social technologies that constitute the world of experimental science (Kohler 1994) – are inherently unstable and path dependent (Pickering 1995), driven 'from behind' by their own history and dynamics rather than a teleological quest for a given future (see Rheinberger 1997: 28). Much recent research on scientific practice tends to shift the agency behind the system in question from the inventive researcher mixing his or her labour with the productive material to the material itself. Echoing the position of Latour (1988), Kohler (1994) and Creager (2002) emphasise that the 'standardised' laboratory fly, virus and mouse are organic machines endowed with an agency, colonising the landscapes of laboratories and taking the centre stage of experimental genetics.

The reference to machines should not be taken as mere metaphor. In the classic analyses of Mumford, a machine is a 'minor organism' in that it 'involves the notion of an external source of power, a more or less complicated inter-relation of parts, and a limited kind of activity' (1962: 11). While Mumford sees machines as organisms, Knorr-Cetina treats cells and whole organisms used in the production systems of laboratories as biological machines (1999: 149). Digital genealogies can be similarly regarded as machines, generating – for social, managerial, as well as epistemological purposes – connections, questions and answers (Pálsson 2006 forthcoming). Flies, viruses, and mice, however, do not issue statements about ownership. Nor do family trees, although people often carefully guard their family histories as cultural property, strategically defining the terms of inclusion and exclusion according to the discourse of their times and their personal needs. Who, then, are the owners of the actual components and products of experimental systems and how is property established?

Family histories are essential components of many biomedical projects. Often such projects represent a curious pooling of rather different sources or databases that have not previously been combined – historical, genetic and medical (Pálsson and Rabinow 2004). While each source has its own trajectory and use rights, their collective, synergic assembly for the purpose of exploring the potential genetic bases of common diseases necessarily redefines each of them. The notion of 'bundle of rights' (F. von Benda-Beckmann, K. von Benda-Beckmann and Wiber, this volume) is a powerful tool for examining the complex rules of access and entitlements that emerge as a result of such redefining, not only in specific local contexts but also comparatively as part of the larger anthropological project.

The Book of Icelanders

The Book of Icelanders is a digital genealogical database that has been under construction for several years. Approximately 650 thousand people are recorded in the database, about a half of the total number of people born in Iceland since the Norse settlement in the ninth century. A team of researchers and computer programmers at Frisk Software and the biotech firm deCode Genetics in Reykjavik have compiled the information contained in the Book of Icelanders and designed the necessary programs for displaying and analysing it. The whole point, of course, is not simply to record individuals but rather to be able to connect them to each other. The 'connectivity rate', the rate of documented connections between an individual and his or her parents, is close to 90 percent.

The construction of the Book of Icelanders has drawn upon several kinds of historical records on families and genealogies – the Book of Settlement (Landnámabók, written around 1125), the so-called Family Sagas (Íslendingasögur), church registers, administrative records, censuses, and published registers and national databases. Some of the censuses are only partial lists of farmers and taxpayers while others are relatively complete. Frisk Software in Reykjavík originally began the construction of a genealogical database on Icelanders on its own early in the 1990s, starting with three censuses (1703, 1801 and 1910) which covered the whole country at sufficiently different points in time to minimise overlap, as well as the up-dated national records (Þjóðskrá). The director of the company, Friðrik Skúlason, happened to be a genealogical enthusiast eager to use his programming skills for his hobby. Among the sources available to him was the Icelandic Database compiled by Vasey and others (see Vasey 1996), which in addition to censuses includes digitally stored records on births, marriages and deaths from surviving parish registers (the birth records were originally converted to digital format by the Genealogical Society of Utah). Later on, deCode

Genetics signed an agreement with Frisk Software to speed up the construction of the database by adding information from a variety of available sources, focusing on twelve censuses taken from 1703 to 1930. 'Pretty much everybody', as Skúlason puts it, 'is included.' It is only now that the task of a complete genealogical file on Icelanders has become a realistic one, thanks to modern bioinformatics and computer technology.

There are number of empty spaces in the genealogical database. Part of the problem stems from missing information about paternity. The scale of the problem, the missing pages in the Book of Icelanders, varies from one century to another and from one region to another. Generally, the further one goes back the more erratic the records. For some regions, most of the records of the past have been lost due to fire or negligence. Not only are there empty spaces in available records, there are errors, too. Adoptions pose a particular problem, at least for deCode Genetics and others interested in genetic connections. Sometimes, families have 'purified' their records, possibly to prevent disclosing information about teenage mothers or to avoid an image of inbreeding. Some of those who collected family histories were considered creative or 'poetic' (lýrískir) genealogists, which underlined their reputation for modest respect for genealogical facts. However, recent estimates indicate that the problem is a minor one, for example with an error rate of 0.7 percent in maternal connections (Sigurðardóttir et al. 2000). Often, the genealogical team of deCode Genetics and Frisk Software have had to 'socially construct' the information they have, in the light of their understanding of Icelandic history and culture and the nature of the sources at their disposal, making inferences, for instance, about births, marriages, deaths and family connections. Skúlason, the chief architect of the genealogical database, has likened his task to 'working out a puzzle the size of a football stadium, with half of the pieces missing and the rest damaged and randomly scattered', a gigantic enterprise indeed.

The Biomedical Project

The genealogical database of the Book of Icelanders takes two forms. One version is available to the biomedical company deCode Genetics. In this case, no names are included, only numbers or IDs that allow for the combination of different datasets on a limited basis for particular research purposes. A complex process of encryption, surveillance and monitoring has been designed to prevent any illegitimate use of the data. Such a database, it is argued, combined with genetic and medical data, provides an invaluable historical dimension to the search for genes with mutations and other potential causes of common diseases.

Current work at deCode Genetics typically begins with a contract with one or more physicians specialising in a particular disease with a potentially genetic basis. Through a contract with the pharmaceutical company Hoffmann La Roche, deCode Genetics focuses on research on twelve common diseases. In their practice over the years, the physicians have constructed a list of patients with the particular symptoms in question. This list is passed on in an encrypted form to a research team within the company, which, in turn, runs the information provided through its computers, juxtaposing or comparing patients' lists and genealogical records by means of specialised software developed by the company. The aim is to trace the genes responsible for the apparent fact that the disease in question occurs in families. Such an analysis may show, for example, that of an original list of about 1,000 patients, 500 or so cluster in a few families. In the next step, the physicians affiliated with the research team collect blood samples from patients and some of their close relatives for DNA analysis. In the final stage of the research, statisticians evaluate the results of the genetic analysis, attempting to narrow down in probabilistic terms the genes responsible for the disease. In practice, this is a highly complex interactive process combining different kinds of mapping, in particular genetic maps indicating genetic distances on a chromosome and more realistic physical mapping. Moreover, strategies of gene hunting are adopted and revised both intuitively in the laboratory or at the computer screen and in formal or informal meetings.

These procedures are not, of course, unique to deCode Genetics, not even in the Icelandic context. However, with the so-called Health Sector Database that is expected to cover extensive medical records on Icelanders and family histories going a number of generations back, the power of genetic and epidemiological analyses may grow exponentially, with far larger samples. The addition of the national medical records available since 1915 allows for the exploration of a set of new questions on the interaction among a number of variables apart from genetic makeup and genealogical connections, including variables pertaining to lifestyle, physical and social environments, the use of particular medicine, and degree and kind of hospitalisation. The results may be useful, according to the designers of the project and the medical authorities, for pharmaceutical companies and for the medical service, yielding information about potential drugs, particular genes or proteins, and possible preventive measures in terms of consumption and lifestyle. At the same time, the construction of the Health Sector Database that is still on the drawing board raises fundamental questions about access and property rights. Who are the authors of the Health Sector Database – physicians, nurses, medical authorities, computer personnel?

To illustrate the deCode approach to the exploration of the role of familial relations for explaining differential occurrence of common diseases, it is useful to focus on the team that studies osteoarthritis (hereafter 'OA'), one of the most common diseases of humans affecting joints in fingers, knees and hips (see Pálsson 2004). The OA-team of deCode Genetics was one of the more established teams within the company until 2003, with several permanent members, mostly biologists and technical laboratory assistants, collaborating closely with statisticians and physicians specialising in OA (see Stefánsson et al. 2003). Their project started with the initiative of the physicians. Then the pharmaceutical company Hoffmann La Roche arrived on the scene, and a contract was signed with the clinical collaborators, focusing on two particular phenotypes of the disease, OA of the fingers and hips. Later on, the study of OA of the knees was also incorporated.

Often, it has been assumed that OA 'simply' comes with age. Indeed, the Icelandic term for osteoarthritis, *slitgigt*, refers to the kind of arthritis that develops as people become 'worn down' due to *slit* (drudgery) during the life course. When the deCode project started it was assumed that there was some underlying genetic factor, since siblings were known to have a higher risk than others of hip replacement. However, no one had successfully 'cracked' a complex disease like OA or, in other words, identified the genetic factors involved in the phenotype. The identification of families with the right phenotypes, obviously the critical starting point in work of this kind, is somewhat problematic due to the nature of available sources. S.E. Stefánsson, the leader of the OA-team, explained: 'It's not easy to find well-defined families. One of the problems with past records is that diagnoses often were poor. People didn't know the difference between rheumatoid arthritis and osteoarthritis.' 'By using the "Book of Icelanders"', he suggested, his team was able 'to show that OA is inherited, there is a founder effect. Simply by going back one generation after another. Patient groups have fewer founders than others. They are significantly different from control groups.'

Having established a familial connection, the OA-team set out to locate the genetic factors involved. S.E. Stefánsson elaborated on the relative competitive advantage of the deCode Genetics team thanks to the 'deep' genealogy of the Book of Icelanders: 'Most other groups are looking at sib pairs. They have less resolution than we have for linkage analysis as they don't have the genealogies. We only need to know how people are related.'

By running their encrypted patient lists (of people diagnosed with osteoarthritis) against the encrypted version of the Book of Icelanders, the OA-team explored 'how people are related'. Knowing the genealogical relationships, establishing meiotic distances (the number of links separating any two persons in a pedigree) among the patients, the researchers sought to confirm and narrow down candidate regions in the genome, i.e., regions with genes whose protein products were assumed to affect the disease. The greater the historical depth of available genealogical records, the narrower the candidate region becomes and the narrower the region the less time-consuming the hunting of the genes involved. If this reasoning is correct, when combined with medical and genetic records the genealogical database is a highly valuable resource, an essential component of the biomedical machine.

Kinship goes Online

Another version of the Book of Icelanders was made available on the worldwide web for genealogical enthusiasts and the general public in January 2003 (http://www.islendingabok.is). While virtually public and free of charge, this version is only accessible to 'Icelanders'. Those who are interested in exploring the database have to request a password and as long as they have an Icelandic security number they are provided with access. This version, of course, includes personal names; there is no encryption. It allows users of the Book of Icelanders to trace their family histories and to check in a split second their genealogical connection to any Icelander, living or dead. Overnight, the Book of Icelanders became a popular pastime and a party game. Thousands of Icelanders requested a password, exploring their relations with neighbours, colleagues and friends – and with public figures such as the Prime Minister and the musician Björk.

While the Book of Icelanders would not have been brought into being had it not been for the genealogical enthusiasm of Icelandic scribes and collectors through the centuries and the gene talk of the modern age, once in existence it had important repercussions. The responses were quite interesting. Over the weeks and months following the launching of the

Book of Icelanders on the web the public responded enthusiastically by sending corrections and additions to the company responsible for the maintenance of the database. The company received thousands of e-mail messages from users of the database. Some of the comments were written in an angry mood, particularly messages involving corrections regarding marriage, cohabitation or paternity. The company claims that through the enthusiastic cooperation of the public it has effectively 'hired' a substantial part of the population for free to correct and finalise the database.

A Genealogical Society was founded in Iceland in 1945 to foster genealogical studies, to sustain important historical and demographic documents, and to publish censuses and family histories. The Society now has eight hundred members, it organises several lectures a year, and publishes a newsletter. A few Icelandic companies specialise in the tracing of family trees and the computerisation of genealogies. Also, a number of genealogy enthusiasts specialise in particular families, both for themselves and for anyone interested in their expertise. All of this testifies to the Icelanders' current interest in genealogies.

Obviously, the complete genealogical database on the web, the Book of Icelanders, is revolutionising genealogical practice in Iceland. Genealogical enthusiasts and family historians no longer have to struggle with a variety of obscure documents, past and present, as most available material has now been digitalised and compiled in a single database. Interestingly, the typical user of family histories is no longer an elderly, scholarly male. The Book of the Icelanders seems to be used by both men and women, old and young, from most walks of life. Internet access is fairly widespread in Iceland. Among the early users of the Book were groups of young girls who apparently wanted to explore kinship connections with their friends.

The launching of the Book on the web encouraged Icelanders to think that they are all fairly closely related, suggesting an imagined community based on kinship ties. The current popularity of genealogies and the 'structural nostalgia' (Herzfeld 2000: 78) which it represents, in both Iceland and some other contexts, does not simply reflect excessive playfulness among those concerned; rather the growing role of family histories underscores ongoing social processes, including urban desire for rooting in the rural past and the 'medicalisation of kinship' (Finkler 2000).

The Issue of Ownership

While genealogical information on Icelanders has been in the public domain for centuries, its assembly and use in the digital form of the Book of Icelanders has been somewhat controversial. One commentator offered the following remark, in an op-ed article in the main local newspaper *Morgunblaðið* entitled 'Will the interest among Icelanders in family histories disappear with the arrival of deCode Genetics?' (8 October 1998): 'Now a company in Iceland is recording in one place every piece of information documented in previously published works, including genealogies ... and censuses. Unfortunately, the company is doing this without asking anybody for permission.'

Another critic complained that the spokespersons for deCode Genetics denigrated and made fun of most professional genealogists, eventually eliminating them from business:

> With the appearance of the Book of Icelanders there is a danger that genealogists ... and the publishers of family histories will have to cease their operations, since the financial basis of genealogical publications is gone and it is tiresome to work on ... research on families and relations and the history of the nation if some rascals steal one's work and give it to the public on the Web (Eggertsson 2003).

Significantly, the laws on personal information have recently been changed, as of 2000 (laws No. 77, enacted by parliament on 23 May 2000; http://www.althingi.is), following debates in Parliament on patients' rights and the protection of personal information, partly triggered by the issue of the Health Sector Database. Thus, the recording of genealogical data no longer enjoys all the privileges it had in earlier legal clauses. Increasingly, genealogical records, which have traditionally been in the public domain without restrictions on recording and publishing, are being treated in the same legal fashion as other 'sensitive' personal information. It remains somewhat unclear, on the other hand, how the new laws on personal information will be interpreted and applied with respect to genealogical records and their publication. Genealogical information still represents a diverse and partly gray area in a legal sense. Church records enjoy certain legal protection for a given number of years while the National Records of the Statistical Bureau are open to the public.

The shift in legal framing of genealogical data during the last years has been partly informed by intense public debates surrounding the Health Sector Database (Pálsson and Harðardóttir 2002). These debates, in turn, were partly fuelled by political contests over the commodification of fishing rights (Helgason and Pálsson 1998), a contest similar to other fisheries where 'rights talk' has been dominating, including those of Canada (see Wiber 2000). The Icelandic fishing industry has been radically reorganised in the last twenty years or so with the application of market-based models to fisheries management, the so-called individual transferable quotas (ITQs). Critics argue that the current regime represents 'the biggest theft in Icelandic history', to use a frequent slogan from recent political campaigns, transferring wealth and property from the general public to a few privileged boat owners. Medical and genetic information, it is currently argued, are common pool resources analogous to the fishing stocks in Icelandic waters. Privileged access, permanent or temporary, as a result, should only be granted in return for a return-fee to ensure equity and fairness. While the Icelandic Parliament has emphasised that both resource-bases are public property and that privileged access is only temporary, under some kind of arrangement of public trust, fees have only been applied in the case of the medical database.

The text for the licence granted to deCode Genetics for constructing the database specifies, partly in response to critics of the quota system in fishing, that the company must pay the Icelandic state a certain fee for the assembly and use of the records of the medical service. DeCode Genetics was requested to cover the cost of the agreement on the database, its construction and marketing. Also, it has to forfeit seventy million Icelandic kronur annually (six million EUR) for the licence that will be used for furthering medical research and development. Furthermore, the Icelandic state will receive 6 percent of the annual profit that deCode Genetics may make from using the database. This payment will never exceed seventy million Icelandic kronur. The annual revenue to the state will, thus, amount to something between six and twelve million EUR.

Given the synergic importance of genealogical records for deCode's biomedical project, the issue of access and ownership has been even more contested than their potential infringement on privacy and autonomy. In January 2000, the Icelandic genealogist Þorsteinn Jónsson and his publishing company Genealogia Islandorum challenged deCode Genetics and Frisk Software in the courts for using previously published genealogies whose rights, it claimed, belonged to the company. One of the shareholders in Genealogia Islandorum, it may be noted, was the rival biotech firm Icelandic Genomics Corporation. The spokespersons for

Genealogia Islandorum suggested that scholars working for them had searched original documents in local archives throughout the country (genealogies, farm histories and folklore), compiling massive amounts of information and arranging it in readable fashion, in a series of costly commercial publications. Now, they claimed, their property rights were being violated as others, deCode Genetics, punched in these records, copying and marketing the products of earlier efforts for making profit, partly through biomedical research. In compensation for the 'violation' of its property rights, Genealogia Islandorum requested millions of EUR.

The staff of deCode Genetics rejected the claimants' arguments, pointing out that on their own genealogical facts did not constitute private property. Also they suggested that along with Frisk Software the company had added extensively to earlier compilations by independent research and, moreover, designed its own electronic format of storing and usage. DeCode Genetics further claimed that genealogical information about Icelanders constituted a common heritage and by taking the makers of the Book of Icelanders to the courts Genealogia Islandorum was effectively trying to appropriate genealogical information that had been the joint possession of the Icelandic nation for centuries. Finally, deCode Genetics announced that it would be offering its genealogical program and database for free, in the public domain so as to ensure public access to this important resource. In 1999, one may note, the architect of the database, Skúlason, estimated that on a CD-ROM it would become a best seller for a subscription of approximately 450 EUR.

The case was taken to the Icelandic Supreme Court. During its proceedings the claimants requested that two evaluators be appointed to examine the way in which the digital database was being constructed. In particular, they suggested, the evaluators should:

> establish whether the spokespersons for the Book of Icelanders had chiefly constructed the database ... on the basis of published genealogies or chiefly through their independent scrutiny of original documents containing the information that genealogists usually consult when they compile genealogical documents ..., working on the original documents by means of the methods used by genealogists so as to create a separate holistic work, independent of earlier published genealogies (http://www.haestirettur.is).

The court accepted the claimant's request and appointed two independent evaluators. Their report concluded that the description of the construction of the Book of Icelanders offered by deCode Genetics and Frisk Software was essentially correct:

As a genealogical database, the Book of Icelanders is based on original sources, but in the process of its construction many printed or published sources have also been consulted. The sources that have been used have always been properly cited. This approach testifies to scholarly methods which resonate with the finest procedures applied by genealogists in recent times when composing their writings. ... All published genealogies naturally add to previously available information ..., making it easier at the same time to connect persons and accelerate the process. Likewise, such comparison is necessary to both allow for corrections and to establish cases where different sources fail to agree (*Morgunblaðið* 25 September 2002).

Eventually, the company Genealogia Islandorum was declared bankrupt and its spokespersons withdrew the case against the Book of Icelanders. Many of the genealogical databases and publications of Genealogia Islandorum were bought by deCode Genetics and Frisk Software, adding to the companies' already vast storehouse of biomedical information on the national body. Once the legal issue was settled, the Book of Icelanders was made available on the web.

The password provided for the Book of Icelanders only allows for limited access in the sense that the user cannot explore other families or the database in general. Access, in other words, is egocentric; a person can only trace his or her relationships to other Icelanders and detailed information is only provided on close kin and long gone generations of distant relatives. Thus, the designers of the Book of Icelanders have deliberately, it seems, avoided further legal hurdles involving competition with published works. At the same time, such restrictions prevent others from downloading extensive information from the database, securing the property rights of the companies involved.

The publication and free distribution of the Book of Icelanders on the web is bound to affect the market for books on genealogies that in the past has been a lively one. However, these are radically different kinds of publications. The Book of Icelanders only includes basic facts on dates of birth and death, residence, and occupation, while the printed books on the market tend to provide much 'thicker' descriptions of families and histories, sometimes adding photographs of individuals, families and farms, descriptions that the consumers tend to be interested in. The critical issue under Icelandic law, however, was not one of marketing but rather the extent to which the new electronic database was the result of original, independent work or the reproduction of earlier texts. Icelandic law enacted in 1972 provides protection against violations of the right of authorship. The laws, which were modified in 2000 in accordance with a

European order of 1996, protect authorship of collections of independent works, whether in the format of books or digital files. According to the laws, the protection of authorship is conditioned on contributions to the works in question in terms of financial commitment and contributions. These laws apply to genealogical databases.

The Book of Icelanders is an interesting border case raising questions about what counts as independent contribution and a separate database. Similar questions have been raised by a series of other legal cases on the European front involving, for instance, geographical maps in digital form (Iceland), telephone directories on CD-ROM (Germany), and the linking of news pages on the web (Denmark). The contest over what counts as property and on what grounds is obviously played out in specific contexts with specific concepts and histories, each of which has developed its own bundle of rights. In every case, however, the opinion of the European Court has been consulted before the national legal authority has issued its final judgment.

Conclusions

One version of the Book of Icelanders, as we have seen, the genealogical search engine available on the web, establishes connections that would otherwise remain hidden, managing histories and identities, personal, familial and national. The other version, the encrypted database created for researchers tracing the presumed genetic roots of common diseases, is a powerful navigational aid in the cartography of the human genome, much like GPS technology and remote sensing are essential for modern travellers and explorers. Theoretically, at least, it generates a vast amount of information on the body politic, about useful 'hunting' grounds, the causes of human diseases, and their eventual treatment. For the spokespersons of deCode's project, then, a relatively homogenous population with good medical records (for precise phenotypic identification) is the ideal experimental site for linkage, linkage being, in their view, the ideal method of analysis. For them, the royal road to identifying the underlying cause of pathology is through linkage analysis: 'The most important asset of linkage analysis is its ability to screen the entire genome with a framework set of markers; this makes it a hypothesis-independent and cost-effective approach to finding disease genes (Gulcher et al. 2001: 264)'.

In such a scheme, genealogies represent an important commodity, inviting debates about authorship, property and body politics. As Latour has argued, *'whenever we learn something about the management of humans, we shift that knowledge to nonhumans and endow them with more and more organisational properties* ...: industry shifts to nonhumans the management of people learned in the imperial machine' (1999: 207–28; emphasis in the original).

Because for humans everywhere the body is both the locus and agent of experience (Csordas 1994), it is often represented as 'sacred space' resisting invasion, extraction, commodification and ownership (Campbell 1992; Marshall et al. 1996; Nelkin and Andrews 1998; Scheper-Hughes 2000; Sharp 2000). Anglo-American law and, no doubt, many other legal traditions, do not consistently recognise outright property rights in human bodies and persons. Organs have been typically exchanged within the framework of what has been called rather euphemistically the 'gift' (Gold 1996; Wilkinson and Garrard 1996). Biomedical information, however, does not fit easily into the legal tradition of the body (Greely 1998: 488). Thus, the issue of the human genome is legally complex and unsettled. While some policymaking bodies, including UNESCO, treat the human genome in a symbolic sense as the heritage of humanity, inviting the idea of international stewardship of the genome to avoid potential abuse, there is no legal foundation of such a 'common heritage' concept. Indeed, an alternative approach emphasising the 'familial' nature of human genetic material seems to be gaining acceptance in Western societies despite the growing social and legal fragmentation of the family in the current age (Knopper 1999: 23–24).

One of the early scholarly commentators on Melville's principle of the rights over the fruits of one's labour, Thorstein Weblen, objected that it was difficult to see 'how an institution of ownership could have arisen in the early days of predatory life through the seizure of goods, but the case is different with the seizure of persons' (Weblen 1898: 363). For Weblen, captives, chiefly women, originally served as personal ownership, acting like trophies or insignia of masculine prowess; 'it becomes a relatively easy matter', he added, 'to extend this newly achieved concept of ownership to the products of the labor performed by the persons so held in ownership' (1898: 365). The 'seizure of persons', to extend from Weblen, in the sense of the fractioning and commodification of the body and bodily information, is one of the important new forms of property in the current age of biomedicine. But how should the principle of rights over the 'fruits of labour' be applied to that domain? What exactly constitutes 'fast fish'? The application of the labour theory of property is not as straightforward as it may sound. For one thing, self-ownership need not be taken for granted (Ryan 1994). Generally people are not allowed to sell their organs, although some body parts may be sold, including hair and blood (sperm and ova in some contexts) (Marshall et al. 1996). As to the Icelandic genealogies discussed here, many native scribes and collectors have mixed their labour with family histories through the centuries. This rich local tradition established and developed during the Middle Ages has now been adopted and enhanced by the powerful tools of computers and modern informatics. Perhaps this resource, being neither completely public nor completely private, much like some genetic resources, is best regarded as 'limited common property', to draw upon Carol Rose (see Brown 2003: 239). The distinction between public and private property, indeed, is increasingly seen as problematic. Not only does it misrepresent some of the contexts of classic ethnographic description (see, for instance, Widlok 2001), it also fails to render the complex nuances of new forms of property. Thus, Wiber (this volume) speaks of 'relative publics' in the context of cultural property.

There are interesting parallels between the discovery and exploitation of the human genome and those of distant lands. Some of them are nicely documented in Haraway's (2000) analysis of the advertising of the genome industry. Recent advances in the mapping of the human genome, indeed, remind us of the nineteenth century 'scramble' for colonies. Now that most of the habitat of the globe has been charted, documented and conquered, the West is increasingly turning its attention to the 'remotest corners' of living organism, in particular the human genome. Genes, some people have argued, will be 'the currency of the future' (see Nelkin and Andrews 1998). In many cases, a 'common wealth' of records, genealogical and medical, has been transformed into commercial property. These developments are transnational and occurring at an exponential rate. And they have taken place in a social environment where the partnership of science and the market is considered to be the most efficient means of advancing knowledge and human well-being (Fox and Swazey 1992; Titmuss 1997; Starr 1998). Bodily components and bodily information (genealogies, medical records, and genetic characteristics of individuals and entire populations) are quickly absorbed into the market place where they are exchanged in the form of commodities, partly for the advancement of the big men of science.

Anderson's (2000) study of Nobel Laureate C. Gajdusek, and his transactions with Western medical staff and the New Guinea Highlands Fore, in particular their big men, illustrates the rearticulation of the local and the global in the contest over human biological resources. In the 1950s and 1960s, Gajdusek was above all an author, circulating Fore blood and brains in a communitarian fashion within the reward system of science, for the advancement of the study of 'possessing kuru', a condition variously diagnosed as the result of a slow virus, adjustment disorder, or sorcery. Later on, however, in the 1990s, he became a patent-holder, participating in the commodification of human cells. Anderson concludes his comparison of the big men of New Guinea and the big men of science along the following lines:

> we need to develop more locally specific models of the scientific exchange of gifts and commodities, to consider further the social life and moral weight of scientific things, and to document the cultural differentiation of scientific artifacts, rather than generalise about the global economy of science. But an emphasis on local knowledge should not be taken to deny the importance of global structures and systems. Instead, it challenges us to try to understand global science as a series of local economic accomplishments (2000: 735–36).

While during the latter half of the twentieth century, biomedicine has established new kinds of properties in persons and personal information and ongoing developments in biotechnology and bioinformatics have opened up an entirely new biological and social world, each case represents a particular articulation of the global and the local, a particular kind of bundle of rights to biomedical resources.

References

Anderson, W. 2000. 'The Possession of Kuru: Medical Science and Biocolonial Exchange', Comparative Studies in Society and History 42: 713–44.

Boyle, J. 1996. Shamans, Software, and Spleens: Law and the Construction of Information Society. Cambridge: Harvard University Press.

Brown, M.F. 1998. 'Can Culture be Copyrighted?', Current Anthropology 39(2): 193–222.

—— 2003. Who Owns Native Culture? Cambridge: Harvard University Press.

Campbell, C.S. 1992. 'Body, Self, and the Property Paradigm', Hastings Center Report, Sept.-Oct.: 34–42.

Connerton, P. 1989. How Societies Remember. Cambridge: Cambridge University Press.

Creager, A.N.H. 2002. *The Life of a Virus: Tobacco Mosaic Virus as an Experimental Model, 1930–1965*. Chicago: University of Chicago Press.

Csordas, T., ed. 1994. *Embodiment and Experience: The Existential Ground of Culture and Self*. Cambridge: Cambridge University Press.

Eggertsson, K. 1998. 'Deyr áhugi Íslendinga á ættfræði með tilkomu Íslenskrar erfðagreiningar?', *The Morgunblaðið Newspaper*, 08 October 1998.

—— 2003. 'Kári Stefaánsson vegur að heiðri ættfræðinga', *The Morgunblaðið Newspaper*, 28 January 2003.

Finkler, K. 2000. *Experiencing the New Genetics: Family and Kinship on the New Medical Frontier*. Philadelphia: University of Pennsylvania Press.

Fox, R.C. and J.P. Swazey 1992. *Spare Parts: Organ Replacement in American Society*. Oxford: Oxford University Press.

Gibbon, S. 2002. 'Re-examining Geneticization: Family Trees in Breast Cancer Genetics', *Science as Culture* 11(4): 429–57.

Gold, E.R. 1996. *Body Parts: Property Rights and the Ownership of Human Biological Materials*. Washington, D.C.: Georgetown University Press.

Greely, H.T. 1998. 'Legal, Ethical, and Social Issues in Human Genome Research', *Annual Reviews in Anthropology* 27: 473–502.

Grubb, A. 1998. '"I, Me, Mine": Bodies, Parts and Property', *Medical Law International* 3: 299–317.

Gulcher, J., A. Kong and K. Stefánsson 2001. 'The Role of Linkage Studies for Common Diseases', *Current Opinion in Genetics & Development* 11: 264–67.

Haan, H. de 1994. *In the Shadow of the Tree: Kinship, Property and Inheritance among Farm Families*. Amsterdam: Het Spinhuis.

Hann, C.M., ed. 1998. *Property Relations: Renewing the Anthropological Tradition*. Cambridge: Cambridge University Press.

Haraway, D. 2000. 'Deanimations: Maps and Portraits of Life Itself', in *Hybridity and its Discontents: Politics, Science, Culture*, eds A. Brah and A.E. Coombes, London: Routledge, 111–36.

Helgason, A. and G. Pálsson 1998. 'Cash for Quotas: Disputes over the Legitimacy of an Economic Model of Fishing in Iceland', in *Virtualism: A New Political Economy*, eds J. Carrier and D. Miller, Oxford: Berg Publishers, 117–34.

Herzfeld, M., ed. 2000. *Anthropology: Theoretical Practice in Culture and Society*. Oxford: Blackwell.

Jacobson, C.K. 1986. 'Social Dislocations and the Search for Genealogical Roots', *Human Relations* 39(4): 347–58.

Jones, O. and P. Cloke 2002. *Tree Cultures: The Place of Trees and Trees in their Place*. Oxford: Berg.

Klapisch-Zuber, C. 1991. 'The Genesis of the Family Tree', *I Tatti Studies: Essays in the Renaissance* 4(1): 105–29.

—— 2000. *L'Ombre des Ancêstres: Essai sur l'imaginare médiéval de la parenté*. Paris: Fayard.

Knopper, B.M. 1999. 'Status, Sale and Patenting of Human Genetic Material: An International Survey', *Nature Genetics* 22: 23–26.

Knorr-Cetina, K. 1999. *Epistemic Cultures: How the Sciences Make Knowledge*. Cambridge: Harvard University Press.

Kohler, R.E. 1994. *Lords of the Fly: Drosophila Genetics and the Experimental Life*. Chicago: University of Chicago Press.

Latour, B. 1988. *The Pasteurization of France*. Cambridge: Harvard University Press.

——— 1999. *Pandora's Hope: Essays on the Reality of Science Studies*. Cambridge: Harvard University Press.

Locke, J. 1960. *Two Treatises of Government*. Mentor: New York.

Marshall, P.A., D.C. Thomasma and A.S. Daar 1996. 'Marketing Human Organs: The Autonomy Paradox', *Theoretical Medicine* 17: 1–18.

Melville, H. 1962 [1851]. *Moby Dick*. New York: Macmillan Company.

Mumford, L. 1962 [1934]. *Technics and Civilization*. San Diego: Harcourt Brace and Company.

Nelkin, D. and L. Andrews 1998. 'Homo Economicus: Commercialization of Body Tissue in the Age of Biotechnology', *Hastings Report* 20(5): 30–39.

Pálsson, G. 2002. 'The Life of Family Trees and the Book of Icelanders', *Medical Anthropology* 21(3/4): 337–67.

——— 2004. 'Decoding Relatedness and Disease: The Icelandic Biogenetic Project', in *From Molecular Genetics to Genomics: The Mapping Cultures of Twentieth Century Genetics*, eds J.-P. Gaudillére and H.-J. Rheinberger, London: Routledge, 180–99.

——— forthcoming 2006. 'The Web of Kin: An Online Genealogical Machine', in *Genealogy Beyond Kinship: Sequence, Transmission, and Essence in Ethnography and Social Theory*, eds S. Bamford and J. Leach, Oxford: Berghahn Books.

Pálsson, G. and K.E. Harðardóttir 2002. 'For Whom the Cell Tolls: Debates about Biomedicine', *Current Anthropology* 43(2): 271–301.

Pálsson, G. and P. Rabinow 2004. 'The Iceland Controversy: Reflections on the Trans-National Market of Civic Virtue', in *Global Assemblages*, eds A. Ong and S.J. Collier, Oxford: Blackwell Publishers, 91–103.

Pickering, A. 1995. *The Mangle of Practice: Time, Agency, & Science*. Chicago: University of Chicago Press.

Radin, M.J. 1996. *Contested Commodities*. Cambridge: Harvard University Press.

Rheinberger, H.-J. 1997. *Towards a History of Epistemic Things: Synthesizing Proteins in the Test Tube*. Stanford: Stanford University Press.

Rival, L. 1998. 'Trees, from Symbols of Life and Regeneration to Political Artefacts', in *The Social Life of Trees: Anthropological Perspectives on Tree Symbolism*, ed. L. Rival, Oxford: Berg, 1–38.

Rose, C.M. 1994. *Property and Persuasion: Essays on the History, Theory, and Rhetoric of Ownership*. Boulder: Westview Press.

Ryan, A. 1994. 'Self-ownership. Autonomy, and Property Rights', in *Property Rights*, eds E.F. Paul, F.D. Miller Jr and J. Paul, Cambridge: Cambridge University Press, 241–58.

Scheper-Hughes, N. 2000. 'The Global Traffic in Human Organs', *Current Anthropology* 41(2): 191–224.

Sharp, L.A. 2000. 'The Commodification of the Body and its Parts', *Annual Reviews in Anthropology* 29: 287–328.

Sigurðardóttir, S.A., A. Helgason, J.R. Gulcher, K. Stefánsson and P. Donnelly 2000. 'The Mutation Rate in the Human mtDNA Control Region', *American Journal of Human Genetics* 66: 1599–609.

Starr, D. 1998. *Blood: An Epic History of Medicine and Commerce*. London: Little, Brown and Co.

Stefánsson, S.E. , H. Jónsson, T. Ingvarsson, I. Manolescu, H.H. Jónsson, G. Ólafsdóttir, E. Pálsdóttir, G. Stefánsdóttir, G. Sveinbjörnsdóttir, M.L. Frigge, A. Kong, J.R. Gulcher and K. Stefánsson 2003. 'Genomewide Scan for Hand Osteoarthritis: A Novel Mutation in Matrilin-3', *American Journal of Human Genetics* 72(6): 1448–59.

Strathern, M. 1999. *Property, Substance and Effect: Anthropological Essays on Persons and Things*. London: The Athlone Press.

Titmuss, R.M. 1997 [1970]. *The Gift Relationship: From Human Blood to Social Policy*. London: LSE Books.

Vasey, D. 1996. 'Premodern and Modern Constructions of Population Regimes', in *Images of Contemporary Iceland: Everyday Lives and Global Contexts*, eds G. Pálsson and E.P. Durrenberger, Iowa City: University of Iowa Press, 149–70.

Weblen, T. 1898. 'The Beginnings of Ownership', *American Journal of Sociology* 4: 352–65.

Wiber, M.G. 2000. 'Fishing Rights as an Example of the Economic Rhetoric of Privatization: Calling for an Implicated Economics', *Canadian Review of Sociology and Anthropology* 37(3): 267–88.

Widlok, T. 2001. 'Relational Properties: Understanding Ownership in the Namib Desert and Beyond', *Zeitschrift für Ethnologie* 126: 237–68.

Wilkinson, S. and E. Garrard 1996. 'Bodily Integrity and the Sale of Human Organs', *Journal of Medical Ethics* 22: 334–39.

Chapter 15
Cultural Property, Repatriation and Relative Publics:
Which Public? Whose Culture?

Melanie G. Wiber

In this paper I utilise recent reevaluations of the public/private dichotomy in property theory (Weintraub and Kumar 1997; Geisler and Daneker 2000) to explore the repatriation of objects claimed on the basis of cultural property rights.[1] My analysis is based on two North American cases of repatriation, one from Canada (Kruzenga 2001; 2002) and one from the United States (Milun 2001). First, I rely on the concept of 'relative publics' to ask questions about potential multiple claimants to cultural property (F. von Benda-Beckmann 2000).[2] I also use notions of space and time to think about the role of power both in establishing value for particular units of cultural property, and also to control access (Harvey 1997; Cruikshank 1998; Ku 2000). Cultural property claims are often made in tandem with accusations of the misuse of power, and of the betrayal of cultural groups through the appropriation of their cultural knowledge, secret rituals and religious icons. But there are also accusations of betrayal that drag in very different scales of social organisation – of public trust if objects are treated improperly, or of wider human knowledge systems if cultural rights are allowed to trammel a public interest in scientific research (Brown 1998; Jones and Harris 1998).

While the public/private dichotomy has an intrinsic concept of power difference, the multireferentiality it relies on obfuscates, and as Ku (2000: 221) notes, depoliticises power relations. This allows cultural property claims to be depoliticised as well. Many scholars treat the issue as primarily one that sets narrow private interests against broader public interests (Winter 1993; Messenger 1999). I argue that repatriation or restitution involves the transfer of cultural property between quite different publics, or between corporate groups, as often as it does between simply conceived private and public realms. Critical reevaluation of both the public and the private spheres allows for increased attention to different scales of power. For example, many recognise that claims based on group rights are often problematic,[3] but a notion of relative publics exposes the relative strengths and weaknesses in the way such publics are constituted, in the identification of proper representation for conflicting publics, and of consequences of these power considerations for recognition of property rights.

Commodification adds another layer of complexity that often involves crossing multiple boundaries of social or geographical scale. Finding or imposing meaning on an object at a scale quite alien from that of its original creation or cultural source can damage the original value attached to the object in order to create market value elsewhere. This can involve debasement at the local level, such that the original users no longer feel the object useful for their own cultural projects. Harvey (2001) notes that value in cultural commodities is linked to monopoly rent, or the enhanced income stream created through exclusive control over some directly or indirectly tradable item that is in some crucial respects unique and non-replicable. Since there are few things more unique and non-replicable than 'authentic' culture: 'there are continuing struggles over the definition of the monopoly powers that might be accorded to location and localities and ... the idea of "culture" is more and more entangled with attempts to reassert such monopoly powers' (ibid.: 399).

I focus here on the issue of these continuing political struggles and on the many groups at intermediate scales who are involved in claiming control over establishing market or non-market value. I argue that legal anthropology can contribute some analytical clarity to the analysis of such claims and of those making them, from the perspective of the public/private debate.

The International Legal Environment

Claims on valuables premised on culture have been strengthened by international instruments that address human rights, aboriginal peoples and world heritage.[4] This emerging international law is plagued by problems long faced by the state, including: 'how to institutionalise the recognition of difference in a way that does not essentialise and cement difference' (Randeria 2002: 300). One theme has been to 'celebrate culture' by making cultural diversity a public good, without linking it too closely to rights. Of course, given the so-called 'rights revolution'

(Ignatieff 2000), this stance is difficult to maintain, which may explain why the language of many international instruments obfuscates the tension by conflating 'cultural property' with broader 'public goods', that is, of value to all humanity, as in the following: 'considering that the interchange of cultural property among nations for *scientific* cultural and educational purposes increases the knowledge of *the civilisation of Man*, enriches the cultural life of all peoples and inspires mutual respect and appreciation among nations' (Preamble to UNESCO World Heritage Convention 1972, italics added).

In this quotation, conflation of the narrower cultural value and the wider public value of such property masks significant moral and ethnical difficulties generated by the scientific objectives pursued by the convention. Another example is the more recent UN Convention on Biological Diversity (1992). One clause is particularly telling with regard to relative power differentials. Article 8.j reads:

> *Subject to its national legislation,* [parties will] *respect,* preserve and maintain knowledge, innovations and practices of indigenous and local communities embodying traditional lifestyles relevant for the conservation and sustainable use of biological diversity and *promote their wider application* with the approval and involvement of the *holders* of such knowledge, innovations and practices and encourage *the equitable sharing of the benefits* arising from the utilisation of such knowledge, innovations and practices. (Italics added)

The Convention fails to redress significant imbalances of power with respect to who controls the transfer and how the benefits are allocated.[5] These problems are no less apparent when considering the cultural property laws passed at the nation state level.

Cultural Property Claims as a Challenge to the Political Order

A fundamental problem is that the universalising models of science underlying national and international instruments are rejected by the very peoples they enjoin us to respect. We are all familiar with the way that museums have become sites of conflict over this issue.[6] Cruikshank (1998) speaks to the separate roles that objects take on in their rich cultural life and in the hermetically sealed world of the museum with its essentialising master narrative. She relates a story about a museum calling in indigenous elders to learn more about objects collected half a century before. The expectation was that these elders would speak to the past of these objects, who made them and who used them and for what purposes. Instead, the elders spoke to the present, so that the objects 'took on precise political meanings in terms of contemporary struggles' (1998: 99). Cultural property claims have significance in a *political* context of rights demands, a significance from which museums often feel it necessary to distance themselves. But museums are not politically neutral places since they create chronological coherence through evolutionary models of social and political change that rationalise and naturalise history (ibid.: 113).[7] Cultural property claims are often an explicit attempt to rejoin physical objects to personhood, social order and cosmology, and to thereby challenge political order.

The meanings (and values) attached to objects emerge from human interactions with the material world and with other humans. Particularly in a world which increasingly lacks coherence, material and nonmaterial cultural objects offer a reassuring sense of continuity, as well as a basis for (re)constructing identity and cultural belonging. In this sense, cultural property takes on significance that often gives it a value not originally envisaged by collectors, nor more importantly, by creators. Recognising this fact begins the disentanglement of several badly tangled threads that are simply not captured by the public/private dichotomy, and allows us to address questions that might otherwise be overlooked. For example, who are the *creators* of cultural property and what rights do they retain in their creations? What role does the private individual play in the generation of 'cultural' as opposed to 'public' goods? Who are the 'collectives' that are represented in subsequent cultural property rights claims, and how do they differ from the 'public' of the public/private conceptualisation? Who will be accepted as a member of the cultural group empowered to claim property and who will represent the group in making claims? These and other questions will be illustrated in the following case material.

The Fair Winds Water Drum

The first case involves aboriginal materials collected in the 1970s by the Canadian anthropologist Jack Steinbring during his research in the area of the Ojibwe community Pauingassi, which lies 300 kilometres north of Winnipeg, Manitoba.[8] The materials included a water drum made by a Pauingassi native, Fair Winds, who was known as 'an exceptionally powerful medicine man' (Matthews 2002). The drum was said to be an important tool in both healing and in warfare, having the power of life or death in the hands of one properly trained in Ojibwe ritual practices. Fair Wind's grandson, Charlie Owen was a practitioner like his grandfather and a respected leader in the community. Along with many other Pauingassi residents, he converted to Christianity in the 1970s but maintained an interest in passing on Ojibwe knowledge and culture to the next generation. He agreed that the Steinbring collection should be housed in the University of Winnipeg museum, and he later visited the museum to verify that his grandfather's artifacts were properly treated. However, just before he died in December 2001, Charlie Owen learned that the Fair Winds artifacts were no longer in the museum. The anthropology department, which was responsible for the management of the collection, instituted a search for the missing objects at the instigation of Charlie Owen's supporters.

As reported in the Canadian media, this search established that 'persons unknown' who had access to the collection had taken many of the Pauingassi artifacts and given them to unspecified aboriginal claimants. A number of these artifacts later surfaced in the possession of Eddie Benton-Banai, an Ojibwe leader of the Three Fires Mideiwiwin Society of the Lac Courte Oreille Band in northern Wisconsin, in the United States. He currently uses Ojibwe spiritual concepts to address problems of alcoholism, drug addiction, violence and poverty in Canadian and American aboriginal communities. The Canadian media also emphasised that he is reportedly one of the founders of the radical American Indian Movement or AIM, which had several deadly confrontations with federal forces, including one at Wounded Knee in 1973. According to a media interview in March 2002, Benton-Banai's opinion was that the artifacts were aboriginal and that white persons (whether Canadian or American) had no proper claim to them. He also suggested that the Ojibwe people of Pauingassi had lost their rights in the objects as they were Christian and had let them fall into white hands.

Once this irregular repatriation was reported in the Canadian press, pressure was brought to bear on the University to account for the way a Canadian historical object held in a public institution had been exported to another country. The Office of the Provincial Auditor General was asked to investigate, and that office released a report (Auditor General 2002) that was soundly critical of the university, of the museum and of the persons involved. All of these institutions and individuals, had in the words of the Provincial Auditor General, been entrusted with *public* resources, and had failed to act in accordance with that trust. The report particularly deplored that artifacts entered the United States irregularly, contrary to the Canadian

Cultural Property Export and Import Act, which identifies objects on a Control List requiring a permit for export. While the report encouraged the university to act against those persons involved in the irregular repatriation, it stopped short of requiring that the university make legal attempts to recover the artifacts. This disappointed some residents of Pauingassi who had been following the story since Charlie Owen's death. The report also stopped short of identifying any of the individuals who had taken part in the repatriation. However, the aboriginal news media reported that Manitoba's only aboriginal judge, Justice Murray Sinclair, reportedly a member of the Three Fires Society himself, was one of the players (Kruzenga 2001; Matthews 2002). Charlie Owen was not among those named as aboriginal advisors in the repatriation process, nor was any other member of the Pauingassi community.

While the process of repatriation followed in this case is not well documented, it is clear that the various potential 'publics' who lay claim to the Fair Winds artifacts, and those who represent them, are very unequal in terms of their political and social status. They include:

- Charlie Owen and other descendents and relatives of Fair Winds, who are primarily rural Ojibwe peoples with few connections to the urban, politicised world of provincial or national Canadian society.
- The wider aboriginal national leadership, who often challenge white stewardship of aboriginal cultural artifacts held in Canadian museums and other public institutions.
- The University of Winnipeg, the public institution responsible for the museum collection, which argues that the repatriation did not follow proper procedural channels and was thus invalid.
- The province of Manitoba, one source of public funding for the public institution of the University of Winnipeg and of the associated museum collection.
- The Government of Canada, which through its Cultural Property Import and Export Act, regulates the export from Canada of items 'designated by Canada as being of importance for archaeology, prehistory, literature, art or science' in order to protect the wider interests of the Canadian public.

The case, however, also includes transboundary claimants:

- The Ojibwe Three Fires Society, and in particular, its representative, Eddie Benton-Banai who claims a superior interest as a practicing member of an Ojibwe medicine society which operates on both sides of the Canadian/U.S. border.[9]

• Aboriginal political agents, who argue that the Ojibwe tribal nation as a whole should not be subject to the Canadian/U.S. border restrictions and regulations, and who claim autonomy for aboriginal governance on a wide variety of issues, including the ownership and transfer of rights in cultural property.

From a legal anthropology perspective, I am not so interested in which of these claimants has a superior or more legitimate claim to the materials. Rather, I am interested in the way in which the terms 'public' or 'cultural property' masks the various and important distinctions between the units involved and their relative structural relations within multiple concentric fields of power, widening out from Pauingassi to the international arena of North American aboriginal and white constituencies. The second case further demonstrates these interconnections with elevated political and legal heat, the details of which I draw primarily from Milun (2001).

Spirit Cave Ancestor

The Spirit Cave human remains were found in a burial site in Nevada, in an area claimed by the Northern Paiute tribes. These were housed for many years in the Nevada State Museum. Soon after the Native American Graves Protection and Repatriation Act (NAGPRA) was passed in 1990,[10] the museum tested the Spirit Cave remains through DNA analysis and radiocarbon dating, with dating results of over 9,000 years before present.[11] What sets the Spirit Cave human remains apart from the estimated 52,000 individual skeletal remains held in American museums and universities (Jones and Harris 1998: 253), is the combination of this early date with a subsequent physical anthropological analysis suggesting that the Spirit Cave remains had more physiological similarities with European populations than with modern day aboriginal populations. The analysis was published in an academic setting and subsequently circulated widely in the mass media, which is how members of the Northern Paiute tribe came to hear of the Spirit Cave remains. A subgroup of the Northern Paiute tribe immediately laid claim to the remains, a claim first rejected by the Bureau of Land Management (the federal agency that administers Indian lands under a trust arrangement) on the grounds that there was no evidence for a direct link between the Paiute and the Spirit Cave remains, and then recognised by the Native American Graves Protection and Repatriation Act (NAGPRA) review committee in November 2001.

As Milun (2001: 41) notes, this case rapidly proliferated both the cultural properties being claimed and the claimants to both tangible and intangible property objects. For example, the museum commissioned a physical anthropologist to make a reconstruction of the skull as a centerpiece of a display on the 'most ancient North American yet found'. This created a three dimensional bust, which Milun labels the first virtual Spirit Caveman. The second virtual Spirit Caveman was the photograph of that reconstruction, which appeared on the covers of national media outlets such as Newsweek (Murr 1999) and international, national and local newspapers.[12] There is also a third virtual Spirit Caveman, created when the physical anthropologist involved made a copy of the bust.

In this case as well, claimants are proliferating, to both the original and virtual copies of the Spirit Cave remains, including:

- The Nevada State Museum, which will continue to house the original Spirit Cave remains until all the appeal and counter appeals wend their way through the courts, and who in the meantime continue to prioritise 'scientific' requests to access the virtual or original remains. In accordance with the Nevada freedom of information act, they also continue to release virtual copies to the international press, to 'circulate information paid for with taxpayer's funds' (Milun 2001: 48).
- Representatives of the Northern Paiute tribes, who claim cultural affiliation with the Spirit Cave remains,[13] and who also claim rights to both the real and virtual Spirit Cavemen, citing the collective cultural harm done to them by the circulation of the virtual imagery.
- The physical anthropologist who made the reconstruction, and who is now claiming the bust, the additional copy and all such work done on the remains by her as her own intellectual property.
- Representatives of the academic community, especially anthropologists and archaeologists, who claim it is difficult to protect their scholarly public interest in such human remains since the NAGPRA legislation.[14]
- Representatives of the public media, who resist Indian tribal authority over all representation that has to do with Indian identity as an unreasonable limitation on the freedom of the press – also categorised as a public good.

One approach to such proliferation of claimants is to unpack the simplistic notion of public interest and to examine the relative publics involved and their respective claims to rights of various types. Weintraub (1997: 5) notes that the public/private dichotomy and all relevant dualisms are founded on two interrelated but separate themes: 1) what is hidden or withdrawn versus what is open, revealed or accessible, and 2) what is individual or pertaining only to an individual versus what is collective or relates to the wider interests of a collectivity of individuals. This latter distinction, he notes, can take into account the separation between the wider collective and some subset thereof (part and whole). But this is only the beginning of the layers of complexity in thought and action – used as both normative and descriptive terms such that public versus private distinguishes different kinds of human action – different kinds of human physical and social spaces, different realms of social life (ibid.: 7). As F. von Benda-Beckmann (2000: 151) writes: 'using an analytical understanding of "public" and "private" rather than the specific meanings that these concepts have acquired in American and European legal and political thought, I shall argue that our insight into property rights is improved by recognizing the multireferentiality and relativity of these concepts.'

One problem is that property regimes have always been and will likely continue to be highly charged political categories, laden with ideological significance and subject to 'intense, and at times violent, conflict' (ibid.: 151–52). Cultural property is no less so. I argue that since all but one of the claims listed above were based on some type of public rights and responsibilities (the exception being the intellectual property rights claimed by the physical anthropologist in the Spirit Cave case) a comparative analysis of the 'publics' involved will prove useful.

Analysis of Cultural Property Claimants

Following Weintraub (1997), F. von Benda-Beckmann identifies several constellations of private/public distinctions. These are based on 'paired oppositions', including: 'the contrast between private as intimate, shielded, and personal and public as open and revealed; the contrast between the personal and particularistic and the essentially collective; and the contrast between the political and the nonpolitical' (2000: 153).

These contrasts help to identify the numerous, overlapping but quite different meanings embedded in our concepts of public and private, meanings that draw on quite different levels of scale, of spatial organisation and of types of relationships. In Table 15.1, I list four such contrasts and illustrate their associated meanings. This table does not exhaust all possible meanings, but does illustrate some of the capacity for confusion when the terms are used interchangeably, and especially when various legal understandings are applied to property (F. von Benda-

Beckmann 2000: 154), at both the ideological level and the level of practice.[15]

Table 15.1: *Multiple meanings embedded in notions of public and private*

Contrast	Public	Private
Governance versus non-governance relationships	Relations of legitimate control, authority and coercion through political processes	Voluntary, equal, instrumental and contractual relations, including those of the market
Collective and far-reaching versus individualistic and particularistic interests	Civil society – the arena of active participation in decision making for the common, public weal	Narrow individual concerns, such as domestic or financial arrangements
Broad sociability versus egocentric interactions	Fluid and polymorphous sociability, of broad and largely unplanned encounters	The personal but not necessarily secret life
Open and theoretically transparent versus shielded and set apart spaces	Accessible places of the economic and political order, including the market	Limited access (largely domestic) places

As F. von Benda-Beckmann (2000) notes all law is theoretically public (open, transparent, having to do with governance, in the collective interest), even that law dealing with private issues such as family law; second, the public/private character of property rights is largely determined by the distinction between private and public law and where therein the property object is considered to fall; third, it is useful to distinguish between the theory of property rights and what happens in actual social relations between concrete, rights-holding social units. It is also useful to recognise the political ways in which meanings are selectively drawn upon to distract from questions of power imbalance.

If we consider Fair Wind's drum, for example, the anthropology museum at the University of Winnipeg, as an institution funded by the state, claimed legal stewardship of the artifact. This claim, if recognised, would invest the drum with a public (collective interest, open access, broad relevance) characteristic, requiring that the museum meet an obligation to properly store and maintain it for purposes of scientific and educational use by all members of the wider collective, or at least that subset that qualified under museum protocols. In practice, however, it seems that some department members regularly took Pauingassi objects from the museum for protracted periods without permission, one reason the irregular repatriation of the Pauingassi objects was slow to be discovered (Matthews 2002). There were other practices that influenced the ideal public access, including an informal agreement with Charlie Owen, under which the museum set limits on access for those objects deemed highly sensitive due to their religious or ritual uses.[16] Eddie Benton-Banai of the Three Fires Society, however, was reported to have said that the drum should be placed under the control of a much narrower collective, one restricted to those aboriginal peoples for whom it had specific cultural use value, a community of believers. He is reported (Matthews 2002) to have said: 'I believe that the Spirit directed them to me to take care of them. That's my belief. They weren't sold to me – no deal was made for them. I did not ask for them.' Benton-Banai rejects broader (non-native) custodial control of the drum no matter how constrained by aboriginal requests for limited access.

A similar argument for constraining broad access is made by representatives of the Northern Pauite who have lodged a claim to the Spirit Cave remains, but under much more contested terms. They argue that basic respect for the privacy of the dead should deny any access to either the original remains or the virtual remains. In this case, the Northern Pauite representatives are attempting to constrain much broader collectives, including 'the scientific community' and 'the media'. They have argued that the interpretation and representation of these remains has been one harmful to the individual and collective interests of Northern Pauite people, affecting their status as prior claimants to lands and resources, and resulting in increased levels of vandalism at archaeological sites in their homeland. Both the media and scientific establishments have countered with arguments drawing on their role in society and in the promotion of broader collective interests, one that conveniently ignores the corporate concentration in the former, and the private sponsorship in the latter that together have undermined much of the cachet of the media and of science as vehicles for wider collective benefits (Ku 2000: 222). Nevertheless, many people remain convinced that 'a free press' and 'academic freedom' are both in the 'public interest', more so perhaps because the media and the scientific community thus constrained are both international in scope. A museum and the media are both public according to Weintraub's distinctions, but public at quite different levels of scale.

Scale is a complex issue in discussions of relative publics. F. von Benda-Beckmann (2001) compares a number of Minangkabau public entities and discusses their relative rights in resources. He concludes that it would be inappropriate to restrict classification of the public administrative level to village councils or to state bureaucracies, as lineages and kin groups must also be considered to hold public (collective) rights in some resources. In fact there are many levels of public that might exist between the local and the international. A similar situation pertains to both cases of cultural property discussed here, since theoretically at least, kin groups within larger collectives could lay their own claims. The concept of cultural property was designed (at least in part) to allow the law to recognise this. But the concept has created more questions than it has addressed. For example, has the concept recognised sufficiently discrete categories of potential claimants? If so, who can legitimately speak for such 'publics' and what rights can they claim on their behalf? Who would have access to such property if these claims were recognised? Who else would be disenfranchised? And how would this harm a larger collective of which they are a part? Table 15.2 addresses some of these questions.

Unpacking the Political Content of Relative Publics

Weintraub (1997) makes a number of points regarding the multiple meanings of the concept of public that are relevant here. In the narrow liberalist understanding of public/private, anything not governed by state administration must automatically fall to the private world of the marketplace. This meaning would restrict those considering the future of cultural properties to two narrow options – state governed or governed by the marketplace. Some museum administrators, for example, fear the impact of the market on cultural property should government administration be weakened. In the opinion of some other commentators, however, the state so often fails miserably as custodian that private property rights and the marketplace can only do better.[17]

Second, the examples discussed here highlight the relative political weight of various collectives and their ability to play a role in the public realm. In terms of the classical citizenship model that Weintraub (1997: 10) describes as: 'active participation in collective decision-making, carried out within a framework of fundamental solidarity and equality', most North American aboriginal peoples are simply excluded by virtue of their political status as non-equals. For example, the status of Indians in Canada is controlled to an extreme level by the state apparatus. In this sense, there has been a real undercutting of citizenship in the Weintraub sense of 'conscious collective self-determination'. Natives are subjects, under the governance concept of sovereignty, and as such could be described as 'politically passive individuals who are bearers of rights granted to them and guaranteed by the sovereign' (ibid.). This is as true of their relations with each other within native society as it is of their relations with the dominant non-native society. Thus, the national aboriginal leadership in Canada has often been accused of ignoring the quite different interests of individual First Nation communities, of rural versus urban aboriginal populations, and of Metis versus status Indians. Meanwhile, economists often attack aboriginal special status as unnecessarily restricting aboriginal involvement in 'the world of self-interested individualism, competition, impersonality, and contractual relationships – centered on the market' (ibid.: 13), that is, of civil society in the tradition of political liberalism. Thus, different

Table 15.2: *Unpacking some of the relative 'public' making claims to cultural property – who claims (gets) access?*

Public/ (implied access)	Fair Winds' drum claimants	Spirit Cave remains claimants
Government – state funded institutions ('administered access')	University of Winnipeg anthropology museum; (access under agreed protocols)	Nevada State Museum (unlimited access including international media)
Aboriginal collective (access based on cultural criteria)	Members of Pauingassi (those interested in Ojibwe heritage)	A subset of the Northern Pauite (no access)
Collective of citizen equals (unfettered access)	Canadian citizens (represented by the media)	American citizens (represented by the media)
Collective of practitioners and believers (highly qualified interest group)	Mideiwiwin Society (represented by Eddie Benton-Banai)	Scientific community (all qualified academics)
Accessible and transparent political and economic spaces, such as the market (those with 'resources' to occupy these spaces)	Government of Canada Cultural Properties Import and Export Act (legitimate exporters)	Nevada Freedom of Information Act (media freelancers, media organisations, physical anthropologist who produced the virtual imagery)

representatives in both of the cases discussed here are referring to quite different collectives in their claim-making, and these collectives are vastly unequal in terms of the power they can bring to bear.

Yet another meaning of 'public' illustrates how aboriginal peoples in Canada and the United States are not part of the physical or social spaces in which the rest of society enjoys moments of unplanned sociability and interaction – as in public parks, city squares, cafes and malls. We can ask, for example, is the cultural property tied up in museum spaces accessible in this sociability sense (which Cruikshank (1998) suggests is crucial to their uses in indigenous cultural processes as in narrating history or socialising the young); or, are museum spaces too exclusionary to have spatial and social relevance for aboriginal persons? Perhaps what is lacking in accessing such spaces is 'the background conditions of basic trust, security, predictability, and a sense of shared conventions against which the spontaneity of public life can develop' (Weintraub 1997: 23). Consider too how these sociability spaces, and the trust, security and predictability mentioned above, are connected to the wider political arenas conceptualised in liberal or classical thought. When aboriginals are found socialising in urban spaces, or occupy political or social status within the wider society, they could be said to actually occupy what Weintraub has called *cosmopolis* space – that is a space of heterogeneous coexistence; a space of symbolic display, of physical proximity *coexisting with social distance* (ibid.: 25, emphasis added).

And yet another layer, as F. von Benda-Beckmann (2000) points out, involves non-Western conventions of the public (governance) role of kin groups versus Western conventions of the family as private (non-governance). This cluster of meanings suggests that the descendents of Fair Winds could only claim his drum and other artifacts as private property, which in many cultural contexts would seriously misrepresent the political status and role of extended families. And where do acts done in secret for the public weal fit in? Many ritual and sacred practices of aboriginal peoples of North and South America were aimed at the wider public good of health and good fortune for members of the collective. However, they were often conducted in secret, hidden ways, wherein lay much of their potency. This required that many of the cultural implements used in such practices also be secret and hidden, inaccessible to all but those initiated into their proper use. While they relate to collective and far-reaching interests, these types of cultural property are particularly difficult to reconcile with the other commonly recognised meanings of 'public', including transparency, open accessibility and governance.

Conclusions

I have asked a great many questions about the multi-referentiality of the concept of a public level of ownership in property objects, about the types of objects that might be cultural property, about the social entities that may be holders of such property and about the types of access that might be judged proper by such entities. All of these aspects of the question of cultural property rights can be (and have been) obfuscated by the multiple meanings of 'public'. But the private/public distinctions I have been discussing are relevant for many other highly political questions relating to different types of objects including those less tangible, such as potential biopharmaceuticals (Nigh 2002), cultural practices such as dance, chant, prayer, song, agricultural production, foraging or ritual (see Brown 1998; Sillitoe 1998; Harrison 2002; Kirsch 2002; Nas 2002), the environment needed for cultural survival (Kirsch 2001) and even the biostuff of which humans are made, the human genome (see Haraway 2000; Pálsson and Harðardóttir 2002; Santos 2002; Pálsson this volume). The international legal environment has been creating instruments that endorse cultural property rights without making any accommodation, either to this multireferentiality, or to the political contests and complications which the terminology of the international instruments masks. When cultural property emerges, is contested over, and is allocated to one claimant or another, in aid of one type of public project or another, these meanings can remain deeply submerged. It is only when the types of and political uses for this multireferentiality are explicitly addressed, that the kinds of betrayals mentioned at the outset of this paper are less likely to take place. I argue here that recent criticism of the public/private dichotomy in law and property theory can make a real contribution to disentangling some of the twisted threads in cases of multiple claimants, and perhaps to avoiding some of the more egregious types of betrayals.

Notes

1. My examples will be drawn from aboriginal claims to material objects. For a recent survey article on intellectual property rights and culture see Brown (1998), for a discussion of culture and rights see Cowan et al. (2001).
2. I rely here on cases where competing claims are made on behalf of quite different cultural groups. Julia Krapina (2002) reminds us that many claims for valuable museum artifacts are lodged by individuals on the basis of prior private property rights. She also reminds us that many objects are not claimed at all. In contrast with one of the artifacts discussed in this paper, her museum was never able to find

anyone willing to take either private or public responsibility for a shamanic spirit drum from Siberia, despite the fact that the regional museum in which it was housed was being closed.

3. Of course, many do not recognise the problems here. Sassoon (1999:62), for example, writes 'Nepalese culture belongs to the Nepalese first and foremost, and so do their antiquities'. King (1999: 199), on the other hand, writes: 'cultural property cannot be claimed to be the absolute property of a nation … it is the property of humankind as a whole'. It seems to me to be equally problematic to posit a coherent claimant in the case of caste-stratified Nepal, as it is for 'humankind as a whole'.

4. These include: article 27 of the UNESCO Convention Concerning the Protection of the World Cultural and Natural Heritage (the World Heritage Convention), 1972; the UNESCO Convention on the Means of Prohibiting and Preventing the Illicit Import, Export and Transfer of Ownership of Cultural Property, 1972 and article 15 of the UN International Covenant on Economic, Social and Cultural Rights, 1976. For analysis of these see Shaw (1997: 229–31; 252–54).

5. For the full text see www.biodiv.org/convention/articles.asp.

6. See Gable and Handler (2003) for a discussion of how museums are surviving 'after authenticity'.

7. A non-museum example is the Human Genome Diversity Project that sought aboriginal genetic materials before the: 'populations that could provide more information to elucidate human evolutionary history were in danger of dying out or being assimilated' (Santos 2002: 92). This project was rejected by indigenous peoples not only because of its inherent racism, but also because the U.S. Patent and Trademark Office had recently granted a patent to a human T-lymphotropic virus (HTLV-I) derived from an upland population from Papua New Guinea, which led many to suspect the private profit motivations for such publicly funded research. See also Pálsson in this volume.

8. Steinbring reported that he was concerned about American tourists buying up cultural property of local historical importance. He received a small grant to collect 400 objects, 240 of them from Pauingassi. In a CBC interview, he confirms that he promised members of the community that the objects would be 'protected in perpetuity for the people of the community', that they could visit the University of Winnipeg museum to study them, and that aboriginal wishes would be respected in the way the materials would be managed.

9. According to the aboriginal press, some of the artifacts were returned to Canada a few days before the Auditor General's report was released. Kruzenga (2002) reports that some members of the Mideiwiwin Society met in a 'private ceremony' in Winnipeg on 21 June with 'representatives of the Pauingassi community' to return several items. He does not identify either the representatives for the Mideiwiwin Society or for the community but the reported return does suggest sensitivity among some Mideiwiwin members to claims on the part of the Pauingassi Ojibwe community.

10. This act requires public institutions to return aboriginal artifacts and human remains where an unbroken affiliation can be shown to link them to existing and recognised Indian tribes.

11. Jones and Harris (1998) suggest three variables to consider when demands for repatriation come into conflict with scientific (public) interest. In the case of prehistoric remains, they argue that 'general human interests should take precedence' (ibid.: 257), primarily because scientific study contributes to 'global history' (ibid.: 254) and 'skeletal remains are part of the world's heritage, since the information they yield is relevant to and may even be said to belong to all human communities' (ibid.: 256). But establishing value in this way is often challenged by natives as a result of the political and legal significance that attaches to both who first populated North America and when.

12. Milun (2001) chooses not to further distribute such virtual images, which she argues are at best speculative and at worst racist, positing, as they do, a decidedly European face, hair colour, and skin tones. See Wiber (1997) on race and progress in physical anthropology reconstructions.

13. The Native American Graves Protection and Repatriation Act (NAGPRA) requires that tribes bear the burden of proof to show cultural affiliation with cultural property, using geographical, kinship, biological, archaeological, linguistic, folklore, oral tradition, historical evidence and other information or expert opinion to support their claim.

14. Milun (2001: 48) notes that two commentators on the physical properties of the Spirit Cave remains are both anthropologists involved in the other widely publicised NAGPRA debate that involves the Kennewick Man case.

15. Costonis (2000) comments on this issue of ideology versus practice when he notes that American property scholars resemble theoreticians of light. Those who resemble photon theorists see property as discrete and self-contained, a thing separate from its purported wider social purposes. Other legal scholars resemble wave theorists in that they see property as registering and even incorporating the tensions and values of the social spheres through which it passes.

16. Perhaps in recognition of the creator's *droit moral*, which others might advocate should be ignored in favour of broader public interests (see Costonis 2000: 1845).

17. Costonis (2000) reviews these dualistic arguments. For a broader discussion see Messenger 1999.

References

Auditor General 2002. 'Investigation of the Missing Artifacts at the Anthropology Museum of the University of Winnipeg', Report of the Auditor General's office, Province of Manitoba, http://www.pao.mb.ca/reports/reports_fr.htm

Benda-Beckmann, F. von 2000. 'Relative Publics and Property Rights', in *Property and Values*, eds C. Geisler and G. Daneker, Washington, D.C.: Island Press, 151–73.

———— 2001. 'Between Free Riders and Free Raiders: Property Rights and Soil Degradation in Context', in *Economic Policy and Sustainable Land Use. Recent Advances in Quantitative Analysis for Developing Countries*, eds N. Heerink, H. van Keulen and M. Kuiper, Heidelberg: Physica-Verlag, 293–316.

Brown, M.F. 1998. 'Can Culture be Copyrighted?', *Current Anthropology* 39(2): 193–222.

Costonis, J.J. 2000. 'Casting Light on Cultural Property', *Michigan Law Review* 98: 1837–62.

Cowan, J.K., M.-B. Dembour and R.A. Wilson, eds 2001. *Culture and Rights. Anthropological Perspectives.* Cambridge: Cambridge University Press.

Cruikshank, J. 1998. *The Social Life of Stories: Narrative and Knowledge in the Yukon Territory.* Lincoln: University of Nebraska Press.

Gable, E. and R. Handler, 2003. 'After Authenticity at an American Heritage Site', in *The Anthropology of Space and Place*, eds S.M. Low and D. Lawrence-Zuninga, Malden, M.A.: Blackwell Publishing, 370–86. Reprinted from *American Anthropologist* 98(3) (1996).

Geisler, C. and G. Daneker, 2000. *Property and Values. Alternatives to Public and Private Ownership.* Washington, D.C.: Island Press.

Haraway, D. 2000. 'Deanimations: Maps and Portraits of Life Itself', in *Hybridity and its Discontents. Politics, Science, Culture*, eds A. Brah and A.E. Coombes, London and New York: Routledge, 111–36.

Harrison, S. 2002. 'The Politics of Resemblance: Ethnicity, Trademarks, Head-Hunting', *Journal of the Royal Anthropological Institute* 8: 211–32.

Harvey, D. 1997. *Justice, Nature, and the Geography of Difference.* Cambridge: Blackwell Press.

——— 2001. 'The Art of Rent: Globalization and the Commodification of Culture', in *Spaces of Capital. Towards a Critical Geography*, ed. D. Harvey, New York: Routledge, 394–411.

Ignatieff, M. 2000. *The Rights Revolution.* Toronto: Anansi Press.

Jones, D.G. and R.J. Harris 1998. 'Archeological Human Remains. Scientific, Cultural, and Ethical Considerations', *Current Anthropology* 39(2): 253–64.

King, J.L. 1999. 'Cultural Property and National Sovereignty', in *The Ethics of Collecting Cultural Property*, ed. P.M. Messenger, Albuquerque: The Univeristy of New Mexico Press, 199–208.

Kirsch, S. 2001. 'Lost Worlds. Environmental Disaster, "Culture Loss", and the Law', *Current Anthropology* 42(2): 167–98.

——— 2002. 'Anthropology and Advocacy. A Case Study of the Campaign against the Ok Tedi Mine', *Critique of Anthropology* 22(2): 174–200.

Krapina, J. 2002. 'Heritage and/or property: the Siberian Ethnographic Collections in Russian Museums', paper presented to the Max Planck Institute for Social Anthropology Conference, A World of Cultures: Culture as Property in Anthropological Perspective. 30 June – 2 July 2002, Halle, Germany.

Kruzenga, L. 2001. 'Artifacts Spirited into U.S. by Ojibwe Cultural Society', *The Drum* 9.

——— 2002. 'Provincial Auditor Confirms Allegations', *First Perspectives*, 28 June 2002.

Ku, A.S. 2000. 'Revising the Notion of "Public" in Habermas's Theory – Toward a Theory of Politics of Public Credibility', *Sociological Theory* 18(2): 216–40.

Matthews, M. 2002. 'Ownership of Ojibwe Religious Artifacts', Bowdens transcription of the Canadian Broadcasting Corporation Radio 'This Morning' programme, broadcast 28 April 2002.

Messenger, P.M. ed. 1999. *The Ethics of Collecting Cultural Property*. Albuquerque: The University of New Mexico Press.

Milun, K. 2001. 'Keeping-While-Giving-Back: Computer Imaging and Native American Repatriation', *PoLar* 24(2): 39–57.

Murr, A. 1999. 'The First Americans', *Newsweek*, 26 April 1999.

Nas, P.J.M. 2002. 'Masterpieces of Oral and Intangible Culture. Reflections on the UNESCO World Heritage List. CA Forum on Anthropology in Public', *Current Anthropology* 43(1): 139–48.

Nigh, R. 2002. 'Maya Medicine in the Biological Gaze. Bioprospecting Research as Herbal Fetishism', *Current Anthropology* 43(3): 451–77.

Pálsson, G. and K.E. Harðardóttir 2002. 'For Whom the Cell Tolls: Debates about Biomedicine', *Current Anthropology* 43(2): 271–301.

Randeria, S. 2002. 'Entangled Histories of Uneven Modernities: Civil Society, Caste Solidarities and Legal Pluralism in Post-Colonial India', in *Unravelling Ties. From Social Cohesion to New Practices of Connectedness*, eds Y. Elkana, I. Krastev, E. Macamo and S. Randeria, Frankfurt/New York: Campus Verlag, 284–311.

Santos, R.V. 2002. 'Indigenous Peoples, Postcolonial Contexts and Genomic Research in the Late 20th Century. A View from Amazonia (1960–2000)', *Critique of Anthropology* 22(1): 81–104.

Sassoon, D. 1999. 'Considering the Perspective of the Victim: The Antiquities of Nepal', in *The Ethics of Collecting Cultural Property*, ed. P.M. Messenger, Albuquerque: The University of New Mexico Press, 61–72.

Shaw, M.N. 1997. *International Law*, 4th edn, Cambridge: Cambridge University Press.

Sillitoe, P. 1998. 'The Development of Indigenous Knowledge. A New Applied Anthropology', *Current Anthropology* 39(2): 223–52.

United Nations 1972. UNESCO Convention Concerning the Protection of the World Cultural and Natural Heritage (the World Heritage Convention).

——— 1972. UNESCO Convention on the Means of Prohibiting and Preventing the Illicit Import, Export and Transfer of Ownership of Cultural Property.

——— 1976. UN International Covenant on Economic, Social and Cultural Rights.

——— 1992. Convention on Biological Diversity.

Weintraub, J. 1997. 'The Theory and Politics of the Public/Private Distinction', in *Public and Private in Thought and Practice. Perspectives on a Grand Dichotomy*, eds J. Weintraub and K. Kumar, Chicago and London: University of Chicago Press, 1–42.

Weintraub, J. and K. Kumar, eds 1997. *Public and Private in Thought and Practice. Perspectives on a Grand Dichotomy*. Chicago and London: University of Chicago Press.

Wiber, M.G. 1997. *Erect Men/Undulating Women: The Visual Imagery of Gender, Race and Progress in Reconstructive Illustrations of Human Evolution*. Waterloo, Ontario: Wilfrid Laurier University Press.

Winter, I.J. 1993. 'Cultural Property', *Art Journal* (Spring) 52(1): 103–7.

✝ Notes on Contributors

Franz von Benda-Beckmann is head of the Project Group 'Legal Pluralism' at the Max Planck Institute for Social Anthropology in Halle/Saale, Germany; honorary professor for legal anthropology at the University of Leipzig; honorary professor for legal pluralism at the University of Halle/Saale. He holds a Ph.D. in law (1970) and received his habilitation in anthropology at the University of Zürich (1979). Until 2000 he was professor for law in developing countries at the Agricultural University Wageningen. He has done fieldwork and supervised research in Malawi, West Sumatra, the Moluccas and Nepal. He has written and co-edited several books and published numerous articles and book chapters on issues of property rights, social (in)security and legal pluralism in developing countries and on legal anthropological theory.

Keebet von Benda-Beckmann is head of the Project Group 'Legal Pluralism' at the Max Planck Institute for Social Anthropology in Halle/Saale, Germany; honorary professor for legal anthropology at the University of Leipzig; and honorary professor for legal pluralism at the University of Halle/Saale. She also holds a personal chair in anthropology of law at Erasmus University Rotterdam, the Netherlands. She has carried out research in West Sumatra and on the Moluccan Island of Ambon, Indonesia and among Moluccan women in the Netherlands. She has published extensively on dispute resolution, social security in developing countries, property and water rights, decentralisation, and legal pluralism and theoretical issues in the anthropology of law.

John R. Eidson is a lecturer in the Department of Anthropology at the University of New Hampshire. In his published research to date, he has addressed various aspects of local and regional life in contemporary Germany, including civil society, the politics of identity, social memory, agrarian transition and changing rural property relations. He is the editor of *Das anthropologische Projekt*, a collection of essays forthcoming in the University of Leipzig Press.

Charles Geisler is a professor of Development Sociology at Cornell University and works on issues of ownership, regulation and equity in the U.S. and elsewhere. His recent research focuses on human displacement from protected areas (greenlining), hybrid forms of public-private ownership, and the emergence of socially responsible ownership. He teaches courses on technology and society, environmental sociology, land reform, the history of property and community, and development-induced displacement. Examples of recent work include co-edited books, *Property and Value* (Island Press 2000) and *Biological Diversity: Balancing Interests through Adaptive Collaborative Management* (CRC Press 2001).

Deborah James is a reader in Anthropology at the London School of Economics. Her research focuses on South Africa, and interests include migration, ethnomusicology, ethnicity, property relations and the politics of land reform. She is author of *Songs of the Women Migrants: Performance and Identity in South Africa* (Edinburgh University Press 1999) and the forthcoming *Gaining Ground? 'Rights' and 'Property' in South African Land Reform Programme* (Glasshouse Press 2006).

Esther Kingston-Mann is professor of History at the University of Massachusetts-Boston, a historian of Russia and the Soviet Union and a student of peasantries. Her work has focused on questions of Marxism and rural development, and on twentieth-century peasant encounters with privatisation and collectivisation. Her current book project is entitled: *To Escape from Backwardness: Claiming Property Rights in England, Russia and Kenya*. A forthcoming publication is *Claiming Property: The Soviet-era Private Plots as 'Women's Turf'*, *The Borders of Socialism: The 'Public' and 'Private' Sphere during the Soviet Era*, edited by Lewis Siegelbaurm (Palgrave 2005).

David Lorenzo is a forestry engineer from the Universidad Politecnica de Madrid. For his M.Sc. in social forestry at Wageningen University he conducted research in an *ejido* in Western Mexico. After finishing his M.Sc. he became involved in a research project on community and access to natural resources in the Central Highlands of Peru.

Frank Muttenzer is a law graduate from the University of Basel, after obtaining a Master's in Legal Theory from the Katholieke Universiteit and the Faculté Universitaires Saint-Louis in Brussels, he worked in the field of international law and indigenous peoples before turning to social research at the Graduate Institute of Development Studies in Geneva. His doctoral research takes a socio-legal view on environmental policy and governance in Madagascar and proposes an explanation of deforestation as customary law.

Monique Nuijten is senior research fellow at the Royal Netherlands Academy of Arts and Sciences at Wageningen University, the Netherlands. At present she is involved in a research project on community organisations and forms of local-global governance in Mexico, Peru and Brazil. She has published on land reform and the law, organisation in development, participatory approaches and the different dimensions of state power. Her latest book is *Power, Community and the State: the Political Anthropology of Organization in Mexico* (Pluto Press 2003).

Gísli Pálsson (Ph.D., University of Manchester, 1982) is professor of Anthropology at the University of Iceland. Among his books are *The Textual Life of Savants* (Routledge 1995), *Nature and Society: Anthropological Perspectives* (Routledge 1996, co-editor), *Travelling Passions: The Hidden Life of Vilhjálmur Stefánsson* (University Press of New England 2005), and *Birthmarks: Anthropology and the New Genetics* (Cambridge University Press forthcoming). Currently, Pálsson's research focuses on the social implications of biotechnology and biobanks, environmental change, the life and work of anthropologist-explorer V. Stefánsson, and Inuit genetic history. Pálsson has done anthropological fieldwork in Iceland, Canada, and The Republic of Cape Verde.

Pauline E. Peters is a faculty member in the Kennedy School of Government and the Department of Anthropology at Harvard University. Her research concentrates on the processes of agrarian transformation, particularly agricultural commercialisation, land tenure, property systems, natural resource management, family organisation, gender relations, poverty, and social differentiation. She has conducted research in Botswana and, since 1986, has focused on Malawi. She also works with researchers in universities in other countries of Southern Africa. Her publications include *Dividing the Commons: Politics, Policy and Culture in Botswana* (University Press of Virginia 1994), and

Development Encounters: Sites of Participation and Knowledge (Harvard University Press 2000), as well as many papers and book chapters.

Edella C. Schlager is an associate professor in the School of Public Administration and Policy and Political Science at the University of Arizona. Dr Schlager earned her Ph.D. in Political Science in 1990 from Indiana University. Her research interests focus on coastal fisheries and water use and governance in the western U.S. She studies the emergence and evolution of institutional arrangements devised by local communities to govern natural resources. Her latest book (with William Blomquist and Tanya Heikkila) is *Common Waters, Diverging Streams: Linking Institutions and Water Management in Arizona, California, and Colorado* (RFF Press 2004).

Thomas Sikor received his Ph.D. at the University of California at Berkeley before returning to Germany to head the Junior Research Group on Postsocialist Land Relations at Humboldt University, Berlin. He has conducted in-depth research on agrarian and environmental change in Vietnam and Central East Europe, exploring what, if anything, is unique about postsocialist transformations. He has recently edited special issues of *Conservation and Society* (Sage 2004) on postsocialist property relations and *Forest Policy and Economics* (Elsevier 2005) on community-based forestry.

Toon van Meijl studied social anthropology and philosophy at the University of Nijmegen and the Australian National University in Canberra, where he completed his Ph.D. in 1991. Currently, he is associate professor in the Department of Anthropology and Development Studies and secretary of the Centre for Pacific and Asian Studies at the University of Nijmegen, the Netherlands. He has conducted fieldwork in Maori communities in New Zealand since 1982 and has written extensively on issues of cultural identity and the self, and on socio-political questions emerging from the debate about property rights of indigenous peoples. Among his recent publications are the co-edited volumes *Property Rights and Economic Development: Land and Natural Resources in Southeast Asia and Oceania* (Kegan Paul International 1999) and *Shifting Images of Identity in the Pacific* (KITLV Press 2004).

Oane Visser is lecturer in Qualitative Methodology, Radboud University Nijmegen, the Netherlands. He is also affiliated to the Centre for Transition and Development (CESTRAD) at the Institute of Social Studies, The Hague. He carried out field-work, and comparative research on rural changes in the former Soviet Union. His research interests include: property, farm restructuring, household strategies, social capital and poverty. On these topics he published several chapters in edited volumes and (joint) articles in *The Journal of Peasant Studies, Europe-Asia Studies* and *Focaal-European Journal of Anthropology*.

Melanie G. Wiber is professor of Anthropology at the University of New Brunswick, Canada. She is author of the book *Politics, Property and Law in the Philippine Uplands* (Wilfrid Laurier University Press 1993), and co-editor of *The Role of Law in Natural Resource Management* (Wilfrid Laurier University Press 1996) with Joep Spiertz. Her recent research focuses on new forms of property such as milk and fish quota in the Canadian Maritimes, and on community based management of natural resources.

Index

www.ingramcontent.com/pod-product-compliance
Lightning Source LLC
Chambersburg PA
CBHW072045020426
42334CB00017B/1401